BOOK ME!
How To Become A Successful Working Dancer In Hollywood

Sandra Colton

PINSTRIPED PUBLISHING

Reviews

"It is FABULOUS! She has done a wonderful job!"
-Kate Lydon, Editor-in-Chief - Dance Spirit Magazine (November 2009)

"A bible for dancers."
-Pete Engle, Dance Agent – Clear Talent Group (LA)

"You have really done a great thing for the community by writing this book."
-Jim Keith, Agent/Partner/President – The Movement Talent Agency

"Pick of the Month" – Dance Spirit Magazine (November 2009)
"You probably dream about dancing for Janet and Britney—but sometimes the idea of packing up and making the move to Hollywood can feel overwhelming. Enter Sandra Colton's new book, Book Me! How To Become A Successful Working Dancer in Hollywood. Colton covers all the West Coast dance world basics, from landing an agent and creating a resumé to making connections and building relationships. Worried about auditions? Her do's and don'ts for landing the job, along with her health and beauty tips, will help you look and feel like you've been going out for big-name gigs for years! With a foreword by Brian Friedman and insights from top choreographers like Mia Michaels, Dave Scott and Sonya Tayeh, this book is bound to help you reach your Hollywood goals."
-Michael Anne Bailey,
Dance Spirit Magazine (November 2009)

"Last month, (Sandra) published a book titled *Book Me! How to Become a Successful Working Dancer in Hollywood*, and although its focus is on Los Angeles, much of the advice can be applied no matter where a dancer looks for work. The book is a commercial-dance bible of sorts – an exhaustive, 360-page resource tool packed with dos and don'ts about everything from how to get work visas if you aren't a U.S. citizen, to how to read a contract or audition call sheet properly, to how to apply makeup and dress for an audition."
-Kathryn Greenaway,
Montreal Gazette (December 2009)

"Sandra's book gives dancers insight on the Hollywood scene and the art of navigating the competitive Hollywood entertainment industry in a way that no other has created for dancers. It is filled with Sandra's Sick Tips and secrets to success, BOOK ME! puts dancers on the fast track to getting booked solid in Hollywood. With a foreword by celebrity choreographer Brian Friedman and packed cover-to-cover with stories of over 60 working dancers and 50 top choreographers, you'll be sure to learn something new!"
-Alex Wong (Principal Soloist, Miami City Ballet)
The Winger (November 2009)

Reviews

"Get your mind right before you step into this business. Read *Book Me!* by Sandra Colton for the ins and out of the dance business…"
-Andrea Gilmore, Finalist on 2011 Born To Dance with Laurieann Gibson (BET)

"(This is) a dance handbook/bible. It's so informative and really covers so much information that's pertinent for dancers."
-Jennifer Hamilton, Choeographer, Dancer and Assistant to Marguerite Derricks

"I love the book! Wowee! This is gonna change lives!!!"
-Gigi Torres, Essence Movement Founder & Professional Dancer

"What an awesome collection of information and so pertinent to the biz!!"
-Tammy To, Professional Dancer

"I just wanted to let you know that I haven't quite put it down since I picked it up. I haven't been so excited to read a book since *Breaking Dawn* (part of the Twilight series)."
-Caslin Katsaros, Aspiring Dancer

"Figuring out how to navigate the small circle and tough competition in the entertainment industry is where this book excels."
-Danielle Brown, Publisher, DANCE TRAIN Magazine (Sept./Oct. 2009)

Left to right: Sandra with Dave Scott, Chris Dupre, Pete Engle, Jim Keith, Kevin Stea, Paul Becker, Marcel Wilson, Rodney Chester, Rosero McCoy, Roy Haidar and Bobbie Bates.

THANK YOU!

Copyright © 2013 by Sandra Colton

All rights reserved. **BOOK ME! How To Become A Successful Working Dancer In Hollywood.** Printed and bound in the United States of America. No part of this work may be reproduced in any form or by any electronic or mechanical means including information storage and retrieval systems without permission in writing from the publisher, except by a reviewer, who may quote brief passages in a review.

Published by Pinstriped Publishing,
A Division of Original Girl, LLC
P.O. Box 824, Hollywood, CA 90078

For more Pinstriped Publishing works go online to our Web site at www.PinstripedPublishing.com. Once there you will find detailed information about our authors.

First printing: November 2009
Second printing: January 2011
Third printing: July 2013

Library of Congress Control Number: 2008943717

Colton, Sandra
    Book me! : how to become a successful working dancer in hollywood / Sandra Colton – 3rd ed.
    p. cm.
ISBN 978-0-615-28731-7
Edited by Sandra Colton, Abigail Mortimore, Heather Burton, PJ Graham and Megan Lokis.
Photo editing by Sandra Colton, Danny Essin and ND Capture Photography.
Cover and Part 1-5 photos by Chris Cuffaro courtesy of FOX publicity.

While the author has made every effort to provide accurate telephone numbers and Internet addresses at the time of publication, neither the publisher nor the author assumes any responsibility for errors, or for changes that occur after publication. Further, the publisher does not have any control over and does not assume any responsibility for author or third-party websites or their content. The author, publisher and copyright holder assume no responsibility for any injury, loss, or damage sustained or caused as a consequence of the use and application of this book.

For my mom who always taught me that with a strong work ethic and determination, you can accomplish anything.

For my sister who was always better at everything and let me be part of the act.

For my grandmother, a woman who always speaks her mind, bakes me angel food cake and of course always spoils me.

For my aunt who always shoots straight from the hip and always keeps me in her thoughts.

About The Author

Sandra Colton is a member of SAG/AFTRA, ASCAP and The Recording Academy. As an elected member, Sandra served on the Los Angeles Board of Directors for AFTRA and was appointed to the SAG Dancers' Committee. Along with the 3rd edition release of **BOOK ME!**, Sandra publishes *Dance Track® Magazine, Dance Team® Magazine* and is the creator of the the *Artist Awards*. She is also helping the world laugh at *DanceGiggle.com* and writing her first screenplay & greeting card line called **Spot On!** Sandra was a top finalist on Season 1 of FOX's *So You Think You Can Dance*, performed on the *Tonight Show with Jay Leno* singing backup for both Paulina Rubio and Katharine McPhee and danced in music videos for Snoop Dogg, Justin Timberlake, Chelo, The Game, Katharine McPhee, Raphael Saadiq, Marie Serenholt, Cascada and Too Short. A former *Laker Girl,* Sandra's credits also include commercials for Nationwide Insurance, Fruit of the Loom and Subway, an HBO special with Cedric the Entertainer, *Fashion Rocks, Victoria's Secret Fashion Show,* MTV *Movie Awards, Boston Legal, Viva Laughlin, MadTV, Bring It On: All or Nothing, The Day The Earth Stood Still* and national print ads for *So You Think You Can Dance* and IBM. Sandra has danced on tour with Rihanna and Katharine McPhee and was featured in *Dance Spirit Magazine* and in *BACKSTAGE East/West* as a rising singer. JUST DANCE, Sandra's album, garnered Los Angeles Music Award nominations for Best Pop Artist and Best R&B Song in 2007. Sandra opened for Sean Kingston at Key Club on her Hollywood Club Tour and the music video for her single, *"I Can't Dance,"* premiered on Yahoo! Music in July 2008.

Sandra is currently a graduate student at the University of Southern California. Sandra launched **Original Girl® Magazine** in September of 2008. Graduating with honors from the University of Oregon, Sandra earned her Bachelor of Arts degree in Sociology and Communication Studies. Receiving departmental honors for her completion of the Honors Thesis Program during her senior year, Sandra's thesis entitled, *Biracial Identity Development,* tackled the hard questions persons of biracial decent face when trying to decipher how they will racially identify themselves. Born in Des Moines, Iowa, Sandra has been performing since age 3 and got her start in Las Vegas as an opening act with her sister performing alongside Bill Cosby, Lou Rawls, Savion Glover and the Nicholas Brothers. The sister act, Colton and Colton, went on to win the Teen Dance category on *Star Search* in 1992. Visit **www.SandraColton.com** for more information.

Acknowledgments

In sharing this work with you, I'm excited to also acknowledge some of the people who helped and encouraged me throughout this process. The inspiration for writing this book came from my work as a contributor for a dance blog during the early part of 2008. While writing, I tried to convey the day-to-day life as a dancer and artist in Hollywood, Calif. Sharing knowledge with up-and-coming dancers, I wanted to expand and share more. In this work I want to help others tackle the hurdles of Hollywood head on and skip a few steps along the way.

I would like to thank my agents, managers and mentors in entertainment who have helped to guide my career including Lisa Coppola, Terry Lindholm, Bill Bohl, Lisa Estrada, Laraine Raish, Brian Friedman, Micki and Steve Granger, Shelli Margheritis, Brianna Barcus, Pete Engle, Daniel Hoff, Carrie Dobro, Sheila Crawford and many more.

Foreword by
Brian Friedman

I cannot imagine my life without dance in it. Having toured with and/or choreographed for multiple recording artists including Britney Spears and Janet Jackson, I have seen the ups and downs that all dancers face. Building relationships is as important in a dancer's career as it is to have flawless technique and a consistent performance quality. Sandra displays the discipline, work ethic, talent and professionalism that it takes to have longevity as an artist. I was reintroduced to Sandra during Hollywood Week on Season 1 of FOX's *So You Think You Can Dance*. I called her out in the audition room as part of "Colton & Colton," the tap duo who won on *Star Search* and came to perform at my dance studio in Arizona when I was a teenager. She was all grown up now and surprised that I remembered her. Sandra's got a beautiful face and a great body! She learns the steps, she performs and she adds sugar and spice on top of my routines. Sandra exemplified what I look for which is taking the choreography and bringing it back to me better than I ever thought it could be. She was selected as part of the Top 16 dancers and has worked with numerous recording artists and top choreographers on stage, in television and on film. Sandra has dedicated herself to being a voice for dancers and giving them insight into some of the challenges of the entertainment industry.

In this work, she shares her experiences and offers access to invaluable knowledge about navigating the Hollywood dance scene. By introducing dancers to the realities of the industry, Sandra's helpful tips may shave months to even a year off of what might otherwise be a long and frustrating journey. The stark transition from novice to professional, from hometown dance star to a number at a cattle call, can be both painful and rewarding. Sandra endeavors to make the hurdles more manageable by including advice from top Hollywood dance agents, working choreographers, influential casting directors, a celebrity makeup artist, successful working dancers, representative union management as well as her own *Sick Tips* to make sure that each dancer reaches his or her potential as seamlessly as possible. Working dancers will also benefit from this long overdue compilation. Take advantage of Sandra's selfless attempt to assist her fellow dancers in becoming successful working dancers in Hollywood. Get booked today by adapting to the "Book Me!" mentality.

Never stop learning.
BFree

Contents

INTRODUCTION: MAKING YOUR OWN REALITY

PART ONE:	**PREPARATION IS THE KEY TO SUCCESS**
ONE	Know Your Strengths And Weaknesses
TWO	Greenlight Hollywood!
THREE	The Starter Kit: Your Resume, Headshot And Demo Reel
PART TWO:	**NAVIGATING HOLLYWOOD'S DANCE INDUSTRY**
FOUR	How To Get An Agent And Keep Them Working For You
FIVE	Auditions: Bring Your 'A' Game!
SIX	Got Booked? On The Job Dos And Don'ts
SEVEN	Thank You - Please Stay. The Choreographer's Cut!
EIGHT	Dance: In Film And On Television
NINE	Your Career Path…You Can't Always Take Every Job!
PART THREE:	**I'M VERY THAT! MASTER MARKETING**
TEN	Dance 10 - Looks 10!
ELEVEN	Master Marketing: Selling Yourself, In A Good Way
PART FOUR:	**CONTRACTS: YOUR RIGHTS, RATES & RESIDUALS**
TWELVE	If You Don't Value Yourself, You Become Valueless!
THIRTEEN	Money, Money, Money! How To Make It, Save It And Have It Work For You!
FOURTEEN	Booked Solid? Building Your Brand With A Business Plan
PART FIVE:	**CAREER PATHS AND THE DANCE COMMUNITY**
FIFTEEN	Be Part of the Community!
SIXTEEN	Career Longevity And Transitions
SEVENTEEN	Hollywood: The Intersection Of Art And Commerce
PART SIX:	**THE FINE PRINT**
	Special Thank You's
	Works Cited
	Photographers And Recommended Reading
	Appendices A-N
	The Backstory

Introduction:
Making Your Own Reality

In 2005 Nigel Lythgoe, Executive Producer of FOX's *So You Think You Can Dance*, while critiquing my solo routine to Gwen Stefani's *"Hollaback Girl"* said that I looked like a tap dancing cheerleader and he didn't believe that I'd been given the chance to show all of my talent.

I recall the day I first met Nigel during the Hollywood Week auditions. Dressed in hot pink knee-length Dickie's shorts, white tank top and brand spankin' new plaid print Converse shell-toed shoes, I thought I was supa fly! Nigel asked if my shoes were new and I replied with an energized, "Yes!" He then said, "You know what we do in England?" He then proceeded to pick up his right foot and put a small black smudge mark on the clean white part of my shoe. I looked at him as if he had lost his mind. This was the beginning of my journey through Hollywood Week, a small black smudge on my brand new shell toe! Furious, I walked right into the room with choreographer Brian Friedman. I had a great time learning his combination and even gained a little respect when he announced in front of the entire room during my performance of his combo, "That's it. That's what it should look like!" I felt immediate validation and I remember that feeling like it was yesterday.

On Season 1 of *So You Think You Can Dance*, I wound up in the bottom three and booted after performing a tap solo. Yes, I was the first finalist kicked off, and yes, I am a trivia question on the Internet! I'll admit, I was very bitter for a long time. Not for being booted but for not being able to showcase all that I can do. On the show, I was introduced as a go-go dancer from Las Vegas, Nev. In my case, yes…I did go-go in Las Vegas but I was also a *Laker Girl* prior to being on the show. Jonnis Tannis was also eliminated the same week and we suffered through a very long week of being sequestered in Long Beach, Calif. with bodyguards at our motel by the road. *(At that time, the results show did not air the next day as they do now.)*. In 2008, I was selected to be part of the print, television and Web ad campaign for Season 4 of *So You Think You Can Dance*. I've also been lucky enough to navigate my way through Hollywood and work with top choreographers like Hi Hat, Marty Kudelka, Brian Friedman, Marguerite Derricks and Kenny Ortega as well as recording artists such

Sandra and Jonnis after being eliminated on *So You Think You Can Dance (Above)*.

INTRODUCTION: MAKING YOUR OWN REALITY

as Rihanna, Mary J. Blige, Justin Timberlake, Katharine McPhee, Snoop Dogg and Paulina Rubio. The reason I share this with you is simple. From the bottom three to the top can definitely happen. For me, I'm not satisfied with being just another dancer in Hollywood. I strive to be the best performer I can be, in addition to passing on knowledge to other dancers along the way.

This book is <u>not</u> about how to become a successful ballerina, there are a slew of books on ballet that can help you. This book will <u>not</u> teach you how to dance. **BOOK ME!** is written from an insider's perspective on Hollywood and gives you helpful tips on how to reach your goals, skip steps that dancers have encountered as challenges along the way and give you a leg up on the competition. Is it OK to be "a dancer" in Hollywood? Yes, of course it is! But, you can be "a dancer" anywhere. The majority of dancers who are "successful working dancers" are well versed in many areas of entertainment. This book will help you filter the Hollywood entertainment industry and show you how to put your best foot forward in this very small tight-knit community.

Check out the first of my many SICK TIPS below:

SICK TIP #1:
NEVER SETTLE
Never settle! You must always hustle or you won't have a career, you will have a hobby!

At the end of each section will be a series of <u>BOOK ME! WORKBOOK EXERCISES</u> for you to complete. Make sure you complete these, as this is a great part of your preparation for your future career. There are five total, one at the end of Parts 1-5. Each will have a red background. You will also see a few **FUNNY YOU SHOULD ASK...** sections that are frequently asked questions that stood out to me. An example is below:

BOOK ME! WORKBOOK EXERCISES

FUNNY YOU SHOULD ASK...
WHAT IF I GET A DATE AND TIME FOR MY AUDITION AND THE DAY DOESN'T MATCH THE DATE?

Check to make sure that the day (Monday) matches the date (July 27). Don't assume that one or the other is correct. Call and check with your agent if the day and date do not match to find out which one is correct. You don't want the discrepancy to cost you the job!

INTRODUCTION: MAKING YOUR OWN REALITY

You will also find what I like to call a <u>FAST FIX</u>! These will look like the following:

| FAST FIX
I LOST THE BACK TO MY EARRING!
OR
MY EARRING WON'T STAY ON! | SIMPLE INSTRUCTIONS TO A SNUG FIT:
• Find a pencil
• Rip off the eraser
• Push the earring through to keep tight on your ear lobe
• Do this for both earrings
• Consider investing in tiny plastic earring backings
Carry emergency earring backs with you just in case you have earrings that clasp or close with snaps but still need the addition of a snug fit. These ensure they stay on through a big hair toss or head whip. |

These helpful and quick fixes will be a lifesaver when you have that unanticipated emergency on set.

To conclude each chapter you will find what I call, *Sandra Says...* chapter summaries. You'll find a brief summary and quick bullet points with chapter highlights. Look for the two black pages with white text like the example below:

You will also find a "POINT TAKEN" section in each of the *Sandra Says....* chapter summaries. These are things that I wish someone had told me along the way that might have better prepared me for the entertainment industry. Do some "EXTRA CREDIT" along your journey to Hollywood also! See below:

EXTRA CREDIT: HOLLYWOOD OR BUST BUCKET LIST!
Start that <u>Hollywood or Bust Bucket List</u> before you get yourself on the move. Include things you want to do in your dance career and in life. Make it your own & make it as realistic or unrealistic as you want. List things you want to do like: Travel around the world, swim with sharks, dance on the *Grammy Awards* or on *The Late Show*. Whatever you want, write it down and go do it!

BOOK ME! HOW TO BECOME A SUCCESSFUL WORKING DANCER IN HOLLYWOOD

PART ONE

PREPARATION IS THE KEY TO SUCCESS

CHAPTER ONE

KNOW YOUR STRENGTHS AND WEAKNESSES

Dance is an amazing gift that is so truthful in the stories it tells. Through young and old voices, bodies badly broken down and youth that have swiftly taken its reigns, dance is life. To me, dance has a heart that beats for all who seek to know it. The art form is not ashamed to tell the story of an abused wife, not too proud to jump for joy and never too good to halt creativity in youth from continuing to change its path. Without a foundation there would be no springboard to jump from.

Hollywood's dance scene has evolved to incorporate so many new and different styles that have become so commercially viable in today's advertising market. Whether on stage, in film, on television, in corporate industrials, in fashion shows or on the Internet, dance is being showcased in many different types of ad campaigns by telling the audience, "This is fun, young and hip!" Basically claiming that if you like what you see, you'll like our product. With companies using dance more and more, the opportunities for dancers have increased drastically.

Dancers in Hollywood have a unique task: Succeeding in the best dance market in the world. When people look for great dancers they come to Hollywood. I'm not saying there aren't great dancers working in New York, Chicago or Orlando. I'm telling you what you already know or else you wouldn't be reading this right now. If you want to tour with Lady Gaga, Madonna or Janet Jackson, be in music videos with Usher, perform on award shows with Christina Aguilera or back-up Ciara on *The Tonight Show*, then you come to Hollywood to make those dreams a reality!

CHAPTER ONE

SANDRA'S DEFINITION OF AN L.A. DANCER:

A funk-*Chanel* fashion-forward beat-ologist who creates life out of space, imagination and innate musicality that continually transforms their unique sense of self and shape into a wearable and impermeable freedom we call skin.

WHY DO YOU WANT TO BE A DANCER?

Ask yourself this question and be serious about your answer. The answer might vary depending on where you live and who your idols are. You may want to be famous, make lots of money or tour with recording artists like Justin Bieber, Ne-Yo or Rihanna. Whatever your reason may be, remember it once you arrive in Hollywood. This reason will drive your success. Let me repeat this.

YOUR REASON FOR WHY YOU WANT TO BE A DANCER WILL DRIVE YOUR SUCCESS!

I vacationed to New York one summer and was introduced to Gus Johnson, a CBS Sports anchor. Now a good friend, I can say that Gus is the person who really set me straight. Fumbling around for where I wanted to live and what career I wanted to have, I met him for coffee and we talked about my past career endeavors. Although I've had regular jobs along the way as an office manager, hotel operator and community relations coordinator, he broke it down for me in one sentence. He said, "It sounds to me like you should pursue your dance career." Then he told me to read a book called, *The Alchemist*, by Paulo Coelho. Not really knowing exactly what I wanted to do with my life, I returned to Las Vegas, read the book and decided that I was going to pursue my dreams in Los Angeles.

In the summer of 2001, I came to Los Angeles to audition for the NBA's Los Angeles *Laker Girls*. I didn't make the team and went back to Las Vegas defeated. I survived an entire day of dancing from the across the floor combination to the jazz and hip-hop combos to our introduction to the judges and lastly the freestyle section. Then I was cut! So close, but it wasn't my time. I started work as a go-go dancer at Mandalay Bay Hotel and Casino's Rum Jungle nightclub in Las Vegas. The next summer I came back to Los Angeles and auditioned for D.D.O. Artists Agency. They signed me and I returned to Las Vegas to pack and move to Hollywood. Determined to make it all the way through, I auditioned again for the *Laker Girls* and this time I made it onto the team for the 2002-2003 season. Knowing what I wanted to accomplish, I worked on my skills and had a stronger audition.

KNOW YOUR STRENGTHS AND WEAKNESSES

I was ready to make the team. The move was, should I say, full of unexpected surprises. I was working for Mike Rice, owner of Inversion Entertainment and Gymcats Gymnastics in Henderson, Nev. He said I could borrow his work truck to move my stuff down to L.A. only if I promised to get an oil change for him. So I immediately got an oil change for the truck and headed to my apartment in Las Vegas. In my hurry to get things done quickly, I forgot my car remote for the apartment gate. Now I know we've all done this next part. I waited for the exit gate to open and went in the "out" gate. Unfortunately, I made the cut a little shorter than expected and rammed the entire passenger side door into one of those tall yellow guard posts. The side door was wrecked and now I had a flat tire. Not good, not good at all. I jumped out to check the door and was flowing with tears right away. I had to get to Los Angeles! I went back to the oil change place and had them fix my tire. They couldn't believe I could do such damage in the span of 20 minutes.

What's a girl to do? I jumped back in the truck, went back to my apartment, this time going in the correct entrance gate, and put my belongings in the bed of the truck and drove straight to Hollywood. As I drove, I knew I was in for a new and different lifestyle. I was looking forward to a whirlwind of experiences I'd never seen before. Upon arrival, I received my first parking ticket at my new residence. I didn't think to look at the street signs for street cleaning times. After that drama, I went over to have lunch with my friend who was working at Virgin Records. I drove up to the entrance where someone was waiting for the gate to open. The gate had one of those electric arms that lift up and down to gain access to the parking lot.

The intercom wasn't working, so I waited for the car in front of me to go in, and then followed them in. Did I mention that I had a queen sized mattress and bed frame in the truck bed sticking up above the roof of the truck? This particular gate arm did not have a motion sensor and came down on top of the truck, slid across the rooftop and then onto the bed frame and broke off. Yikes! Recapping, I had already slashed up the top of the roof of my boss' truck, crashed the side door into a pole, received a parking ticket and broken the entrance gate to Virgin Records. Sweet! I was off to an amazing L.A. story. After all of the drama, I was finally good to go...well besides the security guards yelling at me. My friend Kim had to come out to rescue me and get me out of the mess of a potential bill to repair the gate. Oh, and that tricky thing of telling my boss what happened upon the return of his truck. I fibbed a little and told him that the crash into the pole happened when I got back from moving my stuff and not on my way out of town. Oops! Sorry Mike. I know. It's fair to say that he wasn't happy. Is there a lesson to be

CHAPTER ONE

learned out of this? A few! Expect the unexpected, always tell the truth and never go "in" the "out" gate. Making it in Hollywood as a successful working dancer is all about being ready for whatever is thrown your way. It is also about making goals for yourself and your career.

SET GOALS

Setting goals for yourself is key while you are pursuing your career. Part of setting career goals is being realistic about what strengths and weaknesses you have. Sit down and make a list of what kinds of jobs you want to book. Look at some of the music videos you'd love to be in, watch DVDs of tours you've aspired to be part of, revisit episodes of past television shows and films involving dance. Take the time to really understand what these dancers possess and what you have that may be able to surpass them and or things you need to work on in order to get to their level. *(See Appendix I of Must-See Dance Films)*. Write down your goals. It's one thing to dream about it; it's another to write them down. Seeing something on paper can help you visualize your dream and make it reality. Be honest with yourself. There are already enough dancers in Hollywood to compete with for jobs. If you can really sit down and say, "I know it isn't my time," or "Maybe I have a few more things to work on before making the leap," then do that. A huge word of advice: Don't waste your time or others. In this business, you may not get a second chance to prove yourself. It is best that you don't add to the chaos if you don't have the skills to back up your hype. If you do, then fantastic. You will give dancers who are already in Hollywood a run for their money and an additional reason to continually challenge themselves to get better.

ASK YOURSELF THESE QUESTIONS:

Technique.	Do you have it?
Personality.	Is it natural or is it forced?
Drive.	What motivates you? Can you motivate yourself?
Passion.	Will you work harder than those who are already in Hollywood?

The responses to these questions need to come from within. Don't lie to yourself because you will only hinder your career. Do you have technique? If you said no, then get into class. Do you have a great personality? Ask yourself if you are outgoing, can make friends and are sociable. Sometimes your personality while on set will either get you a job or hinder you from working with people ever again. Know yourself. Get to know what works with people and what puts people off.

KNOW YOUR STRENGTHS AND WEAKNESSES

A friend of mine is a well-known dancer. His personality while on a certain reality show put him in an awkward position when being called out for his comments regarding a program judge. Reality television can expose all sides of one's personality, but can also edit your personality to suit the purpose of the show. In this instance, the television audience was forced to make their own judgments about his comments. He was very humbled by the exposure. This dancer is true to himself all the time, no holds barred. He is a kind, caring person with an extreme gift of dance and an extraordinary heart. Without taking anything away from his dancing, this is a good example of walking the fine line of editing yourself while on set or shooting straight from the hip. Be prepared for public scrutiny that may end up rewarding you or have dire consequences depending on how you present yourself to the public.

WHAT KIND OF DANCER ARE YOU?

Are you a natural dancer? Do you have a gift? Do you consider yourself a technical dancer, a commercial dancer or both? Are you pursuing a career in a dance company or in film? How do you define a technical or commercial dancer? There are dancers who possess a very disciplined ballet, modern or jazz background who are more likely to be put into a **technical** dancer category. Some dancers possess a more vigorous hip-hop, street-based freestyle that would be placed in a more **commercial** category. Neither is better than the other, unless you possess both. Possessing all of these skills is to your advantage as you can be called for many more auditions because you have a larger skill set to pull from.

SICK TIP #2:
GET INTO THE HABIT

Get into the habit of NOT being in the habit! Realize that Hollywood is an ever-changing environment. While you might get used to a set schedule prior to moving to Hollywood, you need to work on becoming flexible with audition times, rehearsal schedules and the way in which we all communicate via telephone, Internet, text messaging and instant messenger.

TIME MANAGEMENT

Be flexible with not being in the habit of a schedule, but also be able to manage your time efficiently. Work your schedule in reverse and do things outside of dance to maintain balance.

CHAPTER ONE

Sandra says...

- Figure out what kind of dancer you are and why you want to move to Hollywood.

- Hone your skills. Identify and work on your strengths and weaknesses. Be honest with yourself.

- Set realistic goals and a timeline in which you want to achieve them.

KNOW YOUR STRENGTHS AND WEAKNESSES

- Get into the habit of keeping good time management. Being late is not acceptable.

- Seek out knowledge. Make friends with dancers who have done what you want to do.

- Don't take your talent for granted. Use it or lose it (i.e. flexibility or pirouettes).

- Give yourself time to grow. Nothing happens overnight.

> **POINT TAKEN:**
> In my experience, it was the idea that I could be a dancer whenever I wanted to that made me love the art so much. When I step on stage it is mine to own. With this in my back pocket, I'm free to pursue anything and everything. With dance, I've found my calling and if it's your calling too, you will make it your own.

CHAPTER TWO

GREENLIGHT HOLLYWOOD!

WHAT TO DO BEFORE YOU MOVE TO HOLLYWOOD

Prior to moving to Hollywood, try taking the following steps outlined to see a dramatic improvement in your ability to adapt to your new life in the city where anything is possible.

TAKE A TRIP
When I say take a trip, I mean go all out. Not financially, but with your research of the area. Look for more than just good dance studios. Get the low down on affordable housing, places you might want to shop, find dance agents' offices and take a tour of film studios. A great tip for those moving to Hollywood who can't visit is to simply go online to look for housing.

CHECK OUT THESE WEB SITES:

- www.Craigslist.com
- www.WestsideRentals.com
- www.Apartments.com
- www.Roommates.com
- www.ForRent.com
- www.FastRental.com
- www.LATimes.com
- www.Rent.com
- www.Sublet.com

University Web sites with residential postings:
- UCLA - www.BruinLiving.com
- USC - www.TrojanListings.com

GREENLIGHT HOLLYWOOD!

TO DO LIST WHILE ON YOUR TRIP TO HOLLYWOOD:
- Locate the studios where most auditions are held and visit them. *(See Appendix D)*
- Pre-program telephone numbers to all of the local dance studios in your cell phone. This way if you want to take a class you can call ahead and ask if the scheduled teacher will be there or if there is a substitute.
- Pre-program all industry phone numbers to your phone (i.e. Agency & Union contact). This will help you if you are at an audition and need a contact number in case of an emergency. *(See Appendices at the end of the book for contact information)*

MAKE A FRIEND
You are more likely to make it through your initial move if you know someone in Hollywood. With six degrees of separation, you are bound to know someone who lives here or in the surrounding Los Angeles metro area.

GET INTO DANCE CLASS AND CHANGE YOUR MENTALITY
Make the most of getting into class. When you go into a class, you must have your mentality set to achieve something. Having the idea that you are going to class just to "dance" or to "feel good" are valid points. Honestly, they won't get you anywhere in Hollywood. If you want to go take a class to just "dance" or to "feel good," DO NOT take a class at any studio where you may be seen by a potential employer, choreographer or agent. Take those classes on your own time and make sure that they are at a studio that has good teachers but none who hold your future in the balance. Of course, you want to improve your skills. And yes, you want to impress everyone. But, NO, you do not want to work out the kinks in front of the very choreographers that you are auditioning for. Get that done elsewhere.

BRING YOUR 'A' GAME TO EACH CLASS
When you decide to take a class, you must have the mindset that you will perform each combo like you are at an audition. Get out of the mindset of being in training mode when taking class. Be in work mode! Put yourself front and center and practice good audition etiquette (as described in Chapter 5.) Book the job in class and take classes that show your strengths. Make sure to introduce yourself to the teacher/choreographer after you knock their socks off and take the time to thank them when the class concludes. You want teachers to ask you to be part of their video reel and say, "Hey great job, what's your name?" You want them to ask you to be part of their next project.

CHAPTER TWO

TAKE THE CLASS YOU DON'T WANT TO TAKE

Get a class schedule from every dance studio and then do something crazy like take the one you don't want to take. Maybe it's line dancing, belly dancing or musical theatre. Chances are you'll hate it. But, you may end up loving it. Most likely you'll learn something and meet new people. You may also be able to add a new skill to your resume.

Before you move, work out your strengths and weaknesses as best you can. Once you arrive continue to work on those weaknesses, find new and different strengths as described in Appendix A. If you book the job in class, so to speak, you will be more recognizable to that same teacher/choreographer at your next audition for them and are more likely to book the job from there. The "**BOOK ME!**" mentality is key. Go in thinking you're going to book the job in class and it will transition to your audition mentality as well. This does not, however, mean you are rude, or conduct yourself in an arrogant manner. There is a difference between arrogance and confidence. Conduct yourself in a confident way and present yourself with your talent first. Don't be cocky. In some instances cockiness can get you the job but it may also cost you the job. Micki and Steve Granger were my dance teachers when I was growing up in the Bay Area. They had a sign spanning wall to wall above of the studio mirror stating,

"THE WAY YOU PRACTICE IS THE WAY YOU PERFORM!"

If you practice with showmanship, technique and the mentality that you want to be the best all times, then it won't be so hard when it comes time to audition to maintain that performance level. It will come naturally.

DANCE STYLES FREQUENTLY PERFORMED AT AUDITIONS

• Acro	• Hawaiian	• Modern
• Adagio	• Heel-Tech®	• Nia
• African	• Hip-Hop: Popping, Locking, Krump, Top Rock, Animation	• Polynesian
• Ballet		• Punking
• Belly dance		• Quickstep
• Capoeira	• House: Jacking, Lofting, Footwork	• Square dance
• Bollywood		• Swing
• Boogaloo	• Irish Dance	• Tango
• Burlesque	• Jazz	• Tap
• Cheer/Drill team	• Jazz/Funk	• Trance
• Cirque-Infused: Silk	• J-Setting	• Viennese Waltz
• Dancehall	• Latin: Salsa, Mambo, Rhumba, Samba, Cha Cha, Paso Doble, Jive	• Voguing
• Fire groove		• Waltz
• Folk dance		• Waving
• Fox Trot		• Waacking
• 4-Inch Funk®	• Lyrical	

Today's dance environment is filled with such a fusion of dance styles that it isn't enough to only know how to perform a ballet combination of "tombe, pas de bourre, glissade, grande jete." People don't always call out the moves in jazz-funk or hip-hop. You'll hear, "Boom bah, whack, shimmy da da, crack!" In a ballet class you should be able to hear the combination called out and perform it without any demonstration but with the other combo, you need a little more show-and-tell to really understand what your next move really should be. With each style collaborating and fusing with one another, you are constantly learning.

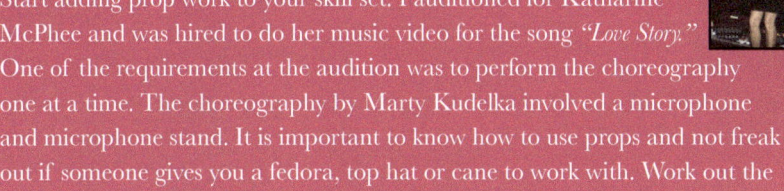

SICK TIP #3:
WORK WITH PROPS

Start adding prop work to your skill set. I auditioned for Katharine McPhee and was hired to do her music video for the song *"Love Story."* One of the requirements at the audition was to perform the choreography one at a time. The choreography by Marty Kudelka involved a microphone and microphone stand. It is important to know how to use props and not freak out if someone gives you a fedora, top hat or cane to work with. Work out the kinks and you'll have a jump start on everyone else.

RELAX AND RELOCATE

Prior to moving, I put together a guide called **R&R: RELAX & RELOCATE**. You can customize your own guide. Designed specifically for you and your frequent Hollywood travel points. This is simply a bound, organized way of having all of the information you need to get to around. Included are essentials like directions with maps to and from the grocery store, the library, dance studios, movie theaters and nightclubs.

Use Google Maps or MapQuest and make sure you have the directions printed out to all of the places ahead of time. It's very easy to get turned around in Los Angeles, and even more frustrating when you're rushing to get somewhere you've never been for an audition. Keep a *Thomas Guide* or *MapQuest US Road Atlas* in your car. You can purchase these at bookstores like Barnes & Noble or Borders Books. You can also use the GPS on your cell phone.

My cautionary traffic rule: Give each freeway 45 minutes to one hour of time in my planning. According to the U.S. Census Bureau in 2006, there are just under 10 million people living and working in L.A. County and many come in from out of town each day to work. Don't miss an audition because you didn't plan ahead.

CHAPTER TWO

I found myself locked out of an audition for choreographer Marguerite Derricks at Evolution Dance Studio, as she is definitely one of the most on-time choreographers in town. Don't be mad because the choreographer didn't get to see your stuff. Get there early!

FIND YOUR OWN STYLE

Dig deep and find what style works for you. If you're a goth or punk guy, then be that. If you're a girly girl, then be that. Don't be afraid to show a touch of personality. There may be two blonds, with same body type, same eye color and same skin tone up for the same job at an audition. You might be the blond that happened to wear the shirt that said, "Out of your league" and it may get you the job! Personal style is crucial in Hollywood.

A friend of mine used to wear this funky belt that had the name "Steve" spelled out on the belt buckle. She would always get questions from casting directors like, "Is that your boyfriend?" It was actually her ex-boyfriend's belt but she liked it so much that she kept it when the relationship ended. This was a moment for her and the casting director to chat and make a lasting impression. When she leaves her auditions, the casting directors will remember her for her audition and for their conversation and when reviewing headshots might say, "Oh yeah, that's the girl with the ex-boyfriend Steve." It's all about figuring out a way to leave a lasting impression. Find yours. Remember though, talent first! Don't rely on a gimmick to get you to the next level. There are a many great dancers in Hollywood and at the end of the day it may just come down to how you look. Uh oh! Did I just say that? Um...yeah, I did!

IT MAY JUST COME DOWN TO HOW YOU LOOK!

Remember that very important point but don't rely on it all the time as your excuse for not booking a job! Figure out what helps you make it through tough times.

TATTOOS AND PIERCINGS

Sometimes being an individual with tattoos, piercings and or oddities is an asset and sometimes it hinders your ability to book jobs based on what the particular client is looking for that day. Remember this note of caution when going in for that really big tattoo across your entire back or the piercing that connects your ear to your nose to your eyebrow to your belly button. While personal style may get you some jobs, it may exclude a lot of other very lucrative commercial ones as well. Try to find ways to compromise if possible. Find sweat-proof body makeup that works well with your skin tone to cover up tattoos if required for a gig. As a *Laker Girl*, I was not allowed to have any visible tattoos and I have one on the middle of my back. This was easily covered for each game with some body makeup. Problem solved. Try to find ways to help yourself if you want to go out for an extremely commercial gig while maintaining your personal style at the same time.

TRAVEL PREPARATIONS

FIND RELIABLE TRANSPORTATION

Make sure that you have a valid driver's license. You don't want to have issues on the road on the way to a gig or audition. Go to www.dmv.ca.gov for more helpful information regarding the California Department of Motor Vehicles for license and registration.

If you do not own a car, then you may be relying on friends to take you to an audition or on public transportation. It is sometimes more economical to carpool to an audition but many times you may be asked to stay and your friend may not. This may create awkward tension between you two and it may be easier to find public transportation to and from auditions or gigs. Go to www.Metro.net for information.

GET A PASSPORT

You may get called to do a gig out of the country. Being ready for your overseas adventure at a moment's notice is crucial to help your agent better represent you. Make sure to have the appropriate documentation available. If you do not currently have a passport, visit the U.S.P.S. Web site at www.USPS.com and enter your local zip code to find the hours of operation and what is required to obtain a U.S. passport. Expediting passports is not cheap, so having one prior to moving to Hollywood is beneficial. It also helps when you are filling out forms while at a work location or on set to verify identification.

PUT ALL OF YOUR DOCUMENTATION IN ONE PLACE AND UPDATE YOUR INFORMATION WITH YOUR AGENCY

I heard a story the other day about how a super model had a chance encounter on an airplane while talking with a photographer. He wanted to book her but she didn't have photos to show him. He asked to see her passport and after viewing it she was booked on a job a few days later. I mention this as a reminder that it may just be something that gets you work, so don't overlook any photo opportunity.

CHAPTER TWO

INTERNATIONAL STRUGGLES

Recently I've become more and more aware of the struggles facing international dancers wanting to come to live and work in the United States. A friend of mine was on the Canadian version of *So You Think You Can Dance* and came to Hollywood to take classes this past summer. He asked for my help in finding a way to get a working visa and relocate. Unfortunately, it is hard for many dancers to obtain the sponsor they need in order to work in the U.S. A few of the dance agencies will sponsor dancers but they must be "extraordinary." There are already so many amazing dancers in Hollywood that it doesn't make much sense for agencies to sponsor overseas dancers to work here since the talent pool is already so large. Dancers are to have "extraordinary ability" by the government's standard in order to further their acceptance by U.S. Immigration with an 01 Visa. An **01 Visa** is a type of visa granted to non-immigrant persons who possess a "special talent" in their recognized field. Persons with "extraordinary ability" need to have their agent, manager or employer file a petition on their behalf to begin the process in addition to the performer supplying one or multiple letters of recommendation by leaders in their professional field attesting to their talents.

If you are looking for help in coming to the U.S. to live and work as a dancer, my first piece of advice is to contact immigration attorney **Kevin Levine at (310) 207-8889 or (800) 95-Immigration.**

12400 Wilshire Boulevard, Suite 1005
Los Angeles, CA 90025
Fax: (310) 207-8889
E-mail: contact@horitsu.com
Web site: www.horitsu.com

LOS ANGELES IMMIGRATION RESOURCES
American Immigration Lawyers Association
www.AILA.org

U.S. Citizenship and Immigration Services
http://www.uscis.gov/portal/site/uscis

U.S. Department of State - Bureau of Consular Affairs
http://travel.state.gov/passport/passport_1738.html

www.OnlineVisas.com
www.ArtistsFromAbroad.org

GREENLIGHT HOLLYWOOD!

KEVIN LEVINE, IMMIGRATION LAWYER

"The bottom line is that most of the people that I see have the talent and they usually have the agent who's interested. So it comes down to, what are they coming to the U.S. to do? It is the event that usually holds these cases up and this is where we get into the realities of the business. Where you're coming to the U.S. from doesn't seem to be an issue at all. The biggest issue is the event and (the length of) the event.

YOU NEED TO FIND AN EVENT THAT IS ONGOING AND LONG.

"Of course, if you get the Madonna tour then that's easy, you just show the government the itinerary. But, if you don't do that, typically what a lot of dancers will do is become an assistant to a choreographer. So all of these top choreographers on dance conventions that tour around the United States or the world are frequently asked by international dancers to be their assistants. They'll get a deal memo or a job to assist them with those types of events that are ongoing.

"Sometimes a choreographer isn't associated with conventions but they say, 'We as a choreographer have a need to test, create and teach the choreography that we develop for other projects.' So sometimes you'll be a pure choreographer's assistant. *(See page 310 for more information on becoming a Choreographer's Assistant).* Those have been classic deal memo type jobs that people will attach to the 01 Visa petitions. Once the case is submitted to the government we usually get our answer within about two weeks, but a lot of events are over within that two weeks."

KEVIN LEVINE ON ADDING ADDITIONAL EVENTS TO AN 01 VISA

"The regulations are not crystal clear. There is a narrow way of looking at the regulation and then there is a more broad way of looking at it. From the narrow view you can only add additional events with the same employer that is listed on the deal memo. So if the application is filed by Bloc or M.S.A. (agents) and the deal memo says, 'Convention X,' and then let's say, 'Convention X' adds another show in Phoenix and it's during that six month period where you were approved already, then you can add the additional event. Using the broad view we indicate the regulation in the application by the agencies and let the government know that this person is going to audition and if selected they're going to do additional events based on regulations. This is the way people are adding the additional events about 9 out of 10 times. International dancers should come for short trips to get acquainted with Hollywood and come prepared with more skills and be hungry to find a great gig to keep them here."

CHAPTER TWO
KELLY KONNO

An elite dancer who has worked with recording artists such as Janet Jackson, Justin Timberlake, Michael Jackson, Prince, Ricky Martin, 'N Sync and Pink. Kelly is truly a successful working dancer. She is the co-owner and co-director of *Triple Threat Dance*, a Canadian dance convention, triplethreatdance.com. Kelly is originally from Lethbridge, Alberta, Canada and came to the U.S. to take the stage with the best of the best.

Kelly Konno

"Being a Canadian it was very hard to work legally in L.A. I actually worked illegally for a long time until I figured out how to get my working papers. When I think back, I always knew that there was a way and I didn't let it discourage me too much. You just do what you (have) to do and stay positive. My advice to international dancers is to make sure that they ask for recommendation letters from anyone they encounter, that they've taken class from, work with and get noticed by. Try and find a dancer that was successful in getting their work permit and ask to speak to them to find out how they did it. It's about using every resource to gain knowledge of the process. Don't think anyone will do it for you. My dad told me something that is now my motto in life, 'If it is to be, it is up to me.'

"The competition is going to be fierce. Don't get discouraged when you don't get a callback or the job. I used to beat myself up and let those negative feelings get the best of me. If I'd known that I wasn't going to book a job until the business was ready to give me one, then I would have lifted a little of the pressure that I put on myself. All you can do is do the work (take class, stay fit, don't get messed up in things you shouldn't be doing) and then things will start to fall into place. This is a business and it's not enough to just be talented. You have to treat it like you're training for the Olympics! Take it seriously. Everything you do in your life should be getting you closer to your goal, so when you do something that you know isn't, then you need to check yourself and get back to business."

"I've learned a lot in my 15 years in the dance business. There is no room in this business for laziness, lack of responsibility, bad attitudes or big egos. You want to have longevity in this business and in order to achieve that you must always stay hungry and humble...by staying in class or working on your craft every day, as do many passionate artists. Stay strong, positive, healthy, passionate, hungry, humble, excited and genuine. I want to wish everyone reading this the best of luck!"

HOMESICK?

If you know you get homesick and will want to return to your family soon then make plans to do so. There is nothing wrong with planning ahead. This way, you know when you'll see them and won't dwell on it once you're living in Hollywood. Is it bad to want to visit family? Of course not! Now, if that's all you can think about then you should probably be somewhere else.

To be perfectly blunt: If you come to Hollywood and find it too difficult, don't have the drive or have recurring feelings of moving back home, then spend your time in pursuit of a career opportunity that better suits you. I know it sounds cruel, but this is the harsh reality we live in. Entertainment is the hardest industry there is and if you don't have the drive to push through all of the obstacles then you are one more person standing in the way of someone else's dreams! This is not in any way an attempt to discourage you from pursuing your dreams but instead is a wake up call to all of the people who move to Hollywood who don't put the necessary work into making their dreams come true.

If you think this is harsh, this is nothing! You must have thick skin in order to handle the rejection you will encounter as part of the never-ending audition process in Hollywood. One day you might be too tall, the next too short, the next the wrong ethnicity or just plain too good or too pretty to stand next to or behind the artist. You never know why you didn't get the job but the audition will come and go and you need to be able to brush it off and move swiftly to the next one without pause!

COPING WITH REJECTION

I cope by knowing that if I do my best at an audition, whether I book the job or not, I'm satisfied.

TO PARENTS OF DANCERS

For parents of dancers who read this book you may want to sit down with your child to really discuss some of the rejection they will face as a part of auditioning. Prepare them by enrolling them in all styles of dance classes, take a summer trip to Hollywood and really have a heart-to-heart with them about why they want to choose dance as a profession.

Many parents try to live vicariously through their children. Pushing your child into a tough industry because you may have wanted it for yourself will never make your child want it for him or herself if the desire isn't in them from the start. Once your

CHAPTER TWO

child decides that they're going to move to Hollywood, the best thing you can do is to be supportive. Be realistic about the industry and don't sugarcoat things. Reassure them that no matter what happens with their career, you will always be proud of them. Teach them prior to moving to Hollywood about the dangers of drugs, alcohol, body image related illnesses as well as good nutrition. Instill a good work ethic and respect for their elders. Make sure that YOU are a good role model at home so they know right from wrong. Parents have the right to be proud of their child, but also be aware that with success comes pressure. The entertainment industry is pressure enough and parental pressures can create an added stress on auditioning.

Talk to your children about going to college. I've never heard anyone who went to college and then decided to pursue their dance career say that they regretted the experience. Some people feel the need to come to Hollywood right out of high school. Others may take a different route to their professional dance career by attending a university and obtaining a degree in dance or another field. It is hard to say which has a better timeline for success. Eventually your body will not be as viable as the young kids in town. Your career transition may continue in another field of entertainment and maybe it won't. With a college education, you can afford to make a different life when your body doesn't respond to that *'triple pirouette drop down to your knees and jump right back up'* combo anymore! Every dancer's career has ups and downs with right and left turns. No path is ever the same.

Parents should also be proactive in their child's dance career. If your child emphasizes that he or she would like to pursue dance as a profession, do your research. Reach out to your child's dance studio owner and teachers and find the resources to make connections in Hollywood. Send them to dance conventions to take classes from different choreographers to learn all genres of dance and teaching styles.

As someone who doesn't have children but does have a mom, I can say that being famous isn't everything. My mom loves me no matter how many jobs I book. She always holds me to a high standard and expects me to do well at auditions but she never doubts my talent nor does she hold me back. She was a hard act to follow, as she was valedictorian of her high school class. She set a good example for my sister and I, taught us to never settle and always pursue our dreams. Set that example for your child at an early age because having a solid foundation prior to moving to Hollywood will definitely help them make better decisions once he or she makes the move. Scholarship programs are available at Millennium and the EDGE. Look into these programs as another option for helping your child continue their dance education.

TO DANCERS WHO ARE PARENTS

Dancers who are also parents will face additional challenges while pursuing a dance career in Hollywood. Tyrell Washington is a parent and dancer in L.A.

TYRELL WASHINGTON

A gifted dancer and up-and-coming choreographer, Tyrell's credits include *Dream Girls*, *Norbit* and *You Got Served* as well as touring with recording artists such as Beyoncé, Rihanna, Destiny's Child, Ashanti, B2K and many more. Tyrell is the father of two young children who has figured out how to balance his life as a successful working dancer. Tyrell stressed that it isn't just about your kids. You really need to have your priorities straight. Every situation is different and how each person deals with them is also different. Tyrell said, "I told myself, I can't let my child be an excuse as to why I couldn't succeed. You need to use your child to go even further, as your reason TO succeed and make a better life for them." He wanted me to get across that dancers who are also parents still need to live their own lives! When things get hard, you need to rise above them because he pointed out that, "Excuses will only hold you back." It isn't good dance etiquette to take your child to an audition but he admits that at times he had to bring them along because he couldn't find a baby sitter or anyone to help at the last minute. He even booked a job because of his child being so friendly in the waiting room. Know that if you put your mind to something, and really work at it, anything is possible. Tyrell said, "As a parent, you are accountable to your children to be successful because you have to put food on the table and clothes on your child's back. Stand up or sit down and watch other people succeed. Keep your head up on this journey."

TO DANCE STUDIO OWNERS

For studio owners, I encourage you to infuse ideas from this book into your programs, increase the number of dance styles you have in your curriculum and most importantly evaluate the way in which you teach dancers to hone their skills, take care of their bodies and build their self-confidence. I'd like to recommend a few things that you, as dance studio owners, might be able to offer your students. For the dancers reading this, if your studio does not offer some of my ideas on the following page, ask them if they might be able to in the future.

CHAPTER TWO

SANDRA'S TOP 15:
SANDRA'S TOP 15 IDEAS DANCE STUDIO OWNERS CAN DO TO HELP PREPARE STUDENTS FOR A SUCCESSFUL DANCE CAREER

#1 - SCHEDULE A BOOK ME! INTENSIVE
Contact me today and I'll come out to teach my BOOK ME! Intensive. The intensive consists of either a one or a two-day workshop. To schedule an intensive send an e-mail to: sandra@sandracolton.com.

#2 - HIRE CHOREOGRAPHERS TO TEACH MASTER CLASSES
Get your dancers used to taking class from multiple teachers with new and fresh ideas on dance. They can be celebrity choreographers or local choreographers from the university dance department in your area.

#3 - HOLD MOCK AUDITIONS
Audition dancers with new and different choreographers to help your students better prepare themselves for the likelihood of not booking every job once they move to Hollywood.

#4 - TRAIN STUDENTS IN MULTIPLE DANCE STYLES
Encourage students and their parents to pursue multiple dance styles in their dance training regimen in addition to exploring outside activities such as gymnastics, vocal training and an introduction to comedy.

#5 - BE HONEST WITH YOUR STUDENTS
Be honest with students about their skill level and don't sugarcoat the obvious. I don't care how much parents are paying you, be realistic with students so they don't have unrealistic expectations once they get to Hollywood. This doesn't mean to dash their hopes and dreams. This is meant to help them get into more classes and be better prepared for the type of competition that they will face once they arrive in Hollywood.

#6 - ADD A FINANCIAL WORKSHOP TO YOUR CURRICULUM
Hire someone to teach students the basics about managing money, saving for their future and planning out their goals. You can also suggest they purchase the **BOOK ME! Workbook** to help students set goals, figure out finances and keep track of their bookings. Go to **www.ColtonCollection.com** to purchase this companion book.

#7 - PROMOTE ENCOURAGEMENT AND GROWTH
Encourage your students to achieve their maximum potential, even if that means they outgrow your studio.

#8 - TEACH DANCE ETIQUETTE
Teach students good dance etiquette and to practice away from the mirror.

#9 - REFRAIN FROM TEACHING "DANCING SCHOOL" STEREOTYPES
Do NOT teach students rehearsed facial expressions and nip lip singing and mouthing counts in the bud. Encourage students to find a performance quality that is <u>real</u> not faked, taught or rehearsed. Some call these the alphabet faces or vowel faces (a, e, i, o, u...or oooh). Examples of what <u>NOT</u> to teach are below:

#10 - TEACH DANCE HISTORY
Hold a regular "Dance Movie Night" to teach your students about the history of dance on film and television.

#11 - DON'T FORGET THE BASICS
Teach every student a time step, how to hold for applause, make an entrance and project to the balcony.

#12 - KEEP UP YOUR ENERGY
Remember your own passion for dance because students feed off of your energy.

#13 - OFFER PARTNER CLASSES
If possible try to offer partnering classes and bring in specialty teachers for ballroom and adagio training.

#14 - GIVE A COMPLETE CLASS STRUCTURE
Make sure to warm-up and cool down your dancers for every class.

#15 - VENDING MACHINE SNACK SWITCH
Offer nutritious snacks and water in your vending machines instead of unhealthy candy, soda or quick fix energy drinks. Include storage devices like CDs, DVDs or USB flash drives so dancers can burn or record music from a class.

CHAPTER TWO

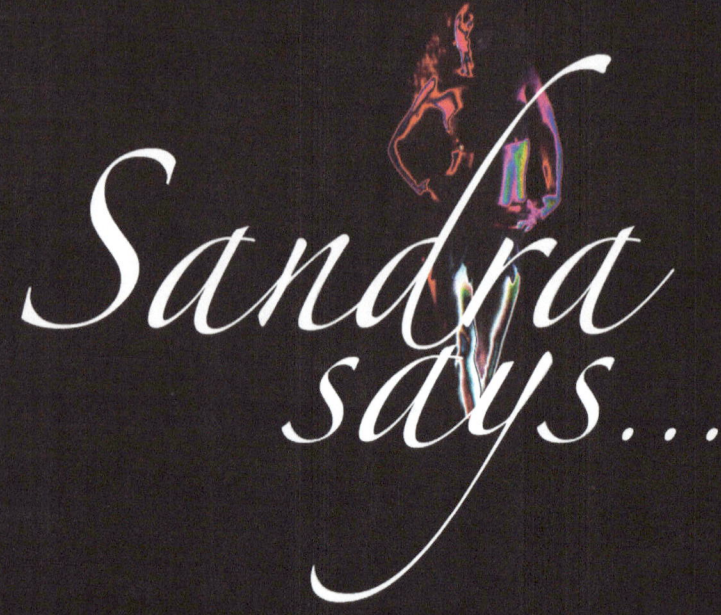

Sandra says...

- Take a trip to Hollywood and see the sights. Scope it out!

- Bring your 'A' Game and take as many classes as you can in as many styles as possible!

- Change your thinking to the *BOOK ME!* mentality.

- Find your own style and create a signature move!

- Get a passport and be ready to travel the world. Prepare yourself physically and on paper.

- Parents and teachers need to be realistic with their children and students about their skill levels.

- Dancers with children: Don't let your child be your excuse for not pursuing your dream!

> **POINT TAKEN:**
> It isn't enough to just be talented. You need the "X" factor. You know you're talented. The part you didn't bargain for are all of the other people who came to Hollywood with their talent too. Yeah, it's a party! Well, not quite. Take care of the small stuff before you get to Hollywood so you can focus on making a name for yourself when you arrive.

CHAPTER THREE

THE STARTER KIT: YOUR RESUME, HEADSHOT AND DEMO REEL

There are many different ways to format your resume. The basics of a resume are simple. Your resume should not exceed one page in length, should be cut to fit 8" x 10" and needs to be prepared in a readable font size and type style. I asked Go 2 Talent dance agent, Lisa Coppola, "What should be listed on your resume?" She replied, "It's simple. Your resume needs to answer these three questions:

> **STANDARD INDUSTRY RESUME QUESTIONS**
> - **What project did you work on?**
> - **Who did you work for?**
> - **What role did you play?**

You can also add outside information like skills you may have that are specialties." She added that, "People want to know if it means anything to put down that you worked for Madonna. When people look at your resume who are in a casting director or director position then that might matter because it is interesting, but if you're auditioning for a recording artist, it's all about how you audition in front of the artist." In my own experience, I can say that casting directors often look at my resume and have commented not that I was on *So You Think You Can Dance* but that I was a *Laker Girl*. People identify with things on your resume that they know. J.C. Gutierrez, commercial agent at M.S.A., added insight for resumes that he has noticed stating, "Although it isn't good to put your commercial work on your resume, sometimes ad agencies will notice that you've worked for a particular production company or director, and hire you because they have a good working relationship with those companies or people." You never know what part of your resume will jump off the page to a particular person, so it is good to put your best work on your resume and keep building your credits. You may have to limit your resume once you've accumulated credits beyond the scope of a one-page resume. Agencies will give you their logo and address to add to your resume for your own updates. Every agency will have their own likes and dislikes for formatting your resume.

FAQ: WHY CAN'T I ADD MY COMMERCIALS TO MY RESUME?

It is important not to list commercials on your resume for one simple reason, conflicts! Even if you don't currently have a commercial running, a potential employer or casting director might not know that. They may see that you've worked for Pepsi and just assume that you are still obligated to the brand for usage. They may also look at your resume and see Coca-Cola and dislike the brand so much that they don't want to use you just for that reason. Never list your commercial work on your resume. Only state this line under the commercial heading on your resume as shown below:

COMMERCIALS
List available upon request

With this noted, casting directors can see you've got commercials under your belt and if they need to know what conflicts you currently have running then your agent can provide them with a list.

FAQ: SHOULD I LIST MODELING EXPERIENCE ON MY RESUME?

If you have an extensive modeling history, then definitely list your experience. It is important for people to know what you've done. If you modeled for Calvin Klein or Christian Audigier, then fantastic! Try to focus on the dance part of your resume and only keep your modeling experience listed until you can add more dance work.

TRAINING AND SPECIAL SKILLS

List your training on your resume. If you've choreographed for dance teams, can ride a unicycle or can tap dance, then make sure to include this on your resume as well. Those with limited performance experience need to list their training. Highlight that you trained at Alvin Ailey on your resume if you attended their dance program. You might showcase that you mentored under a well-known choreographer or were on scholarship at the Edge. These are all things that can help a potential employer know more about your background and who you've worked with.

CHAPTER THREE

> ## SICK TIP #4:
> ## SPICE UP YOUR RESUME WITH SKILLS - DON'T FIB!
> Build your resume with skills to let potential employers know how versatile you are. Do **NOT** add skills that you do not have or embellish your abilities because you may be called to demonstrate these credentials at an audition. If you make yourself out to be an amazing juggler, break dancer or skate boarder and can't back it up you essentially make a fool of yourself, embarrass you and your agent and waste the time of the casting director. Make accurate claims and perfect your skills so you can add them accordingly to your resume.

FORMATTING YOUR RESUME

Most resumes will be formatted in a standard industry, three-column layout. Each agency will like something different but as stated before, they all say the same thing: The project, who you worked for and the role you played. Some may only have a two-column format, which will generally state the project name and director or choreographer's name. A few examples are below to highlight variations you will see in the standard resume format.

MANY RESUMES WILL STATE THE INFORMATION LIKE THIS:

Rihanna Tour	Dancer	Chor. Tina Landon
Mary J. Blige (Tour Skeleton)	Dancer	Choreographer: Hi Hat

SOME RESUMES WILL LIST TELEVISION AND FILM LIKE THIS:

The Day The Earth Stood Still	Principal	Dir. Scott Derrickson
Boston Legal	Supporting	Director: Pamela Stevens

SOME RESUMES WILL EVEN LIST EXPERIENCE LIKE THIS:

Bring It On: All or Nothing	Cheerleader #1	20th Century Fox
Legally Mad	Singer #2	David E. Kelly Prod.

Work with your agent on formatting your resume. I have 5 resumes including 2 dance resumes, (L.A. and N.Y. versions, where the headings are adjusted to reflect my theatrical background for New York at the top and TV/film at the top for L.A.), a commercial resume, a theatrical resume and one with management representation.

THE STARTER KIT: YOUR RESUME, HEADSHOT AND DEMO REEL

You may develop a few more resumes than this based on your skill set. If you have a lot of comedy in your background, you may end up with one devoted entirely to your comedy credits or to your specialty. Personalize your resume for each genre of entertainment, so you are prepared for an audition that requires you to position yourself differently. For instance, let's say you are auditioning in New York for a Broadway musical. You would want to highlight your theatre experience first on your resume. If you audition in Los Angeles for a film, then you would want to highlight your film experience first. Below are a few examples of resumes that include Tre Holloway, Anthony Scarano, Yanick Thomassaint and myself.

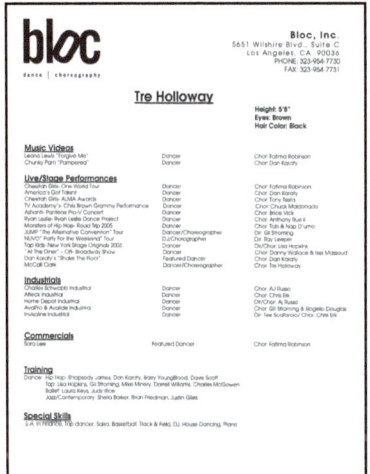

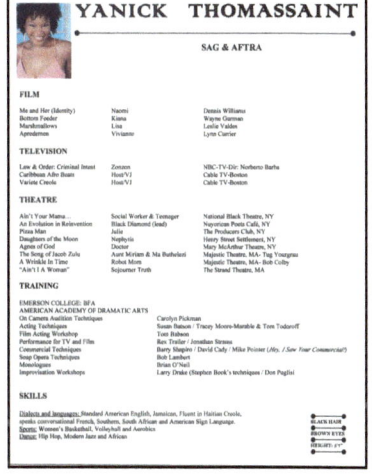

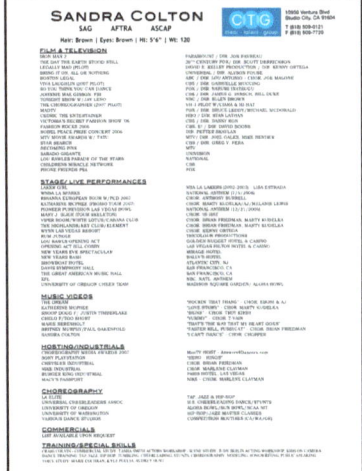

CHAPTER THREE

Add a so-called "stupid-human trick" to your repertoire because many times you'll be asked to do something unusual or unique. *(See Appendix A for a list of unique skills.)*

SICK TIP #5:
THE PLEASURE "PRINCIPAL"

Janet Jackson had a song called, *"The Pleasure Principle."* I loved it, but I can't tell you how many times I've seen people misspell the word PRINCIPAL on their resume. In Janet's case, it is spelled correctly for the song context. When putting it on your resume, you must spell it PRINCIPAL. Different spellings = different meanings. If you spell the word like this, PRINCIPLE, THIS IS WRONG when using it on your resume. Make sure you are using the spelling, PRINCIPAL. This is the correct way to accurately describe what type of role you played on screen when creating your resume credits.

DO YOUR RESEARCH

A great way to find out more about the dance industry is to brush up on the past. Read up on what's going on now and create your own future. Check out Appendix I for must-see dance movies, watch some of your favorite choreographers online teaching classes at dance conventions or simply talk to them at one of the many dance studios in town. Below are some resources that have information on dance styles of your favorite choreographers, industry insights and knowledge that will take you further on your path to success.

ONLINE DANCE SERVICES AND WEB SITES

www.Answers4Dancers.com
www.Article19.co.uk
www.ArtsJournal.com/dance.shtml
www.Ballet.co.uk
www.BoogieZone.com
www.DanceChannelTV.com
www.DanceInsider.com
www.DanceHelp.com
www.DanceMarathon.org
www.DanceMuseum.org
www.DanceOn.com
www.DanceParade.org
www.DancePlug.com
www.DanceView.org
www.DanceViewTimes.com
www.DanceVision.com
www.ExploreDance.com
www.NDEO.org

THE STARTER KIT: YOUR RESUME, HEADSHOT AND DEMO REEL

Here are some Web sites that can help you get more acquainted with the Hollywood dance scene. There is also dance and entertainment industry publications listed below that feature what's new in entertainment. It isn't enough just to know how to dance; you must be a student of the game. You must want to be "in the know" and really seek out opportunities.

DANCE PUBLICATIONS AND WEB SITES

DANCE Magazine	www.DanceMagazine.com
DANCE BEAT Magazine	www.DanceBeat.com
DANCE SPIRIT Magazine	www.DanceSpirit.com
DANCESPORT Magazine	www.DanceSportMagazine.com
DANCE TEACHER Magazine	www.Dance-Teacher.com
DANCE TEAM Magazine	www.DanceTeamMagazine.com
DANCE TRACK Magazine	www.DanceTrackMagazine.com
POINTE Magazine	www.Pointe.com
MOVMNT Magazine	www.Movmnt.com

ENTERTAINMENT INDUSTRY AND UNION PUBLICATIONS

THE HOLLYWOOD REPORTER	**SAG/AFTRA PUBLICATIONS:**
BACKSTAGE EAST/WEST	THE CALL SHEET (SAG newsletter)
VARIETY	SAG/AFTRA MAGAZINE
L.A. WEEKLY	BROADCAST BULLETIN
L.A. TIMES	MUSIC NOTES (AFTRA newsletter
LOS ANGELES MAGAZINE	for recording artists)
INTERVIEW MAGAZINE	
ROLLING STONE MAGAZINE	**AGMA PUBLICATIONS:**
RADIO AND RECORDS	AGMAzine
BILLBOARD MAGAZINE	
*THE CALL SHEET	
(Formerly THE ROSS REPORT)	

These industry publications will give you a head start in knowing who's who in Hollywood. You can start reading most of these publications prior to moving to Hollywood. Subscribe to *Dance Track Magazine* today. Purchase **BOOK ME!** and the **BOOK ME! Workbook** at **www.ColtonCollection.com**.

CHAPTER THREE
PREPARE FOR YOUR MOVE WITH RESOURCES

MAKE A CALLING CARD - HEADSHOT

Resources such as a resume, headshot or comp/zed card will help you be prepared upon arrival. These will be covered in Part Two of the book but keep in mind that it is good to come to Hollywood with a resume and headshot ready to go. Once you move you can meet with an agent and he or she will let you know which photos work for you.

My first Hollywood agency audition experience was for D.D.O. Artists Agency. Bill Bohl was running the audition and I was extremely nervous. They kept me through the jazz and hip-hop audition rounds and then asked me to come in to sign me the following week. I said, "No Problem! I'll be there!" Once in my meeting with D.D.O., I filled out all of the paperwork and showed them that I had already taken headshots. They asked me to format my resume with the D.D.O. logo and get them pre-stapled headshots and resumes when I had a chance. I immediately went to Kinko's *(now FedEx Office)* and put my resume into their agency format, printed copies and stapled the headshots to them. I rushed back to D.D.O. a half hour later and gave my new resumes to the assistant. They were very impressed that they had my materials so fast and even better that the agency could start sending me out on calls immediately. I went out on an audition that week. This showed them that I was ready to work and that I was serious about booking jobs.

HEADSHOT TRENDS

Headshots used to be black and white but now color is in! Look at different types of headshots to make sure you have one that stands out in the pile. Keep your headshot current, not just for the trend but also with your look. If you cut and dye your hair then your headshot should reflect what you look like in person. Directors, casting directors and choreographers hate to bring in people based off of picture submissions from agents and find that the people look nothing like their headshots in person. Keep the retouching of your headshot to a minimum. If you have to change a background that is fine, but if you start to manipulate too many of your facial features then the basic look is altered and you won't be able to recreate it in person. Not only does it give those casting a more difficult job, but you can hurt your chances of being called in for any future auditions as well.

Although this is a groovy picture this won't work as a headshot. Make sure to have professional photos taken to present at an audition.

TRADE FOR TEST SHOTS
Casting notices are posted by photographers who are looking for subjects to take test shots of in exchange for copies of the photos. You get new photos and they get practice and photos for their book. It is a great way to network, gain experience in front of the camera and have different looks to use for marketing yourself.

BE WARY OF PHOTOGRAPHY SCAMS
Although photographers do take legitimate test shoots for their books, there are also ones out there who do not. Be diligent and do your homework. Don't ever put yourself in a compromising situation. If you get a chance to meet the photographer, do it in a public place, bring a friend to your shoot or schedule several meetings before ever doing the shoot. This is your career; take control of it from the beginning. You never want to be in an unsafe environment or be forced to do something that isn't in your character.

MULTIPLE LOOKS
Take multiple looks while doing your photo shoot so you can really make good use of the time. This means take some photos with your hair up and down or in a ponytail. For the boys, take photos scruffy and clean-shaven as well. Don't be pigeonholed by only taking dance shots. Also ask for your photos on a CD or DVD so it is easy to upload them to your computer or burn one for your agent to go through. Always credit the photographer.

I've included a few different types of headshots that are examples of dance headshots as well as headshots that work for theatrical and commercial submissions. Commercial headshots differ from theatrical ones in that commercial shots usually tend to have a more smiley, friendly approach and theatrical shots tend to have a more serious and focus-driven look to them. The photos below I took prior to coming out to Hollywood. These worked for a while but I eventually invested in new shots that created more opportunities for my career.

CHAPTER THREE

OK, so those were a few pictures from my childhood. Now, let's get down to business, here's a few from my first move to Hollywood. I took these in Las Vegas with photographer Jerry Metellus.

The 3 headshots in black and white worked but I also wanted to have a few in color. You can always shoot in color and then change the photo later to black and white. You cannot, however, shoot in black and white and then change it into color. Adding color in later takes time and money.

The photo on the right was my dance headshot. Showing my shape, hair and a bit of movement worked well for me. I used the sunglass photo as a headshot as well as on my business card. Next, I've added a few newer shots that I currently use at auditions.

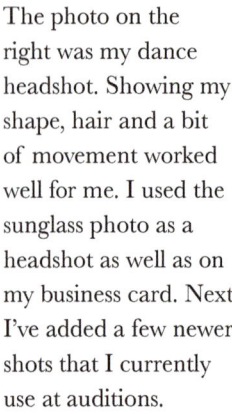

THE STARTER KIT: YOUR RESUME, HEADSHOT AND DEMO REEL

The headshots above are examples of the range you may want depending on the audition you are attending. Most auditions for dance will require you to hand in a headshot that shows your body as well as your face. My primary dance headshot is the middle photo with the pink sports bra. It has an intense look with a body shot as well. My hair is pulled off of my face so you can see my facial features. Included are a few alternative shots like an urban photo, a police officer and even one that many have said resembles Rosario Dawson or Eva Longoria a bit in the bottom right corner. You will be told not to wear white in photos, but sometimes on brown or tanned skin, white can make your photo pop when people are looking at them online. Next are a few more photos that show variations from dancers.

Photos in the red and white tank tops would be considered more commercial. The straight hair, police officer and urban photos would be considered more theatrical.

BOOK ME! HOW TO BECOME A SUCCESSFUL WORKING DANCER IN HOLLYWOOD

CHAPTER THREE
TAMMY TO

You've seen Tammy in the *"Fergalicious"* video with Fergie, on *Saturday Night Live* with Mariah Carey, as part of the Celine Dion *"Taking Chances"* world tour and as part of the Rockettes Christmas Spectacular. Tammy has created some great options for headshots. Video lead girl (below), business (top left), dance/body con-

scious (middle photo on left) and very commercial (bottom left). It is important to note that with so many different looks, Tammy is able to submit herself online for different jobs as well as give her agent options to select from when they submit her. This gives her an edge on the competition, which may only have one look to submit for all jobs. Gigs that need a lead video girl who can also dance will come up frequently. Make it easier for casting directors to cast you in the role by showing them a picture of you already playing the part they are looking to fill. In this case Tammy would submit the photo above and not the commercial photo on the left unless the project calls for this type of lead girl.

THE STARTER KIT: YOUR RESUME, HEADSHOT AND DEMO REEL

JASON WILLIAMS

Jason's credits include *MadTV, High School Musical, HSM 2, HSM 3: Senior Year* and *Fame (2009)*. Photos below show Jason as the guy next door and a hot video guy.

BECCA SWEITZER

These two photos show different sides of Becca. Giving body and sass in one and in the other a focused face with piercing eyes. Becca stands out from the pack in

both photos. Becca's credits include touring with J. Lo, *Austin Powers: Goldmember, Starsky & Hutch, That 70's Show, Cold Case (Asst. Choreographer), Dancing with the Stars,* the role of Darla in the movie musical *Hairspray* and so much more. She continues to expand her resume as a choreographer.

CHAPTER THREE

Headshots generally include the performer's name like Yanick Thomassaint (middle photo), but depending on what your preference may be you can also include your agency information. This may get a bit difficult if you spend money to print 1000 headshots and then switch agents. If this occurs, most often your agent will supply you with a few address labels to cover up the old agency information until you can reprint headshots either without the agency information or with the new agency information on them. If they don't, it is your responsibility to affix the correct contact information. You may opt to use photo paper like Tre Holloway (top left), or use three photos like Paula vanOppen (top right) or use a horizontal three-picture layout like Crespatrick de los Reyes (below).

THE STARTER KIT: YOUR RESUME, HEADSHOT AND DEMO REEL

BEFORE YOU SHOOT YOUR HEADSHOTS
MAKE YOUR PLAN FIRST!

If you decide to take photos prior to moving, make sure that you have a plan in place. You don't want to end up wasting money but do want to be prepared with a headshot when you arrive. You may want to take heed to these preparation techniques for future photo shoots as well.

SICK TIP #6:
PORTABLE DRIVES ARE LIFESAVERS

Get a portable USB flash drive and have your high-resolution headshot and industry standard resume on it and with you at all times. You never know when you'll need to print it out in a jiffy! Remember also to save a copy of your resume and headshot in your e-mail account just in case you don't have your portable drive with you. This will also help if you need to e-mail it to a potential employer while out of the country or if your agent is on holiday.

PREPARING FOR YOUR PHOTO SHOOT

1 - Clean all of your wardrobe selections prior to your photo shoot. No wrinkles.
2 - Hang all of your clothes up so you can see them. (No wire hangers.) You don't want to go to your photo shoot and have forgotten your wardrobe. Hang your wardrobe on your front door so you can grab it on the way out.
3 - For commercial headshots, do not wear white. Wear bright, solid colors.
4 - If planning to get a haircut, do it at least a week ahead of time, so your hair has time to adjust and lay down the way you want it to.
5 - Go over hairstyles a week in advance to go with each outfit for a smooth transition from one look to the next.
6 - Get your nails done. Both men and women should do this to have a very clean look. Clear polish or a buff is all you need to accomplish this.
7 - Make sure to bring accessories. Don't over accessorize but make a clear choice when adding jewelry to an outfit. Pack accessories with your clothing and keep it to a minimum.
8 - Bring extra shoes, makeup, hair styling products, body lotion, spray bottle with water and Johnson & Johnson's baby oil gel. Make sure you've covered all of your bases just in case. Include a lint brush to remove any fuzz.

> Try to plan your photo shoot far enough in advance where you aren't stressed out. Get a good night's sleep for high energy and great shots!

CHAPTER THREE

MAKEUP AND JEWELRY FOR HEADSHOTS

Creating a great headshot requires makeup that doesn't scream, "I have makeup on!" Keeping it simple is the best thing to remember. See Chapter 10 for advice on makeup. Keep jewelry to a minimum and do what is right for you when wearing religious symbols in headshots.

THE IMPORTANCE OF A DANCE REEL

Dance reels can be costly so you need to pick and choose your best footage wisely. Avoid images that are blurry or out of focus. Try to show your best assets as a dancer and eliminate long intros or offensive music. Be current with your song selection and try to make sure that each selection and edit are deliberate and make sense in the overall presentation. Agents are busy and only want to see your best work. Label everything with your contact information. Make sure you include your name, telephone number and e-mail address. This may sound redundant, but people forget to include contact information all the time.

Make sure that your reel doesn't exceed five minutes. Grab their attention at the beginning and make sure to hold it for two minutes. Agent Laney Filuk of Bloc Agency stated that, "Dancers tend to put a full routine on or they'll put a competition routine on (their reel). What they have to understand is that an agent can usually tell the type of dancer (they are and if) they want to sign (them) in about two counts of eight or maybe in about 25 seconds. Dancers (always) just do a full body shot; nothing's ever pulled in where you see the person up close or even how they sound. As simple as it sounds they should probably slate themselves." *(See Chapter 5 - Auditions to learn more about how to slate).* Have a short reel and long reel available. You may impress an agent with a short reel and he/she may want to watch more. It's always good to be prepared with a short version and an extended version so you have a more in-depth look at your abilities. If you don't have enough footage, don't throw one together and repeat footage. Hold off on making this until you have enough to make it worth your time, effort and money.

FAST FIX

HEAD-SHOT/ RESUME

RESUME/HEADSHOT IN A JIFFY!
Need your resume and headshot to be printed, stapled and flawless for an audition, but you ran out? No biggie.
- Print out a color copy of your headshot and resume at home or at FedEx Office, Staples, Office Depot or your local copy store.
- Grab a few extra sheets of paper and place in between the two to add thickness, or print your headshot on photo paper
- Staple on all four sides and voila! Headshot/Resume in a jiffy!

THE STARTER KIT: YOUR RESUME, HEADSHOT AND DEMO REEL

SICK TIP #7:
UPLOAD YOUR PHOTO SHOOT ONLINE TO VIEW

Upload your entire photo shoot for a small fee at Argentum on Sunset Boulevard. After Argentum uploads your session, you can log on and have your agent view them. This saves time and money. No more printing a billion 4x6s.
(See Appendix F for Argentum's contact information.)

EXTRA CREDIT: VOICE OVER DEMO

You've got your headshot, resume and dance demo done and ready to go. Now add a bit more to your repertoire. Ever consider that you may be able to use your voice for work as well? Creating a voice over demo is simple. You may have a pleasant speaking voice that would be great in commercials for companies like Geico, or maybe you have a quirky voice for cartoons. Capitalize off of this also. Record a long block of television programming. Sit down and write down the ad copy from a series of commercials. Record a variety. Include something fun and quirky like a coffee commercial, a sassy, *"I've got a hot date tonight,"* beauty commercial for soap, lotion or perfume, and a serious commercial for state police or D.U.I. penalties. Write down the dialogue from each and then practice it. Record yourself with your cell phone and play it back. Once you've got it down, find a local recording studio or simply record it on your home computer audio program like GarageBand®. Add a bit of background music that matches the type found in the original spot. Make each snippet on your demo short and sweet, no one will listen to you go on and on. Create a small slice of what your vocal stylings offer and you may just land yourself a primo spot by just having it when someone asks, *"Do you do voice overs too?"* It's always nice when you can say, *"Yes, I'll e-mail you my demo!"*

BOOK ME! WORKBOOK EXERCISES - PART 1

Some **BOOK ME! Workbook** exercise topics from Part One of this book are listed below. Purchase the **BOOK ME! Workbook** online by going to: **www.SandraColton.com**

- Map out your move or your visit to Hollywood.
- Outline a plan to bring your skills up to your fullest potential.
- Research the history of dance and detail your part in its future.
- Prepare yourself for immediate entry into the industry.

CHAPTER THREE

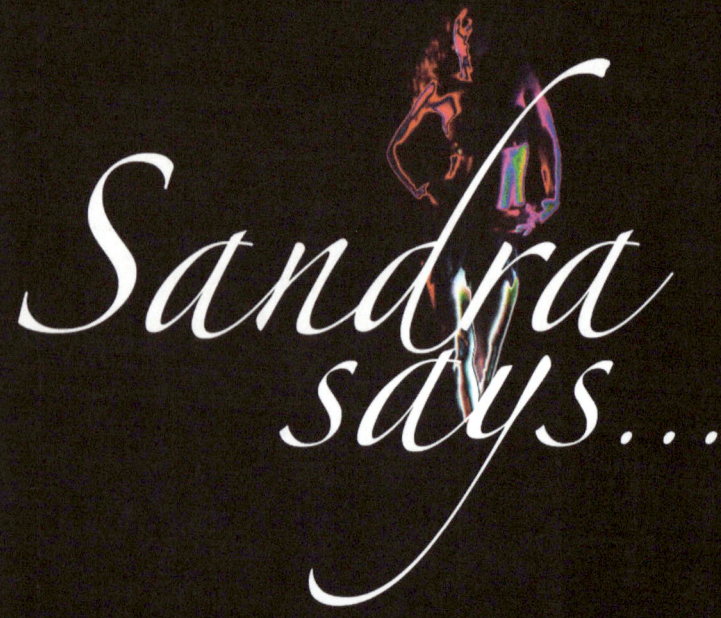

Sandra says...

- Create your starter kit today. Include your resume, headshot and demo reel. Create the package!

- Try to branch out and acquire some special skills to add to your resume (i.e. skating, singing or comedy).

- Do your research and read industry publications like *Variety*.

- Create your dance demo reel and focus on your strengths. Keep it tight and don't make it too long or you'll lose the agent's attention.

- Work on securing great headshots that pop! Work with a reputable photographer and take multiple looks.

- Package yourself for success and you'll be a step ahead of the rest once you arrive.

- Be yourself. Find your own personal style and rock it!

> **POINT TAKEN:**
> You may not have the most credits on your resume but that isn't what matters. The quality of the work you've done and the presentation in which you package those quality experiences is what matters most. Yes, being able to recognize well-known choreographers' names on your resume is great. Be you and that along with your talent will take you far!

PART TWO

NAVIGATING HOLLYWOOD'S DANCE INDUSTRY

CHAPTER FOUR

HOW TO GET AN AGENT AND KEEP THEM WORKING FOR YOU

Many dancers like to contact agents while out of town to show their interest in representation. FYI: Agents don't want to know that you're coming to town. They want to know that you're in town and ready to work. So yes, it is OK to place the call regarding interest, but know that you'll get more attention placed on your inquiry if you are in Hollywood and not in another state. This just shows that you are here and prepared to go on an audition if called.

The dance world in Hollywood practically demands that you have an agent or some sort of dance representation in order to be called for auditions. Looking for an agent and finding one that you gel with is always a task. Try to make sure that you are in the hands of someone who is reputable and most importantly, is a franchised agent. A **franchised agent** is a firm, corporation or person who has an agreement with SAG/AFTRA to follow rules set forth by the union when handling dancers who perform work under their jurisdiction.

Some of the top dance agencies in Hollywood also have branches in New York, Las Vegas and Atlanta. Clear Talent Group, Bloc, Go 2 Talent Agency, D.D.O. Artists Agency, Trio Talent and McDonald-Selznick and Associates are the top dance agencies in Hollywood. (*See a more complete list of agency addresses and phone numbers in Appendix B.*) Other agencies that have recently added dance departments are ACME and CESD. Recording artist, Ciara, has also opened her own agency, Universal Dance and Talent Agency (UDT) with branches in Los Angeles and Atlanta. Most dance agencies will post their auditions as an open call on their Web site. (*See Chapter 5 - Auditions: Bring Your 'A' Game! for more detailed audition definitions.*)

CHAPTER FOUR

Be seen in person. This is the method I would recommend when trying to find an agent. Another method is to submit a query letter along with a video demo reel. You can contact the agency via e-mail and include links to clips for them to review. Find a sample query letter is in Appendix L. The basics of the query letter should answer the following questions:

> ### AGENCY QUERY LETTER QUESTIONS
> - **Who are you? (Name, where are you from?)**
> - **Why are you writing the agency?**
> - **What can you offer the agency?**
> - **List your dance background/credits/training.**
> - **List your contact information and if you live in Hollywood or if you will be visiting the area soon.**

Each agency has their **submission requirements** listed on their individual Web sites. Please refer to their Web sites for updates on these requirements and open call listings. You can also ask for a referral from someone who is with an agency who can attest to your skills as a dancer. Most submissions are not returned so don't send your only copy. Be on top of your game and make multiple copies just in case one is lost in the mail or erased.

> ### SICK TIP #8:
> ### MAKE THEM WANT YOU!
> The best way to get an agent is to have some buzz around you. Shine while in class or stand out in a performance piece to get the word out about your skills. Make agents want you and you'll find yourself interviewing the agent instead of the agent interviewing you.

GOT AN AGENT - NOW GET THEM WORKING FOR YOU!

After signing with an agent, you will need to fill out paperwork. This usually includes a contract, stat sheet, talent check authorization form, a W-4 and I-9 forms. Make sure to sign your contract and get a copy of the signed contract for your records. Agencies update the information and skills you list on your **stat sheet** into their databases so that the information is readily available when they receive an audition notice. Make sure that after you submit your stat sheet, if you update your skill set with another dance style or activity, that you also update your agent's records. The talent **check authorization form** is filed so that your agent can act on your behalf when collecting monies due for any project you are hired for that was booked through the agency.

Your agent will put together a **deal memo** when you book a job. This is similar to a one-sheet that outlines in short form the details of the project for which you will be contracted. A deal memo normally includes the project's pay rate for rehearsal and shoot days, rehearsal and work dates, etc. See Appendix M to see a sample deal memo. Provide your agency with a copy of your government issued identification (i.e. California State driver's license, U.S. passport and Social Security card). When I signed with my agency, I made a copy for them that had all three items on one sheet of paper so that they could file it and not need to look for it in multiple places. Keep a copy of all of your records in a safe place in case your agency needs a copy of a pay stub or a contract you signed while on set. Fill out the **IRS W-4** form accurately. This is where you will fill in your personal tax allowances. Your agent is not your employer and for all non-union jobs you will receive a 1099 for your year-end taxes. *(See Chapter 13 for more information about IRS withholding forms).*

COMMUNICATION WITH AGENTS IS KEY TO YOUR SUCCESS

Giving your agent the necessary tools to work with will help your career in the long run. If your agency is sending you out on calls that don't fit the type of work you see yourself doing, make sure to talk with them so you can devise a plan together to get you out on the calls that you envision for yourself.

FAQ: WHY AM I NOT GETTING ANY AUDITION CALLS?

It may be that your pictures aren't getting you the audition. It may also be that agents are asked to only send their top 5-10 dancers and you haven't been there long enough to get that ranking. Call your agent and talk with them about upcoming opportunities to be seen by choreographers in order to build your resume and reputation in the community. Some agencies have lists that show page headings for each choreographer and the dancers they have booked. A choreographer may call an agency to direct book dancers they have worked with before. The agent simply opens up the book to their page and begins suggesting names of dancers. This may also be another reason.

FAQ: SHOULD I HAVE ONE OR HAVE MULTIPLE AGENTS?

As a performer, you may aspire to incorporate different aspects of the entertainment industry into your career. Acting in commercials or film, comedy, theater and voice-overs can bring on a whole set of new challenges. Some agencies represent across the board for all genres. It is your call if you would like your dance agency to also represent you in its commercial, theatrical, choreography, print, voice over, sports or literary departments. Do <u>NOT</u> assume that because you are already represented by an agency for dance that you will automatically be represented by the agency in all departments. Most agencies require an additional audition with the head of each department. You may also consider having multiple agencies handle different parts of your career.

AUDITION NOTICES, CONFIRMATIONS & CANCELLATIONS

With technology rapidly advancing, people are thinking of fonder days when auditions weren't so last minute. Agents would have to call a home number and leave a message for performers about upcoming auditions. These days, performers are lucky if agents are given a day's notice to inform clients of potential auditions and callbacks.

Check your e-mail, voice mail and text messages to make sure you haven't missed an audition call or callback in your junk e-mail folder. Automated text messages are issued now to cell phones, audition notices are sent out by L.A. Casting and Actors Access as well. *(See Chapter 11 for more marketing tools)*. Create an alternate e-mail specifically for business for your audition notices. Sign up for an answering service if you don't want your personal cell phone number to be used. Google Voice is a great option as well. Confirm with your agent via e-mail or by phone that you received the audition call and if you will be attending the audition.

PULLING A NO-SHOW

Do not confirm and then be a no-show at an audition. Yes, you may forget about an audition, sleep through it or get stuck in traffic, but do not deliberately confirm for an audition and then not go. This is disrespectful and eventually, you will not be called. Agents prepare lists of names and the only ones allowed to audition are on the pre-confirmed lists. You might take a spot by confirming that could have gone to someone else. When you don't show up, choreographers might then have to re-think their vision based on who is in the room. Don't think they won't ask why you weren't there if they were expecting you. The community is small. Pick and choose your choices wisely.

DANCE AUDITION BREAKDOWN

The Dance Audition Breakdown (D.A.B.) should include everything you need to know about an audition. It will be the who, what, when, where and more to your audition. If the breakdown you receive is incomplete, it is your responsibility to ask the right questions to make an informed decision on whether to attend. Chances are if your agent is calling you, you're right for the project but if you don't feel right, you don't have to go. If you choose not to go to an audition, be professional and let your agent know that you won't be going. Don't make them track you down to see if you can fit it into your schedule.

D.A.B. QUESTIONS TO ASK:
1 - What is the audition for?
2 - When is the audition? (Date, time, location)
3 - When does the job work? (Rehearsal dates, performance dates)
4 - Who is the choreographer? What is their dance style?
5 - What type are they looking for? (Height, ethnicity)
6 - How many dancers are they looking to cast for the project?
7 - What is the rate for the project? (Union, non-union, Dancers' Alliance)
8 - Was I requested? If so, why? Do they need a specific style of dance that I do?
9 - What picture did you submit? Do I need to go with a certain hairstyle based on the picture you (your agent) submitted to the casting director or choreographer?

Sometimes your agent is given very little information and they are not able to provide every detail. You need to make your own decision. Let's say your agent tells you the audition is an open call and they are looking for young/hip types, (for example, iPod). In this case, make sure to bring a sack lunch and a change of clothes because you might be there for a while, and note, most iPod auditions do require you to sign multiple release forms. Get approval through your agency first. This is a standard procedure for their ad campaigns but it is always good to ask your agent whenever you are asked to sign any kind of release.

If you are given all of the details, then make the best decision for your career and keep it movin'! Agents are busy and they don't have time to baby-sit you on the phone while you make up your mind. They are placing calls to all of their clients who fit the type for each job. So make it snappy because while you're deciding, someone is holding on the other line trying to confirm.

BOOKING OUT
If you know that you are going out of town, it is common practice to **book out**. This is just making a simple phone call to your agent(s) to let them know what dates you will be unavailable. It is common courtesy to do this, so your agent doesn't place phone calls to you for an audition not knowing you're unable to attend. Make sure to check back in with your agent when you're back in town so they are aware you're ready to go!

CHAPTER FOUR

UPDATE YOUR RESUME/HEADSHOT

Keep your headshots and resumes up-to-date with your agency. If you added teaching or choreographing to your skill set, make sure to update your resume not only on your end but with your agency as well. Don't wait for your agency to tell you they can't send out a packet with your headshot because they ran out, make sure to keep them plentiful so you always have a shot at upcoming jobs.

VISITING YOUR AGENT

Be a constant in the eyes and mind of your agent(s). This doesn't mean to only call them on the phone. Visit your agent also. This doesn't mean stalk them. This means to occasionally check in with them. When making your grand entrance, please make sure to look your best! You want to always make a good impression. When you leave, they need to say, *"Wow, she looks good!"* Or, *"He'd be great for that new gig with XYZ Choreographer!"* You never want them wondering what happened to their potential star or asking themselves if you're looking tragic going out on audition calls.

AUDITION/BOOKING TERMINOLOGY

<u>AUDITION</u>: What you attend in order to be seen for a job that needs roles cast.
<u>CALLBACK</u>: The second/third/etc. audition you attend in order to be cast.
<u>BOOKED</u>: You got the job!
<u>ON AVAIL./ON HOLD</u>: You've been selected as one of the possible dancers and the casting director or choreographer has put you on notice for the specified dates of work.
<u>DIRECT BOOK</u>: You're fierce, honey! Your agent was contacted and you were hired directly without any audition.

SHOW ME THE MONEY

Each agency will keep a percentage of the rate you make for your job. Sometimes their percentage will be on top of your rate and it won't come out of your check. Agencies make money on commissions from jobs that you book and from the residual payments from those jobs as well. Most agencies earn 10% for union clients and 20% for non-union clients. **"Client"** in this respect is you, the dancer, not the project client for which you will do the job *(i.e. Recording artist, film project)*. Make sure that your checks are accurate when you receive them from your agency. Yes, it is their job to calculate their percentage and deduct it from your check. It is also your responsibility to be diligent about checking that the amount paid is correct, the amount deducted is correct and that your paycheck is accurate.

FAQ: WHEN WILL I GET PAID FROM A COMPLETED JOB?

As a general rule, payment is due to your agency for a non-union job within 30 days of completion. You should then receive payment from your agent within their designated timeline, which is usually a two-week turnaround time to process checks. Most agencies invoice the client the day following the completion of the job. Clients can process invoices quickly and some not so quickly. With union jobs, production companies must comply with a specific deadline and are penalized for late payment. In some instances, you may be paid directly from a job. It is your responsibility to make sure that the percentage that should be taken out is done correctly. Contact your agent and confirm that they've been paid separately or find out if you need to cut them a check for their percentage. It may be a hassle but without an agent sending you to the audition, you may not have known about the job at all. *(See Chapter 12 - If You Don't Value Yourself, You Become Valueless! for more on unions).*

FAQ: WHAT IS MOST FAVORED NATIONS OR "MFN"?

In relation to dancers' pay rates, the favored nations clause generally means that if one dancer is paid $500 for a job or buy out then all dancers will be paid the same rate. This is not for all jobs. Ask your agent for more details or go to http://en.wikipedia.org/wiki/Most_favoured_nation for an in-depth look at MFNs.

SICK TIP #9:
CUTTING A SEPARATE DEAL

The people you work for may want to contact you for another job. When contacted directly for a job make sure to have all dealings go through your agent. Not just because it is the right thing to do, but because if you enter into a contract and don't involve your agent, then your agent won't be able to negotiate or help you to get out of a contract if you need to.

AGENTS SPEAK

I interviewed agents at the top five dance agencies in Hollywood. These are the people from whom you will seek representation and the ones who will evaluate your level and promise in the dance industry in Hollywood. Agents Laney Filuk (Bloc), Pete Engle (Clear Talent Group), Terry Lindholm (Go 2 Talent Agency), Rodney Chester (Trio Talent), Jim Keith (Movement Managementat) and Christopher Freer (D.D.O. Artists Agency) lend their advice to dancers on what they look for at their open call auditions, how often they hold their agency auditions, some of the key mistakes dancers make, entertainment and industry tips and how to adjust to the small dance community. Are you on their radar?

CHAPTER FOUR

LANEY FILUK - BLOC
DIRECTOR, DANCE DEPT.

SC: What do you look for from dancers at open auditions for Bloc?
LF: I look for a lot of things, not necessarily the obvious ones. We're in a very visual industry, very visual. Everything has a lot to do with on camera and how you look on camera. I'm looking for a look and it doesn't necessarily have to be a classic or a quintessential kind of beauty look. It can be something that is unique, anything that draws attention to them or visually draws you towards them.

There are so many elements that are required for you to be successful and it's more than just the obvious like how fast they pick up, how much they enjoy the audition, all sorts of things. I like to see if people are punctual, people that are friendly and nice and courteous to the other dancers in the room. To me, if they submit a nice looking headshot and resume - that creates a good impression. It means they're already somewhat prepped professionally as opposed to just a snap shot and a resume that's not really professionally done.

SC: What do you expect of new clients?
LF: The best thing I expect is a good form of communication. If someone is able to do that and be interested in developing a relationship with their agent by coming into the office to see us or talking to us then I'm more understanding about the other things that they can't get done. Sometimes those things include really good professional headshots, or they can't make all of their auditions because they have to have a part time job. For me, that's half the battle because the other things will come.

CHRISTOPHER FREER
CLEAR TALENT GROUP
FORMER DIRECTOR, DANCE DEPT. (N.Y.)

I met Christopher when I first moved to Los Angeles where he worked at D.D.O. Artists Agency. Currently the Director of Dance at C.T.G. in New York, he helped me adjust to life in L.A. and has great advice for dancers.

CF: Start networking as soon as you get to the city. Treat each audition as an opportunity to better your relationship with that director, choreographer or casting director.

JIM KEITH
THE MOVEMENT - A TALENT AGENCY
AGENT/PARTNER/PRESIDENT

SC: Which is better for you, having a dancer submit a demo reel via mail or attend an open call for your agency?

JK: I appreciate the e-mail and the hard copy submission but here's the deal: When you go into an audition situation chances are you've never done the combo. Chances are if you're not seasoned you've never worked with the choreographer before or don't know their style. So I need to see you, how quickly you pick up and retain choreography. That DVD or YouTube link you sent me, you could've been working on that combo for months. You could look the bomb. I've seen kids compete, doing crazy tricks on stage and then I would teach them a master class and the kids could barely do a *chaine in plie*. If the person has a great look and they are also filling a need that we have, and I hate to be racial and sexist, but it is broken down into male/female, race and look. If you are a 5'7", blond-haired, blue-eyed female who's a good jazz technician, well I'm sorry to say it, but I really don't need any more of you. But if you're a female, Asian breakdancer then I have a need for you because I don't have many of those.

I prefer the live audition. I get to see how you're going to show up. I get to see the wardrobe that you selected and I get to see how quickly you retain choreography and how well you perform. Nothing is rehearsed. In essence, I get a good taste of how you would look if you were in an actual audition setting. If dancers send us a hard copy or e-mail submission, we'll keep that on file and then contact that dancer for our next round of auditions. We'll let them know that we've received their submission and contact them at a later date to let them know the designated day and time of our open call.

SC: What do you expect from your clients? Anything they should understand up front?

JK: Clients don't get that if you don't make money, we don't make money. So we want them to make money. Here's the 'Ah ha!' moment for a lot of the dancers in my orientations. I bring them all in when I sign them and talk to them for about two hours. We only make 10% because we only do 10%. If we did more, we would make more. So the rest of the 90% lies where? With the dancer. A lot of dancers don't get that. Out of that $100, I'm making $10. And that's only because I'm sitting behind a desk, I'm on the phone and I'm clicking buttons all day long. I'm not out there...telling you what to wear. I'm giving you suggestions...not pulling outfits in your closet. I'm not there with you in class. I don't know whom you're talking with, who you're networking with. I'm not there with you at the audition. I don't know how your freestyle looked. Basically, we see (dancers) at the first audition and then we don't see them again until they actually perform.

<u>SC: What is the role of an agent?</u>
JK: My job is to find you audition opportunities, book you accordingly if you book the job, negotiate your contract and a rate for you, make sure you get paid, paid on time and make sure you're protected and credited. That's it! That's all we do. All the rest is up to the dancer.

<u>SC: Do you have any advice that can help dancers once they get an agent? Anything to help them understand what their role is?</u>
JK: A lot of dancers, when they get agents, especially in the beginning, they sit back and kind of put their feet up and wait for the phone to ring. Your job as a dancer in this city is to make people, places and things look <u>cooler</u> so more people buy them. Bottom line. Whether it's a Gap jean jacket, a can of Coca-Cola or the pop artist in front of you who can't sing so she needs 12 backup dancers. Really that's it. Your job is to enhance people, places and things. You're used as a tool to make something look better so more people purchase it. Because the majority of the population that is viewing that TV show, that is viewing that commercial, that music video has no idea about dance. They have no idea how many years you trained or what you had to go through. The dancer doesn't realize that we have some amazing technicians who don't work. And then we have girls who know a lot of people, are really attractive, know how to dress for auditions and book all the time, and they can't even spot. **And they book all the time!**

<u>It's about 3 things. After you get an agent, one of those things has nothing to do with how good you are. So you will still be the best dancer in the room and still get cut.</u>

It's about who you know, how good you look and how well you sell!

What used to always cheer me up was if I knew I (messed) up and I turned around and everyone was 5'8" then I knew it wasn't me. If I turned around and everyone was Asian, then I knew it wasn't me. If I booked the job and I looked down the line and there's another guy who looks exactly like me I know why I booked it because it's called being a **bookend**. A lot of dancers aren't aware of that stuff.

TERRY LINDHOLM
President, Go 2 Talent Agency

SC: What advice about the business side of dance can you can give to new performers coming to Hollywood?
TL: In the information age, there is so much more out there about how to be a smart, savvy performer. The power is in the talent's hands. Every decision that is made is in the talent's hands. People have always said to me that talent is everything. But the caveat to that is, <u>talent</u> coupled with <u>knowledge</u> is everything. There are a lot of talented people and you wonder why they don't make it. Sometimes you see people, and they sit back and wait for other people to do the work for them. Being an ex-performer, I think that if you wait for someone else to do the work for you then you're the only one that's at fault, because no one's going to care about your career more than you do. However, we all strive to align with people that believe in us more than others.

SC: What kind of challenges do performers face intersecting their business with their art?
TL: Is it about you or more about the craft? We are in a business where those things collide head on (and) because you are the craft (is) where I think people run into some difficulties. Yes, sometimes creativity suffers but I think that it is all on a case-by-case basis. Sometimes people get tied up in the business side a little bit too much and then they forget that by doing so they can push opportunities away. Unfortunately, there's never going to be a perfect contract. Even though we would like to get everything we want, we can only push so far. This situation could apply to any type of job that you're in. It's never going to be perfect. So yes, there are some people that push jobs away and they're their own worst enemy because they want it to be perfect every single time.

Dancers often feel taken advantage of and feel they need to protect themselves, which is good, but again being savvy doesn't mean inflexible...it means realistic. All business is all about give and take. I think people that have less of a give and take approach may see negative effects in the way they audition because...if they are focused elsewhere, walls may begin to form making them less accessible. So then, yes, that affects the craft. I think that there are positive ways to be very business and very artistic at the same time because unless you can be comfortable with your business you're not going to be able to free yourself up to be artistically open. It's all about management and how you manage both sides.

CHAPTER FOUR

SC: Do you have any advice for parents who are moving their children to Hollywood to pursue a career in dance?
TL: It is very difficult. If it were just specifically for dance, there are not that many projects for young dancers. We have consistently maybe two or three per year. If you move at age 12, then you'll be uprooting your life knowing that you're going to come into a time period at as early as 13 or 14 where somebody could be 18 years old and play 15 or 16. So you're going to come into a really dry spell at that point. It'll be even more difficult because of age restrictions. So if it's just for dance, I would really do a lot of research and talk to as many people as you can about that. Make the decision because you've made the decision not because someone is promising you something.

If it's a little bit younger of an age, then that may be a different story, depending on if your young dancer acts or sings as well. The volume of work opens up for commercials, film and television. The more educated (you are) the better it will be for you. There is also work in big cities across the country, (i.e. Dallas, Chicago, Detroit or Orlando). There are reputable agents and work there. With tax incentives for films, you can get your feet wet doing that and it prepares you for what L.A. will be like. So you know what commitment the child really has and know how they're going to react to the pressure of auditions and the pressure of not getting every audition. It's all about teaching a child how to deal with that kind of stuff because it's hard for an adult.

SC: There are plenty of dancers who have talent but no drive. What advice can you give the dancers who lack the drive to pursue their dream because it didn't come the way they thought it would or in the time period in which they wanted it to?
TL: Sometimes you (the agent) want it more than they do. My gut says find something that you absolutely love and do it. Every career is going to be hard. If you don't have the drive, then it probably isn't the best choice. Life is hard. You're constantly being knocked. It didn't happen the way I thought it was going to happen. Sometimes people make mistakes because it doesn't happen the way you think it's going to go. I see people, especially here in Los Angeles, get caught up in the hype or caught up in the cycle of what the next job is. Often that can be very frustrating and so they think that maybe they're not loving it as much because it's really just a machine. This is one of the things that happened in my career. I forgot that there was also a love/passion side of dance.

RODNEY CHESTER
Trio Talent Agency
Director of Dance And Choreography

SC: What do you look for when you have agency auditions?
RC: We try to find versatile people with a spark that we really feel like (in) what's going on today, that they can really fit in that mode and work as a dancer. We usually have open calls maybe two to three times a year. It sort of depends on seeing what we need and we go from there, but at least two each year. We always try to instill in our people to not stay stagnant in dance but to try to just move over into doing commercial workshops so that you do have more longevity. The kids these days are coming out so young. Now we're trying to talk to the kids and tell them, even the young ones to start taking commercial workshops and start venturing out doing other things.

SC: Do you have any advice for dancers who may get frustrated when they are overlooked by veteran dancers, even when they smash an audition?
RC: That's never going to change. As time goes on when you're working with an artist on tour and then the tour comes back around again. It's always gong to be there. (Rehiring the same dancers). We tell people to go in and do your best and your time will come. It is frustrating for a lot of people because they don't understand and they don't get it. We try to educate them and let them know it's never going to change and that it's always been this way. Choreographers and casting directors are used to certain people, even with commercials. Some casting directors book the same people for all of their commercials also.

SC: Tips for the inevitable scenario of coming to Hollywood as the hometown hero and being faced with the fact that you are in a town where everyone was a star back home?
RC: When you come from a town where you were the star and then move here and you're not working right away, a lot of people give up quickly.

It's difficult and a lot of people leave. It's a reality check.

Now the turn around is more positive. A lot of kids are getting it a little bit better because they are understanding what it is when you come here. You need to get in front of the choreographers that work all the time. You have to get to the studios where there's a lot going on and be in the middle of that.

CHAPTER FOUR
PETE ENGLE
CLEAR TALENT GROUP
DIRECTOR, DANCE DEPT.

SC: What do you look for when auditioning dancers?
PE: It depends on what audition it is for; if it's for hip-hop or for jazz for instance. For the technical auditions, we're certainly looking for technique, but overall we're looking for someone to bring something special to the table. Make yourself stand out. What makes me want to look at you and say, 'You're going to come into the agency and you're going to start booking jobs.' Do you have the confidence? Is there that extra spark? That's what we're looking for and that's what you see in auditions when working dancers are in a real job audition scenario. The ones that book jobs are the ones that have that extra edge, that extra performance quality. Of course, you have to be a good dancer, whether it be a technical dancer or you've got the style of the particular hip-hop, but you have to have that extra star power. The top agencies that are around right now have pretty strong rosters. They're pretty challenging and competitive places to get into. So you've got to prove that you're going to get into the agency by being one of the best, not as someone that's not ready to be represented. In some cases, that performance quality comes with time, so we also look for potential. We look at everyone and say, 'OK, maybe they're not quite where we want them to be but we can see them developing into that.' When we're at auditions, I'm looking for someone to excite me.

SC: How often do you hold auditions to look for new talent and how many new clients do you usually sign from those auditions?
PE: We try to hold auditions about three times a year. It really depends on the turn out. From our point of view, we're pretty pleased with our roster, so technically we could leave an audition not finding anybody.

Our last audition, we had 500 people and we signed 5.

One of the mistakes that new dancers make, and it's nerves too and not being used to it, but sometimes it feels like we're watching a class. I feel like saying, 'No. This is the moment you should be dancing for your life.' Sometimes we lose that. It's hard and sometimes I feel for the situation. We may cut six groups in a row and the energy may die in the room, but you've got to be able to rise above that to prove that you deserve a spot. That's what we're looking for. The people that have that kind of drive, that kind of awareness to really say, 'This is why you need to represent me.'

SC: Do you have any advice for dancers after they sign with your agency?
PE: Dancers are representing themselves and the agency. In the dance world news travels quickly. You don't want to start getting a reputation of someone that's hard to work with or have attitude issues. Pretty soon half the town is going to know and it can negatively affect your career.

SC: Is there one specialty that you would like to encourage dancers to work on?
PE: If there was a specialty that I think all dancers should look into or develop it is certainly tumbling. We always encourage as many specialties as you can (master). The more versatile of a dancer you are the more your agency can market you.

SC: Would you or do you represent dancers who have limitations or disabilities?
PE: It's not whether or not an agency would represent a dancer with a disability, it's more a question of who is hiring. (It's about) identifying the projects that would be able to use a dancer with a disability. It is certainly something that we would consider but there would have to be a discussion with the talent that explains there would be some challenges and limitations on the types of jobs they could do based on their ability to complete them. While dancing for a recording artist, there can't be one dancer that is standing out more than the others. There is a certain continuity that has to exist amongst the group of dancers. It can be challenging and it may depend on the disability as well; the range of movement. Certainly we're open to seeing different types of dancers whether they have a disability or not. The job of the agency is to provide opportunity for its clients. The questions then would be, 'What opportunities could we provide for this person? Are there enough opportunities? Are we connected in the areas that could open those doors for them?' It depends on the project and would be a case-by-case situation.

For example, we represent a b-boy out of Canada who does not have complete use of his legs. He break dances with arm braces and that is very unique. There are certain jobs that probably wouldn't be able to use him. For instance, jobs looking for a break-dancer that could also dance and match a group. But, there could be a commercial or other opportunities because of his original ability. A person who is hearing impaired; it doesn't affect a range of motion. It may affect some communication issues, but it is very different. You never know what kinds of projects are going to come up. I can imagine Madonna, or someone like her, bringing someone on tour with him or her that had a disability but also performed an amazing talent. I can also see them not being able to bring someone because they may or may not match the rest of the dancers.

CHAPTER FOUR
JOEY ANTONIO
DANCE IS LIFE!

I wanted to introduce to you a dancer who is a positive example to all of us. Joey Antonio is a dancer who also is hearing impaired. After talking with agent Pete Engle about the challenges a dancer faces that doesn't have limitations, I contacted Joey to really understand how he makes dancing without being able to hear the music look so easy. A gifted dancer, he wants to share his craft with the world, create with fellow dancers and aspires to work with recording artists on tour, on television and in film. He made a lasting impression as part of the dance crew ASIID who gave exciting performances on *Randy Jackson Presents America's Best Dance Crew*. He wants to inspire dancers, disabled or not, to live out their dreams. Excerpts of our interview shed light on his inspiring story.

JOEY ANTONIO ON DANCING TO THE MUSIC

"I started dancing when I was only 4 or 5 years old. My family used to have parties every weekend back in the day! Every time they danced, they attracted me to their movements, to the music (noise to me). I began following them as if I was learning in class. I always watched Michael and Janet Jackson, Aaliyah, TLC and many others while trying to imitate them. I've always loved to dance. I'm profoundly deaf, meaning without my hearing aids, I cannot hear anything at all. With the hearing aids, I can understand speech by lip-reading. Growing up hearing-impaired, honestly, it was tough but I cannot say that it's a disability because it isn't to me. I've learned that life is too short to be down about what you have or don't have. I do have my moments, but I make sure that after I go through it, that I understand that I have a choice to either live my life to the fullest or just throw it all away. **I CHOOSE TO LIVE IT!** The past is the past. Learn from it, grow and move on!

"As a hearing-impaired dancer, it's almost twice as hard for us than for a hearing person. First, you cannot hear the music…you don't know what the beats are. You're going to have to feel the rhythm from others and memorize the timing while they are moving to the beats. You have to really commit to it. One of the important things I've learned in the dance world is that it's really tough. Don't ever let anyone see you at your weakest point because sadly, it's a competition world. Don't even tell anyone that you're hearing-impaired or anything like that. You don't need any pity. You're there to dance and work your butt off! Believe in yourself. With no belief, nothing will happen. Don't ever let anyone stop you from doing what you love to do…Anything is possible."

Funny You Should Ask...
I have an agent; do I need a manager too?

In most cases you will be just fine having only an agent. Most dancers who have managers have reached a certain point in their career where they need someone to really focus their career path. Agents are different than managers in that managers are not procuring you work per se; they are guiding your career. Agents can help guide you as well, but if you are just starting out, you probably don't need both.

YOUR AGENT IS NOT GOD!

Life was pretty good when you could just go to class and dance all day long and just live in the choreography without having to coordinate an outfit, map out directions to an audition, confirm with an agent, book out with your schedule, inform choreographers of scheduling conflicts, learn new and different personalities at work every day...blah, blah, blah, blah...this could go on forever.

In the Hollywood dance community, you need to adjust almost with the changing of the hour. The one thing that I came across when interviewing dancers and choreographers was that your agent is not your boss and some went as far as stating, "Your agent is not God!" Many dancers think that you are working for your agent. You are not. They are working for you. In essence, you must work to get an agent's attention and keep it. You must not rely on them to always get you work or to tell you to get in gear and work on the skills you are lacking. Their word is not the absolute, end-all-be-all statement of what it is that will define your career.

This is not in any way to put a negative light on agents whatsoever. It is meant to give you the opportunity to take charge of your career, handle your business and be ahead of the game and not trailing behind it. Follow up with your agent, as they do get busy. They do, although we might not think it, have lives outside of calling you for auditions. Remember, they are human too and do make mistakes. You do your job and they do their job. It is a working relationship. I say relationship to mean equal partners working toward the same goal. The partner you have in your agency has many relationships to work on with all of their clients whereas you only have yours with them to focus on. Do your part to the best of your ability and not in a nagging way at all. Be courteous and respectful. You're the product that they are selling. If you don't have anything that people want, you won't sell. Above all, if you don't treat your career with any focus, neither will your agent(s).

CHAPTER FOUR

Sandra says...

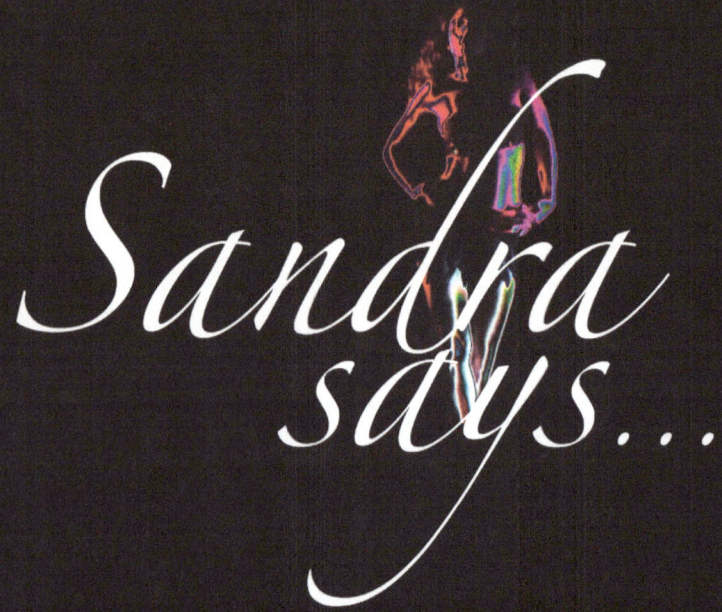

- Create a buzz around you. Make agents want to find out who you are instead of the other way around.

- Audition in person to let agents see how you learn choreography and perform. Hard copy submissions are accepted but don't show how you perform live!

- Communication with agents is key to a healthy working relationship.

- Dance Audition Breakdowns: Ask the questions you need answers for like the project name, audition location, the pay rate and work dates.

- Follow the money. Make sure to keep accurate records. This is part of your job.

- Make an annual appointment with your agent to talk about your career.

Point Taken:
With the raw fact that you can be beautiful and have not one ounce of talent looming out there, let me make one thing crystal clear: You can also be the most unattractive person by most general societal stereotypical terms and have tons of talent and work a lot. Both extremes will work in show business. Trust me.

CHAPTER FIVE

AUDITIONS: BRING YOUR 'A' GAME!

Just like athletes who play professional sports have their seasons, so do professional dancers. It is crucial to anticipate and be well informed about upcoming events all year long. If you don't get a call for an audition and you know that the *American Music Awards* are coming up, reach out to your agent. Be a student of the game and don't be left on the sidelines. Before I even tackle what to do at an audition, I'd like to showcase a few annual events that we should all know are coming up on the **Hollywood Dance Calendar**.

KNOW YOUR SEASONS AND KNOW THE HOLLYWOOD DANCE CALENDAR

Dancers make their living in a variety of ways. Hollywood has so many opportunities through television and film that you need to always be savvy and know trends for pilots, award shows, seasonal tours and holiday spectaculars.

A major source of exposure comes through the coveted award show. A great way to keep up to date is to check in with ***The Envelope*** on the **L.A. Times** Web site at **http://theenvelope.latimes.com**. Here you will find an award show calendar as well as information about the nominating process, deadlines, film festivals and more.

I've put together a list of award shows to demonstrate just how many there are. Not all of the shows listed use dancers and those that use the most dancers have an asterisk next to them. These include most music-based shows such as the *Grammy Awards* and the MTV *Music Video Awards*.

AUDITIONS: BRING YOUR 'A' GAME!

Listed below are the current award shows televised yearly and the month in which they usually occur:

FALL

Primetime Emmy Awards (September)
Creative Arts Emmy Awards (September)
BET *Comedy Awards* (September)
**Fashion Rocks* (September)
*MTV *Video Music Awards* (September)
*VH-1 *Hip Hop Honors* (October)

*Spike TV *Scream Awards* (October)
**CMA Awards* (November)
**Latin Grammy Awards* (November)
**American Music Awards* (November)
**BET/J Virtual Awards* (November)

WINTER

**Billboard Music Awards* (December)
Gotham Awards (December)
Spike *Video Game Awards* (December)
DGA Awards (January)
SAG Awards (January)
Golden Globe Awards (January)

**CBS *People's Choice Awards* (January)
Academy Awards (February)
**Grammy Awards* (February)
NAACP Awards (February)
Writers Guild Awards (February)

SPRING

BET *Rip the Runway* (March)
*Nickelodeon *Kids' Choice Awards* (March)
*CTV's *Juno Awards* (March)
**Academy of Country Music Awards* (April)
**TV Land Awards* (April)

**Billboard Latin Music Awards* (April)
VH-1 *Rock Honors* (May)

SUMMER

Daytime Emmy Awards (June)
Choreography Media Honors (June)
*MTV *Movie Awards* (June)
**BET Awards* (June)
**Tony Awards* (June) – American Theatre Wing

*Spike TV *Guys Choice Awards* (June)
ESPN *ESPY Awards* (July)
*FOX *Teen Choice Awards* (August)

*Employ dancers frequently.

The television events listed above are scheduled events that are subject to change and/or cancellation. Although dancers are regularly hired for most of these shows, there are a few including the *Golden Globe Awards*, *SAG Awards*, *Writers Guild Awards*, *DGA Awards* and *Creative Arts Emmy Awards* that do not regularly use dancers during their ceremonies.

CHAPTER FIVE

Each year dancers also have the opportunity to perform in televised events for national charitable organizations, pageants, world events as well as specials, industrials and sporting events. I've put together a few events that have occurred and can be anticipated in the future.

TELETHONS/FUNDRAISERS
Jerry Lewis M.D.A. Telethon (Labor Day Wknd)
Children's Miracle Network (June)
Chibad Telethon (September)

PAGEANTS/WORLD EVENTS
Miss America (January)
Miss U.S.A. (April)
Miss Universe (June)
Miss Teen U.S.A. (August)

TELEVISION SPECIALS/TELEVISED INDUSTRIALS
Rock and Roll Hall of Fame Induction Festivities (April)
Macy's Passport (September)
Victoria's Secret Fashion Show (December)
Grammy Award Nominations Concert LIVE (December)

PRE-GAME/HALF-TIME SPECIALS OF SPORTING EVENTS
NCAA Men's Football (August-November)
BCS Bowl Championship Series (January)
NFL Super Bowl (February)
NFL Half-Time Specials (February)
(i.e. *Jimmy Kimmel Live!* and *MTV)*
NFL Pro Bowl (February)
NBA All-Star Game (February)
NCAA Final Four (April)
NBA Finals (June)
MLB All-Star Game (July)
WNBA Finals (October)
MLB World Series (October)

LOCAL RADIO CONCERTS/MALL AND SEASONAL EVENTS
KIIS FM (102.7 FM) – <u>Wango Tango</u> (May) and <u>Jingle Ball</u> (December)
Power (106 FM) – Powerhouse (June) and Cali Christmas (December)
<u>L.A. County Fair</u> - <u>www.LACountyFair.com/</u> (Aug. 30 - Sept. 29)
Beverly Center (Winter Performances) / Sherman Oaks Galleria (Summer Nights)
<u>LA Tap Festival</u> (Usually in August - Go to <u>www.LATapFest.com</u>)
<u>Paris by Night</u> and <u>Asia</u> are also a yearly showcases that highlight Asian dancers. Contact Shanda Sawyer (Coordinator) for more information about *Paris by Night* and Kristen Denehy for *Asia*.

Some shows may not be listed like VH-1's *Big in... Award Show* because they may get revamped and are not televised for a year or come back with a different type of award show in a few years. Award shows come and go. The *Billboard Awards* did not have an awards program in 2007. Most come back stronger than before with a new concept and a larger budget. Always keep your ear to the ground for new shows that keep dancers working.

AUDITIONS: BRING YOUR 'A' GAME!

The *World Music Awards* is another show that has varied in its televised broadcasts. Usually a non-union show, it is filmed overseas and is rarely done in the U.S. Also look for tributes, holiday specials such as *Dick Clark's Rockin' New Year's Eve* and arts specials such as the *Kennedy Center Honors* that will always have musical guests and sometimes even highlight the works of dance professionals.

Late night television shows such as *The Tonight Show with Jimmy Fallon* or *Late Night with David Letterman* and variety shows like *Saturday Night Live* are more frequent employers of dancers with recording artists. You occasionally see dancers or choreographed scenes on sitcoms like *Scrubs* or on *The Ellen Degeneres Show* in addition to dramas like *Ghost Whisperer*, *Eli Stone* and *Glee*.

TOUR SEASON

Tours happen all year long. Some recording artists will kick off a tour overseas to get the kinks out prior to the U.S. leg of their tour. Scheduling really determines where and when recording artists tour and what venues they play. You may be on a world tour, U.S. tour, regional tour, radio or promo tour or simply a showcase series for an independent artist. There is no rhyme or reason to a tour schedule. Being on the road is long and grueling but if you have the right team around you, it could be the best time of your life.

TELEVISION (PILOT SEASON)

A **pilot** is usually considered the first episode of a series. Pilots are produced between mid-March and early-May in what is known as **pilot season**. Pilots are shopped to different networks in hopes of being picked up for the fall network lineup, which is usually announced in mid-May. If rejected they can be shopped to other networks or shelved altogether.

SICK TIP #10:
COMMERCIALS – THINK AHEAD!

We have all seen television commercials where cute cheerleaders are used to sell beer during the Super Bowl, as well as festive dance-inspired Gap commercials during the winter holiday season. These are not filmed in November for December, these are well thought out, pre-planned marketing and advertising campaigns that include commercial spots to run during highly viewed television programs like the finale of *American Idol*, *Dancing with the Stars* or the Preakness. Remember that it may seem timely that you're watching these commercials, but you want to be in them. Think ahead.

CHAPTER FIVE

AUDITION REQUIREMENTS

Most people will tell you that their best audition was the one they did in the car ride on the way home. Make the most of your auditions by following some of these helpful hints.

BEFORE YOU AUDITION
- Print out the directions from MapQuest.com or invest in a GPS system
- Think about your wardrobe
- Google/YouTube the choreographer and their style
- Google/YouTube the recording artist/television show/product
- Check the audition time
- Put together your audition bag
- Set your alarm for a good wake up time

CALL TIMES
A **call time** is the time you are to be available and ready at an audition location or on a job site. Know when your call time has been scheduled. Don't worry about other people's call times. Worry about your own. For many commercial call times, they are very specific and may be down to the minute of the hour. Casting directors get very upset when their schedule runs long. Adhere to your call time for any commercial or film audition as well as dance calls or you will delay the person following you.

Agency Call Times: Each agency has a separate call time for their dancers.

Women vs. Men Call Times: Women are seen at one time and men are seen at a different call time.

Union vs. Non-Union Call Times: Union members are seen at one call time and non-union dancers are seen at a different call time. (Generally speaking, union dancers are seen first on union projects and non-union dancers are seen second.)

Open Call vs. Specialty Call Times: An open call time is where all dancers are seen at once. Specialty call times are given for dancers who have an additional talent such as tap, ballet pointe, flamenco, ballroom, fire or hula-hoop work, etc.

BEING EARLY IS BEING ON TIME
Punctuality is an asset. If you are early then you're on time. If you're on time then you're late. If you're late, someone's probably already booked the job.

AUDITIONS: BRING YOUR 'A' GAME!

FAST FIX: DRIVING TIPS My friend Jessica Lynn shares great alternate driving routes:  Instead of Santa Monica Boulevard, use parallel side streets Fountain or De Longpre.	DIRECTIONS TO THE 10 FREEWAY: • Take Vine Street - Vine Street turns into Rossmore • Turn right onto Wilshire Boulevard • Cut onto Rimpau *(on your left)* • Go to Pico Boulevard • Turn right onto Pico Boulevard • Cross over La Brea Boulevard • Turn left on Cochran Avenue • Turn right on Venice Boulevard • Turn left on Fairfax and follow signs to the 10 Fwy QUICK AND PAINLESS: • Avoid Highland Avenue to the 101 Fwy, take Cahuenga Boulevard or Argyle Avenue to the 101 Fwy to avoid traffic • To studios in Burbank from Hollywood: Take the 101 Fwy, exit at Barham and cut over the hill, OR take the 101 Fwy to the 170 and exit Burbank Boulevard. Turn right off the Fwy • From Hollywood to Pasadena/Glendale: Don't use the 5 Fwy. It's easier to backtrack on the 101 Fwy and exit at Barham Boulevard • From Hollywood - It's easiest to exit at Barham and take Forest Lawn to get onto the 134 Fwy • There's not much you can do about the 405 Fwy...sorry!

PARKING DILEMMA

Parking delays occur like on trash pick-up day. You may pull up to a side street that you would love to park on in order to jet right into the audition location. Big problem, already-emptied trash bins line the street blocking any chance of securing a prime spot. The car engine is running and you're thinking, if only the homeowners were here right now to put their trash bins away. Now, I'm not saying to drag them onto the property, but I have shimmied them into a much better position on the sidewalk in order to secure a spot. It's not for everyone, but if they've already been emptied and are strewn up and down the street blocking a parking space ripe for the taking, you may shimmy one or two yourself.

Trash cans blocking a good parking spot.

Neat and tidy with room for a car!

CHAPTER FIVE

> ## SICK TIP #11:
> ## PARKING TICKETS & WHERE TO PAY THEM
>
> No one wants to get them, but if you do, you should know where to pay up! Read signs and know what the consequences will be if you find yourself in the very sad predicament of receiving a parking ticket while at an audition or on set. No one wants a boot on his or her car or to be towed for too many parking tickets.
>
> Parking violations bureau payment centers allow you to pay by phone, mail, in person or on the Internet. City of L.A. (www.lacity-parking.org).

PUTTING TOGETHER YOUR AUDITION BAG

Items that you might need at an audition can add up, so bring what you need to survive the longest audition possible. Here are a few must-haves below:

DANCER'S MUST-HAVE SURVIVAL KIT

- Water
- Sneakers and heels
- Briefs or biker shorts and skirt
- Deodorant
- Towel
- Change of clothes
- Safety/Bobbie pins
- Hair brush/comb
- Baby powder for shoes
- Tissues/Visine
- Business card
- Light snack (Powerbar, granola, apple)
- Makeup (for men and women alike)
- Telephone (Always on silent, of course!)
- Extra headshots/resumes/mini-stapler
- Hair essentials (scrunchy, gel, hairspray)
- Toothbrush and toothpaste
- Simple jewelry (for the ladies)
- Dance belt (for the gentlemen)

ADDITIONAL SURVIVAL ITEMS

FOR GUYS:
- Shoes for hip-hop that also fair well for turns or jumps
- Wear an outfit not dancewear unless specified (crucial for guys to look masculine)
- Button up or collared shirt
- Hoodie, jacket or sweats

FOR GIRLS:
- Layers - From baggy to tight
- Wear something that makes you look and feel good

FOR BOTH MEN AND WOMEN

- Sheet music for a Broadway musical audition
- Zed or comp card for a modeling call
- IPod/CD of danceable music (in case you have to supply the music)

AUDITIONS: BRING YOUR 'A' GAME!

DANCE AUDITION BREAKDOWN (D.A.B.) AND ETIQUETTE TO LIVE BY

Key parts to most auditions include signing in, slating, photos, logging in with bar codes, learning and performing the combination, height lines, type casting and freestyle performances. It seems like a lot, but every audition starts with the same question before you leave your house, "What am I going to wear?" Most of the time the people casting don't know the look they want until it's staring them in the face. Dancers who dress with their own style in addition to having a functional wardrobe that means, "ready to dance," are the ones who look comfortable and stylish at the same time.

WHAT TO WEAR TO AN AUDITION

AUDITION NOTICE WARDROBE STYLE NOTES		
• Young	• Cool L.A.	• Hot, sexy and ready to dance
• Cosmopolitan	• Hip-Hop	• Hip, cool and trendy
• Simple or neutral	• Body-conscious	• Girl or guy next door
• Classic business	• Dance attire	• All-American

I held an audition and asked people to arrive dressed as if they were going to a specific dance audition, camera-ready with wardrobe specifications like the ones above. Although you are generally given a wardrobe style to go to your audition in, it is best to add your own flavor to it if possible. In photo #1, Paula vanOppen is giving you a <u>Rocker Vibe</u> but also at the same time <u>Hot, Sexy and Ready to Dance</u>. With the fitted logo t-shirt, vest and leggings, she could easily dance in the shoes she's rockin'! Add her accessories in and cool hairstyle and she's ready to *work*! In photo #2, Tre Holloway mentioned he studied business in school, so it was fitting that he auditioned in <u>Upscale Business Attire</u>. Photo #3 has Ellenie Galestian dressed in a <u>Body Conscious /Ready To Dance</u> outfit. She could also fit an <u>Athletic/Sporty</u> wardrobe audition notice. Ellenie came prepared and asked if I wanted to snap pictures in any other looks. She had a whole bag full of options and threw on a <u>High School/Cheer-Inspired/Girl-Next-Door</u> look for photo #4.

BOOK ME! HOW TO BECOME A SUCCESSFUL WORKING DANCER IN HOLLYWOOD

CHAPTER FIVE

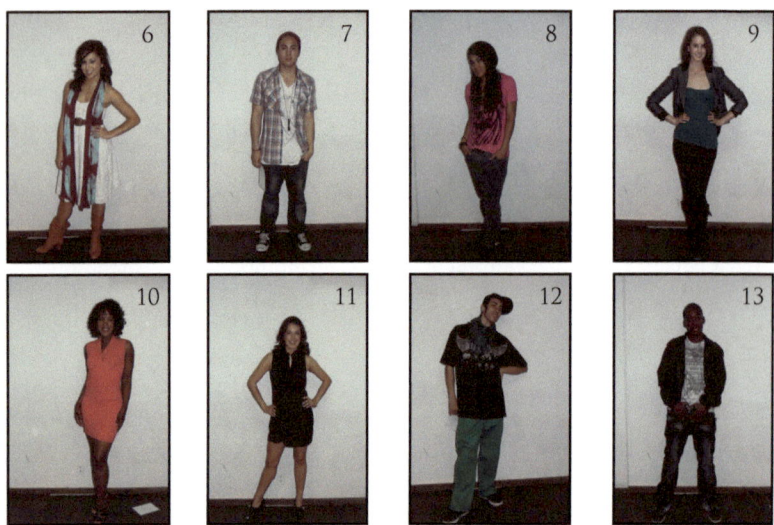

Photo #6, #7 and #8 show dancers with a few variations of a Hip/Trendy/Cool L.A. look. Dalila Muro in photo #6 is showing multiple layers with the cinched belt at the waist, while Crespatrick de los Reyes has a layered t-shirt/jean look in photo #7 and Isla Rose in photo #8 accessorized her ensemble with a more casual vibe. Valeska Mosich-Miller came ready for the catwalk in boots and a cropped jacket in photo #9, as she is also a model as well as a dancer. In photos #10 and #11 we can see an Upscale Club/Evening look from Yanick Thomassaint in #10 and Sandra Enriquez in #11. A few versions of an Urban/Hip-Hop look can be seen in photos #12 and #13. Giving color in #12, Anthony Scarano also accessorizes with a scarf and cap and Dalphe Morantes ties in the jacket with a cool belt in photo #13.

By asking dancers to come in wardrobe specific attire to an audition, casting directors and choreographers want to have you, the dancer, give them an idea of what the final product will look like. This is your time to put your own personal style into the wardrobe description. Sometimes you will get a specific wardrobe note. I auditioned for a Target commercial and was asked to wear a red t-shirt and khaki pants and tennis shoes. They were very specific to the look they wanted to see, as it is one of the ways they identify their employee uniform. Don't stray from an audition wardrobe note too far because you might end up looking out of place. You may go to an audition and be the only one in a cheerleading outfit while everyone else is in baggy clothes. This indicates one of two things: You're at the wrong audition or you're the only one who got the right audition wardrobe notes!

For commercial auditions, it is good to wear bright solid colors, avoid prints, plaids, white and black for camera. It is also good to note that when you are asked to bring your own clothing to a shoot to avoid logos or emblems that denote a brand, as this is usually not approved for use. Dressing the part does matter. Look around at what people who are booking jobs are wearing and take notes.

> ## SICK TIP #12:
> ## FASHION TREND
> I am not against wearing camouflage ever, but I used to go to every hip-hop audition and see all of these girls in tight tops and camo pants. I was so over it and thought that it just looked so unoriginal. For me, I'm not the one to start doing what everyone else does. If the costume is camouflage, sure I'll wear it. To start wearing what the fad is seems like you are compromising your own personal style. You can always make the new trend into your own style or add your own flare on top of it. Fashion trends change, just make sure that you create your own look and don't walk into the audition along with 15 other girls, or guys for that matter, wearing the same camouflage pants. Set yourself apart. You can still be hip-hop with your own unique flavor!

AUDITION ACCESSORIES

A general rule of thumb with audition accessories is: If you can't dance in it, don't wear it! Many times your accessories will get in the way of a great audition. Bangles that keep running up and down your arms, hoops that keep getting caught in your hair, sometimes even your hair itself can hinder your performance at an audition. Guys may want to practice in hats as well. Whether it's a baseball cap or a derby, at some point in your career you will wear a hat. Ladies may wear hats also, but this occurs more often for men. If a backwards baseball cap is your style then make sure it doesn't fly off during an audition and trip up the next guy. For men and women, piercings and accessories may be stylish but partnering can get dangerous. A ring may cut someone's hand, or worse, you may rip out a belly ring during a lift or possibly get caught with an earring. Minimize your injuries by keeping your accessories down to the essentials so that you know you can perform your best.

DO YOU HEAR CRICKETS?

I've been really open about the dance industry and now I'll let you in on the awkward truth. Ladies and gentlemen, there's something I like to call,

NAKED AUDITION SILENCE!

CHAPTER FIVE

Yes, it is exactly what it sounds like. You will, at one time or another, probably attend an audition and strip down to those bare essentials. It may be toward the end of the audition or at the very beginning. A choreographer may say that they don't want you in any baggy clothes or that the job is in silhouette and they need to see bodies. So know this now, it isn't an effort to degrade you. No dancer ever says, "Hey, I want to get up this morning and go to an audition to strip down to my itty bitty bra and panties!" OK, someone does, but most don't! There will be an awkward silence and then you will just start talking to your neighbor. Trust me, it'll happen. Just maintain confidence, suck it in and know that we're all in the same boat. Guys, this may also happen to you as well. Just be shirtless and sexy! Check out an actual photo of the naked audition silence, LOL!

AUDITION SAFETY AND COMFORT

Often you must be in funky or less-than-appropriate street attire to walk from your car to the audition venue. For the ladies, wear something to cover up so you feel safe, especially in the evening hours. On a comfort note, bring flip flops to walk to and from an audition and slip on those heels at the last minute to save your pretty feet. If you are in a skirt then boy shorts are a must when auditioning in skimpy attire. Just slip off comfy sweats at the last minute and you're ready to go. Remember to always keep it classy! Ladies wearing skirts with only thong underwear underneath...not so much! Cover it up - if it's meant to come out, trust me, it will on its own.

> ## SICK TIP #13:
> ## HAIROGRAPHY 101
>
> Brian Friedman has been known to use some sexy hairography. I say, "Live it, love it and learn it!" Adding head rolls and intricate details can make hairography add an extra half count to an extra full count to a move. Ladies, please practice dancing with your hair down. This is an added bonus once you move here because if you can figure out a way to style your hair and perform with it down and not be distracted by it, you are way ahead of the game.

AUDITIONS: BRING YOUR 'A' GAME!

AUDITION TERMINOLOGY:
SIGN-IN/SLATE/PHOTO/BAR CODE/HEIGHT LINE/ TYPE CASTING/INTERVIEW

The audition process for music videos, recording artists, television shows, cruise lines, theme parks, films and industrials are all different but the terminology will remain the same.

SIGN-IN

To keep an audition running smoothly there is a sign-in process that takes place. Usually you are asked to sign-in with your name, agency, agency contact (which is your agent's name), agency phone number and sometimes your contact phone number and e-mail. You do not have to supply your contact information if you do not want to. Your agency information is enough. Sometimes there are too many people to do this and a choreographer may choose to type cast first before asking for people to sign-in. They may also teach a combination and then make a cut before asking you for headshots and resumes. At commercial and theatrical auditions, there will always be a sign-in sheet. *(Example SAG/AFTRA Exhibit E sign-in below)*.

When signing in, write your contact information legibly. The last thing you want to do is not hear your name called because the choreographer butchered it or can't read it. Remember the number you signed in with. This way if you don't hear your name, you can ask around to see what number they are on. At commercial auditions don't forget to sign-out! This is crucial if you are a union member. The casting session may go longer than anticipated and there are penalties for keeping you there longer than one hour. Get into the habit of always signing out even if you are there for less than one hour. Below is a color key with the fields that need to be correctly filled in by you at the audition.

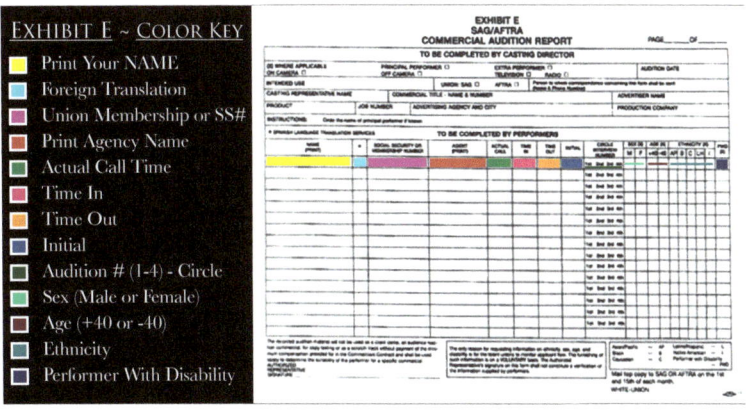

BOOK ME! HOW TO BECOME A SUCCESSFUL WORKING DANCER IN HOLLYWOOD   75

CHAPTER FIVE

The fields on an Exhibit E *(listed on page 75)* - The SAG/AFTRA Commercial Audition Report is very easy to fill out. Fill in your **name** in the first field. For a foreign **language translation** check the second field or let the casting director know. Fill in the rest of the fields accurately as to your **agency name**, (for Clear Talent Group I put the abbreviated C.T.G. in this field), **sex** (male or female), **age** (over or under 40) and your **ethnicity** *(AP: Asian/Pacific, B: Black, C: Caucasian, L: Latino/Hispanic, I: Native American)* and if you have a disability make sure to check the **P.W.D.** box *(Performer With Disability)*. In the field where you are to put in your **call times**, your actual call time is the time your agent gave you as your given appointment time. The **time in** and **time out** are the times in which you arrived and left the audition. If you arrive early, great! But that is not your actual call time, that is your **arrival time** or your time in. Complete this portion accurately because your start time for when you calculate the time you've spent at the audition will not begin until your actual call time. This is very important for overtime calculations.

SAG/AFTRA - GLENN HIRAOKA *Interview Conducted prior to sag/aftra merger
National Director, Stunts, Singers, Dancers & Safety Dept.

"Performers who do not sign-out from an audition will not receive the overtime payment required by the Commercials Contract. It is incumbent on all performers to sign-in and out from auditions. These commercial Exhibit E sign-in and out sheets are under the control of the casting director, and the signatory company (advertising agency or advertiser) is responsible for paying overtime monies when a performer goes into overtime. This contract provision will help the casting director to ensure that performers are seen on a scheduled basis throughout the day and for efficiently managing the audition process.

"The Guild recommends that auditioning performers do not write their Social Security numbers on the Exhibit E Sign-In sheet. The occurrence of identification thefts should bring a greater awareness to the performer whenever Social Security numbers are requested. For the commercial audition sign-in sheets, it is recommended that a performer write **"On File"** in the space requesting your Social Security number. If any audition overtime payments become due, then the casting director or advertising agency can contact the Guild or the agent and request the information." *(For overtime rates see Chapter 12 - If You Don't Value Yourself Then You Become Valueless).*

SLATE
Slating is just a term to identify you on camera. At the conclusion of a dance audition, you may be asked to slate your name, height, agency, etc. Look directly into

AUDITIONS: BRING YOUR 'A' GAME!

the camera, and with your own unique personality, say your name and any other information requested. If you are asked your age and are not comfortable saying that you are 35 years old because the role calls for a 22 year old, you by law do not have to state how old you are. You can, however, state that you play 18-25 years old or whatever age range you and your agent have discussed. Show personality during your slate. I've said my name in Spanish, sang my introduction or given a cute hair toss at the end. Make it count. If a casting director is specific and asks you to be very straight with your delivery of your slate, don't add extras. Follow their instructions so they don't have to re-shoot you.

PROFILES

For your profiles, give a slow turn from looking direct to camera to one side then back to camera and then to the opposite side and back to camera. Keep your eyes looking at the camera until the last second your head changes to the profile side. Always have something behind your eyes like Herman Chan in photo #14. While shooting the pilot episode of *Legally Mad*, Director Kenny Ortega explained how he wanted to see that we had a secret behind our eyes and to show a fire or light during the performance. Your profiles are no different. Don't lose the intensity behind your eyes just because you are changing your focus away from the camera. In Yanick Thomassaint's profile, (photo #15), her hair is covering her stunning features. If you hair covers your face, pull it back into a <u>lifted</u> ponytail off of your neck (photo #16). This creates a nicer profile and elongates your neck (photo #17).

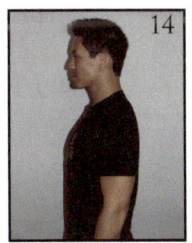 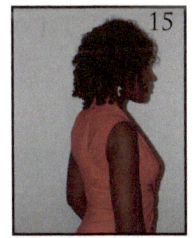  

SHOW YOUR HANDS

To show your hands, place both hands in front of your face (photo #18) and then flip them to show the other side (photo #19). Don't flash them so quickly that the casting director can't get the shot. Take your time.

CHAPTER FIVE

HEIGHT LINE

Being asked to do a height line may be key for the vision of the director or choreographer. Make sure to get into one quickly, don't waste time and make sure to be accurate. You may also be asked to take off your shoes to be measured on a wall for height.

SICK TIP #14:
TRICKS OF THE TRADE (HEIGHT)

Strategy is key! Would you go into battle without being prepared? <u>NO</u>! Why is an audition any different? Know the artist you are auditioning for. This means, you should know how tall they are too! *(See Appendix H-1 and H-2 of recording artist heights.)* If you are slightly shorter than the artist, wear taller heels and punch up your hairstyle. If you are taller than the artist, slick you hair down, and wear flats or a boot with a shorter chunky heel. Even out the playing field. Think like you're going to book the job no matter what the height requirement is.

TYPE CASTING PROCESS

Type casting is a way to put people into ethnic, height or specialty-based categories in order to cut down the number of dancers at an audition based on a pre-determined number of cast members. It is unfortunate, but it's a way to narrow the field before even getting started.

FILLING OUT SIZE CARDS AND INFORMATION FORMS

You may be handed a size card to fill out. Fill out your measurement information. Know your sizes. If you don't know them, no one else will. Fill out contact information with you agent's information. Do <u>NOT</u> put your Social Security number on this form. If you are booked on a job, your agent will handle the payment details and you will be asked to fill out IRS forms that will include this information. Know the difference between a W-2, W-4 and I-9 form. *(See Chapter 13 for more info).*

AUDITIONS: BRING YOUR 'A' GAME!

KNOW YOUR BOUNDARIES

On your size sheet, there may be questions that ask you what you are willing or unwilling to do (i.e. Are willing to work as an extra? Availability for certain rehearsal and working dates.) The size sheet or questionnaire may also include questions regarding if you are comfortable with nudity, semi or implied nudity or suggestive choreography. Do NOT feel as though you have to say "Yes" to these questions. These are to determine what the casting directors or choreographers can consider you for throughout the audition process. Some men and women feel very comfortable with their bodies and are OK with being part of body painting or being dressed in very limited or suggestive clothing. The people who feel this way should check "Yes" in that box and others who don't should check the "NO" box on these questions. Never feel pressured into saying, "Yes" to something you don't feel comfortable with. In the end, you are the one deciding how your career path will go. The way you begin your career is how it will continue.

SICK TIP #15: PRINT YOUR OWN SIZE CARD STICKERS

Most size card information is listed in the same exact format and if it isn't, most likely it asks the same questions just in a different order. Make your own size card stickers by creating a Microsoft Word document on your computer and filling out the necessary information in the square block format. Purchase labels from Staples, Office Depot or Office Max that are blank so you can create your own size. Print them out, perforate them and have them handy at your next audition call. This will save you time and energy. While others are focusing on filling out the paperwork and wondering exactly what size their waist is, you can focus on listening to the music, doing the combination one more time or just zoning out all of the nonsense.

AUDITION ORGANIZATION TECHNIQUES

Know your sizes, bring your bar code *(see page 241 for more information)*, attach it to the back of your grocery store rewards card so it is with you all the time and organize your auditions with a simple chart *(See example Audition Tracker in Appendix K)*.

AUDITION TRACKER FORM		
FIELDS TO INCLUDE:	• Date • Client/product • Agent/manager • Casting Director/choreographer • What medium? Input one of the following: (TV/print/film/industrial/Internet/commercial)	• Clothing • Callback • Callback date • On avail. • Booked • Dates worked

BOOK ME! HOW TO BECOME A SUCCESSFUL WORKING DANCER IN HOLLYWOOD

By making this chart, you can list your auditions, the choreographers or casting agents you auditioned for, list what you wore and remember it for the callback. Also use it to evaluate how many jobs you are booking, getting a callback and/or being put on avail. for. Highlight your bookings and callbacks in different colors. Figure out what the difference was in your performance at the auditions and note reasons why you may have booked one job over the other or why you're being put on avail. and still not booking the job.

AUDITION ETIQUETTE

A few rules of engagement exist in the dance world. There is friendly competition and then there are people who just do not know how to conduct themselves while auditioning. Don't be fooled that the choreographer doesn't see poor audition etiquette. It may cost you the job.

#1 - KNOW YOUR SPACING AND BE COURTEOUS

When you are learning the combination, give a good zone between you and the other dancers. If there isn't any room, don't worry, just do your best. Be conscious of who is in front, on the side and behind you. You don't want to bump into others, step on feet or unintentionally whack someone in the face. I've had my fair share of stiletto jabs to my feet and they didn't feel good!

#2 - LEARN QUICKLY AND FIGURE OUT WHERE TO STAND

Time waits for no dancer! In an audition, you will do your best if you are a quick learner. With a large group attending auditions, choreographers do not have time to keep repeating steps. If you are a slow learner, try to work on picking up material quicker. Go to the front in the beginning of an audition to get a head start on the combo instead of starting from behind. The quicker you learn, the more time you have to put your personality into the steps and perform it without focusing on what comes next in the combination. Every dancer has a different learning process and I don't want to discourage any dancers by saying that you must be a quick learner. If you learn best in the back and then want to come to the front that's fine. If you want to stand to the side of the choreographer to learn then that's great also. Do what works best for you.

I personally like to stand directly behind the choreographer in the center of the room simply for the fact that I can tell when I'm not doing something exactly right because my moves will be off from the choreographer. Secondly, I know that when they normally turn around to watch the combination, I'm right there in view. You may have your own method to picking up choreography. If you aren't a quick learner then work on this skill, as it will help you tremendously in the long run. If the choreographer asks you to switch lines, SWITCH LINES! If they ask the front rows to bend down so the back rows can see, KNEEL DOWN SO THE BACK ROW CAN SEE! This is just good form and good karma. When asked to perform the routine in small groups and not to do the material on the side, DON'T DO THE COMBO ON THE SIDE! There is a reason that you are asked not to do the combo, IT'S DISTRACTING! Refrain from doing this or step outside to get an extra run through on your own.

#4 - KNOW WHEN AND WHEN NOT TO ASK QUESTIONS. WHAT IS THE CHOREOGRAPHER'S PREFERENCE?

Some choreographers don't mind answering questions and breaking down the combination over and over. Most choreographers are on a strict timeline with room rentals and getting footage of auditions back to their respective clients in order to cast the job. If someone asks a question, pay attention to the answer. If a choreographer makes a change to a move, make the correction yourself. Don't ask the choreographer a question like "Wasn't the head on '5' a minute ago?" Make the internal correction for yourself and if the choreographer changes the combination while teaching it, make the change then too, unless it is something terribly crucial to a move that makes no sense with the actual timing of the piece. You don't want to already be on their bad side for calling them out in front of the whole room. Most of the time when a move changes and ends up on other counts, it is by mistake and other times it is very deliberate to see how you adjust to constant change.

#5 - KNOW WHEN TO BLEND AND WHEN TO SHINE

At many auditions, you will hear a choreographer say to put your own personality into the combination. This does not mean you have the liberty to change the steps. This means you have license to throw your own flare on top of it to make it "your own." If you simply do the choreography the same as it was taught without anything extraordinary to make you stand out then you will in turn just look like plain Jane and probably not book the job. I was at a commercial audition where the casting director separated us into groups of five and we were asked to create our own dance routine to the song *"Fever."* They wanted no overt sexual movement, no smiling, just straight-faced non-robotic movement to help sell their product. In essence, strip yourself of all "face" and emote from within, through the eyes and without anything coming across even remotely sexual. This task, for some, was ex-

CHAPTER FIVE

tremely hard to do as in this industry we all know that sex sells! But for this assignment we were forced to really come up with some intricate choreography that showcased the product without limiting our movement as dancers. So it was back to basics. We pulled out lifts, pirouettes and kicks.

Knowing when to blend and when to shine is an art in itself! This was an opportunity to work as a group. You may be also be asked to show your individuality. Find moments within bits of choreography where you can instinctively make them your own. There is a difference between making something your own and pulling the eye away from a recording artist. If you're a backup dancer for Britney Spears, Madonna or Ne-Yo, then of course you have some serious dance skills. The routines choreographed for these artists emphasize the need for high-energy all the way through. They do not suggest that you can take a moment to run to the side of the stage to throw in your fouettes to show off. You are there to support the artist, not steal the spotlight. On most tours, the artist will take a moment to introduce the dancers. This is your moment to go all out. The artist hires you to complete a vision, not steal the stage. Know what your role is on tour. Never upstage the artist.

#6 - KNOW THE COMPETITION
At auditions, you will start to see the same people. As an African-American, light-skinned girl with long curly brown hair, I frequently run into many dancers at auditions with my similar look. You will too! Take notice, make friends and exchange contact information. Look to the right and left of you when at an audition and find out who is booking the job over you or who is asked to stay in the final group. These people are your competition. If these girls or guys book more jobs than you, start paying attention to what they are doing and start figuring out how to get an edge over the competition.

#7 - SEEK KNOWLEDGE
Learn from watching. If you've watched the competition and made friends, why not ask them to teach you something. I know, pride gets in the way of anyone ever asking for help. If you don't ask, then at least watch and learn. If you didn't get the move during the audition, you can ask the choreographer when his or her next class will be. Advance your skills and your ability to perform them when called to.

#8 - BE RESPECTFUL OF THE AUDITION SPACE
Auditions are held at rehearsal halls and venues of all kinds. Be respectful of other rooms that might have classes running, auditions in progress or any number of

things including office staff trying to run a business. Do **NOT** park in reserved staff parking areas. Clean up after yourself and be courteous to employees working at the audition facility. My mom used to say, "I'm your mother, not your maid." Make sure you don't leave your trash for others to clean up.

#9 - GENERATE BUZZ
This is your time to break the mold a bit! Have fun and show everyone what you've got. It's your audition, so go out there and make a name for yourself.

#10 - BE GRACIOUS
If you don't get called to stay, don't make a face. Choreographers see those! It may not have been your gig. Sure you can be disappointed, but don't make a scene. Try to be gracious and remember to thank the choreographer after you're done.

SICK TIP #16: OH NO SHE DIDN'T!

Sometimes there may be an audition in which you feel as though you were amazing but still got cut. Ouch! I know. It stings a bit. Having spent time, energy and money on viable headshots you may want to rip your headshot right out of the choreographer's hand. DON'T DO IT! Unless the choreographer says, "Hey, I know you spend your hard earned money on your headshot and if I don't call you, feel free to take it with you. I don't want to waste your headshot if you could use it for something else." Then sure, go ahead and request your headshot back. But don't be a *"Bitter Betty"* and storm up to the choreographer or their assistant and make a scene when you get cut if they haven't already offered that option to the group. It doesn't reflect well on your character and who knows if you might get a call for something else if they keep it on file. I got called by Fatima Robinson for a job in 2007 from a headshot that she had from 2003. It had my old agency information and old cell phone number on it. You just never know where it'll end up and you don't want to make a scene over not being kept at an audition. Keep it movin'!

AUDITION HURDLES TO CLIMB

BUT I ONLY KNOW IT WITH THE LYRICS!
Dancers have been taught with eight counts and with boom-ba ah's for years! Choreographers teach steps to counts, lyrics and sometimes subtle nuances only they can hear in their own heads. Be prepared to learn all types of count method-

ologies. If the choreographer has just taught everything to the lyrics and then you ask, "Um, can you break that down into counts," they might just tell you, "No!" Some might do it but others expect you to learn it the way they teach it. Most choreographers are former dancers and they hear or feel the music. Work on your own musicality and this will save you in these types of auditions. Start taking from a variety of teachers. If you have grown up learning from the same teachers and are used to the way they teach, it may hinder your progress at an audition with someone who teaches faster than you are used to or counts in a different manner.

THE DREADED FREESTYLE

Many dancers who are technically trained do not feel comfortable doing any kind of freestyle. This is where I'd like to say, "Get over it!" Find your freestyle no matter how long it takes you to put something together. My friend Christian Vincent put it best when he said, "Get a 'Freestyle A' together and a 'Freestyle B' together. And maybe even a 'Freestyle C.'" As long as you can put a combo together that you feel comfortable with, no one will know it wasn't created on the spot. You will be in your own groove and it will eventually become natural.

FORGETTING THE COMBINATION...DON'T STOP - KEEP GOING!

If you are in a group performing the combination and are asked to freestyle before or after it, know the combination. Don't spend so much time on your freestyle that you forget the combination. It will weigh better that you did a simple freestyle and hit the combo rather than an extravagant across the floor freestyle and then forgot what you just learned. What if you mess up? The best dancers make you watch them regardless of if they mess up the combination or perform it flawlessly. They won't let it come across their face that they just made a mistake. How you recover may matter most to your audition. Of course, you want to perform with perfection and personality, but if you mess up, make sure to keep going! The last thing a choreographer wants to see is you freak out over messing up. Choreographers will interpret this as your inability to find your way back into the piece in their future projects. Pull it together and get back into the choreography if you can or freestyle it out. Whatever you do, keep going!

PARTNERING AT AUDITIONS

With the success of ABC's *Dancing with the Stars* and FOX's *So You Think You Can Dance*, the amount of auditions with partnering has increased. We are seeing more and more dancers being asked to do lifts with partners at auditions that they've never tried before. Get a leg up on your auditions and seek out a few partners to practice with. My friend, Kelly Connolly, is a perfect example. She arrives at auditions prepared with different partners based on the style of dance, whether it be swing, cheerleading or adagio, she's got it in the bag. Rehearsed lifts, transition steps and confidence in her partner is key. *(See more on Kelly Connolly on page 90).*

Some auditions will be broken up into an all-girl audition and then an all-guy audition. Then they will bring both men and women back to a callback and ask you to partner up. In this case you are put in a situation where you hope to find someone that you've partnered with before. If not, try to go over moves with a new partner the best you can. Most choreographers in these types of situations know that many dancers are working together for the first time and are really looking for chemistry or the potential for chemistry. Don't stress out in this situation, just focus on the task at hand. Be safe when trying lifts with new partners. Ask for a spot if you're feeling a little shaky or offer one to others if you are willing to really brace someone. Never offer to spot anyone if you aren't fully committed to catching or bracing a fall. Better to be safe than sorry if you are trying a stunt or helping to prevent an injury.

CRASHING AN AUDITION

Is it OK to crash an audition? Um, probably not! But there are those times where you may just be able to sneak in. A word of caution: Choreographers put out calls for specific descriptions and you do not want to waste their time or yours by trying to get into an audition for a type that you do not fit. You may also want to know that dancers hate it when someone books a job that they were up for by someone who didn't even get a call to attend the audition in the first place. I personally used to hate to see people get to come to a callback for an audition when they weren't at the original call. Bypassing the first call to me seemed like cheating a little bit. But as my career progressed, if I wasn't able to make a first call sometimes I'd be given the luxury to come straight to the callback. For new dancers, this sucks! You make it through cut after cut and then they bring in some veteran (a fierce dancer, probably working a job at the time of the first audition call) and they go straight to the callback or direct book the job without ever auditioning at all. Yes, this will happen. And maybe one day you will be the one being direct booked to the job.

SPECIAL NOTE FOR COMPETITION KIDS AND CHEERLEADERS

It is very easy to spot someone at an audition that grew up going to dance competitions a.k.a. "convention kids," just as it is easy to spot someone who was a cheerleader for many years. This is not a bad thing to show technique or special skills.

CHAPTER FIVE

Unfortunately, the industry will want you to shed a few of those layers and create a new shell around those skills in order for you to be marketable and not so cookie cutter. I don't intend to offend anyone by saying this because I was also a cheerleader. I know dancers with competition backgrounds who have had to mature their presentation when auditioning and this is not to say that the skill isn't there, it is just the package that needs to be remolded a bit. This does not mean that if you move to Hollywood and are 15, 16 or 17 years old that you can't look young. It does mean that your visual presentation needs to hold a certain presence when taking the floor that does not readily scream, "I'm performing in a competition." Trust me, Tony G. has scripts for *Bring It On* movies for a few more years. Never fret, you can do 2-2-1s, toe touches and herkies at specialty calls in the future.

SICK TIP #17:
KNOWING WHEN TO GET AHEAD

You will attend an audition that has multiple call times and see dancers teaching their friends the choreography as they exit the audition. You may be the one to ask someone who was just in the audition room to teach it to you. This may help or hinder your chances in the audition. By learning part or the whole combination, you may go into audition and find that they are teaching a completely different combination. You've now wasted time and energy learning a combo and now a brand new one is taught for your audition. The best advice I have is to learn the choreography directly from the choreographer. Your friend might teach it to you wrong or the person you thought was your friend might deliberately sabotage you. Just wait for your call time, that's why you have one.

DIVERSIFY WITH TACTICS
TO GET A LEG UP ON THE COMPETITION

Some practices at auditions are completely out of your control. From how many people show up, to who the choreographer is, breakdowns of each role and many other factors that you can't change even if you wanted to. You **DO** have control over a few things like diversifying your skill set, perfecting your picture-taking skills as well as taking care of your skin, hair and body.

THE PROMISE OF A POLAROID

Although Polaroid has stopped making disposable film, casting directors and choreographers still have stock left. A picture can say a thousand words and most auditions will include at least one close-up and one body shot. Most pictures are digital these days, which means <u>FOREVER</u>! Below are a few tips to help you look your best that actor **Eitan Loewenstein** outlined that have helped me at many an audition.

"***Get down to or below the level of the photographer.*** Tall people know that they look really silly in photos because the photographer is typically below their eye level when they shoot. In the photography business this is referred to as shooting 'up someone's nose.' The bottom of the chin is featured as well as anything that happens to be living in the actors' nasal passages. Combat this (by getting) down so your eyes are at the level of the camera or even an inch or two below. Spread your legs apart so you don't have to hunch over. ***Don't let your chin fly away.*** For some reason when you aim the camera at people they tend to throw their heads back trying to look like a 'bad ass gangsta.' Well, it's just as bad as being shot from below, so don't do it. Tilt your head down slightly, very slightly. Think of aiming your nose at the bottom of the camera.

"***Don't point your nose directly at the camera.*** Polaroid cameras are wide-angle cameras. They're meant for shooting big group photos. So they distort things at close range (where most commercial audition pictures are taken). So by aiming your nose slightly to the right or left of the camera (and still looking straight at the camera) you prevent your nose from looking bigger than it actually is. This is a very slight tilt. Don't overdo it. Aim at the left or right side of the camera with your nose. That's it. Perfect, you look beautiful. ***"Get away from that wall.*** Every session runner (casting assistant or choreographer's assistant) shoots photos against a wall because it makes for a neutral background. They also use a flash, which casts a shadow on the wall. Avoid a dark, sharp shadow floating behind you. Make sure you're not leaning against the wall. Put your hand behind you...try to space yourself six inches to a foot away from the wall to minimize the shadow but not annoy the photographer (and last but not least) ***relax.***"

SPECIALTY SKILLS - YOU NEED THEM!

Next up are a few dancers with specialty skills that are exciting and out of the norm.

CHAPTER FIVE

MELISSA "MYRTLE" GARCIA (AERIAL)

A talented singer and dancer who has toured with Celine Dion and more, Myrtle also has a few aerial skills in her bag of tricks.

"The aerial community has increased drastically, although there are not many auditions or projects that incorporate it. What hurts the audition availability is that there aren't very many facilities for it. Usually you have your demo reel and submit that for your audition. You generally get called in to do a job from your reel. Aerial is definitely getting bigger because of shows that incorporate it like *Cirque du Soleil* and *Circus of the Stars*. Projects like industrials, music videos and tours are starting to (incorporate aerial). It is dangerous, so be smart (when) training for it. You could really get hurt. Do your research and be really smart in choosing an instructor. As the co-owner of Playback Studios located in Van Nuys, Calif., we've just started our own aerial classes. Come by and hang out for a while!" Go to www.PlaybackStudioLA.com for more information about the aerial class schedule. You can also find classes at Hollywood Aerial Arts, www.HollywoodAerialArts.com or at Edison Downtown, www.EdisonDowntown.com.

JILLIAN SCHMITZ (POLE DANCE)

A friend of mine is the very accomplished, trained dancer, Jillian Schmitz. She's worked with and assisted choreographers such as Marguerite Derricks, Joseph Malone and many others in the television and film industry. I asked Jillian how she added pole dancing to her skill set and she replied,

"I learned from other girls who knew how to do it, and practiced any time I had a chance. Once you know the basics the rest is just placement of arms and legs, momentum and strength."

Although hopping on a pole looks like a raucous good time, creating the illusion of floating takes a lot of upper body strength. Not all dancing in Hollywood requires this specialty. My mom would actually like this specialty not to be included in my book but I think it is important to note that if you are comfortable with your body, able to perform the flexible, strength and transition elements and are willing to submit yourself for these specialty roles, then master it and add it to your resume. Although the flip side of pole dancing includes a path aimed toward a more seedy atmosphere, this I do not wish to advocate. My point is that these roles do exist in Hollywood. Jillian is brilliant in all dance styles and can jump into this role if called on because she's got mad skillz! *(Check out USPDF competition highlights).*

TIMO NUÑEZ (FLAMENCO)

With credits including *So You Think You Can Dance*, *Rules of Engagement* and the movie *Rent*, Timo has taken the lead on flamenco dancing in Hollywood. He has been training since he was 8 years old and grew up dancing with his sister in Santa Barbara, Calif. With a Spanish heritage, his grandmother made sure that he enrolled into dance classes.

"Flamenco is extremely unique in that you're combining a whole bunch of technique that we see in L.A. all the time. You need to have a ballet background for the most part. I mean there are gypsies who are just totally raw, who've never stepped a day in a dance class in their lives. But to be a technical flamenco dancer you need a ballet background and you need to have a really good ear. A lot of the percussion of the feet is often related to that of a tap dancer or clogger. With modern day flamenco you have things that (can) sometimes resemble hip-hop or modern dance. So I really feel privileged to be a flamenco dancer because I get to use so many different emotions and so many different characteristics of dance, it's not just one thing. The technical difficulties are in the rhythms. The dance is so complex because there are so many different rhythms; like in traditional Irish and Indian dance styles as well. You need to be so familiar with each rhythm of flamenco and each one calls for a different emotion. You really need to be up on your knowledge. I'm still not there; I'm still learning all the great colors of flamenco.

"The way I'm using flamenco today in Los Angeles is slightly different. I'm trying to relate it to more of a mainstream audience. I'm trying to make sure that people who are in the commercial industry can understand that flamenco isn't just an old art form that is only supposed to be seen by people who love flamenco. I've done flamenco to hip-hop music and people have gone crazy. I want to make sure that people know that it can be marketable in different ways. A hip-hop dancer can take a flamenco arm movement and it could be the hottest new thing. We've seen (this) with Bollywood mixing with hip-hop as well. People are so open minded and creative and I get to use it for more than just authentic flamenco shows. The flamenco scene in L.A. has had its up and downs. Right now, I feel like it's getting hot again. Back in the '80s and '90s it was huge! The El Cid Restaurant in Silverlake used to be the big headquarters for flamenco. It's starting to really explode now. The Fountain Theatre has an authentic flamenco show there every other Sunday. It started up during that era that I spoke of and has been around for a long time, run by co-founder, Deborah Lawler. She's been very committed to the flamenco dance scene."

CHAPTER FIVE

DANIELLE HAWKINS (ROLLER SKATING)

Danielle leaves it all on the dance floor and has taken her skates from the rink to the set! This talented working dancer has appeared dancing and skating in music videos for The Dream, Mya, T-Pain, The Pink Spiders, Chris Brown, Brooke Valentine, Jessica Simpson and Sean Kingston. She's also danced with Miley Cyrus on *Hannah Montana* as well as in *Bring It On: Fight To The Finish* and *Seventeen Again*.

"I have been skating since I was 2 years old. I just kind of learned from watching and not being scared to try different stuff. I am kind of a dare devil and always have been. Even as a kid, I would try the crazy stuff just to prove I could do what the boys did. I don't go on very many calls for skating because it isn't that big or widely recognized in Los Angeles. Skating is a lot bigger in places like Chicago, Atlanta, New York and even the Bay Area. I will say that I have had more commercial and theatrical auditions for skating.

"Skating does give me an edge in certain auditions. I skate on traditional quad skates. It's a very soulful thing that has a lot of history and culture involved. It's definitely not something that everyone can do, so when I display (my skating ability) at auditions it gains attention and makes people think outside the box of regular dancing and choreography. They get excited to try and use it in their projects. I am definitely a rare breed when it comes to skating. Very few dancers actually can do what I do. ***Some can skate, but there is a big difference between being able to SKATE and being able to ROLL!!!*** You can be the best dancer out there but skating is a total different thing. Even standing on a pair of skates...you will see the huge difference in balance. If you are looking to take a class, you can take skate lessons at AMF World On Wheels. They have had skating lessons on Saturday morning for over 15 years."

KELLY CONNOLLY (PARTNER STUNTS/PET OWNER)

Kelly's credits include Orbital 360, Cybex print ads, Hip Hop Abs®, *Weeds, Dancing with the Stars, Year One, A Christmas Carol (2009), CSI: New York, Days of our Lives, Malcolm in the Middle, Cold Case, The Shield* and *Bolden*. She is a great partner dancer and does many styles but she also has a star pet named ***Mister***! Mister is a Pomeranian with cream and sable coloring. He's a super hero and trained at Le Paws for roles in commercials and film. They have headshots together and he even has an agent! "My dog loves to do jump spins and he sings to the song, '*Who Let The Dogs Out?*' He does the '*Ruff! Ruff!*'"

DOMINIQUE KELLEY (TAP)

A tapper since the age of 9, Dominique's credits include the first national tour of *Bring in 'da Noise, Bring in 'da Funk* and the European tour of *Black and Blue* when he was 13 years old. You have seen him in *The Producers* (movie), *Across The Universe*, *FAME* (2009) and *Bolden*.

"It's not that I wanted to learn tap, I think that tap wanted to learn about my body. You know what, my mom got me those patent leather shoes; I looked like a little black Billy Elliott in class. All of a sudden, I just started to excel in tap. Then after doing dance competitions for two years, I was the only little black boy that was really tapping. There aren't that many auditions in L.A. for tap. You have to introduce tap to them like a friend of yours. You will go in and try to knock out the audition but at the end it's like, 'Before I leave, let me introduce you to one of my best friends.' That's when you put on your tap shoes.

"Keep practicing. A lot of people complain that they don't get this or that job or this opportunity. At the end of the day, your feet will speak for themselves. **<u>People will find out who you are if you are really putting it down</u>**. It doesn't necessarily mean you have to be in every tap festival, be in every competition or be in every show. Instead of complaining about it, go into the studio and <u>work on your feet</u>. Work on foundational elements so that by the time that preparation meets opportunity you'll be able to shine! There are specific tap dancers that book a lot of work and they have great feet. I compare them to a lot of the best b-boys (who) are great at free styling but when it comes to choreography they can't do it at all. Some tap dancers are great at improving and great in a cypher circle but when it comes to learning the choreography, they go down in flames. That's when you have to have your own voice and you have to bring something to the table, as well as knowing your foundational elements.

"No matter what I say I do, no matter if (people) see me do ballet, or whatever the type of dance, whether it's with footwork or if it's with house they're like, 'Oh my God, you're such a tap dancer.' If it weren't for tap, I wouldn't be where I am right now. Tap has opened so many doors and not only that, it has helped me to edge out the competition because in California, and specifically in Hollywood, you don't really see people bringing out their shoes and really laying it down. You'll see some people shuffle off or do wings or whatever, but they're not really having a conversation with their feet. The best teachers are the ones that you gravitate towards. Take a breadth of classes because everyone is different. Even Greg Poland will give you swing from back in the day. Go to classes that make you do stuff on

CHAPTER FIVE

both the right and the left, which are going to help you with your improv and give you foundational elements. Do a soft shoe one day and then do something in a harder hip-hop the next. Do something in a 5 count or in a 7 count, not necessarily a standard 4-4. You need something that is going to challenge you. **Tap keeps you grounded, no matter who you are.** You can think you're on top of the world and then you'll meet a little kid from East Bumble Dolly Dinkle Tap School who will wear you out! But they may not have the heart you do, or the experience you do, or the knowledge you do. With tap it's all about how clean your feet are. If there's somebody cleaner than you then you need to pull up! You might be able to fudge with hip-hop or with some modern elements but <u>***with tap, you always know where you stand***</u>."

ETHNICITY AND CULTURAL AUDITION NOTICES

CH: "For all the Asian Americans: Be proud of where you are from and or what nationality you are. Don't ever lose that! We are still minorities in this industry, but we are making a mark and slowly getting out there. If you can speak the language or do whatever the traditional dance is for that country, it's always a plus! Don't get offended by stereotypes but simply educate others and represent the Asian community. I am Japanese. I do not get called in to specific casting directors more because of my race. Unfortunately, we are all just Asian-American in their eyes. I do find that I get called back in to casting directors because I give it my all at every audition. As long as you are professional and give it your best, they will see that!"

CHIEKO HIDAKA

Chieko has worked with Christina Aguilera, Gwen Stefani, Keyshia Cole, Black Eyed Peas, Omarion, Mya and Paulina Rubio.

LIZ RAMOS

Liz can be seen in Enchanted, Rent, El Cantante, Dirty Dancing 2: Havana Nights and more!

LR: "Casting directors who specialize in Spanish-speaking projects are **Tepper Gallegos** and **Blanca Valdez**. They have a big hold on Latin commercials and TV shows. They will bring dancers in to read for Spanish-speaking parts because they like the energy dancers bring. I think the best line I ever heard was from Nancy O'Meara at the 1997 *Oscars™*. She said, *'Happy to be here, easy to work with.'* I've kept that in mind and that just shows you that a dancer can work for a long time if they have the dedication and professionalism behind it!"

MUSICALITY, RHYTHM AND KNOWING THE BEAT

Dancers all think they have such gifted musicality. Not to put a damper on your parade, but many are not directly on top of the beat and continue to hear parts of music that just really aren't there to account for their lack of timing. Knowing the music is another part of your job. Additionally, dancers who have knowledge in music beyond thinking in counts of eight that can also jump in if a conductor asks them to go from the 4th bar or take it from the chorus, the hook, the bridge or reprise of the song, will have an advantage over those who do not know what this kind of terminology means. Most songs have an introduction, multiple verses and choruses, a bridge and an outro. There are pre-choruses that occur before a chorus and additional breakdowns, which is where most dance sections occur with recording artists. This allows the artist to do the choreography full out without having to sing and dance at the same time. Be aware of the use of this terminology and how to count yourself in if a conductor or musical director instead of a choreographer is leading you.

Listen for distinct breaks in music at auditions because the choreographer may not count you in to start the routine. Find the intricate changes in music, close your eyes and really sense and feel the changes in the arrangements. Songs are words and music together and usually have melodies to them (generally two melodies - one in the verse and one in the chorus). A song generally goes from the **intro** or the **introduction** into the **verse**. The verse will flow into a **pre-chorus** or straight into the **chorus** or the melody of the song (or what some call the **hook**: the catchy phrase or melody that people remember the most and is repeated generally without variation). The song structure continues in most cases to a second verse into the pre-chorus or chorus or into what is called a **bridge**. This is another melody that is more of an interlude or a climax of the song that brings it another element a sort of surprise or hint of change. Following the bridge is generally a chorus repeated and an **outro**. There may also be a **break** or **breakdown** where a percussion or instrumental solo is performed. Dancers usually find this to be the rhythmic more intricate section of choreography.

DORIAN HOLLEY (SINGER/MUSICIAN)
VOCAL COACH FOR AMERICAN IDOL

"If you have never sung before, when you don't have the experience as a singer, it is like trying to speak another language. If you are going to be in this business and you want to be versatile then get into a music class or a voice class. Get into a choir at church. You don't necessarily have to become a singer like I am but if you want to

CHAPTER FIVE

maximize your employment ability then you have to study these things. It's not something that people are going to learn on the gig that day if you don't already have some skill.

"If you get with a musician for four hours, you can learn music pretty quickly; especially since dancers are already used to breaking down time in a particular way. You can advance in music in a year or two. Church choirs allow people to learn songs quickly and new songs weekly. Take a night school class at a community college (i.e. Santa Monica Community College) or get a private vocal teacher. Get with a singer or musician and barter some dance lessons for trade with music or singing lessons. When the band director gives the artist direction to come in on the 4th bar in, the dancers usually don't understand that direction. For a dancer, you would normally count in groups of eight counts unless doing a ballet piece in groups of three. For almost every pop song, it would be in groups of four, every bar is 4 beats. It would be unusual to find one that wasn't except in some ballads... but you can still break that down. So a song that is in 4-4 time: Counts #1, 2, 3, 4 would be one bar, 8 counts would be 2 bars and 16 counts would be 4 bars. For example: Let's say we do a 4 bar intro, (which would be 16 counts or 2 counts of 8 for most dancers). Dancers begin to move on the downbeat of verse 1 (which is on count #17 or the 3rd count of 8 for dancers). So count #17 is considered the beginning of the 5th bar. It might sound confusing but once you get the hang of it, you'll be one step ahead."

DORIAN HOLLEY ON THE HIERARCHY THAT EXISTS ON STAGE

"What it really boils down to is just envy. The band members hate the singers because they think the singers get all of the camera attention. And the singers hate the dancers because the dancers stand in front of everybody. What I can't figure out is this: Why on the pay scale does it go the other way around? The singers usually get paid more than the dancers. It is changing in some respects for some but not on all fronts. The way that it can change even further is for dancers to command the respect. And one of those ways is for dancers to know the vocabulary, know what they are talking about when they say we're going to start at the bridge and the bridge is at bar 32. Knowing where that stuff is because it is important. It's not about sitting there throwing your weight around. It's about knowing what people are talking about when they are discussing these things. When you speak the language they can't talk over your head. In my opinion, it's not over your head; it's just a different language. You speak Spanish and I speak French and another person speaks Latin and we're trying to do this thing together. But they use it over you in that way because they are envious of you and one department thinks that they are better than another department. For me, if a person is really serious, you do everything you can to make yourself hirable. It's not about getting some jobs dancing with somebody. You want to work as long as your body with allow."

KNOW YOUR FACE
Many times you may have to simply rely on your facial expressions to land you the job. A mere reaction to something like tasting the best grape juice ever, showing the disappointment in not getting the birthday gift you wanted or even laughing the right way to a joke are examples. Look in the mirror and really know your face. This will apply more for commercials, television and film.

A class that has been recommended to me is the facial expressions class by Bobbie Chance. This is a Saturday afternoon class for only $25. Bobbie Chance states that, "The Expression Session works on the actor, not the role. It is all emotional work and is extremely passionate, opening the actor to be emotionally available so that the actor can express whichever emotion is required by the role." (www.BobbieChance.com)

CHANGE CLOTHES
Practice quick changes at home. Try taking off a jacket in a relatively short time while dancing. Then increase difficulty. Remove your jacket and pants and put on a skirt or shorts. Then remove a full outfit and put on a new one and change shoes from sneakers to heels or vice versa. Time yourself and don't panic. Stay calm and avoid missing a key article of clothing, buttoning something incorrectly or hindering your fellow dancer's ability to perform their own quick change.

SICK TIP #18:
KNOW WHO YOU ARE
Practice your answers to the personality questions below with friends and family. Reveal what you want and make your answers sound spontaneous and memorable.

- What is the craziest thing you've ever done? Your best and worst trait?
- Who is your idol and why?
- If you could work with anyone, who would it be and why?
- Do you work well with others? Are you a team player?
- Are you registered as a Democrat, Republican or Independent?
- What religion are you? Are you straight or gay?

CHAPTER FIVE
GO BIG OR GO HOME
Another type of challenge for a dancer who is used to performing in small venues is making the leap to a large stadium. Performing with Rihanna at Wimbley Arena in London is vastly different than performing *"Run, Run, Rudolph"* in front of the cast and crew of *Boston Legal* or saying my lines as part of *The Day The Earth Stood Still* with actor Robert Knepper as the only other person in our scene. Engaging an audience is difficult in an arena, as you must project to the balcony seats while on television you must transmit the same energy through a camera lens for the viewers at home. This can be a huge challenge but well worth meeting.

ACCESS NOT GRANTED
Be wary of music video "behind-the-scenes" footage on set. Any and all footage taken of you will require a release form. Past camera crews have exploited female dancers by claiming to conduct interviews with them while on the other end of the camera lens they are focusing on cleavage, legs or other body parts. This is an intentional effort to try to exploit dancers and paint them in a light where they are more on display for looks than for talent. Don't get me wrong, this is Hollywood and there is something to be said for looking good. However, in these cases, you need to make sure that the behind the scenes camera crew is a legitimate organization and you've signed the appropriate releases.

If it's MTV's *Making the Video*, then you've seen these episodes where they really do capture the 'making of the video' and are not trying to capture models, dancers or featured ladies half-naked in the dressing room. There will be illegitimate camera crews wanting to take advantage of you in certain situations whether for monetary gain or just for personal gratification. Be aware of your surroundings, and contact your agent if there is a situation you do not feel comfortable in. You are there to do your job and should never be in a position where you feel unsafe or exploited.

TRADEMARKS AND SINS
Now that you've spent some time figuring out who you are, let's take a look at some of the things that work for some but not for all. The next few examples are of what I like to call **Trademarks and Sins**. These are the signatures for some people that just look downright awful on other people or look really bad on all dancers no matter who you are! I'd like to begin by saying that I would like to thank the dancers who helped me with the illustrations.

AUDITIONS: BRING YOUR 'A' GAME!

TRADEMARK #1: GUM CHEWING

Aisha Francis is a pro at this and works it into her personality while she's on stage, whether she's got gum in her mouth or not. Now, she can work it, others cannot! So don't even try.

TRADEMARK #2: FINGER IN THE MOUTH

Jessica Lynn has this move down and embodies it. Many have tried but only a few can really pull off the grown and sexy like she does.

TRADEMARK #3: THE NASTY GIRL DIP AND WIPE

Now, I know it sounds vulgar because it is a little nasty. For some, the drop to the ground and the slow hand through the crotch on the peel up with a little hair whip is attention grabbing. Others who try this move that are off balance in their heels and/or just not sexy should refrain from this move!

SIN #1: STANK FACE

So many dancers believe that to do real hip-hop and have the intensity of the genre, you must give the **Stank Face**, not true! I had to have my dear friend James Alsop demonstrate a series of stank faces!

JAMES GIVING THE STANK FACE!   JAMES ALSOP
from Step It Up & Dance on Bravo.

SIN #2: DIVA STANK

This is even worse when you try to dress up the stank face and give it Diva status. I personally had to illustrate this one, now you know why it shouldn't be done. Yuck!

TECHNIQUE SIN #1: SICKLED FOOT AND PIGEON -TOED

Try not to turn your foot in.

TECHNIQUE SIN #2: POSTURE (SWAY BACK OR SLOUCH)

Rotate those shoulders back and tuck your butt under. Straighten up!

TECHNIQUE SIN #3: SKI SLOPED HANDS AND HYPEREXTENSION

If you have a tendency to do these naturally, work on making you extremities not slope or over extend.

SKI SLOPED ON LEFT, FLAT ON RIGHT

BOOK ME! HOW TO BECOME A SUCCESSFUL WORKING DANCER IN HOLLYWOOD

CHAPTER FIVE

Sandra says...

- The <u>Hollywood Dance Calendar</u> is important as many award shows employ dancers.

- Know your audition call time, learn quickly and dress the part.

- Leave with plenty of time to park and play nice with everyone.

AUDITIONS: BRING YOUR 'A' GAME!

- Be assertive, sign-in legibly and slate with intention. Stand out when it's your turn and blend when necessary.

- Don't be your own worst enemy at auditions. Go in and do your best. Leave knowing that you did a great job and if they think you are right for the part, then it'll be yours.

- Get feedback from choreographers. Talk to them and ask them what you can work on.

POINT TAKEN:
You will continually have to prove yourself at each audition. Be consistent and on the ball. Don't slack off just because people are starting to recognize you. That is when people start watching you more, shouting your name to rev up the crowd in support of your turn. Serve up whatever the choreographer is cooking! Most of them like it HOT!

CHAPTER SIX

GOT BOOKED?
ON THE JOB DOS AND DON'TS

CONGRATULATIONS!
NOW YOU NEED TO KEEP YOUR JOB!

Many times there will be factors that you contribute to being dismissed from a job and sometimes it has nothing to do with you at all. Outlined below are a few tips to making sure you have the best "on the job" experience as possible.

WHAT TO DO ON THE JOB!

DO #1: ARRIVE EARLY

Arrive early for your call time. Arriving late is just disrespectful to your choreographer and shows that you don't take the job seriously. Look up directions the night before. If you leave your house with an early arrival planned, even with detours and the possibility of getting lost you should still be on time. Establish yourself in the rehearsal hall or on set. Sign-in with an assistant director, request a call sheet, warm up, rehearse if you've already learned the choreography or simply relax for a bit.

SICK TIP #19:
KNOW YOUR STAGING

Don't be that dancer who, when an artist goes the wrong direction on stage, doesn't follow them or stays on center even when the artist has moved off center. Don't be the "I was in my spot, she wasn't" dancer! Follow the artist or guide them back. That's your job.

GOT BOOKED? ON THE JOB DOS AND DON'TS

UNDERSTANDING THE CALL SHEET

It is imperative that once you arrive on the job site of a television show, film set or music video that you are prepared for whatever is thrown at you. Understanding the **call sheet** is important to getting your questions answered and your problems solved before they even occur. You will receive a call time the night before a shoot unless called in for a last minute role or as a replacement.

Call sheets list all of the key people and their job titles to accurately account for who is in charge of each part of the production process. All talent and their call times will be listed as well as the choreographer, stylists, set designers, director, catering and more. Pay attention to who is listed, as you may want to send a thank you card to a director who you had great chemistry with on set, or a choreographer who you would like to send additional footage to. Keep in contact with hair stylists and makeup artists for future projects. Call sheets will also list the shoot day's weather forecast, the production company information (just in case you'd like to request a copy of the footage), the local hospital in case of an emergency and the call times of the other cast members.

SAMPLE CALL SHEET (TV PILOT)

CALL SHEET Unknown Production, Inc.	TITLE OF SHOW	DAY/DATE:	Tuesday, March 10, 2010 Day 11 of 12
Production Office: 555-5555 Production Fax: 555-5555	CALL TIME 12:30 P.M. SHOOTING CALL 2 P.M. Pilot - Title of Show report to: Stage 20 (Crew Parks at Gate 10)		PROD# 300000
Executive Producer: John Doe Executive Producer: John Doe Producer: John Doe Director: John Doe		SUNRISE - 6:55 a.m. SUNSET - 5:59 p.m. Weather: Cloudy - Light Wind (S 6mph) 5% Chance of Rain Low Temp: 34 High Temp: 76 Hospital: UCLA Medical Center (5 miles) AD Phone: Questions? Call John Doe @ 555-5555 Lunch 6:45 p.m.	
Episode / GL: Pilot/300000			
NO FORCED CALLS WITHOUT PRIOR APPROVAL OF UPM ALL CALLS SUBJECT TO CHANGE BY THE UPM OR AD'S** **NO CALL TIMES MAY BE CHANGED WITHOUT UPM OR AD APPROVAL**			

DESCRIPTON	SCENE	CAST	D/N	PAGES	NOTES	LOCATION
Int. store (green screen) John lures Lisa	SC9	1,4,6	N2	6/8		PHANTOM, STAGE 20
Company Move to Phantom NY Street						
Int. Harlem Club To Complete Coverage of Club Scenes	SC10	1,2,3,4,5 18A,18B,18C	N2	2/8		PHANTOM UNDERGROUND CLUB
Company to Move to Phantom Stage 20						
Int. House John talks to Wendy (Laundry Room)	SC 19B	11,4,8,9	D1			PHANTOM, STAGE 20

#TALENT	NAME	CHARACTER NAME		CALL	SET	REPORT TO
1	Jane Doe	Character Name	12P	1P	11A P/U @ Hotel, To Phantom, St 20	
2	Jane Doe	Character Name	11A	12P	Rpt to Phantom, Stage 20	
3	Jane Doe	Character Name	1P	2P	Rpt to Phantom, Stage 20	
4	Jane Doe	Character Name	1P	2P	Rpt to Phantom, Stage 20	
5	Jane Doe	Character Name	1P	2P	Rpt to Phantom, Stage 20	
6	Jane Doe	Character Name	1P	2P	Rpt to Phantom, Stage 20	
18A	Jane Doe	Character Name	1P	2P	Rpt to Phantom, Stage 20	
18B	Jane Doe	Character Name	1P	2P	Rpt to Phantom, Stage 20	
18C	Jane Doe	Character Name	1P	2P	Rpt to Phantom, Stage 20	

#	STAND-IN/PHOTO DOUBLES/ATMOSPHERE	CALL	SET	REPORT TO
TOTAL:	4 (SI) Stand-Ins, 50 BG (Background)			

CHAPTER SIX

The sample call sheet on the previous page is for a television pilot. You'll notice a few things that may or may not be on a call sheet for a music video or commercial (i.e. a numbering system for talent). Production identifies the cast that is needed for a particular scene with their number, which is also noted on the left-hand side of the call sheet. The #1 may be the star of the TV show or film whereas on a music video call sheet, the recording artist would be listed first. For a music video you may also see a column heading for an agent's name and contact information, artist management, label contact and production company. The call time and on set times are listed next to one another. This helps to know how long you have before your first on set call, which will mean the cycling through hair and makeup needs to get done within this time frame or that your run to craft service might need to happen within those two time periods. You may also have a rehearsal or run through for the camera scheduled between these time periods as well. Do not stray from where the P.A. or A.D. tells you to be. No one wants to hunt you down.

On a commercial call sheet you may see information for the ad agency hired to produce the commercial for the client. For example, Johnson Advertising may be hired to produce a commercial for Lucky Charms cereal. Vendor information is listed for camera equipment companies, casting, catering, craft service, insurance, messenger services, shipping, sound, payroll, Honeywagon, hotel, travel, trucking, VTR equipment, storyboards or walkie talkies. The electronic, art, visual EFX, motion control, choreography, beauty, grip, camera and production departments and equipment or editorial agencies may all be listed individually as well. Production assistants are usually listed so get familiar with these people. Be kind to everyone, from craft service to production assistants to wardrobe, hair and makeup. Today's P.A. is tomorrow's Spielberg! You never know who you'll meet and where you might run into them again. Or worse, who will tell someone else how horrible you were to work with and how you shouldn't be working on a project and not get hired for a job because of your last gig.

SICK TIP #20:
ROAD CLOSURES ARE NO JOKE

Pay attention to signs. "No parking on Sunset Boulevard after 4 p.m.," means you are guaranteed to get a ticket or be towed. Traffic challenges occur at intersections with few left-hand turn signals, on freeways, and during special events like the Santa Parade, Tournament of Roses Parade, Gay Pride Parade, Mann's Chinese Theatre *Walk of Fame* dedications, the Hollywood Bowl and film premieres in Westwood and at ArcLight Cinemas.

DO #2: MAINTAIN YOUR LOOK

It is imperative that once you book a job that you maintain your look. If a choreographer hired you because you had long hair, don't chop it off before the first day of rehearsal. Big NO-NO! Maintain your look throughout rehearsals unless specifically asked to change it. If you are asked to change your look after booking a job, you do not have to. It might mean that you may not keep the job based on the refusal of the new look, but if you have headshots and zed cards freshly printed and are asked to completely overhaul your look for a one-day gig, this may not be worth it to you.

On the other hand, I've seen a few people do radical changes once being booked on the Janet Jackson tour in 2007 where they chopped their hair and dyed it jet black. This I can totally understand. If it is for a major artist and a significant period of time, sure why not?! If you're out on tour, you probably will be able to afford new headshots upon your return that reflect your new look. *(Find more beauty regimens in Chapter 10).*

DO #3: ARRIVE PREPARED FOR YOUR GIG: WHAT TO BRING

• Varied dance shoes	• Headshots/resumes/biz cards
• Snacks/water/Propel singles	• Cell phone and charger
• Money for parking meters	• Kneepads
• Change of clothing/bring layers	• Travel toothbrush/toothpaste
• Towel	• Dental floss/breath mints
• Makeup and small mirror	• Eye drops/throat lozenges/Tums
• Feminine products & baby powder	• Ibuprofen/Advil/Excedrin/Tylenol
• Oil blotting tissues and Kleenex	• Flexible straws/ Sharpie to label water
• Double stick Hollywood tape	
• Bobbie pins/wig cap	• Batteries/plastic silverware
• Screw driver (tap screws)	• Health regiment (band aids, ace bandage)
• Sewing kit/nail kit	
• Shoe kit/shoe shine	• Tide to go or shout wipes
• Body lotion/cleansing clothes	• Magazines, busy work, etc.

For your "rehearsal bag" simply make an extended version of your "audition bag" from Chapter 5. Never assume that you will be provided lunch on set or at a rehearsal hall. Always prepare snacks or stop and pick some up prior to getting to your rehearsal location. You want to replenish your body because of the calorie burn you'll be doing.

DO #4: KEEP ACCURATE RECORDS

Jot down your start and finish times as well as your breaks to keep an accurate rec-

CHAPTER SIX

ord of your work schedule. Agents need these details to make sure your paychecks are accurate.

DO #5: HYDRATE, REPLENISH AND MAINTAIN ENDURANCE

Great snack must-haves for on-the-job rehearsals:

• Water	• Raisins
• Juice	• Bananas (potassium)
• Protein/granola bars	• Gatorade
• Chex mix/trail mix	• Apple

DO #6: KEEP IN TOUCH: CELL PHONE DOS AND DON'TS

Charge your cell phone the night before. Purchase multiple chargers, so you can have one at home and one to travel in your audition bag. While at work, do not visit your cell phone every five seconds. Use your cell phone during designated breaks. The last thing any director or choreographer wants to do is ask you to get off your cell phone and pay attention. Put your phone on vibrate or silent, but remember to activate the ringer upon leaving.

Do check your cell phone for information updates from your agent. You never know if your agent may call you to advise you of pertinent information regarding your job. While shooting a music video, my agent called to let me know about wardrobe specifications and to tell me not to sign any contract or release as the client/artist's management had not yet returned the deal memo for the job. Keep in contact with your agent while on the job if there are questions that arise.

DO #7: REDUCE INJURIES AT REHEARSALS AND ON-THE-JOB

Many injuries happen prior to your gig actually happening. While rehearsing for the Mary J. Blige tour, the first day of our rehearsals with choreographer Hi Hat included an injury to one of the dancers where she tore her achilles tendon. This kind of injury is not something people readily prepare for or can avoid but it is an example of what can happen prior to getting on stage to perform. Injuries can also occur from fatigue due to long rehearsals. Keep your fitness up and know your body. Warm up and stretch before rehearsals even if others aren't. Be in tune with your aches and pains and wear comfortable dance shoes during rehearsal. If performing in high heels, most often choreographers will teach you the material in sneakers and then switch over to heels.

SAVE YOUR FEET WHEN POSSIBLE!

DO #8: ASK ABOUT YOUR PERFORMANCE SHOES
Speaking of feet, it is a great idea to ask about what shoes you will be wearing during your performance. Ask if you'll be able to rehearse in them before getting on stage. It may not be possible but if it is, then you are ahead of the game.

DO #9: INVEST IN AN INCIDENTALS RESERVE CREDIT CARD
Hotel room incidentals on the job may require a hold on a credit card. Do not use a debit card as it will charge the card immediately and withdraw (in theory they say but it really is in actuality) your funds directly from you account. These funds normally take 7-10 business days to be refunded to your account even if no charges are brought on your room account.

Don't be misled on tours with multiple dates in foreign countries. Hotel holds should be taken care of by management and you should only be responsible for room charges (i.e. room service). With multiple city tour dates, you are not liable to place credit card holds on each room when traveling from one city to the next every day. I normally turn off the long distance phone capabilities. Artist management should still be able to call your room. I use my cell phone for all of my phone necessities while away or the Internet.

DO #10: ALWAYS KEEP RECEIPTS AND CHECK YOUR HOTEL BILL
It is always good to keep your receipts for your own personal tax returns. Always check your hotel bill when checking out. Make sure that your room does not have any charges prior to you leaving. Disputing charges in foreign countries after leaving a location is difficult, so be proactive. The tour manager may check out all of the rooms at one time. Even if you're tired and just want to get on the bus, get confirmation on your own that nothing is left outstanding on your room.

DO #11: SEND THANK YOU NOTES
Be gracious and keep your lines of communication open with your employers.

DO #12: NETWORK WITH FELLOW DANCERS
Make sure to reach out to your fellow dancers by exchanging phone numbers and e-mails. Keep in touch and let them know when you have an upcoming gig! Support your fellow dancers!

DO #13: SEPARATE YOUR PERSONAL LIFE FROM YOUR WORK
It is important to have a separate work and home life. You may have friends who

CHAPTER SIX

are dancers and hang out with them as well as work with them. Try to branch out in the industry and include more types of people in your circle. Has anyone ever told you, "It's all about who you know?" Well, it really is.

DO #14: OPEN YOUR EYES, TALK TO PEOPLE AND LISTEN
Pay attention to the roles people play on set or at a performance. Talk to people. Listen to the director when he's calling for action, setting up shots and making quick decisions. Take in your surroundings, watch how the choreographer works with the artist and management, and decipher who does what on a job site. Why are there so many assistant directors? *(See Chapter 8 for on set job descriptions).*

DO #15: BE A LEADER, NOT A FOLLOWER
Always put your best foot forward as a leader. Set a positive example.

DO #16: MAKE LOVE TO THE CAMERA – ALWAYS GIVE 250%
Unless told different direction, you need to make sure to look through the lens to the audience at home unless you are playing a character and interacting with others in a scene. Then your sight line would depend on the scene and your direction. When you are performing in concert the audience needs to feel your energy!

DO #17: BRING AUDITION CLOTHES TO YOUR REHEARSAL
Be prepared. You may be at a rehearsal and get a call to go to an audition directly following your rehearsal. Have clothes with you. Have an emergency bag with you just in case. This way you can head straight to the audition without having to go home.

DO #18: BE AWARE OF YOUR STAGE SURFACE
Being comfortable on your dance surface is imperative! Often you will not get on the stage before the actual performance. Check the surface and make sure that you can dance on it, that there are no nails sticking up or slick parts. Many award show productions use Windex glass cleaner or Pledge to shine floors between takes. Prepare yourself for a dangerous dance experience. Wipe off your shoes before entering a slick surface and put shoe grips underneath the toe of your stilettos.

FAST FIX: SLICK FLOORS	• Mop the floor with a bit of soda (**Do NOT do without asking**) • Shoe grips (Add to bottom of shoes)/rubberize soles • Bring hair scrunchies to tie around your shoes • Use a shoe scraper to rough up your shoe soles

GOT BOOKED? ON THE JOB DOS AND DON'TS

DO #19: AVOID THE DANGERS OF BODY OIL

We all want to look great and have shine on our legs, gloss on our lips and flawless hair. Unfortunately, we may be contributing to an unsafe dance surface. On stages where makeup artists and stylists are lathering on the body oils, this may potentially ooze onto the dance surface depending on the choreography of the piece. I prefer to bring Johnson's baby oil gel to the set as it still has the shine of regular baby oil to bring out the fabulous features you have but with a little less slippery outcome. This gel will stay on you rather than all over everything else.

DO #20: HAVE FUN!

This may seem like a lot of things to remember, but while doing all of the 19 things listed previously, don't forget to HAVE FUN! Ultimately, your job if done right shouldn't seem like a job because it is what you LOVE to do! Dance! Get out there and have fun while at work. Make the work look great and enjoy it at the same time!
Think about all those people who auditioned and would love to be in your place.

DANCER TO-DO LIST WHILE AT REHEARSAL OR ON SET

- Write down start and finish times
- Ask for a call sheet
- Ask permission to video during rehearsal so you can practice at home
- Read your contract on set and contact your agent with any questions <u>PRIOR</u> to signing

Now that you've learned my top 20 things TO DO on the job, it's time to go over a few things that may hinder your chances of ever getting another one. This isn't to scare you because sometimes, people are just that good that choreographers and directors will put up with their antics to have them do the gig. But that doesn't happen very often! Remember, that you are replaceable. Not by loved ones or friends, but in this industry if you are causing problems, most likely you won't be around the next time to hinder a production. So heed the warning now to avoid problems in the future.

SICK TIP #21: TRIP I.D. AND MEMORABILIA

Keepsakes from your travels are great for scrap booking later or just to have to reminisce about. Hold on to I.D. badges, backstage passes, airline luggage tags from your trips overseas or award shows. You won't regret it!

CHAPTER SIX

WHAT NOT TO DO ON THE JOB

DON'T #1: ARRIVE LATE
I think I mentioned this before. Is it sinking in? Don't make it a habit.

DON'T #2: CHOREOGRAPH OR DIRECT
Unless asked for your opinion on certain moves or transitions, do not choreograph or direct on the job. The client hired choreographers and directors for that. It can get very touchy if you start giving suggestions every other move. Choreographers will ask you for your opinion if they want it.

DON'T #3: GOOF OFF
Pay attention during rehearsal. Focus your energy on the work at hand and you will be better off. Choreographers don't want to have to reel you in. You don't want to have the reputation of someone who goofs off too much and doesn't take the job seriously.

DON'T #4: BE A SLACKER
Pull up at all times. When asked to be "full out" make sure to give your full energy. Actually, you shouldn't have to be asked to go "full out." You should be giving it your all every time. If you aren't at your highest performance level, your fellow dancers may have to continue to grind out routines over and over until your performance level is up to par.

DON'T #5: GET CALLED OUT ON ALREADY CLEANED MATERIAL
Lock in key changes and cleaning notes to memory. Make sure that you are making your changes each time. Choreographers are not happy when they have to continue to correct you after they've made corrections during a cleaning session.

DON'T #6: LEAVE FOR BREAKS AND RETURN LATE
When given 5-minute breaks or lunch during a rehearsal, don't come back late! Don't take liberties while on the job. Yes, of course, when you have a meal break this is your time and you can eat, talk on the phone, read a book or do whatever you choose. Don't decide to go to eat at a place that takes a long time to prepare your food when you only have an hour or 30 minutes. Practice good judgment.

DON'T #7: CONSTANTLY ASK WHEN YOU'RE GOING TO BE DONE
Your agent should tell you the schedule for your rehearsal and the hours in which

GOT BOOKED? ON THE JOB DOS AND DON'TS

you will be working. I've seen many dancers annoy choreographers when asking them, "How much longer will we be going for?" Some have another audition to get to or they feel the need to be somewhere else. If you don't want to be there, I'm sure there is someone ready to take your spot. Remember why you moved to Hollywood and put your game face on!

DON'T #8: MISS AN AIRPLANE FLIGHT

If you are scheduled to be on a flight, don't miss it! You will more than likely pick up the cost to change your ticket. Because of the nature of U.S. airport security when traveling, it may not even be possible to get onto another flight, especially one overseas. You may miss your job entirely because the flight you were supposed to be on was the only one that could get you to the performance city in time for the show. Here are a list of airports in and around Los Angeles and their Web sites.

AIRPORT NAME	AIRPORT CODE	AIRPORT WEB SITES
Los Angeles Intl. Airport	LAX	lawa.org
Burbank Airport	BUR	burbankairport.com
Long Beach Airport	LGB	longbeach.gov/airport
Ontario Intl. Airport	ONT	lawa.org
Las Vegas Intl. Airport	LAS	mccarran.com

LOCAL AIRPORT ADDRESSES AND PHONE NUMBERS

Los Angeles International Airport
1 World Way
Los Angeles, CA 90045
(310) 646-5252 Phone
Airport Lost and Found:
(310) 417-0440

Bob Hope Airport
2627 North Hollywood Way
Burbank, CA 91505
(818) 840-8840 Phone
Airport Lost and Found:
(818) 840-8830

*Check baggage weight limits and handling fees as well as security restrictions prior to traveling. Always travel with an itinerary and travel contacts for production or artist management.

Ontario International Airport
2900 East Airport Drive
Ontario, CA 91761
(909) 937-8653 Phone
Airport Police Lost and Found:
(909) 937-2700

Long Beach Airport
4100 Donald Douglas Drive
Long Beach, CA 90808
(562) 570-2600 Phone
Airport Lost and Found:
(562) 570-2640

McCarran International Airport
5757 Wayne Newton Boulevard
Las Vegas, Nevada 89119
(702) 261-5211 Phone
Airport Lost and Found:
(702) 261-5134

CHAPTER SIX

It is your responsibility to get to your gig. Your flight may be cancelled due to weather and you may have to figure out a way to get there by car or bus if your train ride is detoured. Think outside the box. Don't just give up. You may not be able to get in touch with a tour manager, agent or relative while stranded. Pick your head up and pull through. Don't ever give up without trying to figure out an alternative plan if you are stuck.

AIRPORT PARKING

Parking your car at the airport can get expensive. Rates for long term parking range from $9 - $30 per day depending on what parking lot you choose. In my own experience, it is easier to park and shuttle to the main entrance at the Burbank Airport than at LAX. Make drop off arrangements ahead of time or plan extra time as you may wait a while for shuttles to transport you from the parking lot to the terminal at any airport.

INTERNATIONAL FLIGHTS AND TRAVEL SUGGESTIONS

Plan ahead for international flights. Make sure to bring your passport and government issued identification. Pack lighter than normal, as you never know how terminals in other countries are structured and how far you will have to walk with your luggage. You also do not want to incur extra charges for your luggage being over the weight restrictions if you bring souvenirs back. Purchase a sturdy suitcase with wheels so you don't strain your back trying to carry around a large duffle bag. Pack a smaller bag to carry with you to venues. Mark your bag with an identifiable ribbon or luggage tag to easily spot it on the baggage claim carousel.

SICK TIP #22:
FROM THE PLANE TO THE STAGE

Flight delays and other unforeseen circumstances may contribute to your untimely arrival to a performance venue. Figure out exactly what you have to do in order to get ready on the fly. Know what you need to fix your hair and put your makeup on in the van on the way to your show. Be prepared for anything because the show must go on!

DON'T #9: UPSTAGE THE STAR

I mentioned this earlier, but it deserves a second go around. Don't upstage the celebrity you are working for. It is imperative that you do your job to the best of your ability but there is only one artist on stage. Upstaging the artist may lead to your dismissal. Walk the line very carefully between being the best you and stealing the spotlight.

DON'T #10: GOSSIP ON THE JOB
The dance community is small and it is very likely that what you say about a dancer or artist will get back to them or the artist's management. Watch what you say about fellow dancers. If you don't have anything nice to say then don't say anything at all.

DON'T #11: ENTERTAIN TOUR LOVE
Ah, the sweet smell of tour love, I mean lust. While out for extended periods of time on tour with a recording artist, your friend and fellow dancer may start to either annoy you with their quirky habits or start to look pretty hot depending on the surroundings and your relationship status back home. Try to avoid, if at all possible, the "tour love" scenario. That means with fellow dancers and never with your recording artist employer. Now I know, if it's love, then it's love! But most of the time, it's lust combined with a nice little cocktail! Proceed with caution while on the road because if you find yourself romantically involved with someone in week two of a thirteen-week tour, and your "relationship" doesn't last, you might be in for a very long bus ride! Be careful what you wish for and remember that when you get home, what happened on tour usually has a way of trickling through the grapevine of the dance community. On the flip side, you may find your soul mate. If you do, please call me! I'd love for you to tell me I was wrong and give me the opportunity to congratulate you.

DON'T #12: DRINK ALCOHOL OR DO DRUGS
Be an asset, not a liability while on the job. If you have an affinity for drinking in excess or a drug of choice, get help. You do not want your agent to get a call that you cannot perform because you are ill from drinking too much the night before. Nor do you want anyone to be called because of an emergency related to this kind of behavior. Curb your appetite for alcohol and if you need assistance contact the phone numbers below for help.

DRUG AND ALCOHOL ABUSE HOTLINES AND WEB SITES

Los Angeles Alcoholics Anonymous Web site:
www.lacoaa.org/find_meeting.php

Center for Substance Abuse Treatment
U.S. Department of Health and Human Services (800) 662-4357
Crystal Meth Hotline (888) 9NO-METH

Narcotics Anonymous
www.na.org

CHAPTER SIX

DON'T #13: BOMBARD CELEBRITIES WITH PHOTO REQUESTS
It is best to make a photo request with an artist's manager or production assistant so not to have every dancer break out into paparazzi during rehearsal or before a performance. Wait until there is down time to ask and try not to seem like a bug-a-boo. You also don't want to come off like an uber-fan. Ask politely but don't nag. William Shatner was sweet and took a pic with me on the set of *Boston Legal*.

DON'T #14: COMPLAIN ABOUT WARDROBE
My wardrobe on set has included a Buzz Lightyear costume in a Disney commercial, Nike athletic apparel and dancing in my undies in a Fruit of the Loom commercial. You may find yourself in an outfit that you would be scared to show your friends or you may love it and want to keep the fantastic frock. Stylists are hired to capture the vision of the writer, choreographer or director. Don't complain about something they want you to wear unless it really does not fit you and you will not be able to dance in it.

If this is the case, it is better to let them know up front that you cannot move in the clothing or the shoes. I performed on the *Victoria's Secret Fashion Show* as a silhouette dancer in the *"Sexy Back"* performance by Justin Timberlake. In the fitting the stylist asked, "What size shoe do you wear?" I replied, "I'm a size 8." The stylist then said, "So do you want a 7 or a 9?" After the initial shock I said, "I'd much rather cram my foot into the 7 than have my foot be swimming in the size 9." She apologized as they were unable to get everyone's shoe sizes and I totally understood. Dancers must be willing to jump in and take one for the team. Stylists may not have your shoe size, so suck it up and make due unless it is a complete hazard to your ability to dance.

DON'T #15: BRING YOUR GIRLFRIEND/BOYFRIEND TO THE SET OR REHEARSAL
Super un-cool! Don't bring your girlfriend or boyfriend to the set or a rehearsal. It is distracting, unprofessional and not to mention unauthorized at any venue.

DON'T #16: BE DISRESPECTFUL OF PERSONAL & PHYSICAL SPACE
Regardless of your sexual preference, be respectful of personal and physical boundaries no matter how comfortable you feel in a rehearsal or tour situation. Do not force your fondness of an individual on them whether you are straight or gay. No one should be forced to confront that type of situation while on a job.

DON'T #17: BE AN "I'M NOT..." DANCER!

Don't be the one who says, "Well, I'm not going to..." If you don't want the job then don't take it or don't audition for it. Sometimes you may have extensive floor work, long nights and extreme working conditions. If you start saying you're not going to thrash your head one more time, or you're not going to go full out until show time, you may as well throw a negative energy on the whole project. Don't bring everyone down because you don't want to do some aspect of the job or don't want to rise above whatever obstacle stands in your way.

DON'T #18: PLAY PEEPING TOM

Men and women are in close quarters sharing dressing rooms. Many individuals feel comfortable changing or doing quick changes in the same changing areas. Be respectful, both men and women. Do your job and try not to play the role of the *"Peeping Tom"* or *"Peeping Tina."* Ladies, try to find a separate area if you feel uncomfortable with the environment or contact your agent. Men can also offer to leave the area while letting the ladies change.

DON'T #19: LIP SYNCH OR MOUTH YOUR COUNTS

Whatever you do on the job, do **NOT** lip synch behind a recording artist. There is only one lead singer on stage. Even if the artist isn't singing live, you must not move your mouth to the words unless specifically told to on background vocal portions of the song. You must also not mouth your counts. It's one thing to practice and say the counts as you go, but do not visualize them on stage. It is distracting and you will look like an amateur on stage.

DON'T #20: GET INTO ANY PHYSICAL FIGHTS

The last thing you want is to get fired from a job because you can't get along with your co-workers. You may think that physical fights don't happen in the dance world, but trust me when I tell you that they do. Get along with your fellow dancers and authority figures. Know when to let things simmer instead of continuing to escalate a problem. Don't stoop to a lower level. Always take the high road.

DON'T #21: BE A DIVA

Don't be a DIVA. It won't help your career. Enough said.

TOURING WITH A RECORDING ARTIST

Next up find valuable information about being on tour with a recording artist, how to handle being away from home and travel tips.

CHAPTER SIX
JAMIE KING

Celebrity director and choreographer, Jamie King is the man behind the top live tours from some of the best known recording artists like Madonna, Britney Spears, Celine Dion, Spice Girls, Ricky Martin, Rain and Christina Aguilera to name a few. Not limiting his credits to only stage, music videos, television, film and commercials, Jamie has also created the Ultimate Hip-Hop Inspired Workout called *Rock Your Body*™ *with Jamie King* and also partnered with Nike to create the *Nike Rockstar Workout*™ *with Jamie King*. Having worked with so many celebrities and capturing the creative vision for projects that have won *Emmy® Award* and MTV *Video Music Award* nominations, I want dancers to learn from his vast knowledge and understand exactly what he looks for when casting projects.

SC: What do you look for from dancers at auditions? Do you have any tips to really standing out that you watch for?
JK: I want dancers who are themselves and express who they are - individuals are more interesting to me than a type.

SC: What do you expect from dancers on the job?
JK: Professionalism and adaptability.

SC: Having been the force behind some of the most well-known concert tours, are there tricks of the trade you find helpful to dancers who may be going out on tour for the first time?
JK: Save your money and enjoy the experience - take advantage of the traveling and see the sights and experience the different cultures. The world is much bigger than just North America.

SC: Do you have any tips/advice that you can provide for dancers to help them make the transition from dancing on stage to dancing on TV/film (or vice versa)?
JK: Listen, watch and learn from every experience.

SC: Do you have any advice for dancers on how to really create a name/brand?
JK: Work hard and never think anything is impossible or out of your reach. Anything is possible so never limit yourself - if you want something, then make it happen and do not wait for someone to give it to you!

GOT BOOKED? ON THE JOB DOS AND DON'TS

TOUR TIPS

As a performer you are always being watched. It is the nature of a dancer to walk into a restaurant and be recognized as a dancer because of your posture, how you're dressed, your body type or just the fact that you have a presence. While on tour and traveling in large groups be aware that you are representing the artist or project for which you were hired. Know the appropriate place to talk about issues with rehearsal, payment discrepancies or your particular opinions about your employer. Generally these are topics to curb in public places.

SIDE GIGS

Some dancers have been lucky enough to teach classes while overseas and plan mini-trips ahead of time based on their tour schedule. Your priority #1 is the gig that brought you to that country. If you miss your tour bus or flight because of your personal plans, that's no excuse! Know how to deal with being paid in foreign currency and the strength or weakness of the U.S. dollar. You will have a work visa while on tour in foreign countries but this does not cover your side gigs at dance studios. You are required to report this income to the IRS. Be diligent about setting up classes legally and with the proper documentation. Don't be denied at the immigration/customs counter for any illegal activity while in a foreign country.

MAINTAIN INTENSITY

Performing on tour is exciting for some as they can constantly improve how they perform each show and for some it may be boring doing the same show 200 times. It doesn't matter if it is your first show or the last; perform it at your highest level because it is the audience's first time seeing the show.

BE RESPONSIBLE FOR YOURSELF

Be responsible for your wardrobe. If there is a designated wardrobe staff then let them handle it and give you instructions for after show placement. Don't leave it up to tour employees to call the venue because you left your shoes on stage during your quick change. What you take to the stage is yours to bring with you to the next performance unless otherwise specified. Every tour is different. Be respectful and minimize issues for the road manager to address.

SICK TIP #23:
PHONE HOME FOR LESS
Save money and make a temporary international plan with your cell phone carrier. Use e-mail, iChat or AOL IM and Skype at www.Skype.com.

CHAPTER SIX

OVERSEAS TRAVEL TIPS
- Look up foreign exchange rates prior to departure at www.ExchangeRate.com.
- Pack more efficiently by looking up the weather at www.Weather.com.
- Bring or locate a plug converter as U.S. cords may not be compatible.
- Be careful with men's hair clippers and women's hair dryers. Plug converters and electronics may exhaust the hotel room power. Short-circuiting due to converters may cause them to completely fail.
- Check weight limits on airline luggage to curb fees.
- Add your trip mileage to your flight rewards cards.
- Avoid travel jokes at ticketing counters. Airline security won't find them funny.
- Travel with a small amount of cash for emergencies. Don't rely on your ATM/debit cards or credit cards in foreign countries. Many ATMs may not have the same symbols as used on the back of U.S. bank or credit cards. It is best to carry some cash to exchange upon arrival just in case your cards do not work.
- No drugs or drug paraphernalia!
- Get permissions for any prescription drugs you need to take.
- Stay with your group, do not stray off on your own (travel in groups).
- Take pride in being from the U.S., try to avoid American stereotypes and be careful when arguing with people over charges on food, baggage, etc.
- Lock your belongings up in your room on tour.
- Don't put your purse/backpacks on hooks in airport bathrooms.
- Look into traveler's insurance.
- Keep your passport current.

Travel sizes of most products for hair and body are essential for overseas maintenance. Most of the time you'll be on a bus, airplane, train or even ferry to get to your next performance location. Storing your luggage underneath is highly likely. Even with this being the case, you may still not want to carry large bottles of conditioner or shampoo around with you. Look for travel sizes of those items as well as face wash, cleansing towlettes and body wipes. You may get on the bus and not have an opportunity to shower prior to moving on to your next location to sleep for the evening.

BE SAFE AND REPRESENT YOUR COUNTRY WELL

Some of the best jobs you audition for in Hollywood will take you overseas. The last thing you want to do is end up detained for any illegal activity while overseas. It will be very difficult for you or your agent to navigate your way through legal troubles. You do not want to put any burden on the tour manager to have to assist you in any problems that you brought on yourself. Make an important file with copies of your driver's license, Social Security card and passport. Give a copy of these forms of identification to your agency. Try to fit them all on one page.

GOT BOOKED? ON THE JOB DOS AND DON'TS

UPHILL BATTLES WHILE OVERSEAS

You may encounter a few challenges while on tour, especially while in a foreign country. It is natural for people to form clicks. Make the best of an awkward situation if you're the odd person left out. Send postcards home to loved ones, friends and family! Jump on the Internet and communicate if you feel homesick and check in with your agent if you encounter problems or unexpected rehearsals and/or added shows. Know the crew that you are traveling with and get to know what they do. It is part of your job to be aware of how things work in this business.

Don't be another dancer who just does their job and goes home. Be the one who is on their game and is aware of their surroundings while doing their best on stage and off. It's kind of like the difference between being a cheerleader who looks good in the uniform and can perform the routines and the cheerleader who has the looks, performance and pays attention to the calls being made on the field. Now, I feel like I can say this because I've been in the company of both types. Ones who want to know all there is that's going on in the game and those who don't like the sport, but love the job. Be a student of the game and understand the inner workings of what's going on around you and it will help you be better at your job. Trust me, not every venue on tour will be the same stage dimensions or hold the same crowd capacity. The artist may not do his or her own sound check either. If given the opportunity to do a walk through, <u>DO ONE</u>! There should never be a time where management has said, "If you want to do a walk through, go ahead," and you don't go! Know what type of stage it is, the divets and the drop off. When the lights go out and you only have so much light to work with, you'll need to know your spacing. Applying your makeup is normally your responsibility on tour. Get to know what works well for the types of venues you're performing at. *(See Chapter 10: Dance 10 - Looks 10! for more information on makeup and beauty regimens.)*

INSIDE THE WORLD TOUR

I'd like to introduce you to a few friends who have been around the world and back again with recording artists Justin Timberlake and Beyoncé. Check out some advice from successful working dancers Dana Wilson and Heather Morris.

DANA WILSON
JUSTIN TIMBERLAKE WORLD TOURS

HEATHER MORRIS
BEYONCÉ WORLD TOURS, GLEE

CHAPTER SIX

SC: Any tips for dancers who are going on tour for the first time?
DW: Life on tour is VERY unnatural. You are subjected to some very late nights/early mornings. Try not to sleep your days away. Instead, keep your health and stamina up by hitting the gym (usually free in the hotel). Write in a journal and take plenty of pictures, because you are going to want to remember this. Lastly, get out of the hotel! Go explore and learn about the city and its people. Remember, most people pay to travel and see the world. You get paid to. Take advantage of that.

HM: Keep yourself in check 24/7. Be safe when you're out and about with others. Making poor decisions could wind up costing you your job or even hurting your career.

SC: What do you think are some of the challenges while being on tour?
DW: Eventually it becomes hard to work, play, eat, sleep (and) breathe with the same people. Your co-workers become a second family. You will fight, make up, love each other and hate each other just like brothers and sisters do. I maintain, however, that the hardest part of being on tour is coming off of it. Tour is like a dream. Surreal. Coming off the road is like waking up.

HM: Challenges are sleep, of course. You're constantly on a bus or flying, so you always feel overworked or lethargic. Bring vitamins and drink tons of water. Also spending is a nasty habit on tour. Take very good care of yourself! Your sleep and health are sincerely the most valuable assets to keeping you from getting injured or sick. It gets to be pretty tiring and hard on your body to sleep in different time zones or in a different bed every night. Keep up a healthy diet too. You're confronted with the challenge of not having convenience on the road. With food, you're forced to eat limited things. As hard as it is, try to be smart with your money and not blow it all because you're 'having fun.' You'll end up regretting it later.

SC: Are there any secrets to maintaining your home life while away?
DW: Well, I got rid of my place when I went on tour, so I lucked out on that one. I had all my bills on auto *(automatic withdrawl)* and tried my best to stay in touch with friends and family.

HM: I videotaped and snapped hundreds of pictures (during) the tour, which I felt afterwards was a very smart decision as well. I posted pictures on MySpace and Facebook and people could keep up with where I was or what I was doing on tour!

SC: Describe the friendship/boundaries that dancers need to adhere to while walking the fine line with artists when you're on the road.
DW: Although there is a time and place to 'clock out' and have some fun, remember that the artist is ultimately your BOSS...And you eventually have to (and want to) 'clock back in.'

HM: There's a fine line. Even if an artist does seem super comfortable with their boundaries and wish to cross the line of friendship, don't let that happen. Now, I'm not saying don't be friendly or be rude, but it would do you much good to spare their reputation and not to give them any incentive later to fire you for telling your friends too much information! Just respect the artist's status for their fans and the media.

SC: While touring with a recording artist, your formations will change due to venue size, your song will have different edits based on the TV show, your choreography might change if you do a house remix, etc. Any advice for dancers on being flexible, remembering the changes, techniques that help you focus best, or examples of something you never thought you'd be doing as a dancer?
DW: I had a print out of every stage we ever used and would block out formations using people's initials, or even colored highlighters to map out nasty traffic patterns/formation changes. It never hurts to have an MP3 of the mix on your iPod! Be very nice to the sound guys/musical director and they may give it to you if you promise not to share.

HM: As a dancer, it's a little silly to have an 'independent' mindset. What I mean by that is, you're NOT the most important person out there, no matter how talented you are as a dancer. You're there to do a job and you want to do a DARN good one at that so just LISTEN very thoroughly and always be patient with others.

SC: Are there any drawbacks to being on tour? What are some of the highlights, perks and advantages of touring with a recording artist?
DW: The perks of being on tour with an artist: You get paid to travel and perform in front of screaming audiences all around the world and you have consistent pay check$$$ *(very rare in our world)*. Some drawbacks: It's very difficult to continue training/taking class. You may begin to feel out of the loop, as it is hard to stay in touch with friends, family and even trends in the dance world.

HM: Drawbacks: Eating and sleeping habits. Take care of yourself. Highlights are the places you get to see. Take hold of every place you go and get to see.

CHAPTER SIX

Sandra says...

- Arrive early. Be on your gig from moment one.

- Read the call sheet and know the day's work schedule.

- Be a leader on the job, not a follower. Don't gossip. Be responsible and have some fun too!

- Separate your personal life from your work life.

- Be prepared for long days. Communicate with your agent if you have problems but don't constantly talk, text or BBM while at work. Remember, it is a job!

- Always say goodbye to the choreographer or director before leaving. It shows that you want to be there.

- Every job is an audition for another job. You want to be asked back.

> **POINT TAKEN:**
> While at work, do a good job and have a little fun while there. The best jobs are the ones where you get your work done and the people you are surrounded with make the environment an enjoyable one. Be the person that everyone wants to work with. Try to keep an upbeat attitude and a great work ethic and people will flock to you.

CHAPTER SEVEN

THANK YOU - PLEASE STAY. THE CHOREOGRAPHER'S CUT!

"THANK YOU. PLEASE STAY!"
Generally these phrases mean, **Thank you for coming**. **Please stay; we'd like to see more of you**. Hearing them from directors, casting directors and choreographers is a frighteningly stressful situation because you always want to hear "Please Stay!" Sometimes it doesn't work out that way.

KNOW CHOREOGRAPHERS AND THEIR ASSISTANTS
A great way to find out what is current in Hollywood is to go to dance agency Web sites and watch choreography reels. Check out past projects and go to choreographer's individual Web sites to see what they're doing now. It is important to do your homework before auditions as well. Know what style you are going to be asked to do. Find out what the choreographer likes and dislikes. Do they love leggy women? Are they in love with gritty urban fashion? The worst thing you can do is to thank the choreographer after you've auditioned and say, "Thank you so much. My name is Sandra, what was your name again?" Not a good idea. Been there, done that! Not a good feeling. Know whom you are auditioning for.

CHOREOGRAPHERS SPEAK
Here are words of advice from a few friends who happen to be your potential employers. I asked each one to give advice to dancers. Some were specific to auditioning skills, while others gave on-the-job tips. Everything must be taken in and absorbed. Know their faces and really listen to what they are saying. Try to be a sponge and really retain all of their suggestions and comments. It isn't enough to listen to people at an audition say, "I want you to do this move." Really try to understand the place in which it comes from.

THANK YOU - PLEASE STAY. THE CHOREOGRAPHER'S CUT!

There is always a reason for the movement, not just an arm on "1" or a ball-change on "2-3." There is always a story to tell, an audience to excite, a rhythm to explore and even better, knowledge to be gained through each experience working with creative directors, choreographers and even your fellow dancers. You aren't doing your job by only listening to the counts and watching the movement. Learn from their comments and apply them to each audition, job and in your life. These aren't just lessons to be played out on the dance floor, they are lessons that impact your life everyday. All choreographer photos were not available at the time of publication. A few credits are listed for each choreographer, as there are too many to list them. Some of the following choreographer comments may be repetitive. I've included them, as I believe having them come from so many respected choreographers may help to really emphasize their importance.

ADVICE FOR DANCERS FROM TOP CHOREOGRAPHERS

KEVIN MAHER
"I look for personality, good work ethic and energy. I tend to like people who are introverts, nerds or dorks in real life and then turn into beasts on the dance floor!"

NKOTB (World Tour 2008), Mariah Carey (Charmbracelet World Tour), Britney Spears ("Piece Of Me")

TONY G.
Bring It On Again, BIO: Fight To The Finish, Alvin & The Chipmunks: The Squeakquel

"I look for dancers to be professional and aware. Dancers who take direction, from signing in to patiently waiting. Be prepared for anything and everything. Lastly, limit your questions. I expect dancers to be on time and keep their talking to almost none while rehearsing. Those are my big pet peeves also. I truly lose respect if you're not on time. Rely on you and (your) ability to adapt to the changes in genres in our industry. Never let anyone say, 'You can't.' Always challenge yourself to your fullest and remember that YOU make dreams happen not the one just talking about it. Passion, passion and passion!

"Make connections professionally and hold off on making them friendships. I wish I were told to believe in myself more than another. I have all the tools to move and progress and I can't leave all that in someone else's hands. Be passionate, driven and aggressive. It's okay for doors to close, just be ready for the main ones to open. Stay in control of your journey. If you have an agent, remember they work for you and not the other way around. Lastly, take classes to become stronger and better."

CHAPTER SEVEN

BENJI SCHWIMMER

"I think more than anything there is always that invisible X-Factor only few truly have. You can have all the training in the world and be as hot as they come but in the end, you either have it or you don't. Talent is best seen in class. Impress your teachers, take class, and you'll see that the word flies quickly as to who you are and what you're all about."

So You Think You Can Dance Winner Season 2, C. Aguilera

TONY TESTA

"When I'm auditioning dancers for a job, I look for people who OUTSIDE of the room, and OUTSIDE of their talents, are respectful and have good energy. The kind of person that you hire is a direct reflection of you as the choreographer. When putting a team together, one bad apple can make a project painful and leave your employer with a bad taste in his/her mouth. It's just a good rule of thumb… you never know when someone is watching, and your actions can overpower your talents."

So You Think You Can Dance, Janet Jackson, Dance on Sunset

LUTHER A. BROWN

"In dancers, I look for appearance, originality, flavor (style), ability to pick up choreography and personality. The best way for a dancer to prep him/herself is to take classes from a wide variety of teachers. When they find a style that matches their strength, they need to master it. While they are mastering their style, they still need to take other classes - so they get used to doing anybody's style."

Diddy, Brandy, Mario, 2007 CHM Best Choreography "Nike"

GUSTAVO VARGAS

"I look for style and detail but most importantly that they feel the music and are having a great time doing so. I'm all about having a good time and having fun. I want to work and be surrounded with that energy."

Along Came Polly, Strong Medicine, Be Cool, Dance Like We Do

You Got Served, Performed with Missy Elliott, Justin Timberlake and Will Smith

DANTE SEVIN

"I look for a peaceful entry from a person coming in to see if they get along with people. Then I look for style and presence. Give it your all 'til you have nothing left."

SANDRA COLTON

THANK YOU - PLEASE STAY. THE CHOREOGRAPHER'S CUT!

ADAM PARSON

"It's important for a dancer to be able to let go of their individual style and adapt to the style given, while keeping their personality. I'm not crazy about clone dancers, I appreciate (that) we all have our favorite styles, but doing X's choreography with Z's style will usually get you cut. Know what your body is doing at all times!"

CHRIS DUPRE

"At auditions, I look for someone who moves me...who can take what I give them and deliver it back with brilliance and style. Talent and self-confidence play a huge part in that. Someone who is focused and on their gig, because I don't like to repeat myself and LOVE when people are two steps ahead without me having to ask them to be. Someone who I can get along with and plays well with others. The dynamics of the company that's assembled can make or break any job. And someone who stands out in a crowd!"

BRIAN FRIEDMAN

"I watch for the dancer that is a star. I need for them to be able to hold the stage on their own. I don't like dancers that blend in. I like for them to know who they are as an artist and be confident in their own skin. I expect nothing less than perfection. If I am showing up and doing my job, I want the same from them. I like dancers that learn quickly and are never lazy. I also love dancers that have no fear...no matter how crazy the piece may be or how difficult the steps are, they throw themselves into it with no inhibition. My advice to dancers is to save your money and purchase property as soon as possible. Invest and set up for your retirement. You can only dance for so long, so pay attention to transition careers and start learning about that career before you are too old to dance and end up looking for that *next thing*."

SONYA TAYEH

"You can't teach passion and heart. It's innate, it's an energy that exudes through a dancer and for me, makes them stand out more. That's what I look for or feel for. I don't want to work with a machine. I want to work with a dancer who has to dance, not one who's trying."

BOOK ME! HOW TO BECOME A SUCCESSFUL WORKING DANCER IN HOLLYWOOD

CHAPTER SEVEN

HI HAT

Step Up 3-D, Step Up 2 The Streets, Missy Elliott (M's "Pass The Dutch," "Get Your Freak On."

"At my auditions, I look for the dancers that are confident, but not arrogant. Dancers that are determined and stand in front of the line learning the choreography. Dancers that try to replicate the moves exactly how they are taught to them. When a dancer is asked to freestyle, for that dancer to be able to show their own style that is fresh and unique. I am big on personality when a dancer performs, so even if a dancer may not pick up quickly, their personality may be the thing to draw me in."

JERRY MITCHELL

"Acting, acting, acting. For me dance – particularly dance – in musical theatre is an extension of the storytelling in the book and the lyrics of a show. Most of the choreography that I work on, in most of the shows that I work on, tries to continue to tell the story in a form of a dance. So therefore, when I'm auditioning dancers, I'm looking for great actors. They're the ones that I'm attracted to, the ones that make me watch them. They have that extra something.

Hairspray, Legally Blonde, Gypsy, The Full Monty (B'dway)

"It's not just about the steps, it's what's behind the steps. Of course, the other elements of a great dancer that I require – or like to have in the room – are desire, determination, drive and discipline. I call them the Four D's. I like people in the room who like to be in the room. That really makes the experience of creating a new musical the most exciting for me."

Justin Timberlake, Pink, Elton John, Marques Houston and commercials for Sprite, Sony and more.

JAYSON WRIGHT

"What I look for from dancers on a job is the ability to perform as well as execute the choreography. A lot of times dancers can learn steps but when they get on stage the charisma behind those steps is not there. Challenging themselves with different styles is the best way to improve their overall technique, which leads to being a more well-rounded dancer."

EDDIE GARCIA

"You wouldn't come to a party empty handed, so every time you come to dance bring something!"

Janet Jackson, Ja Rule, Sheryl Crow, Bringin' Down The House, Fantasy (Las Vegas)

THANK YOU - PLEASE STAY. THE CHOREOGRAPHER'S CUT!

MIA MICHAELS

"I look for dancers who come into an audition and a project with an open mind, prepared to work hard. I'm drawn to the dancer who is looking to learn and grow. Someone who is not only strong in technique and style but who also has a willingness to explore their own individuality within the given movement. I feel that this exploration is so important because it brings a raw, organic texture to the movement and also challenges the dancer to expand the limits of their craft. This in turn allows the creative process of the project to take on its own unique direction. Thus, ultimately helping to produce a great final product."

SYTYCD, Céline Dion's "A New Day" (Caesar's Palace), Cirque du Soleil "Delirium" (World Tour)

CHONIQUE SNEED

"I look for a unique look, strong sense of presence and confidence. Someone who pays attention to detail and style in the choreography, and picks smart places to add their own flavor, so I can see who they are as a dancer."

Britney Spears, Paulina Rubio, Christina Milian, Nike "Made to Move" Campaign

GALEN HOOKS

"At auditions, I look for dancers who can inspire me within the first 8-count. Dance with your entire body, which includes your face! It brings life to even the simplest of choreography. Be respectful! If you end up booking the job, follow through on what you offered at the audition. Don't slack off because you've been hired. Instead, be excited to start the hard work. I love dancers who can figure out how to fix problems on their own.

Hilary Duff, Jonas Brothers, Fergie, '08 Choreography Media Honor for Ne-Yo MV "Closer," Dancing with the Stars w/John Legend and is an elected member of the Board of Directors for AFTRA L.A.

"If you need to travel across the stage in 4 counts but you keep bumping into another dancer, figure out your traffic! BE ON TIME! I still am and always will be a dancer, not just a choreographer, so I always expect dancers to put the hard work into their jobs that I do when I'm in their position. As long as you're passionate about dance, the hard work will be fulfilling."

CHAPTER SEVEN
DAVE SCOTT

"My auditions go through a few stages – the reason for this is I look for more than your dance ability.
• <u>Work Ethic</u> – I want you to go hard and not hold back and be willing to stretch your body to the limit.
• <u>Spirit</u> – You've got to be a pleasure to work with and work well with others.
• <u>Individuality</u> – I like artists (dancers) with a sense of individuality. This is an inspiration to my creativity depending on the extent of the content for the particular project. ***Be yourself – go hard and stay humble.***"

LISETTE BUSTAMANTE

"Dance can be both singular and a gift to share. It's knowing when and how to share your fire that creates the ultimate experience for you and your audience. I'm attracted to the fire when I'm watching someone perform, when it comes from an honest place, there's nothing like it. If you can always go back to why you love to dance, you find direct access to igniting your flame. The difference between a good dancer and a great dancer is the ability to access that within yourself."

JASON SAMUELS SMITH

"Technique, vocabulary and a demonstration of a strong foundation of tap history and tradition are always attractive elements to the eyes and ears of a choreographer. But the X-factor that can outshine these components is what we call in the tap community "fire," better known as passion or desire. When a dancer demonstrates this type of love and passion for the art, the level of energy is elevated, thus increasing the chances of that dancer leaving a positive impression, and possibly booking a gig. Passion will not compensate for a lack of technique and skills, but it can be the difference between standing out and blending in at an audition."

FRED TALLAKSEN

"You are being evaluated from the second you walk in the door. Come early and be friendly! Learn to smile when you are nervous and try to have fun while being respectful. A positive attitude will get you noticed and make you desirable. Make sure your photo looks exactly like you. Once you leave, you are being chosen with your photo. The team lines all the photos up on the table and starts arranging them in different combinations to see who fits together best. You would not believe how many times we look at a photo and say, 'Who is she? Was she even here today?' And then the photo goes in the 'NO' pile!

"Answer all of your phone calls and e-mails every day. If I call a dancer for a job and they don't call me back. I never ask them a second time. Yes, I want talented dancers, but more than that, I want a dancer who loves to dance and wants to work hard. If they are professional and have a great attitude, I will push to hire them on every project I work on! Leave your drama at the door. Most of the time that you are on a job, you are not even performing. The dancers who are easiest to get along with and are 'low maintenance' will be asked back again and again. Never leave a rehearsal or shoot without saying goodbye to the choreographer. It is disrespectful and can give off the wrong impression...An impression that you do not want to be there! And the next time, you probably won't!"

TABITHA AND NAPOLEON D'UMO

"The industry is SMALLER than you think and a great reputation will help close the deal at an audition. Next to talent, the most important quality is professionalism. Los Angeles is full of talented hungry dancers and choreographers don't need to waste their time with dancers who are drama."

FRANKIE ANNE

"Dancers at auditions - Your mind, body and spirit come into play...full tilt! Be prepared at all times, no excuses, be focused on what you need to accomplish, don't let your mind stray to any worries. They will only be your nemesis and pull you down. Above all, trust your talent, have a great time, enjoy the dance and remember this is a business and you are so fortunate to be in it."

CHAPTER SEVEN

KEITH YOUNG

"What I look for from dancers at auditions and on the job is susceptibility, determination and most important, willingness. I feel I can work with any level of talent as long as these things exist. A helpful tip: Don't let what you can't do...stop you from doing what you can!"

KEVIN STEA

"First and foremost I look for expression. Yes, it's important that (dancers) get the steps, but HOW they convey the story of the movement is more important to me. Do they go into autopilot with their face when they dance, or show every thought? Do they find moments to communicate to the audience or can you just see them counting?

When someone is really performing, I can forgive a lot of mistakes in the choreography. In an ideal world, I'm looking for people that can hold a stage or camera shot all by themselves. There's a comfortability and awareness in great performers that usually takes some life experience and practice. I jump when I find young people with those qualities. That can't be taught, but choreography can always be cleaned. I look for professionalism on the job. Be on time, leave the attitude at home, ask questions if you need to and pay attention. One should be able to not simply perform and clean in a mirror, but know how to replicate their performance without one. One should be able to feel the difference between holding their arm at '3 o'clock' and holding their arm at '4 o'clock', without looking around. I look for people who can adjust themselves on set, who see their surroundings and make their choreography smaller or bigger or travel further according to on set circumstances. People who adjust for safety and share issues with me or my assistant if they can't be figured out organically."

TJ ESPINOZA

"I look for an artist. I believe in order to dance behind an artist you must be one yourself. I look for a connection to the people they are performing for. If I was at home, or at a concert watching them I ask, 'Could they relate to me and tell me a story?' They don't necessarily need to pull focus but they need to pull at my heart. When you're good they expect it, so be better."

THANK YOU ~ PLEASE STAY. THE CHOREOGRAPHER'S CUT!

MARCEL WILSON

The Wayne Brady Show: ABC, The Show in the Sky Las Vegas, Dreamgirls

"I believe versatility is the key to success for dancers. It allows performers to say 'Yes' to anything. Limiting yourself to one style of dance only limits the endless opportunities a performer can have. I think it's important for dancers not to modify the choreography unless told to do so. I've worked with many dancers who change the vision of what the choreography is suppose to be. It's very disrespectful and could affect future work."

KENNIS MARQUIS

Jennifer Lopez, P. Diddy, Ludacris, LL Cool J, Juelz Santana, R. Kelly

"Be versatile in dance but also know how to communicate and network. Know that there are also politics in the music business that play into dance as well. It's almost like playing cards. Like playing spades, throwing out the right card at the right time. If you don't have any cards, no one wants to play with you. You may have an agent but you need to have a good relationship with your agent. It's like having a relationship with a girl or a guy, it doesn't work without communication. Relationships with choreographers are important too. Put yourself out there, make yourself available but don't look too desperate. Dancers don't like to give themselves critiques. Keep up with what you have, but be real with what level you're on. Train and stay in class.

"At auditions, it depends on what the job is for but as a professional dancer, you should always be on point, have hair done, nice shoes...it's all about marketing someone. I look for personality and work ethic. On the job, my pet peeve is talking. If I'm in a moment and someone says, 'Maybe do that.' I don't want someone to help me with the choreography, I don't really tolerate interruptions. There's no 'B' or 'C' choreography...**no sideline choreography**."

AAKOMON JONES

Usher (One Night Stand Tour), Madonna (Sticky & Sweet Tour), Center Stage: Turn It Up, Dreamgirls, Jennifer Lopez

"I look for the ability to execute combinations as they've been taught, not individual interpretations of my choreography - the opportunity to express your own style comes when I ask you to freestyle. I expect a level of humility and hard work from dancers first and foremost, (which) I try to express throughout my career. My biggest pet peeve of all time is when male dancers dance like women. If I'm hiring a man, that's most likely what I want to see. My advice would be this (generally speaking), your success is only as deep as your struggle."

CHAPTER SEVEN

JASON MYHRE

"It depends on the audition but the thing on the top of the list is that MEN dance like MEN and the women can keep up with the men but still being girls. That's what I look for, as well as if their look will match the artist/project, so that they compliment each other. As

Paulina Rubio, Rihanna, Janet Jackson, Aerosmith and PCD.

Tim Gunn says, 'Make it work.' Fill in the blanks yourself. If I don't like it, I will give you something to do, but make it work from point A to point B without being told. If you can't figure it out then ask. I get annoyed with dumb questions that, if you think about it, you could answer it yourself. Be a smart dancer! Know it's a game and that 75% of it is how you look and who you know, then comes talent. Know that there is a right job for everyone. If your look isn't right for one artist, it might be great for another. Make sure you can blend well and pick up details. I can't think of any choreographers that wouldn't want their dancers to dance like them. Watch for the details, take a correction and fix it right away."

FATIMA ROBINSON

"One of my main things: I really try to assemble a group of dancers that I'm going to have a good time with, that are going to have good attitudes, that are not going to be too, 'it's about them and not about the project.' I look for people who are having a good time when they dance. At commercial auditions I would advise people to come in fresh-faced, not a lot of makeup, not a lot of stuff going on because it distracts from (the client) being able to see

Dreamgirls, DWTS, Public Enemies, Aaliyah, Black Eyed Peas, Fergie and more.

you dance. You really should just go in as simple as possible, minimalistic. Go to my Web site WhatDoYouDance.com and make sure you're integrating yourself into the community! While not impossible, it's very rare that someone lands here in Los Angeles and books their first job. There are so many people out here that have been working for a long time. New dancers get in the mix."

Step Up 3-D, Step Up 2 The Streets, Center Stage: Turn It Up, Stomp The Yard, You Got Served, Glee

HARRY SHUM JR.

"I would rather hire a good dancer with personality than an amazing dancer with none. Remember that the dance industry is a business. If you're dancing for a living then learn as much about the business with the same intensity you have for dance. Trust me, you will understand when the time comes. Dance is what music looks like."

THANK YOU ~ PLEASE STAY. THE CHOREOGRAPHER'S CUT!

ROSERO MCCOY

"What I look for in dancers is originality. I like people who take my steps and do the steps but put their personality behind it. I like people when they come in and they go over the top because I can always pull you back. I like people with a lot of energy and when dancers come in very confident and know the steps.

"I think dancers are coming in with their tricks and the good thing now versus back in the day is that a lot of people aren't falling out of them. The biggest thing about it now, is that if you come in with tricks make sure you can pick up choreography too. The difference between dancers that can just do those tricks and dancers who can do those tricks and do choreography is huge. If you can do a great freestyle but not the choreo then we can call you in for one day on the set but if you can do them both then you get paid for the rehearsal days because I need to teach you the choreo and you're on the set that day because you can do tricks too! So I like the dancers who can do both. I like it when a dancer is very professional, when they're on time and when they don't complain."

PAUL BECKER

"When I'm holding an audition, I'm always looking for someone who can tell a story. I always look for the actors in the group because a lot of times in choreography for dance and musicals, it requires an extra something. I want them to be able to pick up my choreography but I don't, personally as a choreographer when I'm teaching at an audition, don't like doing two hundred counts of eight and wearing the dancers out. I know how nerve-wracking auditions are so I usually just give them...like three to four counts of eight. This is so they can learn the choreography and actually perform it how they would perform on the day of a shoot for me. Because they only have four counts of eight to remember they can actually give a true performance instead of learning twenty counts of eight and giving a really nervous performance because they are trying to remember the steps.

"As dancers we are physical movers and a lot of questions can be answered by just watching, especially on set. Every count doesn't need to be set while we're creating. It's usually the beginners who ask a lot of questions. Some people ask questions just for the sake of being seen and noticed at auditions. What will get you noticed won't be the questions that you ask, it will be your dancing and your energy."

CHAPTER SEVEN

MATT CADY

"At auditions I love dancers who pay attention to a correction. A lot of them think that all they have to do is live in their own essence, and it's not just about that. It's about being clean as well. Yet, on the other hand, some dancers worry too much about being clean and forget to perform! If nothing is happening in the face, I'm sorry, I'm bored. It has to be a happy medium. I look for cleanliness and the performance aspect.

ABDC (Fanny Pak), The Choreographer (Finalist), Natalise.

"On the job I expect respect for my creative process. There needs to be flexibility from the dancers in the aspect that I, the choreographer, don't always know fully what is going on. A good amount of time of rehearsal will be used toward experimenting with different movements, different staging ideas, different moments within the piece. It's not just about the choreography and formations – I need to make sure the overall picture evokes the correct feeling and message. Being in this industry for the last 5 years, I've definitely met my share of dancers who don't like to 'work' for it. They expect the choreography to just come easily and don't see the value in cleaning the movement of all the dancers together. If a piece isn't clean, then all the creative work that went in, won't be seen! There's no point to do it, if you can't see the point to it...but I mean, hey, it's fine, I just won't ever use those people again."

ROMAN VASQUEZ

"A lot of dancers become disappointed or upset when they are not selected, given they, and I will use the words 'smash' or 'killed' the routine. It even becomes frustrating if you have been auditioning for quite some time and see no results. DO NOT TAKE IT PERSONAL. It's just the type the company is looking for. Sometimes it can be out of the choreographer's hands. Always stay positive when auditioning, because you never know if a choreographer is auditioning next to you."

Britney Spears, Christina Aguilera, Jennifer Lopez, EFX (Las Vegas, NV), Celine Dion

MARY ANN KELLOGG

"I don't really audition very often. I don't find auditions give me as much information as when I have a dancer in a working situation. Then I can basically try someone out and give a dancer an opportunity to see how they work. I rely a lot on agents because I find that they've already screened the dancers. I was never a commercial dancer. I started with Atlanta

A Night At The Roxbury, Abuelo (Director), Mad Men, Clueless and more.

City Ballet when I was 14 years old. I danced with Twyla Tharp for 8 years and also worked with Martha Clarke and Philip Glass. I find that I work better with dancers who are trained well and those that continue to train. These dancers are open to the way that I like to work, which is more improvisational. I draw from their experiences. I like to work with people who understand narrative storytelling, which means that I find that a dancer also has to be an actor. That's what's wonderful about working with dancers who work in the commercial world because they are required to be actors."

CHLOE ARNOLD

"I look for someone with great energy and passion. Someone that's not overdone and approaches the audition with a professional attitude. Arrives early and warms up. They should be able to rock the choreography and put their own flavor on it. They should also be able to express themselves clearly with musicality through improvisation/freestyle. Someone that  takes risks and even if they make a mistake, they keep the going with the same vigor. Bring the choreography to life. Come with positive energy and an open attitude to everyone in the room. Great focus and work ethic. A piece of advice I (received) from Dianne Walker by way of Bunny Briggs who said, 'You gotta stay in your own bag.' There will always be someone taller, thinner, lighter, darker, sexier, classier, or technically stronger, but there is only one you. And you must always work to better yourself and realize and recognize your own style and value."

JAQUEL KNIGHT

"Generally, I look for whoever can get the style and the vibe of the choreography correct. Choreography is the easy part, but can you present it how I imagined? It's so much more than the dance to me. I also look at how the dancers carry themselves during the audition. That tells you a lot about how they will act on the job. Good energy makes rehearsals more fun and less stressful and like a job. If it's a job dealing with an artist, I expect for the dancers to always be on their 'A' game when the artist is around. That encourages the artist to want to learn and pull up skill and performance wise. I am not a fan of dancers who are lazy and do not deliver! I can't handle them! You have to want it, crave it, breathe it, eat it, sleep it and everything else possible. You have to feel it in your gut and you must do it for yourself, not for anyone else. If you are already there, then you must stay focused, dedicated and committed. You also (need) to have a passion and a love for it and allow that to show. <u>Only the strong survive</u>."

CHAPTER SEVEN
SERGIO TRUJILLO

"I think that the most important quality is to have a dancer who is not afraid of taking the material that is given to them and creating a character and a world that is appropriate for whatever it is that they are auditioning for. And for them to be able to show a little bit of who they are. There are dancers that are incredibly technical and specific and you love that, but they are empty of emotion and empty of any character-
ization. Especially for theatre, it is important for me to find dancers who are able to create a world.

"L.A. dancers I've seen are very superficial as far as their approach to the material. They are just flash but no essence, no substance. It's so incredibly motivated by the outside as opposed to the in to out. Although the dancers in L.A. are ferocious and they are incredibly passionate, that sort of wears out. They sort of start doing the exact same thing, and it becomes boring. So you go to an audition and try to find that other quality that I'm talking about. On the job I expect them to be professional, to work hard, to deliver and show up, be committed and devoted because what we do is very limited time wise. It is an art, so you better love it."

GEO HUBELA
"What do I look for from a dancer at an audition...hmmmm... maybe it is what I don't look for. I definitely don't look for dancers that walk into an audition with sunglasses on, LOL. What I am trying to say is, I see dancers walking into auditions trying way too hard from the get go. Just be you! Don't feel like you have to play a role or impress a choreographer with your outfit.

"I am all for looking good, image is very important in this industry, but look comfortable in your own skin. You can easily tell when someone is over the top. Come ready to dance and focused on what you are ultimately there for...to book the gig! As a choreographer I look for that spark, that something special in a dancer. When a dancer inspires me, I want be around that, I want to work with that dancer, I want to hire that dancer. That inspiration will compliment my work! Focus on YOU. Stop worrying about everyone else at the audition and focus on how you are going to dance your butt off and impress the choreographer. An audition is not social hour. This is your livelihood and your job. Networking is good, but network the right way and at the right time. Don't get CAUGHT UP in the scene."

LIL' C

Rize, SYTYCD (Judge & Choreographer), Stomp

"I don't look for anything at auditions because I believe if you approach any situation with an expectation you're placing a hindrance upon the person who is auditioning for you. So instead of you expecting to see something or instead of looking for something specific, I might miss out on what it is that they are involuntarily showing me, like fundamentally. So I don't look for things. If I did look for anything, I would look for your strength and anything that you can show me that will communicate that you have a love for the art form of dance. Specific qualities, not physical, sometimes internal. I look for that person's most luminous characteristics.

"From people that I work with, all I expect from them, is that they play their position. Be naked to the situation. People have their fears and things that they are reluctant to do because they feel like they suck at them. They feel like their inner artist will be judged because they're not good at a specific thing or move and have certain uncomfortabilities. I want people to just throw all of that out of the window because nobody in the room is perfect. Let's say we're doing a specific move, I cannot stand when people show their distaste for a specific section of choreography or a specific piece of the music solely based upon the fact that they can't execute it. I hate that. It's like artistically scapegoating. When someone comes in and dancers look around and think the choreography is too outrageous and think, 'Oh my God, why do we have to do this? Why do we have to go to the ground?' Look, it's your job to communicate and help the choreographer find the road map to the X. And the X on the road map is fruition of whatever is in their head. You have to play your position as a tool on the tool belt. If you're a screwdriver, be the screwdriver. If you're a hammer, then (be the) best hammer you can be. Understand that you are a tool. We are all tools. We are all being used for the greater good, for a specific purpose that is bigger than all of us. Let all of your inhibitions go. Don't bring your anchor to rehearsal because the ship of creativity will be capsized if the anchor is not let up. You've got to pull that anchor up!"

SICK TIP #24:
DON'T FIGHT CONSTRUCTIVE CRITICISM

It is important to know that you don't know it all, yet! You probably never will. The gift of dance is that it is always changing, recreating itself in new and different forms. When a choreographer, director or agent is trying to assist you by giving you a note, critique or advice, really take that in. Constructive criticism is there to help you grow as an artist. Never let your pride get in the way of you becoming the best performer you can be.

CHAPTER SEVEN
MONIE ADAMSON

"I am always looking for the dancer who is the most versatile. I will always take the well-rounded dancer who can do all styles of dance over the one who can only do one style well. This way I do not have to limit my choreography. Tips for standing out: First, show up early, never be late to an audition! Second, share your personality in your audition, let the choreographer get  a glimpse of how fun, passionate, quick, and responsible you are. Third, don't over dress the part so that your shoes or your outfit limit your ability to execute the movement full out. It is not a fashion show, it is a dance audition!

"I expect my dancers to always be on time! To always check with me first before heading off to craft service or even the bathroom for that matter without alerting me to where they are going. The dancers that I use again and again, are the ones who are quick studies, capable of picking up choreography quickly and don't get rattled when we have to change movement at the last minute. The dancers I use always keep in mind that this is a job and that they should not be hanging out talking to crew but instead be ready to dance and pay attention to what is going on around them. Not that we don't have fun, but they also know when to buckle down and get to work."

PHLEX

"I look for a couple of different things. Talent, style and look. There may be one that's more important than another depending on the job. Pet peeves, I guess would be plain faces. I am a sucker for personality and presence. I expect hard work and a positive attitude. Energy is everything! Love your craft and continue to train."

CARRIE ANN INABA

"Always respect yourself and your talent. If you do not, it will be difficult to expect others to. Stay true to your own path. Don't try to walk someone else's path. Know thyself and be true to thyself. The road may be long. But the road will be yours! Either way, I wish everyone the best. It can be a tough road, but I think it's an exciting and fulfilling path to pursue as well. Well worth every ounce of sweat put into it."

THANK YOU - PLEASE STAY. THE CHOREOGRAPHER'S CUT!

BRADLEY RAPIER

"I look for those who can best match the choreography taught or freestyle shown to the specific beats and musicality of the song they're dancing to. For me, every detailed move is less important than the groove and style of the dance. Outside of that I look for people who are personable, upbeat, excited to learn and ready and willing to share their talents, but who also have an awareness of others and their surroundings and can be respectful of the audition process. My pet peeves are whiners, moody people and lazy dancers."

The Groovaloos (Founder/Director), Groovaloo (Stage show creator), The Sweetest Thing, Breaking Point

Hyde Park, Latin Froz, WNBA, Diddy

LESLIE SCOTT

"I want to FEEL them dance, not watch them dance! Totally different experience for me watching and for them performing. If their movement is rooted in genuine emotion to the point that when they are out of my sight I can still feel their passion then they will be able to connect and affect an audience after they leave the show, which for me is always the goal. Work ethic and attitude! These are TALENTS that should not be underestimated! I don't care how quickly you pick up choreo, how athletic or sick your movement is, if your aesthetics are gorgeous and ripped, etc. If you don't show up and contribute positively to the team and the project as a whole there is not much I am inspired to do with you. I am so impressed by those dancers that still have the love and commitment for the PROCESS of putting together a show, not just the end result. Those are the people I want on my team. Those are the dancers that give me the gift of an environment to really create my best work. Don't allow your confidence to be rooted in anything external. It's too high risk. Everywhere you go the only person guaranteed to go with you is YOU, so put your strength in that!"

SICK TIP #25:
MAINTAIN THE APPEARANCE OF AVAILABILITY

While interviewing choreographer PAUL BECKER he said, "Always maintain the appearance of availability." I thought he was talking about in your personal life. He meant, if you're at a job and a choreographer wants you to work for them and asks you if you're available, make sure you say, "Yes, I can do it." If you aren't free then work out the details. If you're double or triple booked, they'll understand. You will lose jobs if you hmm...haaa... around!

CHAPTER SEVEN

Sandra says...

- Choreographers have different wants and needs but all of them want dancers to be ready to work!

- Recognize that there are always going to be changes. Be prepared to make last minute adjustments.

- Use common sense if you have a problem.

- The industry has challenges for choreographers too. Be sympathetic to time constraints, long days and music changes.

- Work hard - play hard! Get it right and get out. Perfection is required, so make it happen and put in extra work if you need to.

- Pull up. Work as a team. No one wants to stay late because you're slacking!

- Be kind to choreographer's assistants. They might be your next boss!

> **POINT TAKEN:**
> Choreographers want you to do well. They want to believe that they picked you at the audition and you are going to make their choreography look good. They need great demo reels as well. It is important for you to network with choreographers not out of "wanting to work with them" but from a genuine place. **Being fake is not fierce!**

CHAPTER EIGHT

DANCE:
In Film And On Television

Dance in film and on television can have their own unique challenges, especially for dancers. We are used to having an audience and conveying a performance to spectators. Here are some frequently asked questions and technical terms all dancers should know on set.

FAQ: WHAT DOES IT MEAN TO ARRIVE CAMERA-READY?
This means that if you had to walk on stage the minute you walked in the door, this is how you should arrive. Makeup and hair done, teeth clean and dressed appropriately.

FAQ: DOES THE CAMERA REALLY ADD 10 POUNDS?
Borrowing a phrase from former Alaska Governor Sarah Palin, "You betcha!" It's sad but true! So go out and buy yourself a skinny mirror. Sometimes it helps!

SICK TIP #26:
DON'T EVER WEAR A COMPETITOR'S NAME BRAND
Life is short but these tips will stay with you for a long time. If you're going to a Nike audition, don't wear Puma shoes. If you're doing an Adidas industrial, don't wear a competitor's shoe. Try something that isn't competitive with them like K-Swiss or Keds that you can put your jean over or the new Fanny Pak kicks! Use common sense.

DANCE: IN FILM AND ON TELEVISION
DANCE OBSTACLES TO OVERCOME IN FILM AND TV
NO AUDIENCE - NEW AUDIENCE "THE CAMERA"
No third dimension in television and film creates a different type of dance experience. Shooting scenes without the benefit of an audience reaction or feedback can be quite difficult on a commercial shoot or film production. Recreating scenes over and over while maintaining the same level of intensity can be hard even for the most experienced dancer.

DANCE LIKE A PEDESTRIAN, HUH?
Often casting directors or choreographers will be given the task of finding people who fit the breakdown for a role that requires someone to "move well." This does not mean they should break into choreographed dance that includes leaps, pirouettes and back-handsprings. This may mean that they would rather bring in a trained professional dancer and minimize their movement instead of bringing in an actor that they can't get to move enough to their liking. Most directors would love to have someone do too much and be able to tell them to tone it down, than to have someone who can't do enough to get the shot. This makes things a bit tricky.

At an audition I was told in these exact words, "OK now go ahead and start dancing when I call for action. Well, I mean dance, but don't dance. I mean, you know. Make it pedestrian." I had to scratch my head and think, OK now dance, but don't dance. What would a pedestrian do? I'm a pedestrian sometimes, aren't I? Does that mean dance off beat? Or should I just dance like I have no rhythm? Or should I bust into the 'Carlton' from *Fresh Prince of Bel Air*? I was dumbfounded and had to do this while "not dancing" to a '60s song that I'd never heard before. It kind of helped because not having heard the song before, I was able not to focus so much on the music. Unfortunately, my face told the story. I was so lost.

Sit back while you're in the airport, grocery store or in the mall and just watch people. As a dancer you are training yourself to live within the beat or to find the intricate nuances within the melody of a song. You find musicality as part of your own process to define the rhythm that takes you from one movement to the next. Developing your own unique way of pedestrian dancing will take some of fine tuning so that you capture enough movement to satisfy a casting director but tone down the underlying perfection that screams, "I'm a trained professional!" Try it! Go on...stare at people if you have to! Embody a character you see on the street. The mailman, the delivery guy, or maybe the cute guy or girl walking down the street listening to their iPod. Find an alter ego. Make a choice as to what they feel, who they are, how they live and what their aspirations are. Give them names. Find joy or pain in their ambition, their mode of transportation and really walk the walk of these newfound people and characteristics you've created for them. Then, dance the dance, the pedestrian dance.

SCRIPTS ARE ALWAYS CHANGING

Choreographer **Paul Becker** highlighted that "the script is changing over and over. Let's say I just hired technical dancers and all they have is technique, great lines and they can do choreography really well. If the script changes at the last minute, which it always does in film and TV, where it has more of a theatrical/storytelling emphasis like comedy or if it requires the dancers to speak, you never know and anything can come up. There are so many variables that can come up on set, even on the day of filming, that I want the most versatile dancers as possible. Having versatile dancers helps me as a choreographer."

BREAKING DOWN STEREOTYPES

Some stereotypes do exist in the dance world. Try not to be one of them. A big misconception that still exists is that white girls can't do hip-hop. Not the case. Just look at some of the most commercial and successful dancers like Maryss from Paris or Lady Jules of the BEATFREAKS and you will wonder why these stereotypes still exist.

VIDEO VIXEN VS. LEAD GIRL

Many times ladies are cast in a music video as a lead girl and often are then filmed in the light of the video vixen. There is a distinct difference. Remember what your goal was when you came to Hollywood. If you feel uncomfortable in these roles, don't take the job. You determine your career path. Suggestive movement, compromising scenes of music videos, short films and behind the scenes footage may be to your detriment when trying to substantiate yourself in another field of entertainment. Be a goddess, not a vixen! Choose your path wisely. Most of the girls who are cast in a lead girl role are presented in more of a "girlfriend" light and those cast in a "video vixen" role are set in a scenario with voyeuristic undertones or one that is indulgent in nature to the extent that the woman is objectified and not celebrated for her talent. Some will argue that you can do either and gain the same amount of respect. I respectfully disagree.

RESPECTING THE HIERARCHY

Choreographer and director **Mary Ann Kellogg** stated that "being respectful of the hierarchy that happens in film and knowing who you're working for and with is important. Come with the tools that you need to work and with an attitude that's respectful of the process. The basics: being on time, well groomed, have the proper attire...whether you're in bare feet or tennis shoes, tap shoes or jazz shoes. In TV and film there is an element of working quickly and efficiently, which means no one on cell phones, don't sit down in rehearsal and be involved in the process."

FILM AND TELEVISION SUCK LIFE OUT OF YOUR PERFORMANCE
Choreographer **Rosero McCoy** noted that "the good thing about film is that you get more chances with film; more takes. Film sucks out a lot of the life from you when you dance. You'll notice even when you audition and (record) people on video, sometimes when you look back at it, it doesn't look like the step was done as hard as it should've or could've been done; even if the dancers were killin' it in person. The more over-the-top and aggressive you are dancing in front of me, the better. Let me pull you back, especially when you're dancing on film. Every take has to really count though!"

Choreographer **Monie Adamson** stated, "Probably, one of the keys to the difference in stage performance and TV/film, would be to know where you are supposed to look when performing. Sometimes the choreographer needs you to perform straight into the camera and you need to feel comfortable looking at metal and glass and still be passionate and communicate. Other times you should ignore the camera for it might be right in your face. You need to be good at ignoring (the camera operator) and the fact that he is in your space yet still be able to dance with just as much energy and attack without letting his proximity rattle you and show on your face!"

TIME IS MONEY!
Choreographer **Mary Ann Kellogg** reminds dancers that "Film and television are both very expensive. Often dancers aren't given the amount of time that they need or wish they had to make the performance good. The camera is usually hitting things from many different angles. Do your best on every single take because you never know what they're going to use. Be consistent and if you're asked to do things again for continuity sake. The dance will be made in the editing room. If you can, without disturbing or stepping over the boundary of the hierarchy, get a chance to see the monitor without being intrusive, it will give you a better idea. That little box and that lens see everything!"

RYAN POWELL CHECKING OUT FOOTAGE ON THE MONITOR.

CHAPTER EIGHT

BASIC ACTING TIPS FOR DANCERS

I'm not an acting teacher but I can give you some general insight into experiences I've had on the job, at auditions and some basics that I've learned along the way to help you. I've also listed some classes for acting, comedy, musical theatre and voice training later on page 309 to provide you with further avenues to perfect your craft.

CASTING FACILITIES AND CASTING DIRECTORS

Some things that aren't normally mentioned but you need to know are that casting directors are always casting. You may go in for one project and they may ask you for an additional headshot for something else they are working on. You may also notice that most casting offices have **submission boxes**. Look for them or ask if they have a check-in desk. If the box is full, chances are that they don't check it very often. If it is empty, they probably check it regularly so take your chances with those boxes and submit your headshot there first.

When you go into a casting session, the first call will be with a casting assistant and/or the casting director. Don't worry about shaking hands. Think about how many people they see all day long and how many hands that is to shake. After that visual, you wouldn't want to shake hands with them either. Don't worry about that part, focus on your task: Your slate and what they want you to state on it. Your mark, stay on it and don't fidget or jump out of frame. Dancers are used to movement, which is a big no-no during your slate. Try to stay in frame and give as much personality as you can during your slate. Believe it or not, casting directors want you to do well. They want you to book the job and they want you to make their reel shine when they give it to their client. If you have a scene partner or someone else to interact with on camera, don't upstage him or her or cross in front of them during your audition. If told to cross in front or given specific direction, then go ahead and follow it. But don't intentionally sabotage another person's audition.

In some commercial auditions for food products from brands like Coca-Cola or McDonald's, you may have to "show your hands" as those are a prominent feature when eating on camera. You may have to dance with a chicken mcnugget or pirouette with a can of Coca-Cola. Make sure to always go to these types of auditions with well-manicured hands. If asked to show your hands, make sure to put them up in front of your face palm front then palm back as shown in Chapter 5 - *Auditions*. Try to keep them in front of your face, as the camera shot will be on your face or in a mid-range from waist up. Don't spread them too far from your face, as they will be out of the shot.

DON'T WORRY ABOUT ASKING QUESTIONS
Ask the casting assistant where your eye line should be. They will give you general direction. **Repeat what they say out loud and ask any questions you have at that time.** You usually cannot do things again. If you have done your audition and have another version of the character that you'd like to try, ask if they'll let you do that version. Normally you get one shot. But if you say, "You know, I played it with a hip-hop feel that time, can I try it again with a more Broadway style?" You never know they might say yes! Don't ask every time to do it a different way, do your best the first time. The camera sees desperation whether you are speaking, dancing, singing, etc. If you have the look on your face that you need a job or are desperate to get work, the camera does not lie. It sees inside, backwards and forwards and every which way through you. Don't cheat yourself during your audition, give it your all.

KEEP GOING AND DON'T FORGET YOUR BUTTON!
And DON'T apologize if you mess up. Keep going! Casting directors would much rather see how you handle a flub. Most of these awkward and strange moments of saying the wrong lines or fumbling to get back on track produce what I like to call "moments of brilliance." These moments of brilliance are usually called *buttons*. A **button** is a sort of tag at the end of an audition that made you stand out from the rest, whether planned or unplanned. For example, if you were to do a crazy insane flip, jump, kick into the splits and then wipe your brow while panting out of breath look to the camera and say, "That was easy!" Or maybe you are asked to dance like a "maniac" and have no dialogue whatsoever but during each little break in the action, you give a little nod to the camera like, "You know you want me!" Or "Take that, I'm battling myself!" Whatever your moment of brilliance is, don't ever break from it until the assistant or casting director asks you to stop. You don't want to stop short of having a cool button. Try to keep them individual to each audition. If asked to do it again, don't repeat the same button because it usually isn't as funny, unique or unexpected. Now, if they ask you to repeat what you did the exact same way, then do it. Hey, if you say something witty, the writers may even include it in the actual commercial. If it makes it into the final copy, you may get a bump in pay and writing credit as well.

"WORD PERFECT" OR SOMEWHAT MEMORIZED?
You may be asked to dance and then say a line or two to the camera and then continue dancing. In these situations, you will be provided with your dialogue. Memorize as much as you can, but know that you don't have to know your dia-

logue in what is called **word perfect**. Word perfect is just like it sounds, having the material memorized down to the word - perfectly. This means know what you can and perform it to the best of your ability. Try memorizing the first line, middle line and ending line to make sure you can start strong, have some meat in the middle and end with a bang! Generally, the copy will be provided on a board next to the camera for you to reference. Don't always look at the board. Glance at it if you have to and then move your eyes back to your point of reference. If that's the camera then look to the camera, if it is your scene partner, then look at him or her. When working with a partner, try not to throw your eyes back and forth between their eyes. This can make the viewer confused as to what you're looking at. Focus on one side or the other, but not crossing from one to the next.

In every commercial, music video and infomercial there is always a **hero**! No, I'm not talking about Thor from *Adventures in Babysitting*, I'm talking about the product, the artist or the song that is the focal selling point. Although you are the star in your bedroom, the advertising campaign only revolves around one star and it's not you! When fighting with other dancers for that initial camera time at a commercial shoot because you don't know who is going to end up being a principal in the final edit; try to do your best job at making the product look good. Product first!

WHAT DOES IT MEAN TO BE "BEER LEGAL?"

You may ask friends of yours, "Why am I not getting called to commercial auditions for Bud Light or Corona?" Well, first you might not be the type they are looking for and more importantly you may not be 25 years old or older. There is a mandatory age that you must be, in this case 25, in order to be in a commercial in which the product is an alcoholic beverage. Sorry, if you're under 25, stay under 25 for as long as you can. I myself have been 22 for a few years now. LOL!

THE STORYBOARD TELLS YOU...UM...THE STORY!

In the upcoming sections you will learn key terminology for production on the set of a television show, movie, music video or commercial. The script will generally tell the story but in the case of the commercial, you may get a storyboard giving you a visual depiction of the commercial in frames like a comic strip or even an example of a potential poses.

You may then be asked to either replicate these movements or interpret them with your own style. In any case make it energetic and try to accomplish exactly what they ask of you.

STICKS AND STONES MAY BREAK MY BONES BUT JINGLES WILL NEVER HURT ME!

As a dancer, you will and I mean <u>will</u> go to an audition for a commercial where you are lip-synching the words to a jingle. Advertisers have been known to add "word" choreography to their storyboards. This means that a product may have the new version of an old song or a new jingle where they've put in the words "chicken wings" or "ranch dressing." You may be asked in your freestyle to do motions where you are a playing a rancher simulating a roping move or do a chicken dance on those particular words of the song. You will do these moves, you will look like a dork and you will like it when your residual check shows up in the mail!

Typically, you won't receive any lines to memorize before a commercial audition. You will show up cold (unrehearsed) and learn them on the spot and perform them. For many commercial dance auditions, this is not always the case. You may be required to go online to a casting site to listen to music or look at lyrics so you have an idea of what you will be asked to do. Make sure that if you have a chance to prepare ahead of time that you actually do. Jingles can sometimes be tricky and I've had to learn spoken word poetry for a Subway audition prior to going in simply because of the tongue twisting words. This may not be the case for all jingles but some are down right crazy. Word sequences may be hard to remember and if you forget to lip synch while dancing, try to mouth the word "watermelon." This usually has enough movement in your lips to at least hit some of the words you forget. Do your best. This is serious stuff here!

NO NO AND YES YES

What makes you comfortable? What's your pre-funk? Make sure you are calm. Do not bring in any props unless you are specifically asked to. This is distracting. If you can't read without your glasses, then you should have them on! If you are told to wear glasses and borrow a friend's glasses but can't see through them, then it probably isn't a good idea to wear them. Get a cheap pair from Rite Aid or Walgreen's that have no prescription or pop out the lens. If asked to audition in costume or in character, make sure to slate as the real person you are. If you are going to be speaking with a British accent, speak in your normal voice during your slate so the casting director can tell the difference when you go into your dialect. Dancers like to wear hats but those cast shadows on your face. Slate with your hat off and then pop it on to complete your look. Even though you are in costume, you still have to audition. Your outfit can't do it for you. At the callback, if no one is paying attention to anything you are doing, don't worry, just wait until you are addressed and then turn it on. Also for b-boys and b-girls, when the camera is rolling, shorten your set up time to get into difficult tricks. Casting directors will ask you to jump right into it, which is difficult but they hate the long set up time, especially on the shoot day.

FAMILIES, COUPLES AND BEST FRIEND CASTING

Another common practice is for a family, couple, siblings or best friends to be cast in a commercial together. These can be difficult because the commercial will call for a girl going through the stages of her life, or a family with a young baby, a daughter in her teens and a mother and father seeing her off to college. I was at a casting like this where we were all there to be part of a Latin family. Different variations of physical features made it very difficult to create whole families out of the people who came to audition. Be patient as the casting director knows what the client wants. Sometimes you may not get the part because your counterpart didn't show up. Just move on to the next gig.

DAVID KANG - CASTING DIRECTOR
(MUSIC VIDEO/COMMERCIAL/FEATURE FILM)

David Kang is a casting director for many projects. He now casts for over 25 principal directors and his business is still growing.

SC: Any things you love or pet peeves you hate in a casting session?
DK: I love it when talent come prepared or ask questions before the audition starts. I hate when talent mess up in the middle of auditions and want to start over. They should just improvise and finish the audition. After they finish, they can ask the casting director if they can go again. I love kids, but I hate casting for kids, because whenever I audition them, they bring the whole family which includes their grandma, uncle, sister, mother and father. There should be one parent bringing their child to auditions.

SC: What do you look for when casting for a lead girl or guy/dancer in a music video?
DK: Most of the time, on music videos I get one day notice. When looking for a lead dancer for a video, this is usually a look, so just be yourself. Don't try being someone your not. You were brought into the audition because you have the right look. You just need to make sure you can back up your look by how well you dance.

JOANNA COLBERT - Casting Director
(Step Up, Step Up 2 and Step Up 3-D)

SC: Explain the process you go through in casting dance films. What do you look for?
JC: We call all of the dance agencies. They know we're looking for someone who can act and dance but we'll see everyone because you never know. With a feature film, we normally start with the acting audition and if we feel they're right for the role then we dance them. We'll usually reserve a studio and have all of the choreographers there and the director there and we film them. They go through choreography and then we kind of go from there and start narrowing down.

SC: How do you find the perfect fit for each role?
JC: If somebody makes a mistake, we need to know that it doesn't mean that they can't do the role or it means that they can do the role. It's our job to see through all of that. It's not exactly like auditioning for a company where if you don't do the steps perfectly then you're out. It's a process and we try to be very helpful in saying, 'Give this person another chance,' or 'Look at this tape,' or 'Look at this reel of them dancing.' We try not to make it cut and dry. With Jenna Dewan, she was new to film and already so established as a dancer; such a sick dancer that we couldn't ignore her on any level. Her acting started blossoming and developed with every day that went by. We feel like it's like a gift to...see as many dancers as we can and sort of say well they might not be right for this but they're right for *Step Up 2* or they are right for *Step Up 3-D*. That's also our job (and that) is to have that file in our brain organized well enough where we can sort of put the pieces of the puzzle together.

SC: Do you have any audition preferences?
JC: I am a big proponent of the less is more in the audition room way of thinking. For an acting audition, you need to just put your blinders on, sit in the waiting room, be quiet; don't ask for paper clips and hair bands. Come in and just give me a sense that you know who the character is. It's not a performance, it's not a play and you don't need props. It's a small room. It's very intimate. It's a separate skill and a lot of knowing the skill, is knowing that less is more. It's very subtle. Just kind of click into the character and show me that you know who that person is. That's really all I want.

SC: How do you see the future of dance on TV and in film?
JC: I think dance is here to stay.

CHAPTER EIGHT

TECHNICAL TERMS ON SET/AUDITIONS ALL DANCERS SHOULD KNOW

Here are a few terms dancers should know at an audition as well as key terms while on the set of a television show, film or music video. These key terms are part of your work. It's kind of like knowing how to answer the phone. We all grew up knowing how to answer the phone, but every telephone is different. The keys may be different, it may have multiple lines to answer, but you still know how to do it. You, as a dancer, have been prepared with the choreography or key lines of the scene. You may have different equipment or crew on each job. Maybe they have a small budget and are using a single camera, or maybe this is a huge soundstage where production has a crane and is using multiple cameras at one time. These pieces of equipment are like the telephone you answer. It will be different every time. Your job, however, is the same. Your job is to take direction and deliver the best performance possible. And in delivering this performance you need to know the equipment that might be on set, the terminology a director or choreographer may use to capture the best footage and the people involved to help make this all possible.

The choreographer and director are familiar terms we hear all the time. The choreographer may often times also be the director of a film project like Adam Shankman for *Hairspray*, Kenny Ortega for *High School Musical 3: Senior Year* or Rob Marshall for *Chicago*. When a production starts the **director** is the head honcho in charge! A **choreographer** is in charge of creating the movement of a particular production. Because of the many aspects of their job, a choreographer may have an assistant that may also showcase or teach choreography at an audition or rehearsal. A director has many different moving parts of their production as well. The **assistant choreographer** is also carrying out the desired requests of the choreographer. You may see them cleaning a routine or blocking a piece on stage while the choreographer works with a lighting crew member or fire marshall on pyrotechnics.

DETAILED ON SET DEFINITIONS WITH CHRISTOPHER ERSKIN
I've asked my friend and well-respected director **Christopher Erskin** to help detail job descriptions on the set of television and film productions and some of the things he looks for from talent as well. You may have watched movies he's directed like *Johnson Family Vacation* or music videos by recording artists such as R. Kelly, TLC's T-Boz, Blackstreet and Boyz II Men along with commercials for Tide,

DANCE: IN FILM AND ON TELEVISION

Athlete's Foot and Pontiac to name a few. So buckle up and take note of these important job functions and equipment descriptions along with real on set examples. In the world of film making, whether you are filming a music video, commercial, movie or TV show, nothing moves forward without the written word. So you have to have some form of a script.

TREATMENT (SCRIPT)

A **treatment** is a narrative, a **script**. It's basically a synopsis of your ideas. A treatment is stating what you would do and how you would capture it visually. For a music video, it generally outlines your interpretation musically, a storyline if there is one. If the video is going to be performance based, the treatment outlines how the sets are going to look and how the dancing is going to be, etc.

Example: Music video/commercial process from treatment to completion
A record label or a commercial client has a product they want to sell, (i.e. the artist or product), and the director is asked to interpret the best way to sell that product to the client's audience. For music videos, a director would write a treatment. If the client likes the director's treatment submission better than someone else's idea then they ultimately book the job, sign a contract and are now responsible for delivering that piece of paper; just like a script. Once a director goes into production they are responsible for delivering the words that were purchased by the client. This is the director's path, unless in the middle of the project, the client gives them the authority to veer off in a different direction because of some act of God or they just decide that creatively they want to do something else. In any case, the director has to deliver it. When a director writes that treatment he or she most likely will then talk to the choreographer who has listened to the music. Directors will have some vision for what they want and how it should feel or look, and will convey that to the choreographer. Sometimes, the artist or choreographer is also involved in writing parts of the treatment concept and help in creating the vision for the project. For a commercial, an ad agency is responsible for providing ad copy and a storyboard outlining the sequence of events in the commercial.

COPY OR SIDES

You receive **copy** (words/dialogue) or **sides** (portions of a script) at an audition to read as your dialogue. Your **script** would be the entire body of work for a project just as the material you've learned for dance is called a routine. When auditioning for a commercial, the casting director is required to have a storyboard present with your copy provided. <u>You are never required to have memorized your lines at an</u>

audition. This is why they are provided. Although it is best if you are required to say lines that you have a general feel for them as discussed earlier.

Even though you are not required to know your lines during an audition, you must know them if cast in a role. Showing up to a set without being prepared to do your job is unacceptable. If you aren't perfect in rehearsal and mess up a few steps, you must come to the show knowing what you're doing. No one else is going to show you the next move when you're on stage just like someone isn't going to give you a line on stage. Practice at home.

ON SET CHAIN OF COMMAND AND JOB FUNCTIONS

DIRECTOR

The director is the person who is responsible for the creative vision of the project. Not only that, he or she has been hired to basically creatively deliver the video, film, commercial, etc.

DIRECTOR RYAN POWELL

Example: The director would be like the captain of the ship. The captain has been hired to sail this ship from Florida to Alaska. Because the director has been hired to sail that ship, everyone else works to help facilitate the vision of that director.

PRODUCER

The producer is someone who on the job is very seldom seen. The producer is like a project manager who is responsible financially for it. He or she would be on a ship and they would tell the director, 'I don't care how you get from Florida to Alaska, but get there on time, on budget and without injury.'

CINEMATOGRAPHER OR D.P. (DIRECTOR OF PHOTOGRAPHY)

The cinematographer is the person who is responsible for the look and helps the director execute their vision. He or she would be in charge of telling crew members how everything should be lit and what camera lenses should go in the camera.

Example: If a dancer is dancing out of the frame or out of their light, the cinematographer would tell the director or assistant director that he/she needs to stay in their light or in frame because if you're out of frame, you won't be in the video.

CAMERA OPERATOR
The camera operator makes the vision of the director come alive by obtaining the shots outlined for a project. The D.P. relies on the **gaffer** to be in charge of the lighting crew.

FIRST CAMERA ASSISTANT
The cinematographer is sitting on the camera with their eye up to the eyepiece. Sitting on the side of the camera is a **first camera assistant** with a little dial wheel in his hand. He is using that wheel to keep the subject, (i.e. the dancer), in focus. When he steps off of the camera he uses a measuring tape to measure the distance from the camera lens to the subject. This measurement is done so that he knows what notches and lines to put on the focus wheel. This helps because when moving toward you with the camera or moving with you, now he/she knows at which particular point to turn the wheel to a specific mark because to keep the subject in focus; if that's what they want. Sometimes they want the foreground out of focus and the background in focus. Nevertheless, they are measuring the distance to you to have you either in focus or out of focus depending on what the shot calls for. Some dancers may have a tendency to move from their mark because they believe they are in the way of this act of measuring. Stay put unless asked to move. Generally it is you who they are measuring the distance to. If you are in the way, you will be asked to step aside.

Example: When you have a still camera or digital camera, usually people put the camera setting on auto-focus. Let's say a group of friends are standing a few feet away from you for a photo. Your camera will shutter back and forth in and out of focus for a half of a second and then it will be in focus. Your camera was measuring the distance between the lens and that group of friends to put them into focus, which is the auto focus. There's no such thing as auto focus in motion picture so that measuring happens with a guy or girl and a measuring tape.

SECOND CAMERA ASSISTANT
The **second camera assistant** is the person who uses the **clapstick** *(pictured on the right)*. This usually has the project name, take number, scene name/number written on it. The second camera assistant also loads and unloads the film and assists the first camera operator as well.

FIRST ASSISTANT DIRECTOR (1ST A.D.)
An **assistant director** traditionally is the person who helps the director stay on time, complete the shots they need for the day and helps man and run the set.

CHAPTER EIGHT

You may need several assistant directors depending on how big the job is that you are shooting. Your main assistant director will be called the 1st A.D. If you have a really big job, the 1st A.D. will have a 2nd A.D. assisting him or her throughout the project.

Example: The 1st A.D. will be on set and will go to the principal talent and say, "We need you on set," or asks the crew, "How long is it going to take to get the set lit?" Or "How long do we have before we're done changing over the camera and ready for the next shot?"

SECOND ASSISTANT DIRECTOR (2ND A.D.)

The **second assistant director** or 2nd A.D. is generally the person who is in charge of background talent. This is the person you will seek out upon arrival and sign-in and out with when you arrive and leave your production or rehearsal location for a film, television project or music video unless you are hired as principal talent. For tours and music video rehearsals you will not normally sign-in and out with anyone other than the choreographer, assistant choreographer or artist management. There generally isn't a sign-in sheet either unless one is provided by a production payroll company or choreographer.

Example: Your 2nd A.D. will be the person who will generally escort the extras to the set and make sure things are set up for lunch. Lunch may not seem like a big deal but if lunch is not set up on time and we break to eat and we're waiting another 20 minutes for everything to be set up, that's another 20-30 minutes out of your day that you could've been shooting.

On Set Scenario: The 2nd A.D.'s assistant is called the **2nd 2nd A.D.** Generally, this person will execute whatever duties the 2nd A.D. can't do. The 1st A.D. is with the director. Sometimes they're yelling, "Action," or "Cut." Sometimes they are asking questions about how fast things can be turned over. Let's say extras are crossing the street and cars are moving in the scene, the 2nd A.D. would be the one in charge of all of the non-principal talent or non-principal items. Then there are extras back at the holding area and things that need to be set up at base camp as well. The 2nd 2nd A.D. will deal with those details. Other positions on a production include the **P.A. (Production Assistant)** and **key P.A.**, etc., who all work for the 2nd 2nd A.D.

RULES ON SET

Working in motion pictures and commercials are a lot different than working on a

DANCE: IN FILM AND ON TELEVISION

video set because you have unions and certain rules. On a movie set, a director can only talk to the principal actors, that includes anyone who has a line that has been hired. A director cannot talk to any non-speaking role persons, to extras and depending on the movie, certain dancers, meaning a director cannot talk to them or give them direction. This is because the minute a director gives you direction you get more money and get bumped up to a different category of role. The director must have their assistant director speak to you or tell the choreographer and have them speak to you to give the direction. A director cannot speak to you directly. They can say hello, but cannot give you direction.

HOW COVERAGE WORKS IN TV AND FILM

Watching a minute long scene there could be five-dozen cuts, which would be a lot, but hypothetically, if you look closely, you realize that there are only six angles. A master shot was done from the doorway of the kitchen. Then a close-up from the table and a reverse from the sink to capture that scene. If you watch that back with no sound, you will see that the good actor or performer hit their mark every single time. Not their mark in terms of just dialogue or footing, but in terms of whether they have a drink or a piece of food in their hand. They're holding it the same way every single time and are so precise that when we go into edit, the edits work seamlessly. The same thing goes for music videos and shooting dancers. The really great dancers will hit their marks every time which makes it so easy to cut from one shot to the next. People who do not hit their marks make it harder for the director and editors to have to cut around stuff. You end up cutting in other shots to make it feel like they're sticking the moves when really they're not really hitting them at all.

TECHNICAL INFORMATION:
CAMERA ANGLES, LENSES AND PRODUCTION EQUIPMENT

CAMERA ANGLES

You will be filmed in a variety of shots during your auditions. Because most choreographers are trying to capture multiple people at one time, at most auditions you will be captured using a **wide shot**. There are a lot of dancers who tend to go all *Flashdance* on choreographers and head right up to the table to get their attention like in the stellar scene from the movie. Unfortunately, this doesn't work at all auditions. If a camera is on a tripod and no one is moving it to capture all of the dancing, your moment, although fierce in its own fantastic way, won't be captured for a client to drool over when they're making their selections. They will just see a dancer go out of frame and miss your shining extravaganza. If you are told to stay back and in frame, then do it! Dancers were specifically told at the audition for

CHAPTER EIGHT

Britney Spears' *Circus* tour not to move past a line taped out on the floor. Dancers still did it. Trust me, at the end of the day it won't help your chances. Be amazing, but be amazing behind the line!

During your slate at most auditions for stage, television or film, you will be in a close-up on your face, neck and head or a very tight to medium shot which includes your upper body, torso or face. The casting assistant will normally then pull out from the close-up to shoot a long shot or full body shot and possibly ask you to do a 360 degree turn to show your front and back to the camera. You may also be shot with an extreme close-up or a possible two-T frame that will film you from chest level meaning from the rib cage up.

MASTER SHOT
A **master shot** is the shot that will ultimately tell you where everyone is standing, what everyone is doing and what the entire action is. It's like a wide view of the entire scene. You shoot your master shot so that when you're in the editing room you always have something to come back to.

CLOSE-UP (CU)
You may want a **close-up** on a particular person or dancer because the movement that they are doing is really cool. You may want a series of close-up shots as well.

MEDIUM CLOSE-UP (MCU)
A **medium close-up** is more or less a close-up that shows the face but gets a happy medium between the close-up shot and the mid-range shot.

EXTREME CLOSE-UP (XCU)
An **extreme close-up** is a type of shot that is extremely tight and will isolate a portion of the face like an eye or the nose to get only a specific point in the shot.

INSERT SHOT
Insert shots are generally body parts.

Example: Think about Janet Jackson's music video for the song *"Rhythm Nation."* If you notice, you see a wide shot of the dancers dancing and then maybe the camera moves in. Then, if they turn to the right, you'll see a medium shot of maybe the upper body. They do a combination with their feet and you'll see a low angle of the feet. And then as they turn and their hands do something, you'll see

DANCE: IN FILM AND ON TELEVISION

an insert shot of those hands. Those four shots all cut together will add energy. You get different types of coverage with different lenses. You may also shoot a **wide shot** or a **tight close-up**, which are exactly what they sound like. A **pan** may also be done where the camera moves over a subject or across them. These are all recorded to obtain each **POV** *(point of view)* for the script supervisor.

CAMERA LENSES

The first one will be a master shot and you'll use a wide-angle lens for that. Wide-angle lenses are the lenses with the lowest number. So when you hear someone say, "Put an 18 on there," or, "Let's use a 14 or 21." Those are the lower lens numbers. As you go in for tighter shots the numbers get higher. So if you want to do a beauty close-up, you're probably going to start working in lenses that are 65 mm lenses and higher for those shots. If you work with a wider lens and are close to someone, the more exaggerated it will make the scene. If you use a 14 mm lens and are far away from someone, then you have a wide shot. If you take that same lens and move it four feet away from the dancer and put the camera at the dancer's ankles or on the ground and shoot up, it's going to make the dancer look really tall. For example, people remember when Hype Williams would use the fish eye lens (an 8 mm lens) and how it would mold and obscure different things in videos like Missy Elliot's *"The Rain (Supa Dupa Fly)."*

You will have the following, if you are shooting in 35 mm, 16 mm, digital or in IID: Camera, dolly, cast, crew, sticks (tripod) and a **shot list** (coverage detail).

STEADICAM®

A Steadicam® is not a special camera but is an apparatus to make it easier and more mobile to capture more fluid and smoother shots. The camera is placed on the apparatus, which is a harness that a camera operator wears. The operator is able to walk and even run around with the camera, which is on a stick that has weights, balances and springs in it to keep it 'steady.'

PHOTO COURTESY OF TIFFEN
Steadicam® is a registered trademark of Tiffen.

Example: The Steadicam® was first made famous in the original *Rocky* film. In the movie, they could not figure out how to run up the steps with Stallone and keep the camera from bobbling around with jerky movements. That is when the Steadicam® was actually developed and first used. They could then run up the stairs with him and it was smooth. They could circle Rocky at the top of the steps and after that everyone started using the Steadicam®.

CHAPTER EIGHT

TECHNOCRANE

The technocrane is a particular crane that became famous in the mid-to-late '90s in music videos. The technocrane has a telescopic crane. That crane allows you to pretty much have the same fluidity of a Steadicam®. The Steadicam® unlike the technocrane is limited to the height of a camera

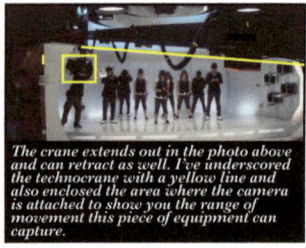

The crane extends out in the photo above and can retract as well. I've underscored the technocrane with a yellow line and also enclosed the area where the camera is attached to show you the range of movement this piece of equipment can capture.

operator. The technocrane can do all that and more but it does have a limited radius. But if you get a technocrane that is 30 feet, and you know what you have and you're only shooting something that is 30 feet wide and 30 feet deep, then anywhere within there, you can move along the ground, follow people side to side or go above them. You can also do extremely fast moves with the technocrane.

BACKDROPS AND STAGE SETTINGS

Backdrops and stage settings vary depending on what the director is trying to convey visually. Some commonly used backgrounds are the white cyc, green screen, black void, pre-constructed sets for television and film along with real life locations and landmarks.

WHITE CYC (PRONOUNCED "PSYCH")

You've seen this in music videos or Gap advertisements where the performers are all dancing with a white background. There's a lot of light that you have to use to illuminate the white cyc so it can be kind of blinding. Many have cautioned about looking directly at the backdrop as it can make one dizzy. Check out the **white cyc** photo on the left. Notice how the white cyc when lit heavily makes the picture

have a bright white backdrop. You may also work in silhouette for an award show or in a Guitar Hero commercial as a body double for a celebrity. Be conscious of each move.

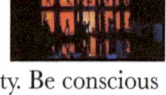

GREEN SCREEN

Green screen is a technology that allows you to matte in any image that you want behind your particular subject, artist or dancer. Think about old movies like the *Wizard of Oz*. Oz seems to go on for a million miles and there

are things moving in the background. They didn't go to a set that looked like Oz. They were on a soundstage with a green background, which allowed them to do what is called **keying**. They keyed in whatever image they wanted to put behind the artist. This process is called keying or **matting**.

BLACK VOID
The **black void** is also used in many music videos to give the appearance of nothingness behind an artist, to draw out all things and with the right lighting can be very effective.

In my interview with choreographer **PAUL BECKER** he talked about his new film with Renee Zellweger called *Cabin In The Woods* where he used motion capture. "There are so many other avenues to explore within dance. Dancers can use their ability for other things that come from dance like movement...this film requires movement for creatures. Choreography and dance are the art of movement. I needed creatures for this horror movie and who better to do creatures than dancers? So there is other work besides doing straight choreography. Motion capture requires dancers with a good physical background and movement for creatures and animals for horror movies and sci-fi projects. With this type of project, you have to start that type of movement from an emotional and connected place with the character. Then you have to build on it and keep adding layers. Keep adding things to the creature like physical traits and then keep building and building upon that."

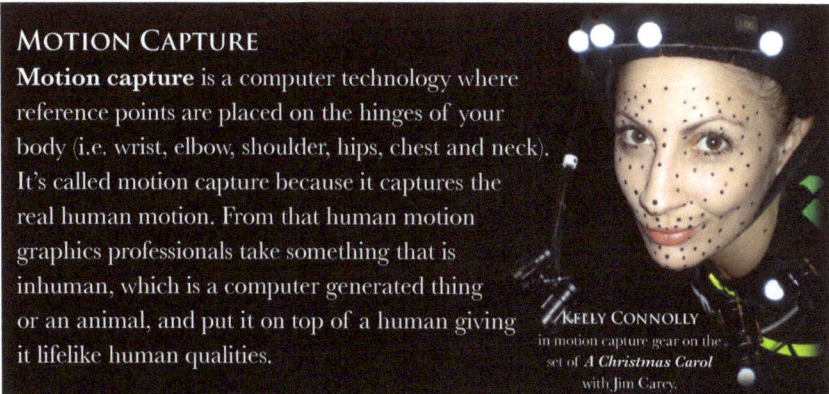

MOTION CAPTURE

Motion capture is a computer technology where reference points are placed on the hinges of your body (i.e. wrist, elbow, shoulder, hips, chest and neck). It's called motion capture because it captures the real human motion. From that human motion graphics professionals take something that is inhuman, which is a computer generated thing or an animal, and put it on top of a human giving it lifelike human qualities.

KELLY CONNOLLY in motion capture gear on the set of *A Christmas Carol* with Jim Carey.

CHAPTER EIGHT

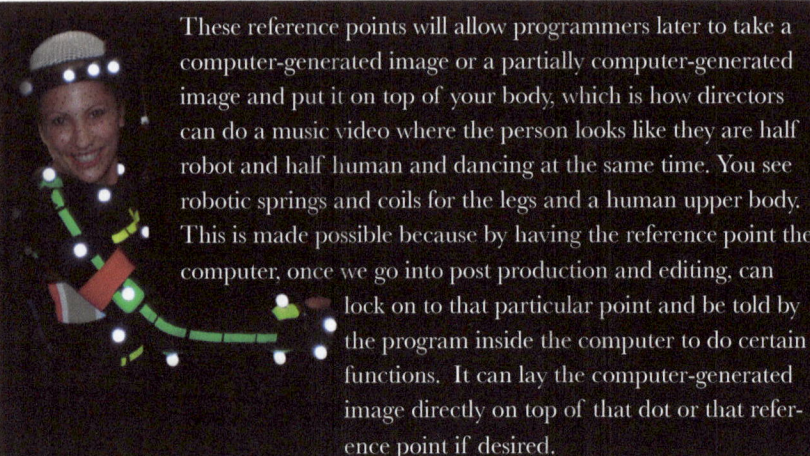

These reference points will allow programmers later to take a computer-generated image or a partially computer-generated image and put it on top of your body, which is how directors can do a music video where the person looks like they are half robot and half human and dancing at the same time. You see robotic springs and coils for the legs and a human upper body. This is made possible because by having the reference point the computer, once we go into post production and editing, can lock on to that particular point and be told by the program inside the computer to do certain functions. It can lay the computer-generated image directly on top of that dot or that reference point if desired.

CGI: COMPUTER-GENERATED IMAGE

If you ever see something that is not real, and it is moving next to something that is real, most likely it is CGI. If you see a dancer dancing next to someone that you clearly know is dead, that was done with CGI. Depending on what the movie looks like, it could be CGI, animated or in 3-D Animation, which is how *Shrek* was done. In *"What's It Gonna Be,"* a music video directed by Hype Williams for Busta Rhymes featuring Janet Jackson, you see drops of mercury, Janet's dress extends forever, there's a river and things are moving, that's CGI. The Justin Timberlake video featuring T.I. for *"My Love,"* directed by Paul Hunter, shows guitars, musical instruments and a wedding band flying in the air. The guitars and all of the things moving behind Justin were all computer generated.

Choreographer **Rosero McCoy** talked about CGI in the *Alvin and The Chipmunks* movies. "Everything was done with CGI. The chipmunks were the only part of the movie that were not human. The first movie had more of a hip-hop vibe to it and the second has more of a rock vibe. I put moves on stand-in chip-pettes and chipmunks so the special effects team could recreate scenes and put them on the real chipmunks and chippettes. The movement has to be bigger to help the animators really see what's going on. Small moves with 'and' step counts versus bigger moves on the full counts of 1, 2, 3, 4, helps to make the movement visible on a larger scale. Everything is seen on film. If you are lurking and you are on camera, the viewing audience will see it. It will be up to the editors to fix it in post production. On stage when you're doing things, sometimes the person in the back is lurking, and you really have to search for his lurking, but on camera it is in your face 100%. Either way, you definitely have to be on your game."

DANCE: IN FILM AND ON TELEVISION

DIRECTIVES/FREQUENT COMMANDS FROM DIRECTORS AND CHOREOGRAPHERS ON SET

Choreographers and directors will use terminology on the set of a television show, music video or film that you will need to respond to with the quickness and be ready when called. Below are a few of these frequently used directives or commands. Again with the assistance of director Christopher Erskin, the terminology is explained in detail.

ON YOUR MARK

When someone says, "**Stand on your mark**," what has happened is that a crew member has put a little X or a dot on the ground and you need to stand on it. The reason that they put that reference point there is because once we have the lens on and have framed up the camera, there is a certain boundary that you have to stand in. That boundary is not only left and right but forward and backwards. That mark allows you to not only stay in frame but also allows whatever symmetry needed while for filming.

Example: It's no different than when you're dancing live and your choreographer says, "Everyone on your mark," or "Back to your first positions." When you hear, "Stay on your mark," or "Get on your mark," we're trying to keep you in frame. It could also be for lighting purposes. If you're not on your mark and you go out of your light and then you see the video later and the other six dancers look beautiful but yet you look kind of muddy and dimly lit, it's because you weren't on your mark or you weren't in your light. If you can't feel the light or you can't see the camera then the camera can't see you and the light won't be on you.

BACK TO ONE

When you hear, "**Everybody back to one**," that means for you to go back to your original position. The position that you started at originally, go back to that place or original mark. Marks are usually given with a tape drawn out in a T shape on the floor.

ACTION

This is what a director or assistant director will call for the scene or background to begin their movement.

CUT

Whether you are a dancer or an actor performing in a scene, even though you

CHAPTER EIGHT

my think that your part has ended, you need to stay in character until the director actually calls, "**Cut**." Anything could be happening from getting extra coverage, if the dancers have danced and they did a pose at the end. You have no clue, a camera could be panning and grabbing little inserts shots of bodies, faces and extra things to go into the final edit. Never break character. Hold the look and follow through because if you break character you have no idea what could be happening. It's like football. Follow through and play until the whistle blows. If the whistle hasn't blown, keep going because the play is not dead.

ROLL PLAYBACK

The phrase **"roll playback"** is a directive to the soundboard operator to begin to play the music. Usually music is cued to a specific section. You may also hear "cue music" as well.

CHECKING THE GATE

Now when you hear, "**Checking the gate**," it basically means you're done shooting a scene and production is ready to move on to a different scene but don't want to move on until the inside of the camera is checked. This is to ensure that none of the notches or perforations of the film are torn or broken, that there's no dirt on the actual film and that somehow the film has not gotten burned or ripped, torn or in any way destroyed. If it is destroyed or damaged in any way or the film has been compromised, and you go to process and edit your film, you will not have that scene. Before moving forward everything is checked. If something is wrong with the gate and it is not clean, we will shoot that scene again for safety.

A more in depth explanation: Before digital cameras, when you loaded film into the camera there were little notches that basically were like a spoke that you put the 35 mm film on top of. As you took a photo, the film would advance and the notches would move the film forward. The gate inside of a moving camera is basically the same thing except for that it spins a lot faster than a still camera does. The reason why they call this portion of the camera the 'gate' is because when you open the camera, it swings open like a gate or a fence. This piece of metal holds the film in place so that the notches can advance the film forward.

LIGHTING (CHEATING TO THE LIGHT/FINDING YOUR LIGHT)

The **key light** is your main light. It is generally the hottest light that will be on you. There is also a **fill light**, which is something that is filling in the shadow side of your body. When asked to find your light, be in the light so you are lit and that you will be

DANCE: IN FILM AND ON TELEVISION

illuminated on film and look beautiful. When asked to, "Cheat toward the light," that means that your body is turned a little bit too far to the shadow side or to the fill light side. So you need to turn a little bit more into your main light or key light.

STAGE DIRECTIONS AND DEFINITIONS

As dancers, one is normally used to taking direction from a choreographer or dance teacher. It is imperative that you know the difference between moving upstage and downstage as well as where stage right and stage left are compared to the camera's view of camera right and camera left. Keeping them clear will make your life easier.

MOVING UPSTAGE AND DOWNSTAGE

Moving **upstage** is to move toward the back of the stage or away from the camera or audience. Moving **downstage** is to move to the front of the stage or closer to the camera or audience.

STAGE RIGHT AND STAGE LEFT

Stage right and **stage left** are the directions to either your right or your left when you are on stage facing the audience.

CAMERA RIGHT AND CAMERA LEFT

Camera right and **camera left** are from the director or the camera's point of view facing you. It is the reverse of stage right and stage left. Just reverse the direction and see it from the camera's perspective. Practice these directions at home.

EXTERIOR (EXT) AND INTERIOR (INT)

Exterior (outside) and **interior** (inside) are the places in which you will shoot.

MOS (SHOOTING WITHOUT SOUND)

The short version of the story is that a long time ago filmmakers from Germany would announce, "Ve shoot mit out sound," hence **MOS**. I kid you not!

CUE CARDS, TELEPROMPTERS AND BACKGROUND

As a dancer you will not have to read from these very often. It is good to review them if you have a chance as you may need to take a cue off of an announcer or host's verbal statement (i.e. a skit on *Saturday Night Live* or on an award show). **B.G.** generally stands for background.

CHAPTER EIGHT

DOLLY

A **dolly** is an apparatus that helps the camera operator move the stationary camera on a fixed line of axis closer toward a fixed point and away as well. It is usually on a track that resembles train tracks but is moveable and can have pieces added to extend the length. This is used in tracking shots as well as pan shots.

LOOPING (ADR)

Looping or **automated dialogue replacement** is the process in which performers must match the dialogue performed on screen that may not have come out clear on the recorded audio from the day of shooting. This usually involves re-recording the dialogue in a recording studio.

Example: Viva Laughlin Shoot

Prior to our shoot day for *Viva Laughin*, we recorded the song *"Fighter,"* by Christina Aguilera which was to be used as our performance track in the scene. This is an example of pre-recording an audio segment. ADR and looping generally are done following the completion of shooting but may also be done in advance for the purpose of lip synching to a track during a performance scene of a TV show or film. In music videos the song is already pre-recorded by the artist and they generally lip sing to the track during filming.

TAKE AND PRINT

A **take** is the term for one recorded sequence on film or audio recording. The filming process generally begins with camera blocking followed by a run through or rehearsal and then by rolling camera for the first take. This is recorded also by the clapstick information as well. A **print** is when the director has ordered a hard copy "print" of a filmed sequence. Cameras for film also take negatives which means that they are able to make prints as well. Prints are ordered in multiples for safety sake and are a very good indication that the shoot is going well.

WRAP

This is when you can breathe easy because your job is done and the shoot is over.

SHOOTING SCHEDULES AND EXPECTATIONS

Movies and TV are shot for economy, not necessarily shot for continuity. You may shoot out of sequence. The script's order has you start off at the house, then you go to the beach, then to the mall, and then a trip across the country and then come back to the beach, mall and house. You may shoot every scene that is in the house,

DANCE: IN FILM AND ON TELEVISION

no matter whether it is in the beginning, middle or end of the script because you're in that house. Production is not going to go across the country and then come back to that house three months later. Production will shoot everything in that house all at one time. The same thing happens in a music video. You will shoot everything that's in that particular set before moving on to the next set. What's the most economical way to get through your day without having to go back and forth? It's like shopping. You try to hit everything that you can at that one store, so you don't have to come back.

CONSISTENCY

A great performer will figure out how to deliver the particular performance that a production needs at that particular time regardless of the time of day or the amount of hours they're shooting. If you get a talented performer, whatever the emotional range is that a director needs you to hit, you take a minute and you hit it like turning on a faucet. The person that can do that will be hired over and over and over because they are reliable, dependable. You have to be ready and be able to deliver on the spot. Remember, time is money and going over budget is not an option.

PERFORMING OFF CAMERA, WHAT?

Something that I was not aware of was that performing **off camera** or **O.C.** will be asked of dancers on many different projects. While performing some cheerleading moves in *Bring It On, All or Nothing*; our audition scene was not so good! That was exactly what the director wanted. After our shots were completed, we were asked to stay and perform the same moves but behind the camera. At first, I didn't understand why. As Solange Knowles and Hayden Panettiere continued to shoot their scenes, the director wanted the added energy for the actors to draw from. The same was true for one of the latest pilots from David E. Kelley. I played a singer who also danced in a scene where the actors were to react to our performance of *"Shake a Tail Feather."* We continued to do our routine although off camera in order for the reaction to our movement to play out in real time. Generally, the actors will be able to play a scene regardless of any extra added elements, but the realness of some reactions and energy in the room is best when the room is buzzing!

SOMETHING FUNNY IS IN MY EAR!

No, that's not a cell phone; it's an earwig. This itty-bitty audio device is a miracle. While on *Boston Legal* shooting the "Green Christmas" episode, I played a singer who danced during the office Christmas party to *"Run Run Rudolph."* This was a

CHAPTER EIGHT

great experience, but I had no idea why I was handed this small little ear plug, or so I thought. The earwig is placed inside your ear in order to hear the music while actors play out their dialogue in the scene. This was given to all three singers so we could continue to perform our routine on stage and at the same time, the actors could be heard while saying their lines. In many instances as a dancer in a film or on a TV show this may occur. This is done to get a clear recording of the dialogue but continue to keep you in time and on beat without having dancers try to count at the same speed and rhythm each time. We did a lot of head whipping so we had to apply some wax on the outside of it to make sure it stayed in, but besides that it was a piece of cake. A friendly reminder: If you take a break for lunch or touch ups and take out the earwig, make sure you hand it to the audio or sound crew member and get the same one back also.

IF YOU DON'T HAVE A LINE, DON'T CREATE ONE!

Sometimes, there will be that one person who wants a line so badly even if it's not your role on the project. Don't yell out, *"Hey!,"* Or *"What's up!?,"* as the Verizon spokesperson passes you and you're dancing in the street. That isn't your role. Play your position or you might get cut from the gig altogether.

TV/FILM VS. LIVE TV AND STAGE

Stage is live. You have one shot to do it. There are no repeats, so if you mess up that is all you have. In film, in order to have a two-hour movie, you generally have to shoot about 60 hours of film. When you see all of the different angles that people are doing, or what is called **coverage**, those angles add to the excitement and energy to the speed of the movie.

A special thank you to Christopher Erskin for sharing his vast knowledge.

SAFETY ON SET - WORKING IN THE ELEMENTS

Part of your job is to maintain your professionalism and your energy. Maintain no matter how late the hours, how tight the costume, how unruly the weather and the amount of water, baby oil, hair spray, lip-gloss, or crazy uncomfortable thing is thrown at you! Production likes to wet down streets to kick up the lights on black pavement. When it is wet it reflects, which is an interesting look. This look may also become your nemesis. Take precautions, do a test run if you have to, and be safe out there. Hanging lights, cords, boom microphones along with expensive camera equipment makes for a nice day at the office!

DANCE: IN FILM AND ON TELEVISION

> **TIPS ON TRANSITIONING FROM STAGE TO TV/FILM:**
> **CHOREOGRAPHER/DIRECTOR MARY ANN KELLOGG**
>
> "You're not going to get the feedback that you do from a live performance. Your performance is being directed by a director or choreographer or by both simultaneously. Pay attention and do what they ask of you because they're the only audience that you have. Help your choreographer. You're all there as a team, as a family to make it happen. The situation and the conditions may be tough at times as dancers are kind of low man on the totem pole in the TV and film industry. Production in general don't understand them and isn't always aware of their needs. Dancers need to be sensitive to that. It's easy to go to the negative but if you try to keep a joyous time, everyone can have a good time because energy begets energy and good will begets good will. Be a team player and take joy and pride in the work that you do. Keep yourself very professional and remember that it is work. Every time you're in front of the 'powers that be' or the director, you should be presentable and put your best foot forward."

SO YOU WANT TO BE ON REALITY TV?

The highs and lows of reality television are overwhelming to some in a positive way and to others in a negative way. In the end, it really depends on the individual person and how much they let the pressures of the weekly grind actually affect their spirit and their morals. For competition dance-based reality programming, there have been some hits and misses. *Dancing With The Stars* on ABC, *So You Think You Can Dance* on FOX, *America's Got Talent* on CBS, *Dance on Sunset* on Nickelodeon, *Superstars of Dance* on NBC, *Step It Up And Dance* on BRAVO, *Taking The Stage*, *Dancelife* and *Randy Jackson Presents America's Best Dance Crew* on MTV have received top ratings! Some that didn't have as much success were *Dance Machine* on ABC, *Your Mama Don't Dance* on Lifetime, *Dance Your Ass Off* on Oxygen, *Dance War: Bruno vs. Carrie Ann* on ABC and *Master of Dance* on TLC.

Already highlighting a portion of my experience on reality television, I hope that you gain some valuable insight into this netherworld of talent and emotional ups and downs and find a way to navigate the long road to the other side. In my interviews with producers, judges and winners and participants of *DanceLife*, *So You Think You Can Dance*, *Randy Jackson Presents America's Best Dance Crew*, *Star Search*, *Superstars of Dance* and *Step It Up And Dance* you will find out how to audition and get on one of these shows, how to win, and most importantly, how to stay humble and ready for the next task after the spotlight fades.

CHAPTER EIGHT
MARY MURPHY
Choreographer/Judge, So You Think You Can Dance

SC: What do you look for when auditioning dancers for So You Think You Can Dance?
MM: Auditions on *So You Think You Can Dance* and other projects are basically the same, but in television we have a shorter period of time. That's the only difference. You have to make an impact with your look, from the second you walk out on the floor. You can go one of two ways: You can go with something very unique that draws us to you, but if it's done in such bad taste that's kind of a scary place to cross. Because if it is bad, and yes it drew attention, but it has already kind of turned us off on you...it doesn't work. If you always stick to classy or a fun/unique (look), I think it can add to the fact that if you can back it up with great dancing, it certainly is an extra plus in your favor. Of course, we're looking for someone who has great lines, great presence...including charisma. That is something that is very difficult to describe to a dancer because it is very hard to find if you don't (already) have it. All we can do is describe it as a light in their eyes, a pureness when they dance, something that radiates from their heart. Everyone who goes to an audition loves to dance or else they wouldn't be there but what's the difference? It's somebody who breaks the walls down, so to speak, and is vulnerable and comes from truly a pure place. That is captivating!

SC: What do you expect from dancers once you've hired them for a job?
MM: I think on a higher level, we expect people to come in with bodies that are well conditioned, well balanced and good posture. Those are the basics. When we have to correct somebody on a posture situation on a professional job; it's just like, 'What?' Dancers now slouch in between (the time) they've gotten the job and when they come to work. They (don't go full out) until showtime. That doesn't make the choreographer feel really confident about that person. When we see somebody that is going full tilt all the time, those people are remembered for the following jobs. The people who were the easiest to get along with during that time; those are the people who are going to have longevity.

SC: Do you have any industry advice for dancers?
MM: Trust me, you never forget, as a choreographer, who was hard to work with. And the next time you see a choreographer, you're sitting around talking about your last job and of course, it's going to come out of your mouth who was the easiest and 'Oh my God, they're fabulous to work with.' And then the next thing that comes out is who wasn't. It's a very small industry, even worldwide!

NORM BETTS
Assoc. Producer, American Idol and Former Contestant Coordinator/Assoc. Producer - So You Think You Can Dance

SC: When casting contestants what do you look for? How can they stand out?
NB: First impression is everything. Mediocre is the norm. We will pass over loads of 'OK to pretty good' singers/dancers. The question we ask ourselves is, 'Would I ever want to hear or see this performance again?' That really determines it all. If it's pleasing to see or hear, for whatever reason, then it's someone we want to consider. It's not always just technique. More often than not it's charm, or a presentation or charisma. Bottom line, when casting for a TV show, you have to be interesting! Period. **_Television has the ability to flatten your personality_**. Things that you may think make you fun or amusing don't always translate well on screen. You have to be bold, fascinating and fearless. Take your confidence to a new level, and if you don't have it, fake it!

SC: As a producer, what do you see that contestants need to be aware of that they overlook about their auditions?
NB: As a string of contestants line up before me I notice one thing more than anything else; they are NOT performing! They are concentrating so hard on their audition that they get lost in themselves. Performance is 90% in the eyes. MAKE EYE CONTACT. SMILE if the performance calls for it. Communicate the message of the song or dance. I've heard incredible voices that stare 20 feet above my head and never engage me. Or they stare at the ground, their face wrought with an intense focus. They will never make it on a show. Perform, perform, perform. Practice in a mirror. Video tape yourself. Work on it! I'd rather take a mediocre dancer or singer that engages me than a great one with a thousand yard stare.

SC: When you were the Contestant Coordinator/Assoc. Producer on So You Think You Can Dance, what things stood out to you that you thought could make or break a contestant's success?
NB: Attitude is everything. Sure, as crew members we like to be treated well. And no one likes an a**hole contestant. But on a reality competition, the schedule is grueling. A ridiculously positive outlook is about the only thing that can help get you through. And if you're looking for long-term success, the contacts you will make behind the scenes are some of the most valuable you will ever make in your career. Impress everyone with your work ethic. Work even harder than the next guy. Show those around you your capacity for learning. Take criticism like it's a precious gift, because it is. Nowhere else will you have the opportunity to surround

CHAPTER EIGHT

yourself with the level of professionals you will encounter on the show. Be a sponge. Take everything in. And be careful not to burn bridges with ANYONE on set. You never know who might be looking for a dancer on another show.

SC: Are there things that come up that you thought you'd never hear and hope not to have contestants ever share again? (The "Do not say that again" or "Audition-killing moment").
NB: As a reality contestant, it's good to have a story; something that makes you easily identifiable to the public. Choose carefully WHAT story line you divulge to the producers. It will stick with you forever. And remember, **_Anything you say on camera CAN AND WILL be used against you!_**

SC: Is there a formula for success on reality shows for contestants?
NB: Look at every winner of the major viewer-voting reality competitions. They generally aren't the best technical dancer or singer. They aren't the best looking. But they are likable. There is something about them that America identifies with. They relate to his/her story. They see themselves in him or her. Find what it is about you that makes you relatable and likeable. Be real. And don't forget that America LOVES an underdog. The front-runner in the competition will almost always peak early and (be) sent home. The voters want to see someone who comes from nothing propelled into stardom, and it makes them feel good when they do! They feel like they are a part of it too. If you aren't competing for viewer votes then that's another ball game. Good luck with that!

SC: Any advice for what voted-off contestants could do to further their careers?
NB: It's much more difficult for a dancer to achieve the same level of fame and fortune than that of a singer. There just isn't a market for dancers. So a dancer has to work even harder to make it happen. The best advice I can offer is to impress those on the show with your attitude and work ethic. They are the people that will remember you and hire you for future gigs. Only one person will win the competition, but every contestant has a real chance at making his or her dream come true.

REALITY DANCE SHOW WINNERS SPEAK

Next, I've highlighted Joshua Allen, winner of FOX's *So You Think You Can Dance* (Season 4), Jon "Do Knock" Cruz of Super Cre3w, winners of *Randy Jackson Presents America's Best Dance Crew* (Season 2) and individually the winner of *Star Search* (2003 Young Dancer Champion), Michelle 'Jersey' Maniscalo from *DanceLife*, Cody Green, winner of *Step It Up And Dance*, Jeff "Phi" Nguyen of the Jabbawockeez, winners of *Randy Jackson Presents America's Best Dance Crew* (Season 1) and Bradley Rapier, founder of the Groovaloos, winners of *Superstars of Dance*.

DANCE: IN FILM AND ON TELEVISION

JOSHUA ALLEN
SO YOU THINK YOU CAN DANCE WINNER (SEASON 4)

SC: How was the audition process for So You Think You Can Dance?
JA: Right before I went to L.A. to be on the show, when we were picked to be in the Top 20, my cousin was killed. He was 14 years old. I wrestled with the thought of, 'Did I want to go on the show and miss his funeral or stay and pay my respects?' I wasn't going to go on the show until my aunt talked to me and said, 'That was what he would've wanted.' He would always come to see me dance. Being so stressed out with a lot of things, finally making it on the show and not really having closure with it was so hard. With the press and trying to make it to the next week, and trying to learn the dance steps within five and half hours, so many times I just wanted to give up. I would sit there and pray and talk to him and say, 'You gotta help me out,' and tell him how much I missed him. I think that God was testing me. He was trying to see how much I loved it. 'How much did I love what I do?' Could I go on a national TV show to be judged in front of millions of people? By three judges each week? Could I handle it with everything I was going through? When I was leaving home I wrote my cousin a long message telling him how much I loved him, and how I was going to do this in his honor and bring it back home. It was funny that I actually did.

SC: How is it now that you've moved to Hollywood and are pursuing your dance career?
JA: It's crazy that I've moved out and live on my own. I have my own apartment and I'm just traveling and making a living at it. I hope it's everything I hoped it would be. I'm steady paying for my rent each month and I'm not even there.

SC: Do you have any advice for dancers who want to audition for So You Think You Can Dance or things that helped you make it to the end and win the title?
JA: Know the reason why you're doing it and when you're there, be yourself don't try to be someone you're not. You can be a brilliant dancer but what makes you different than the person standing next to you? There have been so many good people who never get picked to be on the show. If you can open up and show people who you are and that you can touch people and have people relate to you, that along with your talent is what will help you make it to the end. Never give up on doing what you want to do. A lot of people never get the opportunity to walk let alone dance. It's not called 'America's Best Dancer,' it's **America's Favorite Dancer**. Who is the best dancer? There isn't a best dancer. To me, I could be the best dancer and to you it could be someone else. There are grey areas in television as well. Somebody has to go home, that's the nature of the beast.

CHAPTER EIGHT

JEFF NGUYEN A.K.A "PHI" – JABBAWOCKEEZ
SEASON 1 WINNERS OF RANDY JACKSON PRESENTS AMERICA'S BEST DANCE CREW

SC: How did the Jabbawockeez come together as a crew?
PHI: When we got started, we were all just a group of friends. Everyone was part of a different crew but we knew each other through the dance/hip-hop/b-boy scene and community. Everyone came from a different area. A lot of cats are from the Bay *(San Francisco, Calif.)*, a lot of cats are from Sac *(Sacramento, Calif.)* I'm from Arizona and there are some other cats from down in San Diego, Calif. Gary, who is our fallen member, he pretty much was the bridge between Northern and Southern California. He would go out and session with a lot of So-Cal cats. Next thing you know, friends became friends, and no one really wanted to dog out on their own crew, but they all wanted to still perform together. That's how the mask was born. It was so that we could go perform and no one knew who we were for the longest time. We'd hear people talk behind us because they didn't know who was in the crew. They didn't know it was us because they always thought we were in other crews. So Jabbawockeez was born. We just wanted to show up and kill the night. No one knew who it was, which was the whole premise of the mask.

SC: Describe your experience on Randy Jackson Presents America's Best Dance Crew?
PHI: The show only allowed seven members, Gary was one of them, but he passed. We are ten strong, but some of the others couldn't do the show so we performed with six on the show. We really just did the show because we were representing for our boy Gary; that's what he wanted. So for us, we didn't know how the show was going to be. We knew it was MTV and we had seen *DanceLife*, and other shows, but as hip-hop kids and being really passionate about our culture, (just like a ballerina is and a ballet teacher is really passionate about her class,) that's how we were with our culture, our freestyle, our hip-hop and our dancing. We didn't know how we would be portrayed at all. We went into it and auditioned.

SC: Any advice for dancers who want to audition for Randy Jackson Presents America's Best Dance Crew?
PHI: What will get you far is if you don't have any expectations. Go in and have fun and represent as a crew. What's going to help you as a crew is that you literally have to be a crew. You can't just go and audition for a group because the chemistry is just not there. You have to be with a group of people that you pretty much live, eat, breathe and surround yourself around every day. We're a big family.

DANCE: IN FILM AND ON TELEVISION

When you're on the show, you're going to be put to the test. Everyone's got their own vibe and it's all fun and games, but you've got to have each other's backs. You can't be fighting, or letting anyone's ego get in the way. We just wanted to go out and have fun. If you watched us in rehearsal, we clown on each other all the time. I don't think we really rehearsed. A lot of our dancing and choreography comes from inside jokes. We try to make everything pretty light so that everything flows.

SC: Is it hard to get signed by a dance agency as a crew in Hollywood?
PHI: We tried to get signed as a group with an agency. It was kind of difficult for us because no one really understood the mask in this industry. People would ask, 'Why are there a bunch of kids wearing masks?,' and 'What is it about?' They liked it, thought it was cool, but I don't think that they fully understood it. It was kind of a sticky situation with agents. We weren't really called on too many auditions, we just heard about a few auditions and decided as a crew if it was even the right type of job for Jabbawockeez to really go and audition for.

SC: Do the Jabbawockeez audition as a crew?
PHI: As a crew before the show, we never really auditioned together. We did audition for the bigger dance films like *You Got Served*. As individuals, myself, Rainen and Chris were the dancers who were in L.A. I auditioned on my own as Phi and Rainen was on tour with Gwen Stefani. When *Step Up 2* came out, we just kind of had a big enough name, I guess you could say 'street cred,' like 'ghetto celebrity,' that they knew about us and understood us and what we were about so that's how we got into *Step Up 2*, but that was before *America's Best Dance Crew*.

SC: Do you have any advice for dancers wanting to move to Hollywood?
PHI: Know what you want when you come out here. Learn your business. Be prepared and find avenues other than dance. We've tapped into our clothing line. It takes a lot of time, rhythm, balance and athleticism to do what we do. Whether you're pointing your toe or spinning on your head. Take care of your body and know that it's your temple. It's a part of your business too!

MICHELLE "JERSEY" MANISCALO
MTV'S "DANCELIFE," VH1'S "HIT THE FLOOR", PCD (VIPER ROOM)

Jersey is one of the Pussycat Dolls at the Viper Room on the Sunset Strip in West Hollywood, Calif. She said, "As part of the PCD brand, you have to maintain your body, nails, hair and makeup and it bleeds into your real life as well. Representing the brand to the

CHAPTER EIGHT

fullest is crucial because you can be replaced at any time." When thinking about auditioning for a reality television show Jersey wanted to make sure that dancers ask themselves, "Why do you want to be on the show? What is your reason?" She cautions dancers by saying, "You need to be in the right state of mind and in the right place personally. You have no control over how you're perceived, tweaked or edited. Stay true to yourself, true to who you are and what you want to share because there's no stopping in reality. You can't say, 'OK, stop shooting now, that's enough!' Sometimes they give you your reality and that's a rude awakening." Jersey was relieved to see that when *DanceLife* aired it was an inspiring and uplifting show and really showed some of the struggles that dancers go through to chase their dreams. She detailed how "the reality of dancers is not being able to go to an audition because you don't have money for gas to get there or can't go out to eat." She said, "I wish they could've filmed the struggles after the show. You start to question yourself, 'Am I done? Where am I going from here?' When I'm at my lowest, I can always turn to dance as my friend even though it sounds corny. I know it's mine." She wants dancers to know that, "It's not about money, it's about passion, drive and determination." The highs and lows, ups and downs come so quickly. Jersey encourages dancers to "maintain yourself and stay in the game when the new kids come in. You just gotta come here and LIVEEE!!"

JON "DO KNOCK" CRUZ, SUPER CR3W
WINNERS OF RANDY JACKSON PRESENTS AMERICA'S BEST DANCE CREW (SEASON 2) & STAR SEARCH (2003 YOUNG DANCER CHAMPION)

Member of *Randy Jackson Presents America's Best Dance Crew's* Season 2 Winners SUPER CR3W, Jon was also crowned the Young Dancer Champion on Star Search in 2003. SUPER CR3W doesn't normally audition for television shows or concerts, but decided to pick members of three crews to form SUPER CR3W for Season 2 of *ABDC* on MTV. All of the six members of the crew were known in the b-boy scene internationally prior to appearing on the show but felt a bigger calling to represent for all of the b-boys and their craft. As a crew, Jon notes that they are dedicated and have routines for different strategies when battling.

Having b-boy credits long before that, he acknowledges that for other b-boys "they miss what's on top. That's what I base my whole style on is my introduction." He details how he developed his musicality along the way and that dance is "all about letting your body go free." As a contestant on two dance competition shows, Jon encourages dancers to go after their dream. He said, "I believe in myself and I think that if you have a dream and have heart then no matter what it'll happen. It's all about determination. Give it all you got!"

CODY GREEN
BRAVO'S STEP IT UP AND DANCE WINNER, BROADWAY (WEST SIDE STORY, MOVIN' OUT & GREASE) AND THE 85TH ANNUAL ACADEMY AWARDS

SC: What was it like to win Step It Up And Dance?
CG: The experience on the show was really tough but doing my final dance and finding out that I won at the end was an incredible experience that I will never forget! For me, doing *Step It Up And Dance*, I actually never thought I would do a show like that. The way it worked out though, I was doing **Grease** on Broadway at the time and our stagehands were on strike. So we weren't working at the time, we were actually out picketing in front of the theatre when I heard about the audition for the TV show, *Step It Up And Dance* on BRAVO. So I decided to go to the audition in L.A.

SC: Do you have any advice for dancers wanting to compete on a dance reality show?
CG: Ultimately, when it comes to the competition on the show, you have to remember that it is a television show. That, for you, it goes dance to dance but that there is a larger sort of arc with regards to the storyline of the show (i.e. interviews, reality portions of the show). For my experience, I just wanted to go and do the best that I could in every challenge that I had. I tried to put myself out there in the best light and dance the best that I could each time. And at the same time, leave the rest of the other stuff out of it because it's easy to get caught up in the drama. Because the circumstances are very tense there can be a lot of pressure. But if you can somehow forget about all of that and really focus on doing your best each time and being confident about what you have to offer and be confident in your performance then that is what will come across.

SC: You lived in L.A., what was the experience like coming back from New York for the show?
CG: I'm from Canada originally and attended the Juilliard School in New York but when I was young I would come out to L.A. and take class from a wide range of choreographers. My mom had a company that I danced in and we'd go out and take classes of all different styles for a few weeks each year. This helped me with the various styles we had during challenges on *Step It Up and Dance*. For this ex-

perience, we were housed in apartments while filming the show. The difference between our show and let's say *So You Think You Can Dance* would be that *So You Think You Can Dance* is a week-to-week thing, and we shot all of *Step It Up And Dance's* ten episodes in 21 days. We didn't have any breaks, so if you pulled something or rolled an ankle or hurt yourself at the end of challenge #4, you had to be ready to go at 7 a.m. the next morning for challenge #5. What I realized was that I wanted to be full out all the time but at the same time, the schedule doesn't allow you to go all out all the time because you'll be burned out for the next day. You have to be able to do the next challenge. That was one of the biggest hurdles of doing *Step It Up and Dance* for me.

<u>SC: Were there any challenges that you can help other dancers prepare for?</u>
CG: I was fortunate because I'm comfortable at picking up choreography quickly. For some dancers, that is something they might want to work on if they want to be on a show like this, because you learn it very fast. We would learn a 2 1/2 minute combination in an hour or less and then have to perform it and then go throw on a costume that night and perform it on stage. BRAVO is a popular television station but it isn't a network television station (i.e. FOX, ABC, NBC, CBS, etc.), so the budget for the show was quite a bit smaller. This gives you less time to shoot episodes, which gives you less time to learn the choreography and perform it. You pretty much learn it and do it.

BRADLEY RAPIER – THE GROOVALOOS
WINNERS OF SUPERSTARS OF DANCE

The Groovaloos are the Winners of *Superstars of Dance* (Season 1) and have been a staple in Los Angeles since founded by Bradley Rapier over 10 years ago. Comprised of dancers and choreographers, The Groovaloos also incorporate actors, poets and singers into their shows. Exciting crowds they've appeared on *The Ellen Degeneres Show, Oprah, So You Think You Can Dance, Randy Jackson Presents America's Best Dance Crew* and countless television shows and films. Bradley is the creator of the new stage show called *Groovaloo* with a U.S. tour beginning in the Fall 2009. With a crew that is 25 members strong, they also hold a Groove Night regularly at Debbie Reynold's dance studio in North Hollywood, Calif. Meet people, dance and jam out with some of the hottest dancers on the scene in this community event. Bradley Rapier was kind enough to share his thoughts on dance and his advice on how he's become so successful.

SC: Is it difficult to get the Groovaloos members together at the last minute since a lot of audition notices don't really come with a lot of lead time?
BR: We do get direct bookings, but for some things we still audition and yes, it can be next to impossible to get the crew all in one room! I believe that the booking situation improved with our appearance on *Superstars of Dance*, but scheduling The Groovaloos has always been a challenge and more so in the last couple of years. That's the trade off when you have talented individuals and people in demand within your company. Thankfully we have a strong cross section of members and a history together so we're usually able to pull something out (often just as we're walking in the door, freestyle.)

SC: Are there any qualities you believe someone must possess in order to really achieve a level of success in this industry?
BR: I've generally followed these 5 P's: Positive attitude, perspiration, perserverance, patience and prayer.

SC: As a male dancer, what are some obstacles you've faced at auditions or on the job?
BR: For me the main challenge was internal. When I first came from Canada to the U.S. and saw how many more people at auditions looked like me and kind of had my style, I was a bit lost for a while. So, I went to work on just being myself, with all my quirks. Gradually, I spent less time trying to figure out what each client was looking for or what the latest fashion was and put more effort into bringing something authentic to the table. Of course, you have to be able to learn the choreography at a dance audition, but I'm referring to all that personal style and character. Put the real you out there as respectfully and honestly as you can. I love the saying, **'Be you, until you is what they want.'**

SC: As a working dancer, husband and father, how do you balance your home life and career?
BR: It's definitely a solid mixture of family, friends and faith. Lots of support from family members, friends and of course, The Groovaloos. I'm able to do what I do because of my wife's support. I couldn't imagine a better partner in the journey that has been my life. In all this I am so thankful for the awesome extended family that has been created. My personal belief is that God has had his hand in it the entire time. That is the ultimate strength for me.

CHAPTER EIGHT

SICK TIP #27:
NO ONE LIKES AN UNGRATEFUL WINNER!

On the road of life, the ups and downs will mark your successes and sometimes your shortcomings. What others may call failures may just be your wake up call or catalyst to push you forward to your goal or redirect your focus onto the next great thing! The more success you have the more recognition you will receive. When receiving these accolades, stay humble. Keep working toward new and different goals to keep you relevant in the game. Don't settle, because there is always someone out there that is still working to take your spot, gain the upper hand and creep up at the next audition to outwork you. Don't take your success for granted or those who helped you get there either. Give credit where credit is due and always remember where you came from. Because the same people you see on the way up are the same people you will see on the way down. There is only one place to go where you're on the top and that's down. Staying #1 is the hardest thing you will do. Maintaining the top spot is never easy. Don't burn bridges and always keep in mind that you were once as hungry as the next guy trying to get to your dream!

FUNNY YOU SHOULD ASK...

HOW LONG DOES IT TAKE TO SHOOT TELEVISION SHOWS, MUSIC VIDEOS, COMMERCIALS AND FILMS?

Generally a music video is shot in one to two days depending on the complexity of the treatment. A commercial is usually shot in one to three days and there can be many different versions of one commercial (15, 30 or 60 second spots). A sitcom is in rehearsal for the better part of a week and shoots one episode per week normally in front of a live studio audience. A television series that runs for one hour is shot in a seven-day format and a film that would take an hour and a half to view can take from two to three months or longer to shoot. Some programs are shot in what is called a "live to tape" format which means they are shot in real time and are considered live. The tape of the show may be aired for broadcast later. For example, late night television programs or reality programs like *American Idol* are filmed live and are aired live on the East Coast while the West Coast is shown the taped version. The long shoots and the long days can take a toll on you. Make sure to rest up and get your own work done on your down time. There will be a lot of it. Keep your body warm though, you never know when you will get called at a moment's notice to be at 100% and on set!

TRANSPORTATION

You may be asked to go to a location for a film or television show. It is imperative that you are there on time because many times you are asked to park in a lot designated for the crew. You will be shuttled to another location for security purposes or simply because there isn't enough parking for everyone to be accommodated. Arrive early so you aren't late getting to the set. Yellow signs are frequently used to direct you.

ITEMS YOU MAY WANT WITH YOU ON SET
- A Sharpie (to label your water)
- Straws to sip through to not disturb your lipstick
- Baby powder to keep shoes fresh
- Flower pasties just in case the bra you are given is not full coverage
- Double-stick Hollywood tape
- Sewing kit
- Nail kit (clear polish and remover)
- Shoe kit (cleaner, polish, shoe stretcher)

SICK TIP #28: NO ONE LIKES A SORE LOSER EITHER!

You heard my story from *So You Think You Can Dance* and I admitted that I was bitter. But I never voiced it so loud that I couldn't refocus my energy on proving the voters wrong. I wanted to make sure that people understood that maybe I wasn't the winner of that show, but I am a winner. You are too! Don't ever let one contest put you so far out there with your ego as a winner or so far under as a loser that you forget who you are inside and what you are worth. At the end of the day, I'm a successful working dancer and I am very proud that I've been able to use my skills in the professional world. It is not a good look for you to come out of a contest without class and grace. Be grateful that you had the opportunity to perform in front of millions of people. Yes, go through your grieving period, but pick yourself back up. That is the mark of a true champion! So get up, congratulate the winner and politely ask for a rematch! Just kidding.

CHAPTER EIGHT

Sandra says...

- Time is money in TV and film. Don't waste it!

- Key terms like *treatment, roll playback, check the gate* along with positions like director, 1st and 2nd A.D.s are important. Know their roles.

- Reality TV has many ups and downs. Do your best and know that personality plus talent counts!

DANCE: IN FILM AND ON TELEVISION

- Respect the hierarchy on set. Always look and do your best because you can and will be replaced.

- The camera is now your audience. Love it, live it and put all of your energy into consistent performances for it. Continuity is key! Keep your energy up and make it last.

- Keep your focus on set. With all of the equipment, danger looms. Keep an eye out!

> ### Point Taken:
> Before we start calling you a movie star; let's take a step back. The #1 thing that all dancers should do before they move to Hollywood or right when they get to Hollywood is take a commercial audition technique class. This will help you so much and greatly improve your chances at making a better living dancing on television and in film.

CHAPTER NINE

Your Career Path...
You Can't Take Every Job!

As shown in the *Hollywood Dance Calendar*, there are seasonal times when Hollywood will erupt with an explosion of jobs when there won't be enough singers, actors, comedians or dancers to do them all. Most of the time it is the opposite. Usually there are fewer jobs than qualified performers to do them.

In the case of dancers, we have a unique opportunity in that we can do non-union jobs beyond SAG or AFTRA gigs. Don't count out the small jobs, industrials, corporate events, spot dates, benefits and shows with independent recording artists. Many times choreographers are looking to do a performance piece and will ask you to participate. There are a number of corporate castings which including convention work or industrials that hire dancers for NAPTE or MAGIC in Las Vegas or downtown at the L.A. Convention Center and L.A. Live. Spot dates with new independent recording artists are also a way to make a living and find yourself gaining great experience and footage for your reel.

Longevity in the industry is what dancers strive for. A reputation as a solid dancer who is "on their gig" will benefit you in the long run. Do not forget that in between jobs you can gain a following by teaching your own classes locally or for dance conventions. Many dancers who have been in the industry long enough will start to find himself or herself teaching or choreographing out of the state for different conventions like Jump, Star Struck or Tremaine.

The point of all of this is to make sure you do not limit yourself to only the huge tours, television shows or upcoming films. Although rates may be higher for a television show or film, you may work more days on a convention circuit to fill the

YOUR CAREER PATH...YOU CAN'T TAKE EVERY JOB!

gap. Consider working on a cruise ship, at a theme park or in a touring Broadway production.

CRUISE LINES

If you really want to get out of town and get out on the waves, hit the deck of a cruise ship. This lifestyle is completely different and usually comes with financial gains as you are allotted free room and board along with a paycheck to boot! Below are all of the major cruise lines and their Web sites. Make sure to be diligent about the terms of your contract, what is included as part of your onboard employee status and try to have some fun.

CRUISE LINE WEB SITES:

- Carnival Cruise Lines
www.Carnival.com
www.CarnivalEntertainment.com

- Celebrity Cruise Line
www.CelebrityCruises.com

- Costa Cruise Line
www.CostaCruise.com

- Crystal Cruises
www.CrystalCruises.com

- Disney Cruise Line
www.DisneyCruise.com
http://dcljobs.com/

- Holland America Line
www.HollandAmerica.com
www.HollandAmericaEntertainment.com

- Norwegian Cruise Line
www.NCL.com

- Oceania Cruise Line
www.OceaniaCruises.com

- P&O Cruises
www.POCruises.com

- Princess Cruises
www.Princess.com
http://employment.princess.com/employment/index.html

- Regent Seven Seas Cruises
www.RSSC.com

- Royal Caribbean Cruise Line
www.RoyalCaribbean.com
www.RoyalCaribbean.com/ourCompany/career.do

- Windstar Cruises
www.WindstarCruises.com

PRODUCTION COMPANIES/CRUISE EMPLOYMENT

www.DickFosterProductions.com
www.CruisePlacement.com
www.GaryMusick.com

www.StilettoEntertainment.com
www.JeanAnnRyanProductions.com
www.SixthStar.com

CHAPTER NINE

GISELLE SAMSON
Dancer And ANTM Finalist (Cycle 1)

You might remember Giselle from *America's Next Top Model*. This model/dancer completed an eight-month contract working for Carnival Cruise Lines (normal contracts are usually for 6 months). She details some of her experiences and shares what it is like to dance onboard a cruise ship.

SC: What were the auditions like for Carnival Cruise Lines?
GS: We signed in, handed in our headshot and resume to the monitor. We did a ballet combination, jazz combination, hip-hop combination, across the floor and musical theatre. All of this without making cuts throughout the entire process. Then they (the judges) sit down and talk to you about what their next audition area will be. They travel the country auditioning and then you wait to hear back with a phone call. They could call you the next day or two years later.

SC: What were some of the perks of working on a cruise ship? Any down side?
GS: <u>Perks</u>: Getting to travel around for free to a bunch of different islands and countries. Crewmembers receive ship discounts on merchandise, jewelry, clothing, etc. You are able to see and make friends all over the world; to experience what it's like to perform on a cruise ship also. <u>Drawbacks</u>: Not being able to see your family. You're not allowed to leave at all unless there is a death in the family. You have to get your own calling cards and your own Internet. If you're someone who wants to be in the entertainment business in Hollywood and L.A., you are taking yourself out of that scene for a long time. When you come back, you have to start all over again. It's really weird coming back again. Everyone's kind of different. You feel like you're lost. You have to get to know your friends a little bit better again. You're constantly being watched while on the ship. You're always at work even when you're asleep.

SC: What were the rehearsals like? Does the job differ from jobs on land?
GS: All the bonds that you make (with friends) are the same as other jobs. With that comes drama as usual. If there is a certain cast of people that you get with that are drama, it can happen. The thing with that is that you can't go anywhere. You're on the ship, you're there and that's it. It's kind of like being on tour, on the bus except for you're on the boat. And unlike being on a bus, you can't get off the boat. All rehearsals for Carnival are done onboard the ship, not on land.

YOUR CAREER PATH...YOU CAN'T TAKE EVERY JOB!

SC: What are the accommodations like onboard?
GS: You live in tiny cabins that have bunk beds with roommates, unless you are the singer in the show then you get your own cabin.

SC: Anything that you might caution other dancers about the lifestyle on board?
GS: The only thing that I can say is caution, red flag, **you may become an alcoholic**. The scenario goes like this: Your crazy rehearsals are over. You still have sea days. You're not in port anymore depending on the cruise you're on and there's nothing to do except, eat, sleep, work out and drink. The drinks are really cheap and everyone is like, 'Hey let's go to the crew bar!' And drinks are only $1 for a Grey Goose and tonic. So it's like even when you have no intentions of doing that, it just happens. And then you think, 'Well, you know, it's just an opportunity right now and it won't be like that when you go home.' But then when you go home, you haven't seen your friends and family for so long and they all want to go out with you. So then you're doing the same thing when you get back in town.

SC: Are there height and weight restrictions? Rules about dating amongst the cast or passengers?
Carnival, our ship specifically, had weekly weigh-ins. If you gained more than five pounds you get put on a weight warning and then you're given a certain amount of time to get down to your original size. If you don't then you get taken out of numbers and if you still don't then you can be sent home. Now, it goes the other way, when you lose too much (weight), no one cares. Crewmembers cannot date guests. There is no fraternizing with guests at all. Going to a guest's cabin is grounds for immediate dismissal. Fighting is also grounds for immediate dismissal by the ship's command, the captain. There is gambling but the crew members are not allowed to gamble.

SC: What was the salary like? Any differences between working on the ship and on land?
GS: Great way to save money. Eight months of being gone and I raised my credit score 300 points. Some contracts are negotiable. The average contract is in the range $25,000. That is on the lower end but most contracts are pretty standard. You have full health insurance and you're on a W-2 not a 1099 *(See Chapter 12, If You Don't Value Yourself, You Become Valueless for more information on tax forms)*. You get paid bi-weekly, but you get money every week for your crew staff duties. You have to be 18 years old to work on a cruise. Crystal Cruises requires their cast members to be 21 years old and have ship life experience. Cruise companies are really loyal about re-signing for continued employment on other ships, etc. Also, once you do one full contract (for Carnival), then on your second contract, your friends and family get to go on for a discount.

CHAPTER NINE

THEME PARKS

Every year theme parks in the Los Angeles area cast for show members. Some casting calls also include auditions for theme parks with locations in foreign countries. Recently there was an audition call for Disney's Paris-based theme park. Theme park talent casting includes: singers, dancers, variety performers, parade characters/performers, atmosphere and face characters. Many of these theme parks implement special seasonal shows. For example, Knott's Berry Farm turns into Knott's Scary Farm for Halloween with auditions beginning in early to mid-August. Think ahead about possible employment opportunities when work slows down in the winter months.

THEME PARK LOCATIONS, CASTING HOTLINES AND WEB SITES

Disneyland
P.O. Box 3232
1313 South Harbor Boulevard
Anaheim, CA 92803
(714) 781-4565 General Info.
Disneyland & Disney's CA Adventure
Job Hotline: (800) 766-0888
www.DisneyAuditions.com

SeaWorld of California
500 SeaWorld Drive
San Diego, CA 92109
(619) 226-3815
(800) 25-SHAMU
www.SeaWorld.com
Anheuser-Busch Adventure Parks
http://becjobs.com/

Legoland California
One Legoland Drive
Carlsbad, CA 92008
(760) 918-LEGO (5346) General Info.
(760) 918-5454 Entertainment Job Line
www.Legoland.com/jobs

Universal Studios Hollywood
100 Universal City Plaza
Universal City, CA 91608
(800) 864-8377 General Info.
(818) 622-JOBS Job Line
www.USHJobs.com
www.UniversalStudiosHollywood.com
www.NBCUniCareers.com

Knott's Berry Farm
8039 Beach Boulevard
Buena Park, CA 90620
(714) 220-5200 General Info.
(714) 220-5386 Entertainment Job Line
www.Knotts.com
www.Knotts.com/jobs/index.asp

Six Flags Hurricane Harbor
and Six Flags Magic Mountain
26101 Magic Mountain Parkway
Valencia, CA 91355
(661) 255-4527 Magic Mountain
(818) 367-5965 Hurricane Harbor
Employment (661) 255-4800 Magic Mtn.
www.SixFlags.com/HurricaneHarborLA/Jobs/JobListings.aspx

www.SixFlags.com/MagicMountain/Jobs/JobListings.aspx

YOUR CAREER PATH...YOU CAN'T TAKE EVERY JOB!

PROFESSIONAL SPORTS TEAMS

Auditioning for a professional dance team is also a great way to have a steady gig and paycheck. Although the rates for professional sports cheerleading and dance teams vary; you will certainly have a good and recognizable credit on your resume.

Los Angeles is home to a variety of sports teams. Of them, the most well known would be the NBA's Los Angeles Lakers' *Laker Girls*. Most of the professional basketball dance teams hold auditions in July and professional football around May. Check the team Web sites for accurate tryout dates. Being a part of a professional sports team's entertainment brings many rewards. Below are some of the sports teams' contact names and information for dance or cheer directors.

SICK TIP # 29:
CAPTIVE AUDIENCE

Not only do you have the best seat in the house (courtside or sideline) but you are also in the company of so many industry insiders. As part of the *Laker Girls*, I was able to perform in front of some very high profile celebrities and entertainment industry executives. I note this because Staples Center is a venue where you can invite casting directors, agents and choreographers to watch you dance and see your skills.

NBA

Los Angeles Lakers
Lisa Estrada, Director of Game Operations and *Laker Girls*
www.NBA.com/Lakers/

Los Angeles Clippers
Audrea Harris, Director L.A. *Clippers Spirit*
In-Game Entertainment Groups:
Clippers Spirit (Dance Team)
Clippers Fan Patrol (Gymnastics/Stunt Team)
www.NBA.com/Clippers

NFL

San Diego Chargers
Lisa Simmons, Director *Charger Girls*
www.Chargers.com
www.NFL.com

ARENA FOOTBALL LEAGUE

Los Angeles Avengers
www.LAAvengers.com

Young dancers can audition for the WNBA Los Angeles Sparks *SparKids* or the NBA Clippers *Jr. Jam*.

COLLEGES AND UNIVERSITIES

If you are in school when you move to Hollywood, try to join some of the hottest dance teams in the country. UCLA, USC, Long Beach State University and many others have dance programs.

BOOK ME! HOW TO BECOME A SUCCESSFUL WORKING DANCER IN HOLLYWOOD

CHAPTER NINE

PROFESSIONAL CHEERLEADING/DANCE TEAM AUDITION TIPS

As part of the world famous Los Angeles *Laker Girls*, instructor for Universal Cheerleaders Association, collegiate cheerleader at the University of Oregon and judge for the *Clippers Spirit* auditions, I know how many things go into making it onto a dance or cheerleading team. First you need to watch the team you are going to audition for, know what teams look like, what judges want and give it to them. These teams have been around for a long time and have a definite formula. It is tried and true and is rarely messed with because it works. If you are coming to Hollywood to pursue dance and want to also dabble a little in the professional cheer or dance ranks, audition tips are below for the L.A. Avengers, L.A. Clippers, L.A. Lakers or San Diego Chargers.

IT'S TIME TO RALLY

- Arrive early.
- Don't get intimidated by the returning girls.
- Make sure you are warmed up.
- Bring snacks, water and a towel to dry off.
- Wear a two-piece (half top or sports bra and leotard trunks). Stay classy not trashy but definitely show skin!
- Wear flesh colored tights *(For Laker Girls wear scrunched socks & clean white sneakers)*.
- Wear your hair down (fix it in a way so that it doesn't go in your face and stick there.) Make sure you can move your hair out of your face if it goes there. If you sweat a lot; try not to look like a drowned rat. Make sure that you bring a hair dryer for when you get a break. Trust me it will make a difference.
- Wear good makeup, not *Friday The 13th* stage makeup. Wear something that will show up but is also natural, as the tryouts are in a gymnasium or on a field. You still want to look approachable and also have it last through all the sweat. Full coverage is the best! Purchase MAC or HD makeup to make it last longer. Add lashes, to make your eyes pop. You could end up on the field for part of the audition and it will help to be able to see you from far away. Try not to apply too much eye liner or raccoon eyes. Leave the Eye Black under the eyes to the players on the football field!
- Bring two of the same outfit just in case you sweat through one. You will be given a number to wear and may only get one fresh number so take care of it.
- Bring safety pins just in case you need extras to pin down your number. Some times you are given a sticker. Bring a 3x5 index card and affix the number to

YOUR CAREER PATH...YOU CAN'T TAKE EVERY JOB!

the blank side of the card so you have something to pin through on your clothes. It's best to have a flat number so the judges can see it.
- Dance BIG! - Minimal movements won't get you anywhere. You'll look like an ant on the court or field. Don't flail. Control your moves.
- Cover up any and all tattoos with body makeup. Get a tan! Not orange tan. Get a natural glow tan or something that looks real and not too fake.
- Know the team, coaches and history of the organization. Have an answer ready for <u>WHY</u> you want to be a *Laker Girl* or a *Charger Girl*? Also, remember that many of the same people will judge these tryouts so be careful which audition you go to first. Don't go to the L.A. *Clippers Spirit* audition and say you've always wanted to be a *Clippers Spirit* dancer and then attend the *Laker Girls* audition and say you've always wanted to be a *Laker Girl*. You might be speaking to the same judges. Not the best idea. <u>Audition for the team that you want to be on.</u>
- Focus on you while learning the choreography. Learn quickly and perform it while you rehearse.
- Have a short solo diddy prepared that shows your skills. If you tumble throw that in. If you do great pirouettes then do some. If you've got a great lay out or something flashy make sure to do it. This is the time to show your other skills.
- After the first long day of dancing you will most likely do a lot of paperwork and provide references. Have that information on hand so you don't have to fumble through your phone thinking about who you want the director to call. Write legibly on all of your paperwork.
- You may have an interview. Be straight up with the director. It is way better for you to be honest about your past career or personal undertakings than to have things surface later that could be detrimental to the team.
- At the final callback wear the best outfit you have! The one you wore to the first audition is great. Repetition is good to help the judges remember you.
- Get your nails done, eyebrows waxed and clean up all the rough edges. The judges want perfection.
- Speak when spoken to and make friends while you're there but remember it is a job. You need to look and seem reliable. More importantly with so many games, charity appearances and practices, you need to <u>be</u> reliable.
- Be fit! Make sure that you look toned - not malnourished! You should be proportioned for your height and weight. Some teams do have regular weigh-ins.
- Do not google-eye over players. This is a big no-no! You will sign non-fraternization contracts for most teams to ensure that you know the rules up front.
- Bring a jacket and sweat pants to cover up so your muscles don't get cold.

Have fun and perform up and out. Good Luck!

CHAPTER NINE

CORPORATE GIGS

There are also opportunities to work for corporate production companies who put together made-to-order shows for private clients. E-Plus and Imagination Entertainment are a few that regularly produce full theatrical productions on very grand scales for clients who want production numbers ranging from Broadway reviews, to whimsical fantasy to cirque style artistry. These shows usually include singers, dancers, acrobats, comedians, impersonators and so much more.

Imagination Entertainment
Sam Trego Productions
734 West Beech Street, Suite 100
San Diego, CA 92101
(619) 640-6500 Phone
www.ImaginationEnt.com
information@imaginationent.com

Entertainment Plus Productions (E-Plus)
2324 Halm Avenue
Los Angeles, CA 90034
(323) 969-1756 Phone
www.EPlusProductions.com
info@eplusproductions.com

DOUG JOHNSON
Entertainment Plus,
President And Executive Producer

In speaking with Doug Johnson, he gave some helpful insights into what he looks for from dancers when hiring for an upcoming production.

"When casting dancers for any production, I look for that 'something extra' that seems to explode from them. It's something from the inside, not some fake smile or over sell. I look for dancers who are loving what they are doing, with effortless, flawless execution of the choreography. One thing I have found as a truth over the years, is that most often, the very best dancers arrive first to sign-in. They seem to be more of the business minded types giving themselves enough time to arrive, stretch and center themselves for what's about to happen. Others fly in late, disheveled...THEN, they take another five minutes putting on shoes, fixing their hair; some even talking on their cell phones...ugh!

"I use to call it 'OLD SCHOOL,' but whatever you want to call it, disappearing is what is happening. YES, dancers can do flips, quads, jump splits, and shake their behinds like they are having a seizure, but GOD FORBID they arrive to rehearsal on time, be prepared, professional, with everything that has been asked of them. My theater professor put buckets on each side of the stage just in case one of the performers was sick...he always said 'YES, the show MUST go on...no matter what...unless your head is somehow no longer attached to your body.' I also find that passion for dance has been replaced with passion for being a star. The 'Paris Hilton syndrome' is ruining much of our precious craft. Kids are doing anything and everything just to become a star instead of just enjoying the journey to wherever it takes them. Finally, life is just too short to be a diva. Be kind to EVERYONE. From the person who helps you sign up at the door at the audition, to your costumer, to fellow dancers...word gets around. You are young and beautiful only once, so be good to yourself. The odds are against you so don't let anything stand in your way. Making wrong choices about weight, alcohol, drugs, boyfriends, girlfriends, even family, can keep you from your best. Audition FULL OUT, rehearse FULL OUT, LIVE the choreography from your inside out…enjoy every second of this crazy, insane, fantastic entertainment business."

SICK TIP #30:
EL CAPITAN THEATRE

Working at the El Capitan is an opportunity to have a steady job as well. Movies that run in this theatre change all the time and the pre-show experience changes too with all new live stage shows. Shows are normally on an AGVA contract, have two casts and each dancer works about three to four times per week. An average show day consists of five shows lasting approximately 15-20 minutes per show. Rehearsals on stage are from 5 a.m. - 9 a.m. as the El Capitan is a working theatre. Regular rehearsals are usually from 10 a.m. - 6 p.m. Each show run is different but employment ranges from 6-8 weeks depending on the length of time a movie is in the theatre. Shows and casts are bigger over the summer and winter holiday seasons as they use singers, MCs and characters throughout the year for other performances prior to movie start times. Ask your agent for upcoming auditions and check out this Web site for more information:

http://disney.go.com/disneypictures/el_capitan/

BROADWAY TOURS AND THE ROCKETTES

The Radio City Rockettes Christmas Spectacular tour is a great steady gig and you get to tour the country at the same time. For height requirements go to www.RadioCityChristmas.com/NationalTour.html. For theatre New York is your city, not Hollywood. Not because there aren't opportunities here but because there are so many more in New York. Many Broadway shows tour the country and sometimes plant their roots in Hollywood. *Wicked* had a long run at the Pantages Theatre, which boasts a schedule that includes *Legally Blonde*, *Riverdance*, *The Color Purple*, *Stomp*, *Cats*, *Chicago* and *In The Heights*. In either city you'll need voice lessons.

CHAPTER NINE

GINA STARBUCK, Creator "Art 4 Life"
THEATRE IN L.A. – "WICKED"

SC: What was the audition process like for "Wicked" during its run at the Pantages Theatre? Did it differ at all from a typical L.A. audition?
GS: I would say that musical theatre auditions are pretty different from your 'typical' L.A. audition. It is very important that you come prepared and when they say 'ready to dance,' they mean it! I actually was seen for *Wicked* three times before I booked it. It was running in New York and had a tour out long before it opened in L.A. The first time they kept me through 'til the end. The second, they cut me right away. The third time, I sang twice and learned two different dance combos. Then went through two cuts and a callback. After they saw me the first time, they liked me and kept me on file. But the second time they knew for sure they didn't have a role for me at that time; and musical theatre people are very good about not wasting anyone's time.

SC: What character did you play? Rehearsal/performance schedule and length of your contract?
GS: *Wicked* was my first and only (so far) Equity production contract. I was in the L.A. company of *Wicked* for about a year and three months and played the role of 'The Witch's Mother,' as well as doing some ensemble work. We rehearsed for about a month in New York to learn the show. Then we had one week of rehearsal on stage at the Pantages and about two weeks of previews before we had our official L.A. opening. After that we didn't have to rehearse all that often considering we did eight shows a week! We usually had clean-up dance and/or vocal rehearsals every few weeks. This was all depending upon who was coming in and out of the company…to fit them into the swing of things. We also had random visits from the director and choreographer and/or their assistants.

SC: Was it an interesting dynamic living in L.A. with such a steady gig and paycheck without auditioning all the time?
GS: It is quite interesting! It's like you're here, but not really here! I did my best to keep my face and name out there, but it was very difficult. The steady pay was very nice and *Wicked* is so great to have on a resume!

SC: Any obstacles to overcome or highlights while doing a show day in and day out?
GS: There are many! An eight show a week schedule, especially in a major dance show like *Wicked*, is very taxing on any body. Young or old! The best way to handle it is to train hard, get a good amount of rest, warm up before every show and pray!

YOUR CAREER PATH...YOU CAN'T TAKE EVERY JOB!

While interviewing choreographer **SERGIO TRUJILLO** he had some good advice for dancers wanting to audition for a tour or West Coast premiere of a Broadway show. "You can't go into a *Guys and Dolls* audition dressed like you're going to a music video audition, which happens a lot in L.A. I'm a stickler for having a respect for the art. I hate when people come in dressed in shorts. I toured with a few shows and it was one of the most amazing experiences that I've had. Just because it isn't on Broadway doesn't mean it is a less important production or less of challenge. Dancing on tour is a really phenomenal opportunity. It offers you the opportunity to make a lot of money as well."

GETTING A REAL JOB

No, I don't want one! Urgh! OK, so you are in a quandary. The life of a dancer has many ups and downs. Mostly on the rejection and financial side of things. What to do? Well, suck it up because sometimes you may have to hunker down and get a real job! No. Yes! No. Yes! OK, here are a few jobs that can pay your bills while waiting for your next big break. I never said that they were glamorous!

- Go-go dancer at Hollywood nightclub
- Trade show/convention model
- Personal assistant to a celebrity
- Front desk assistant at a dance studio
- Barista/food server/bar back
- Personal trainer/fitness instructor
- Club promoter
- Television audience participant
- Game show contestant
- Casting assistant
- Dance studio/convention teacher
- Extra?

My personal favorite is office assistant for a temporary staffing agency. These jobs are for a few days only and you can really clarify what types of jobs you are interested in doing with the staffing firm. Below are a few staffing agencies and their Web sites. Go online and upload your resume so that if you ever need them you are already in the system.

Apple One
15165 Ventura Boulevard, Suite 120
Sherman Oaks, CA 91403
(818) 990-4488 Phone
www.AppleOne.com

Comar Agency
6500 Wilshire Boulevard, Suite 2240
Los Angeles, CA 90048
(310) 248-2700 Phone
www.ComarAgency.com

Office Team/Accountemps
3601 West Olive Avenue, Suite 625
Burbank, CA 91505
(818) 391-5501 or 5500 Phone
www.OfficeTeam.com
www.AccounTemps.com

If you need help writing a non-entertainment resume go to www.resume-help.org or search "resume writing help" online.

CHAPTER NINE

The reason I put a question mark next to Extra on the previous page is because the more serious you are about getting into other aspects of television and film, the less extra work you need or should do. It may be how you end up getting your SAG card but it isn't something that you will want to continue afterward. You may end up working as SAG background. There isn't anything wrong with this as the compensation is fair and you may end up getting bumped to a principal role. Be conscious of the parts you accept and remember that you control your career.

> ## SICK TIP #31:
> ## VEGAS IS ONLY A HOP, SKIP AND A JUMP AWAY!
> You can't take every job, but you can get away for a little bit if you'd like. Being so close to Las Vegas is a good thing! Not the gambling. The entertainment. If you want to do a Vegas show like the Show in the Sky, Cher, Bette Midler or even Wayne Brady, there are lots of opportunities to dance in Sin City! For entertainment news check out www.Vegas4Locals.com. You may be able to do short corporate gigs there as well. Many agencies have contacts in Las Vegas to reach out to.

TAKING TOO LONG OF A BREAK

Although you cannot take every job, you also cannot take too long of a break from pursuing your dance career. A dancer's career is short. Being burned out on the Hollywood dance scene is just cause to pull yourself out for a short break doing corporate gigs, taking a vacation, getting a real job to enjoy a steady paycheck and many other reasons to check out for a hot second. Notice, I said <u>second</u>! Taking too long of a break from the industry will force you to come back to an atmosphere of newbies and unfortunately that will also include you! When you re-enter the workforce after hiatus it makes things extremely difficult as there are new casting directors, dancers who have become choreographers, agent turn over, etc. You need a break, you deserve a break, but know the consequences of an extended break. You may come back and get right into the swing of things. Take shorter breaks more frequently instead of six month long breaks. These will definitely help your career stay fresh and exciting for you and be less of a hassle for reintegration.

JINXING YOUR JOBS

After I audition and have booked a job, I try not to jinx the job. I keep quiet about it. You may not want to, but I prefer not to tell my family until I've completed the job so I don't nix it for myself. Jobs will be on the books one day and be cancelled the next. Even if you film a movie and get paid for filming that movie, you may end up on the cutting room floor for any number of reasons.

YOUR CAREER PATH...YOU CAN'T TAKE EVERY JOB!

Funny You Should ask...
What If I'm Not Sexy?

For many young men and women, it is difficult to come to Hollywood and see all the "grown and sexy" being oozed out and thrown all around at auditions. What if you're more of the quirky or the smiley type? This is great! Use your personality to infuse the dance in a way that no one else is. You don't have to grow up over night. You also don't have to take the raunchiness of some auditions to the extreme if you don't feel comfortable. Be you and you will grow into your own version of the "grown woman" or "grown man" that you're meant to be all in due time.

EXTRA CREDIT: DANCER DISTURBANCE

Get up the nerve! I see those guys on the street all the time. You know the ones spinning the sign with the huge yellow arrow that they throw up in the air to get your attention and ultimately point you in the direction of the newest condos for sale or new gadget store grand opening. Yes, you know those guys! I always wanted to get out there and twirl a sign, throw a few of my own moves out there on the dance floor, oops, I mean street corner. Go ahead, grab one of those jobs for a day as a side gig. Throw on your headphones for some great exercise and show-stopping fun.

BOOK ME! WORKBOOK EXERCISES - PART 2

Some **BOOK ME! Workbook** exercise topics from Part Two of this book are listed below. Purchase the **BOOK ME! Workbook** online at: www.ColtonCollection.com

- Identify and communicate the types of jobs you'd like to book with your agent.
- Get the best out of you at every audition. What makes you tick?
- Navigate your way through the Hollywood dance scene - Who's who?
- Detail the career path that works for you.
- Create a back-up plan in case the industry slows down.

CHAPTER NINE

Sandra says...

- You will be busy so you can't take every job that comes along.

- Alternative jobs to working in TV and film do exist. Find work on cruise lines, at theme parks, doing corporate gigs, industrials and touring with a Broadway show for example.

- You might also try auditioning for a profesional dance/cheer team or audition for a seasonal show like the *Rockettes* if you have time.

- Remember that the industry does swell with jobs and also has dry spells. You may look into alternative jobs like waiting tables or office temp work if you need a change as well.

- Give whatever job you take 250%. Be full out on every project.

> **POINT TAKEN:**
> Don't take your jobs for granted because work can go M.I.A. for months at a time. It is best to make sure to have two or three other alternatives just in case the work isn't there to be had. The best thing to do is to have a Plan A, Plan B and Plan C. Then you will always be covered in case an unforeseen dry spell creeps up on you!

PART THREE

I'M VERY THAT! MASTER MARKETING: THE PRODUCT IS YOU!

CHAPTER TEN

DANCE 10 - LOOKS 10!

Don't be mad when another blond walks in the room and you just dyed your hair! This will happen and you will be so furious that someone either copied your look or just can't find their own. You may have mastered it, but you didn't invent it! Trust me, you'll get over it.

In Hollywood, I did say that it might come down to how you look but have you taken a look at most of the A-list celebrities lately? Yes, most of them are gorgeous in some way or another. But really, take another look. Tabloid publications are catching them in their "grocery store moments" and on strolls with their kids. Their "look" has become a different type of animal. Glam is gone on their down time and people want to see them actually living their real lives. Remember <u>YOU</u> amongst all of the hoopla and hype that is Hollywood. <u>Stay true to you</u>! Don't ever let anyone take away what makes you special.

Your physical, mental, emotional and spiritual wellness is also important to your booking success rate in Hollywood. If you are not well emotionally or mentally prepared for the rejection that this town runs on, you will fold under the pressure. In this chapter you will learn ways to look good and feel good by putting your focus on the following: Good nutrition, outside athletic activities to stimulate your flexibility and core strength, understanding the importance of emotional and psychological stability, surrounding yourself with resources that help lift you up and not break you down, take care of your personal and sexual hygiene and lifestyle wellness as well as important contact information to help if you do find yourself damaging your mind and body with alcohol, drugs, poor nutrition, etc.

CHAPTER TEN

OK, now that we've had the pep talk, take heed to some serious maintenance drills! Now, I said don't let anyone take away what makes you special. What I'm also saying is, don't take it away from yourself either. Maintain what you've got! The best way to keep up your look is to eat and exercise in a healthy way in addition to keeping up with a consistent beauty regimen. As mentioned earlier, here is where I break down some great tips on maintaining your look.

BEAUTY REGIMENS FOR MEN AND WOMEN

Hollywood is all about glitz and glamour. In the dance world it's all about sweating in a rehearsal hall and still looking good while doing it! Aisha Francis is a friend of mine who has danced and choreographed for many recording artists. This girl will not be caught dead without her heels, her hair done, her face 'beat' and of course a stick of chewing gum! Oh, by the way,  'beat' means she's fierce! We are in a world that doesn't care that you spent all day in a rehearsal hall. The artist doesn't care that you spent all day auditioning and making cuts to get down to the last few to be presented to them on tape or in person. You need to look your best at all times! Keeping your teeth white, eyes white, hair healthy and skin immaculate is also important to your career and its longevity. The most important thing you can do is to wash your face! Simple as it sounds. The pattern of going from home to rehearsals to a gig to home to another gig to rehearsals, etc. Wash your face. This is where it all begins. A clean face makes a happy "booked" dancer!

ROY HAIDAR
CELEBRITY MAKEUP ARTIST
METAMORFACE MAKEUP CREATOR &
FORMER LEAD EDUCATOR FOR JEMMA KIDD MAKEUP

I sat down with my favorite celebrity makeup artist Roy Haidar and put together my must-have list along with some fun items he recommended to go along with you on every audition and job site to fulfill your makeup necessities.

FAST FIX:

ROY'S FACIAL TIPS

- Keep your face beat
- Moisturize day and night
- Use sunscreen (stay out of the sun)
- Eye crème (very important)
- Exfoliate (dry skin) once a week
- Mask (oily skin) once a week
- Get a facial once a month as a treat to yourself

DANCE TEN - LOOKS TEN!

Makeup Must-Haves (Women)

General Face:
- Moisturizer
- Concealer
- Water-resistant foundation
- Foundation *(crème)*
- Translucent powder

Brushes:
- Contour brush *(cheeks)*
- Highlight brush *(blush and bronzer)*

Eyes:
- Neutral eye shadows
- Glitter
- Eyelashes
- Eyelash glue *(DUO: Black & White turns clear)*
- Eyelash separator
- Eyebrow brush
- Eyeliner *(Crème – Easier To Use Than Liquid)*
- Tweezers – Just in case you need to pluck those brows
- Mascara

Lips:
- Lip balm
- Lip liner
- Lipstick
- Lip-gloss

Makeup Must-Haves (Men)

Overall Face:
- Oil free moisturizer
- Powder
- Concealer (for blemishes)
- Lip balm
- Bronzer

Makeup for Headshots

Hire a makeup artist. Invest because you do not want to have to do a re-shoot. Once you decide on a makeup artist, tell them exactly the look you want. Don't let them just do what they want. Give them examples. Bring magazines or photos that you would like to resemble in your shoot.

Perform test runs if you choose to do your own makeup. Practice. Take photos of what you've done. Practice transitions from one makeup style to your next look. You can buy good makeup products at Rite Aid, Target or CVS/pharmacy. But if you play a little, check out a few brand name products that Roy and I believe make a huge impact!

Sick Tip #32: Open Your Eyes

Be conscious of what you put near and on your eyes. This sounds like common sense, but having your makeup done with the same brushes as twenty other people on set is not cool. Non-sterile environments contribute to pink eye and styes. Glitter eye makeup can scratch the eye as well. Try DUST makeup for eye glitter. Keep a travel kit of brushes so you know what is touching your face.

CHAPTER TEN

FUN STUFF FOR MAKEUP JOURNEYS

- **Adrell:** Fashion lashes
- **Almay:** Eye crème
- **Beauty Secrets:** Nail kit
- **Benefit:** Hula bronzer
- **Biore:** Daily cleansing cloths
- **Bobbi Brown:** Foundations for women of color
- **Carol's Daughter:** Lip butter
- **Christian Dior:** Spray foundations
- **Clean and Clear:** Deep action cream cleanser, oil absorbing sheets
- **Coppertone:** Oil free quick cover lotion spray
- **Cover Girl:** Mascara
- **DUST:** Glitter eye makeup
- **Jemma Kidd:** Brushes, Dewy Glow highlighters, glitter, water proof eye liners
- **Jergens:** Firming body lotion and Natural Glow
- **L'Oreal Paris:** Hip line
- **La Mer:** Gel moisturizer
- **Lancome Paris:** Bifacil *(Eye makeup remover)*
- **Laura Mercier:** Long lasting concealer
- **MAC:** Lip glass, brushes, mineralize skin finish, pigment, Revealing lip glass, Fix + (face hydrator)
- **Makeup Forever:** Body foundations and concealers, HD foundation *(Best foundation on camera)*
- **Natura Bisse:** Oxygen crème
- **Neutrogena:** face wash, summer glow, ultra sheer body mist sunblock
- **Obagi:** Skin care line
- **Revlon:** Mineral powder
- **Rosebud South:** Lip balm
- **Salon:** Bronze spray tanner *(Find at Sally's Beauty Supply Store)*
- **Shu Amora:** Eye lashes
- **Smashbox:** Brow tech and tinted lip treatment
- **Sunnies:** Eye shields for tanning
- **Urban Decay:** Bronzer/shadow/liquid glitter
- **Victoria's Secret:** Eye gloss, the Heidi Collection glitter eyeliner and perfect lipstick *(Malibu)*

SICK TIP #33: SIGNATURE SCENT

Finding your signature scent is another way to claim your individuality. While at a rehearsal, we were all sweating from the grueling workout and had been given a break. All of the dancers scattered. One talking on the phone, another texting, one in the bathroom, another on the computer, another knitting and another feverishly in the mirror trying to nail a step they missed in the last run-through. The dancer in the restroom came out and had sprayed some lovely peach scent that suddenly flowed into the room behind her. Everyone was like, "Yes, somebody smells good!" It immediately changed the focus of the room to something light and positive. Find your signature scent and change the world one sweaty body at a time.

DANCE TEN - LOOKS TEN!

EYE MAKEUP FROM SUBTLE DAY TO STAGE SPOTLIGHTS

START OFF WITH A BLANK SLATE

Begin makeup application having already moisturized. Start on a fresh, clean surface.

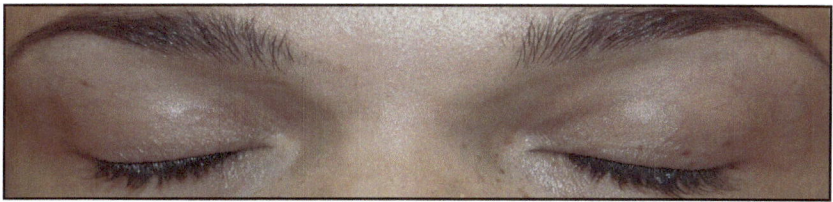

NEUTRAL DAY LOOK

A subtle change with neutral shades can turn your blank slate into a very approachable day look. This can be worn for any casting to give the appearance of a nice beautiful eye without saying, "I'm on stage."

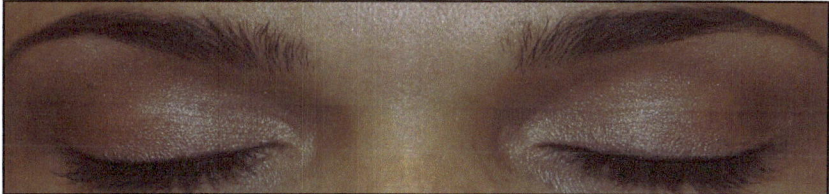

AMPED UP DAY LOOK

Adding a few darker tones, this transitions from a great day look to give more of a statement. Punching up the darker hues of brown gives the eye more definition.

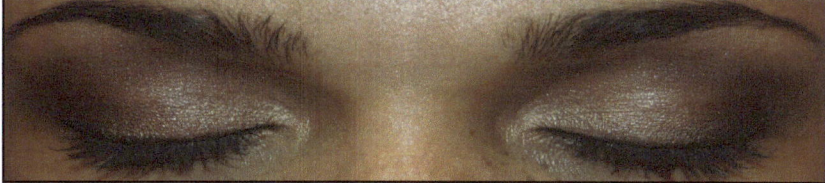

STAGE, HERE I COME!

Go from neutral and natural to shadowy sheik and stunning in 5 minutes. Adding a smokey eye, gave an intensified, more ready for stage or evening look.

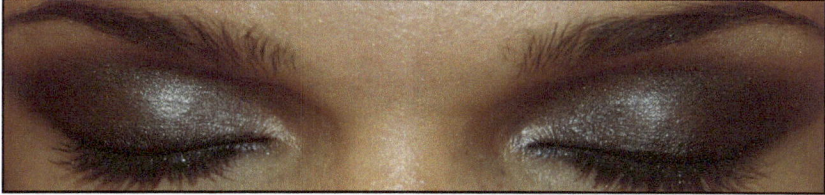

BOOK ME! HOW TO BECOME A SUCCESSFUL WORKING DANCER IN HOLLYWOOD

CHAPTER TEN

EXTREME MAKEUP IS FUN!

Most jobs in the TV and film industry require people to look like real people, but some go to the extreme. This is what makes the magic of Hollywood so exciting! Getting your makeup done by professionals may include additional hours in the makeup chair. Be patient and know that they are creating a masterpiece. You are being transformed into a character and this will only enhance your movement on screen or stage. I've included a few pictures from a gig I did at the House of Blues on Sunset Boulevard for the birthday party of Courtney Love's daughter. The spray paint artist did body makeup on the cast. Ask for business cards of the professionals with whom you work so that if you need a look that requires their expertise, you've got their contact information. Also, pay attention so that you gain knowledge of the process.

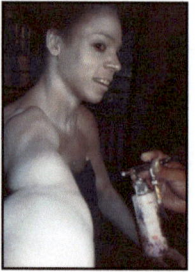 

SICK TIP #34: WASHING OFF EXTREME MAKEUP

There are easier ways to remove this makeup than scrubbing and irritating your skin. Put olive oil or an oil based makeup remover on your body then jump into the shower to help ease the removal with hot water. Body makeup is a pain! Whether you sweat some off or not, don't just lay in it after your performance, remove it so it doesn't clog your pores. Your legs, abs, back and arms aren't used to handling makeup so make sure you do right by them and remove it ASAP. *Well Off* by Origins is a great eye makeup remover.

DANCE TEN - LOOKS TEN!

ROY'S RECOMMENDED READING:
"Don't Go To The Cosmetics Counter Without Me" by Paula Begoun

HAIR
A major part of defining your look is your hairstyle. For me, I've been blessed with locks that have become signature to my look. People ask me all the time what I use in my hair and how I maintain the length and keep it healthy. Since I was a kid, my mom has always used Unicure, a leave-in conditioner, on my hair. It is also called Cure Care. Normally it doesn't really matter what kind of shampoo or conditioner I use in the shower just as long as I use a good leave-in conditioner out of the shower. Make sure to continually change out what you use in your hair to wash and condition it because your hair will get used to certain products and they won't work as well after a while.

HEALTHY HAIR TIPS
- Avoid heat damage: Curling irons/flat irons/blow dryers
- Moisturize your scalp with hair masks: Mayonnaise is a blessing
- Routine trim: Keep those ends healthy
- Avoid rubber bands: Avoid excess breakage
- Brush hair often: Keep scalp stimulated
- Avoid permanent dye/bleach: Try semi-permanent to avoid damage
- Use ceramic irons to minimize damage to hair

RECOMMENDED HAIR CARE PRODUCTS – SANDRA'S FAVS!
- Sea Plasma: Re-hydrant
- Cure Care: Leave-in conditioner
- Frederic Fekkai: Glossing kit
- Herbal Essence Body Envy: 2-in-1 shampoo and conditioner
- Herbal Essence Hello Hydration: Shampoo and conditioner
- Bed Head Superstar shampoo
- VO5 Hot Oil Treatment
- Suave: Daily Clarifying shampoo (Strips hair of nasty built up product)

SICK TIP #35:
BEAUTY IS ONLY SKIN DEEP - LITERALLY!
Remember when you're dying your hair to always use gloves! Imagine dying your hair and staining your hands purple or brown and then having to explain that at an audition the next day. L'Oreal hair color stain remover can do the trick for removal and is inexpensive. I know it sounds like common sense, but people forget all the time to put on those gloves.

CHAPTER TEN

TO WIG, OR NOT TO WIG?

Never forget that you are in Hollywood, film capitol of the world! Many actors, dancers and comedians change their look for an audition and it may be as simple as throwing on a wig to look the part. You may want to invest in a straight-haired wig and a curly-haired wig to help you complete your look and achieve an impossible switcheroo during a crazy day of auditioning. This may also be helpful for ladies whose hair continuously sweats during rehearsals; wigs may be your answer when you need to be ready for a performance quickly.

Hair Extensions, no Hairdo®!

Recently, I was privileged to work with celebrity hair stylist Ken Paves. He has a line of clip-in hair extensions that are AMAZING! Go to www.HairUWear.com. You will be super excited too. I've been requested for jobs because of my hair. Think about investing in a temporary solution like a wig before you go chopping off your hair. You may want to get used to the idea of a short hairdo before you make it a permanent choice. The photo on the left is my real hair length. While in the two photos to the right, I have Hairdo® pieces in for a dramatic change.

MAKEUP AND BEAUTY SUPPLY STORES

Cinema Secrets
4400 Riverside Drive
Burbank, California 91505
(818) 846-0579 Phone
www.CinemaSecrets.com

Naimies
12640 Riverside Drive
Valley Village, CA 91607
(818) 782-2863 Phone
www.Naimies.com

Frends
5270 Laurel Canyon Boulevard
Los Angeles, CA 91607
(818) 769-3834 Phone
www.FrendsBeautySupplyOnline.com

Nigel's Beauty Emporium
11252 Magnolia Boulevard
North Hollywood, CA 91601
(818) 760-3902 Phone
www.NigelBeauty.com

Sally's Beauty Supply Store
12512 Victory Boulevard
North Hollywood, CA 91601
(818) 506-7578 Phone
www.SallyBeauty.com

DANCE TEN - LOOKS TEN!

BROOKE LONG

This former *Laker Girl, Miami Heat Dancer, Charger Girl* and *Deal or No Deal* model has a few tricks of the trade up her sleeve to help some of the female dancers make a good first impression even if they weren't born with the attributes listed on the D.A.B.!

How to make a 'B' go to a 'Full C' without Surgery

"Chicken cutlets are the answer. You can buy sticky bra inserts from Victoria's Secret, Frederick's of Hollywood or ask at your local department store. These will give you the first part of the formula. Start with your sticky inserts and don't put them on over your breasts. Put them on at an angle so that the clasp that holds them together is angled in a "V" pointing down toward your belly button. Spread them farther apart than normal so that when you cinch them in to join the clasp they create more cleavage in the middle. Add on a strapless bra and a regular padded bra over that and you're a bombshell beauty, minus the surgery!" Sandra's demo of before and after is shown below (left to right).

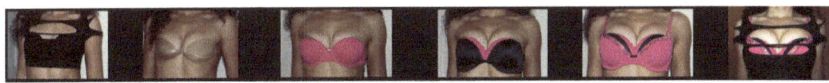

Cut Panty hose – Pull up the Booty. Yes, Seriously!

"By cutting the elastic waist band off of your panty hose and/or fishnets you eliminate that squeeze pushing your skin in and then ultimately out of the top. No more muffin top. You also give yourself leverage for cinching and pulling those panty hose or fishnets up your booty which gives it more shape and no bulky bumps. This will make your bum look very nice!

Tanning

"Plain and simple, tanning makes you look skinnier than pale skin. White skin, if you're not tan, makes you look heavier on camera. Tan skin defines the muscles more so if it's an important job or audition, TAN! Especially if they are requiring you to show your stomach or your butt in a bikini, have tan skin!

Wear Heels And Bevel In Photos

"Don't go to a bikini audition without heels. If they say, 'We need to see your body can you throw a bikini on?' Bring heels with you. Your legs will look so much longer. Flats with a bikini just cut you off. Heels may seem a little vampy and trashy when you're walking in with your bikini on and heels. You may feel like you're in a beauty pageant but on camera it looks way better. Also bevel your foot in at an angle for photos."

CHAPTER TEN

FOR THE GUYS!

Try to make sure that you condition your skin to keep it fresh for when you have to shave down. Avoid razor burn and ingrown hairs by taking care of your skin. Tend Skin products help alleviate razor bumps. Wave caps can do wonders to maintain your locks also.

BODY IMAGE

As a dancer, there are many different body types that work in this industry. Beyoncé has hired full-figured women for her performances, as did the Dove beauty campaign. Assess your body type and really be truthful with yourself as to the maintenance of a healthy height to weight proportion. Maintaining your physique is part of your job. This doesn't mean you need to go to extremes to maintain your body or to improve upon it. Agents are submitting your headshot daily to potential employers who expect to see the toned man or woman in front of them. Maintain your shape for the health of you and your career. Being completely honest, we do live in a time where societal pressures to be thin are the predominant image of what is beautiful. Hollywood lives on beauty but it also thrives on imperfections as well. As a dancer you will be on the go constantly. Some dancers have turned to fitness supplements to curb appetite, speed up metabolism and/or sustain energy. If you feel as though something has changed and may be cause for concern in regards to your eating habits or lack thereof or feel as though you have exhibited exaggerated uses of these types of drugs or supplements, please contact a help center or any of the phone numbers below for treatment options.

HELP LINES AND CONTACT INFORMATION

Eating Disorder Awareness and Prevention, Inc. (EDAP)
(800) 931-2237 Phone
www.EDAP.org

Eating Disorders Anonymous (EDA)
www.EatingDisordersAnonymous.org

National Eating Disorder Association
(800) 931-2237 Phone
www.NationalEatingDisorders.org

Overeaters Anonymous (Los Angeles)
(323) 653-7652 Phone
www.OALAIG.org

Narcotics Anonymous
(818) 773-9999 Phone
www.NA.org

DANCE TEN - LOOKS TEN!

FITNESS

Keeping up with your fitness is key to your success. If there is a series of days without audition calls, make sure you get back in class. Always keep up your endurance. It is especially disappointing for a choreographer to see dancers huffing and puffing during a short rehearsal because they lack the endurance to go full out each time. When preparing for a concert tour, your rehearsals will go 8-10 hours a day for weeks. This is no joke! Keep your stamina and your training at a peak performance all the time so that when you have long rehearsals you are up to the moment and don't drag others down.

If you want a change of pace from attending regular dance classes, join a gym. There are many local gyms, private fitness clubs and corporate giants. Try Equinox, Crunch or a few listed below:

Bally Total Fitness	24 Hour Fitness	Gold's Gym
http://West.BallyFitness.com	www.24HourFitness.com	www.GoldsGym.com

SICK TIP #36:
HAPPY FEET

If you want a more comprehensive guide to taking care of your feet check out *"The Dancer's Foot Book: A Complete Guide To Foot Care"* by Dr. Terry L. Spilken.

ALTERNATIVE EXERCISE

Yearning to get your sweat on doing something other than dance? Try one of the following to get that heart rate up, burn some calories and feel good:

- Spinning
- Capoeira
- Cardio circus
- Aerial fitness
- Pop Physique
- Pilates
- Cardio barre
- Yoga
- Hiking (Runyan Canyon)
- Hip Hop Abs® w/Shaun T

Some of the most important things you can do to elongate your dance career are inside your body not out. Incorporating the right nutrition into your diet is imperative. Also find other exercise methods that really help to maintain your body and its performance level instead of tearing it down. In this chapter, you've heard about what to do to maintain your face, hair, feet and general fitness. Try something new. Think outside the box. Remember that the outside is only as good as the inside. Good nutrition is also key to your career longevity and your ultimate wellness. Your health is not just about if you look healthy, it's about feeling healthy and living healthy. Those are the things that will come across at an audition.

CHAPTER TEN

JEREMY MOWE
Owner, Rip City Strenth
www.RipCityStrength.com

DANCERS AS ATHLETES - CAREER LONGEVITY

"Longevity in the dance community is an extremely complex task since dance itself encompasses such a variety of people and body types. Because dancers are athletes in their own respect, preparation and self-discipline will move you past the competition. Prepare yourself for success and stick to the things that will make you a winner. In order to achieve peak performance, the first step is to maintain your diet and training regimen.

1 - TRAINING YOUR BODY

"As an athlete, define your type of dance style and train your body accordingly. Whether it is through resistance training to become stronger, plyometric training to be more explosive, or elastic training to elicit specific functional movements that only elastic resistance can achieve, you have to plan a routine that compliments your personal style. Training your body is a great way to not only prevent injury and aid in performance but develop self-appreciation and a better self-image.

2 - INJURY PREVENTION AND LIFE CHOICES

"First and foremost, a dancer isn't making money if they are sick or hurt. The most important role you assume is to take care of your body or it will not make you money. A paycheck is more important than the extracurricular activities like partying, late nights or drugs. Establish your goals from an early point in your career. You have to choose what is truly important to you. Be realistic with yourself. Place value on your dreams or they will never materialize. Take your body as seriously as you do your career, the health and longevity of both depend on it.

3 - LIGHTS, CAMERA, ASSETS!

"Whether you are in front of your mirror in your studio apartment lip singing to Billy Ocean's *'Lover Boy'* or on a stage in front of hundreds even millions of people, you have to look good. Looking good starts with feeling good in your skin. **OWN YOUR BODY!** When it's time to perform, this is where your preparation pays off. Spandex is like Miracle Grow for muffin tops. Preparation doesn't mean crash dieting two weeks before an audition or open call to try and lose 10 pounds; it is keeping your body in a constant state of health and wellness. Truthfully, for most to achieve the ideal physique it usually requires dedication and a lifelong commitment to living healthy. If your first thought when you hear of an audition is, 'I have to go on a diet!,' then guess what, you are already behind. On stage should be the last place you worry about your appearance. People will judge you so BE CONFIDENT. By taking control of your body, your poise and preparation will shine through. Your body is a weapon. Keep it locked, cocked and ready to rock!

4 - FOOD IS NOT THE ENEMY - POOR SELECTION IS!

"Maintain the thought that a dancer's body is viewed as the main foundation of their business. Late night runs for fast food after a night of partying probably isn't a good career move. **Just because you aren't overweight doesn't mean you are healthy!** Hold yourself accountable for what you consume. There are many food items being sold that shouldn't even be considered food. The shelves of grocery stores are packed with processed foods that have virtually no health benefits. Just because it is sold as food, doesn't mean that it should be eaten. Stick with foods that are natural and nutrient dense. Avoid partially hydrogenated oils, high fructose corn syrup and any supplements that provide wondrous health benefits yet are sold behind the counter at a gas station. If it has an abnormally long shelf life, there is usually some type of preservative in it. Ask yourself why that pink sugar cookie in the vending machine is always so soft. Preservatives! Without preservatives and dye, processed meat would be a delicious shade of putrid grey and that pink sugar cookie would be hard as a rock in just a couple of days. Read ingredient labels and see for yourself all of the chemicals that the unknowing public induces into their diets. People are literally poisoning themselves from the inside out! Fresh organic foods that you prepare yourself are the best solution. It is not cheap or easy to do, but that extra step is what will elevate you past the competition. Remember, the food industry is a business. Think about that when you walk through the aisles of your favorite grocery store. Just look at all the bright, shiny boxes with toys and million dollar sweepstakes. Advertising and packaging is primarily what you are buying.

5 - YOUR BODY IS YOUR FOUNDATION, DON'T LET IT CRACK!

"The dancer's body is in a constant state of stress. 10-12 hour days for weeks at a time on tour can physically ravage the body. This process is taxing on your immune system but don't worry. Your body has the ability to heal itself with the right tools. I know your legs are sore, back is tired, feet hurt and you can't even hold your eyelid up let alone your arms. Tired? Guess what? So is everyone else! Now is your chance to set yourself apart. Fuel your body and prepare it for recovery by consuming the healthiest nutrient-dense food possible. Then top that off with lots of water and plenty of rest. At least 8-10 hours a night.

CHAPTER TEN

6 - HEALTHY NUTRITION ON THE GO!

"Longevity is established in the infantile stages of your life, thus carrying over into your career and ultimately, the golden years. The foundation of your life, not just your dance career, should be constructed around nutrition and exercise. Diet and exercise go together like Bill Cosby and Jell-O pudding. Avoid falling victim to all the ills of an inactive lifestyle, once again you must organize. You can always make meals ahead of time and take them with you while you travel or are auditioning. Your body requires fuel, so do not avoid feeding it or later you'll suffer the consequences. Malnutrition can have many negative health effects. A few simple guidelines are listed below.

EASY NUTRITION GUIDELINES TO FOLLOW

1 - DON'T OVER EAT

"Make your morning meal the largest meal of the day. This doesn't mean go destroy pancakes and bacon every morning. The morning meal is a great time to eat oatmeal with some fresh blueberries and a few whole eggs. Create smaller meals and eat frequently throughout the day. Try to consume as many as five to eight smaller meals a day. You shouldn't feel like you are stuffed. Eat enough to make it to your next meal. Try to eat in moderation. Remember the advertising tip I gave you about food? Often but not always, when fat is reduced, it is replaced with sugar, and you are right back in the cycle. You can eat gummy worms every once and a while, but if you are on a steady diet of insulin spiking sugar sticks, eventually negative side effects may start to show up.

2 - READ THE LABEL AND UNDERSTAND THE INGREDIENTS

"Soda, candy, anything with high fructose corn syrup or trans fat, certain types of yogurts and packaged foods can have huge amounts of sugar. By the way, just because a label states that there are zero grams of trans fat, doesn't necessarily mean that the product is void of trans fatty acids altogether. When the label is created, it is done on a per serving basis. The FDA requires over a certain amount of trans fat per serving to be listed."

> According to the *FDA's Guidance for Industry: Food Labeling*:
> Trans fat content must be expressed as grams per servicing to the nearest 0.5-gram increment below 5 grams and to the nearest gram above 5 grams. If a serving contains less than 0.5 gram, the content, when declared, must be expressed as '0 g.'

"A company that wants their food product to be labeled as trans fat free may manipulate the per serving content of trans fat. This means that the food product is recorded as having zero on the label when it might really contain some trans fat. Scan the label for partially hydrogenated oils and avoid them altogether."

3 - BUY BRANDS YOU TRUST

"There are many great places to buy foods that you can trust. A few stores that come to mind are Whole Foods and Trader Joe's. Most grocery stores will even have a health food and organic sections. Kashi® makes a lot of great breakfast options as well as snacks and dinner entrée options. They are all natural and usually have a good deal of both fiber and protein, which will help keep you full, longer.

4 - BUY IN BULK AND SAVE MONEY

"Package foods in bags and prepare a few meal options for snacks in advance. A bag of almonds, an apple and string cheese is a great snack. If you are a fan of tuna, buy it in the portable foil packages that tear open. Eggs are a wonder food! Scramble them up with some spinach or hard boil them and take them to go! Salads are an option, just be careful of the dressing. I personally enjoy salsa. It is great on salads, eggs, chicken and even broccoli. I joke with my friends and call my diet the *'Costco Diet!'* I primarily purchase all my food in bulk from Costco. At 6'6", 255 lbs, buying in bulk saves me money and time. Due to my size and dietary needs, I have absolutely no problem eating pounds of fresh broccoli and spinach before the freshness fades. I have noticed that they do not offer a lot of the little worthless things that end up in my hands when I leave the average grocery store.

5 - 'WHAT THE HECK ARE YOU EATING? THAT'S NASTY!'

"Tuna fish with raw spinach mixed in and almonds? SERIOUSLY?! What's wrong with you? My answer is always simple, 'You don't have to like it, you just have to do it.' It's kind of like rehearsing for 18 hours. You don't have to like it, but you just have to do it. Sometimes you need to be your body's parent and say, 'No, you don't need a milkshake and french fries right now!' Practice self-discipline and you will be rewarded. Not every meal has to be a production, but I certainly think every meal should provide you with the nutrients to keep your body operating at its peak performance."

LONG TERM OVERUSE, ENERGY DEFICIENCY, OSTEOPOROSIS AND AMENORRHEA FOR WOMEN AND YOUNG GIRLS

STEVEN J. CHATFIELD
EXECUTIVE DIRECTOR OF I.A.D.M.S. (2001-PRESENT)

Stephen is an associate professor of dance at the University of Oregon and is the director of graduate studies and coordinator of the graduate dance science program. "International Association for Dance Medicine and Science (I.A.D.M.S.)

CHAPTER TEN

is a professional organization that is comprised of medical practitioners including doctors, nurses as well as researchers such as myself and other dance educators, dancers, choreographers, company directors and people who come together and share information about promoting the health and well-being of dancers."

STEVEN CHATFIELD ON DAILY MAINTENANCE

"A lot of (dance) companies these days can't afford to come together and stay together. So there are many situations where a dancer is merely an independent contractor going around and jobbing themselves out for any giving opportunity. Once they get hooked up with a given production, those people in that production, to put it in harsh terms, they just might not care about that individual. It's not their responsibility to keep them healthy, happy and whole. They need to be responsible for themselves when they come into each job.

"As an independent contractor and working with different people all of the time, you are facing different challenges. Each choreographer is slightly different in what they demand from your body, especially with the kind of schedule they expect of you. That's what is going on in this day and age and it makes it hard for the dancer. ***It's very difficult for a dancer to be all things to all people***. The dancer has to take care of themselves and be the one who takes primary responsibility for their fitness and their health so that they can go around as an independent contractor. Maintain your health, your instrument (and) your body in the midst of all of the challenges. If you know what's coming up, it would behoove anyone who is working for X choreographer, and they know that particular choreographer makes such and such kinds of demands, they should begin to prepare themselves ahead of auditioning; certainly ahead of any rehearsal progress should they be given a spot. So that when they get in the midst of the work and the rehearsals...your body has to be ready to receive that information to do it and repeat it.

MANAGING A DANCER'S ENERGY

"Dancers and people who manage dancers tend to have the expectation of them that they are an endless reserve of energy and physical capability and it is just not so. Dancers have to be very careful to manage their energy. A dancer just can't be doing everything everywhere! Teaching classes in the morning, then taking pilates in the middle of the day, then going to rehearsal and then doing a performance at night and then going on tour and then coming back and teaching and continually expecting their bodies to just deliver and deliver and deliver. And then in order to deliver more dancers condition themselves more by taking more conditioning. There's a finite amount of that schedule that people can do.

Dancers need to be able to manage their resources and by resources I mean their energy and their physical ability. The most prevalent kind of injury in dance is what is called an *'overuse injury.'* It is just what it sounds like. You are just doing too much! No one likes to hear, 'You've got to stop doing it.' In reality, that's the kind of moderation that people have to find. To really expect to have a long and fruitful career, they have to not overwork themselves all the time.

"Dancers come out and they think they are invincible, and then at some point in time they learn that they are not invincible and that's when they start looking at people who I call *'the real dancers.'* I mean, if you're just a young buck and you're going off, you really aren't a dancer yet, you're an apprentice, a journeyman dancer. After you've actually survived a little bit of the career and you've figured out that you just cannot do everything all the time, and you come back with a whole new sensibility, that's when I see artists, real dancing artists start to bloom; before that it's all just raw talent. Later it becomes something about the individuals actually expressing themselves. They learn that their tool has some limitations on its capabilities but at the same time it fosters their reinvestment in the expressiveness of their capabilities. Then we get mature artists who are really a pleasure to watch.

I.A.D.M.S. Fact Sheet: The Challenge of the Adolescent Dancer
AVOIDING THE FEMALE ATHLETE TRIAD

Recent research suggests a relationship between exercise levels, nutrition, hormone levels and bone density. Adolescent dancers, like all physically-active young women, are at risk for developing the Female Athlete Triad, a syndrome comprised of disordered eating, amenorrhea (absence of menstruation) and osteoporosis (loss of bone density). Emphasis on low body weight as a prerequisite for success as a professional dancer can encourage the eating disorders linked to the Female Athlete Triad. This syndrome may have long-term health ramifications, with a chronic energy deficit or disordered eating contributing to amenorrhea, which in turn may lead to reduced bone density and early onset of osteoporosis. Young dancers should be educated about healthy eating habits and encouraged to pursue a healthy lifestyle to improve and prolong their dance careers.

DANGERS FOR WOMEN AND YOUNG GIRLS

"One of the most dangerous things for a young woman is that if they are not genetically predisposed to thinness then they tend to under eat. What happens with that is what they are starting to call an **energy deficiency**. With energy deficiency, often times what starts to happen is that they lose their period. While that in and of itself might not seem like such a bad thing to a lot of women, in reality it comes coupled with hypoestrogenemia so they have low estrogen levels as a result. That then becomes very problematic because estrogen is responsible in females for maintaining bone integrity."

CHAPTER TEN

"With low estrogen, calcium starts to leach out of the bone. So you have a bone stemming and a greater chance of osteoporosis. Now, you don't get osteoporosis overnight, it is a long and evolved process but it begins often times in young adulthood with women who are hypoestrogenemic. No matter how much calcium they are eating, if they don't have enough estrogen coupled with it, it just doesn't get layed down in their bones, so their bones don't stay healthy. All of that starts with the whole energy matrix.

"If you're working hard, doing physical labor like a dancer does, at the end of the day, your body takes whatever you give it and supplies energy for that work. Then the other kinds of background processes that happen, the normal homeostatic or nutritive processes like your body rebuilding tissues and taking care of your hormonal health (i.e. the menstrual cycle) and things like that, those all take a backseat to the demands of the energy. Activity takes energy out of the diet as soon as it comes into the body and then the energy deficiency is left for the long term health and well being of the body. So, it doesn't seem like anything is wrong right away but as that progresses things start to go very wrong with the body. It's about energy availability. You have to have enough energy available to do the work and to also maintain your normal body functions.

MALE HEALTH HAZARDS

"In extreme cases, men go through energy deficiency where they can have low calcium levels in their bone, which could start toward osteopenia and osteoporosis. The sterility issue is not as important as it is for women. Men don't suffer from these problems as frequently.

INJURIES OF THE NEW DANCE ERA

"One of the things that is different today than before are the inversions, aerial moves, the extreme gesture or actions and the work on the head. As the movements get more and more extreme; there are more varieties of injury. Previously in the '70s or '80s you would never see dancers with arm, shoulder or neck problems, but now with all of the inverted and gymnastic moves doing spins on the head, or aerial things where sometimes they don't get all the way around, you see all kinds of upper body injuries with dancers. Neck, shoulder, arm and hand injuries are the most prevalent. Most dancers train on their feet, but if they're going to do that type of dancing they need to train in different ways, like a gymnast would train. Get to those places that are going to work hard in their performance and build them up in their training sessions. Keep the body in tune with dance changes and with the demands that are placed on them. We used to stand at a ballet barre and do leg work all day long, but if people are doing things on their hands, then dancers also need to be in the gym working like a gymnast is by doing handstand exercises, flips, cartwheels and inverted exercises."

INJURIES

The best way to prevent injuries is to warm up and cool down before and after auditions, shows, rehearsals and class. Get a good heart rate up and stretch out those muscles. Maintain flexibility, eat right, keep fit and get your rest! You know when you've pushed your body too far. Slow it down with aromatherapy, a hot bath or schedule a day at the spa. Also look into training in **somatics**. Get in tune with your body by learning how to focus and become sensitive to your body's needs with the appropriate response. Check out Burke Williams Spa in West Hollywood or Sherman Oaks and make an appointment by calling (866) 239-6635 or contact the Thai Lotus Healing Spa in Sherman Oaks at (818) 789-THAI (8424) today. They work miracles.

Dancers have a tendency to ignore pain or push through injuries. By doing this you are only continuing to hurt yourself and make an injury worse. I know, people have told you stories of how they danced on a broken ankle night after night after night. Well, if they want to hurt their body, let them do it. Try to take care of your body by not over indulging in painkillers. Seek out physical therapy or alternatives in healing instead. These may include acupuncture, the Feldenkrais Method® or consider the pleasure of a *siesta* to calm your body through a nap. Check out the National Sleep Foundation Web site at www.SleepFoundation.org. Some great information on injury prevention can also be found at www.DanceInjury.org.

HEALTH COVERAGE

Being proactive also means being prepared if you do get injured on set, at a rehearsal or in class. Here are a few things you can do to help yourself just in case:

- Know your medical history & allergies to medications
- Purchase your own health care plan
- Follow safety guidelines on set/rehearsals/class
- Use shoe inserts/get shoes rubbered/wear kneepads
- Have ice packs prepared in your freezer
- Invest in cooling/heating pads
- Prepare an emergency medical kit
- Keep over the counter medicines at home

Medicines:
- Pain relievers
- Lozenges
- Antihistamine
- Decongestant
- Antibiotic ointment

CHAPTER TEN

RECOVERY

If you do get injured, try your best to heed doctors' orders before getting back into the dance scene. You might want to get back immediately and think you are OK. A friend of mine tore her ACL, had knee surgery and underwent physical therapy. She thought she was OK and then re-injured herself on stage. It is about when you are ready but it is also about taking the necessary steps to get back on the horse fully prepared and rehabilitated as well. Dr. Millstein is an orthopedic surgeon and Dr. Weiss is a podiatrist here in Los Angeles if you need assistance with an injury.

LIFESTYLE CHOICES

Beyond the dangers of getting injured on the job are those that are personal choices we must all make when entering into an intimate relationship. My best advice is to keep your work and home life separate. The lifestyle choices you make will affect you and your health. Make good choices with your body and your sexual partners. Below are a few organizations that will be able to provide assistance with questions about personal hygiene, pregnancy, sexually transmitted diseases and testing facilities.

Los Angeles County Health Line
(800) 427-8700

Planned Parenthood
www.PlannedParenthood.org

Los Angeles Gay and Lesbian Center
(323) 993-7400
(888) 295-2429

L.A. Free Clinic
www.TheSabanFreeClinic.org

GAY AND LESBIAN CENTER

In speaking with dancers, some of the resources they were looking for prior to moving to Hollywood involved support groups and help where it concerned their sexuality. "The L.A. Gay and Lesbian Center provides a broad array of services for the lesbian, gay, bisexual and transgender community, welcoming nearly a quarter-million client visits from ethnically diverse youth and adults each year. Through its Jeffrey Goodman Special Care Clinic and on-site pharmacy, the center offers free and low-cost health, mental health, HIV/AIDS medical care and HIV/STD testing and prevention. The center also offers legal, social, cultural and educational services, with unique programs for seniors, families and youth, including a 24-bed transitional living program for homeless youth," as cited from www.LAGayCenter.org. Understanding your sexual health is also important to feeling good and doing your best on the job. In discussing these subjects, you should consult your doctor with the questions you have about pregnancy, STDs and sexuality. Minors should discuss these sensitive matters with their parents in addition to their doctor.

"The L.A. Gay and Lesbian Center's Sexual Health Program offers free sexually transmitted disease screening, treatment and education specifically for the gay, lesbian, bisexual and transgender community (though everyone is welcome). Routine testing is available on a walk-in basis. STD screenings are offered to anyone undergoing HIV testing as well.

"For treatment, same-day or next-day appointments are often available, and you can schedule an appointment by phone or in person at the registration desk. The average visit takes 1-2 hours. It's important to test for STDs on a regular basis; we encourage individuals who are sexually active to get tested every 6 months. Many people who have an STD do not have symptoms, so they don't even suspect they are infected. Fortunately, most STDs can be successfully treated, without long-term side effects, if treatment begins early. Mental health services are also provided including individual counseling, consultations and support groups for anger management, crystal meth and substance abuse, domestic violence, HIV over 50, sex and intimacy, sexual compulsivity and transgender issues.

WHAT IS AN STD?

"STD stands for sexually transmitted disease. STDs are infections that are usually spread by sexual contact such as oral, anal, or vaginal sex or rimming (oral/anal sex), either by coming in direct skin-to-skin contact or by exchanging body fluids like semen, pre-cum, vaginal fluids or blood. Certain STDs may be spread by sharing needles or from mother to child during pregnancy. STDs are very common in the United States and all over the world. Each year, millions of people every year will become infected with an STD. Many people do not know they are infected because they do not have any symptoms.

> HIV/STD Testing McDonald/Wright Building
> Call (323) 993-7500
> E-mail: healthservices@lagaycenter.org
> HIV Testing The Spot - Call (323) 993-7440

WHAT ARE SOME STD SYMPTOMS?

"Depending on the STD and when you were infected, you may have many, one or none of the following:

- *Discharge from the vagina, anus or urethra (the tube that passes urine)*
- *Burning or pain when you urinate (pee)*
- *Itching or irritation of the genitals*
- *Warts or bumps on or around the genitals*
- *Redness or swelling of the genitals*
- *Nausea, vomiting or fever*
- *Persistent sore throat*
- *Sores, blisters, or rashes*
- *Bleeding between periods or after sex*
- *Pain in the abdomen (area below your stomach)*
- *Pain in the testicles (balls)*
- *Jaundice (yellowish skin color)."*

The information above is from www.LAGayCenter.org. Contact your medical professional or the resources mentioned for more help to take preventative measures that take control of your health.

CHAPTER TEN

COSMETIC SURGERY

Many people partake in cosmetic reconstruction of areas they would like to enhance. It isn't something I would recommend, as there are always risks involved in an elective surgery. Be cautious. Be diligent in your research of procedures and the doctor who will perform them and overall please be careful. Many times people want what they don't have and once they get it, they realize that they were great without it. So many people tell me how fantastic it would be to have long curly hair because they have always had short hair. Remember, it isn't the hair that makes you, <u>it's you who makes you</u>. The hair is just one part of your entire being. Hollywood is full of fake, let's try to put some more <u>real</u> into this world of make believe.

> ### SICK TIP #37:
> ### <u>UNION HEALTH FAIRS</u>
> Performer unions also provide health fairs for members. Take advantage of services that include dental care, HIV/AIDS testing, breast cancer awareness, women's health, blood pressure/lung/pulmonary exams, referrals for prostate and PSA exams as well as mental health services.

HEALTHY BODY, MIND AND SOUL

Life is too short to put yourself down constantly and in this business you will hear enough of that on a regular basis. Remember to treat yourself like the beautiful person you are. Keep a positive attitude and always try to uplift others. Choreographer **Leslie Scott** reminds dancers to "be careful of negative self talk. What your mind says your body will follow. If you feel insecure, fat, not good enough, not sexy, etc., it will transcend to others through your movement. Even if you don't feel positively about yourself in that moment I always tell my dancers 'to Act as if.' You would be surprised at the POWER of your mind as your fan not your foe. You are worth it!"

Being full internally is the most important key to your success. Seek out a life coach like Tara Gross Steeves at www.CreateYourLifeInc.com or find your body, mind and spirit through **Nia** at www.NiaNow.com or through **Gyrokinesis** and its fluidity. What helps you with your pre-performance inner workings? What will help you ease tension, stress and pain? Most dancers do not have health insurance and it is crucial to invest in yourself. Find a low cost health insurance provider before or once you move to Hollywood. You must meet minimum earnings criteria for union health plans. For dancers just starting out, this may be a hard goal to obtain and maintain yearly. If possible to be on a family plan with your parents, do that. Take charge of your health!

The Pep Talk

Stand tall as a pillar
Never weaken or break

Be in tune with the sun
No curling, no faltering
No quiver, no shake

Stay green as the rest
And be sure of your growth

Sprout out and act proud
Stand out from the post

As a soldier so effortlessly unafraid
Be you, be one
Be strong, be brave

And yet unassuming
Let one floral or fawn

May you flourish and prosper
And always stay strong

Give us air, give us life
Give us strength, give us might

Take it and give it right back everyday
Okay!?

By Sandra Colton
Poetry Palette © 2003-2013

CHAPTER TEN

Sandra says...

- Feel your best and you will look your best, right? Maintain your body, mind and spirit and your outer shell will follow suit.

- Celebrity makeup artist and creator of *MetamorFace* makeup *Roy Haidar* has solidified your beauty regimen. Keep a fresh face ready for the world and moisturize honey!

- Listen to your body when it is telling you to slow down. Prevent injuries and manage your energy.

- Be healthy with your food intake and your lifestyle. Be safe sexually and get affordable health insurance just in case you're injured.

- Keep your mind balanced. Relax and decompress from the stress with somatics, acupuncture, massage or meditation.

- Garbage in = garbage out. Perform better by eating healthy!

> **POINT TAKEN:**
> Knowing when to say when is always difficult for someone who is living the life of a super hero. You might leap and bound from one tower to the next while jumping into one person's arms and tumbling across the floor! This is a constant push to fuel your energy source, your bones and your psyche. Slow down when you can.

CHAPTER ELEVEN

MASTER MARKETING: SELLING YOURSELF, IN A GOOD WAY

Are you buzz worthy? It's time to start thinking about yourself in a different light. Are you a dancer? Yes! Do you provide a service? Yes, you enhance the visual aspect of a performance whether on stage, in film or on television. Are you marketable as a product? Yes! Are you only a product? **NO!**

PERSONAL WEB SITES

Identifying your strengths and weaknesses and building on those strengths will help you market yourself. The first thing I tell anyone to do is to purchase his or her name as a Web site. This is the easiest way to have name recognition when someone asks, "What's your Web site name?" It is easy to remember if it is your (first) and (last) name (dot) com. **SandraColton.com** is my official Web site. In this instance I'm using my first initial and last initial in capital letters to distinguish between the two words so people can readily tell it is my first and last name. Writing it out in all capital letters works also but can sometimes get lost in translation. Make your distinction and purchase your Web site or **domain** name. MySpace.com/SandraColtonMusic is my music page and I can add people as fans on my Facebook fan page which you can find conveniently located at www.Facebook.com/Sandra.Colton.

If you have a hard name to pronounce or spell, you can also find a way to make it your own. I've always wanted to own www.Sandra.com but it has never been available. You may want to find a way to zero in on your first name as your Web site if it is unique and memorable like Hazel, Stasha or Anya. Many times these are more

MASTER MARKETING: SELLING YOURSELF, IN A GOOD WAY

successful because you can emphasize the uniqueness of the spelling and it becomes more memorable than a first and last name Web address.

A WORD OF CAUTION

You do not have to put every little bit of information on your Web site. With the power of the Internet, you need to maintain a level of privacy. In your contact information, you have the ability to designate how you want people to correspond with you. Giving out a personal e-mail or phone number may be relevant in some cases, but not always the best for keeping your privacy. Decide which is best for you.

Some would ask, "Well I have a MySpace and that's free so why do I need a personal Web site?" My answer is, <u>YOU DON'T</u>. If you feel as though your MySpace represents you and you have no problems getting information out about you, then fantastic. My recommendation still rests with purchasing your domain name and then redirecting it to your MySpace profile. In this case, you will still be able to brand your name by giving people your Web address with your name on it and avoid the cost of maintaining a Web site of your own by redirecting it to your MySpace account. Many third party sites do have their own glitches. Whether it's MySpace, Twitter, Facebook, etc., it is part of the Internet. So if your third party site is down for maintenance and you are unable to access e-mails then this may be a reason to create your own Web site to have complete control and access over where e-mails are going.

WHAT SHOULD I PUT ON MY PERSONAL WEB SITE?

If you put nothing else, put your **name** and your **contact information** on a **placeholder** page. A placeholder page is exactly that. It saves your Web page until you put up your full content. At least put your contact information on this page. There are many ways to approach Web design. Explore the Internet and find sites that you like. Once you have a few in mind, then start shopping for Web designers who can take the parts you like from your examples and create your site.

You can also add things like wallpaper or AIM icons for download to your site.

You may also want to design it yourself. The basics for a dancer to have on their Web site include a bio, contact information, resume, photos and demo reel.

CHAPTER ELEVEN

Most domain selling sites like GoDaddy and FatCow offer web building options included into their domain purchase price. You can also hire someone to create your site for you. Web design can get pretty costly, so I also recommend looking into a few of these books which range from $24.99-$39.99 in price to help you figure out how to create a Web site on your own.

- *Search Engine Optimization* by Jerri L. Ledford
- *Building A Web Site For Dummies* by David A. Crowder
- *Build A Website For Free* by Mark Bell
- *Web Analytics: An Hour A Day* by Avinash Kaushik
- *Web Video: Making It Great, Getting It Noticed* by Jennie Bourne with Dave Burstein
- *HTML, XHTML & CSS* by Elizabeth Castro

MAKING THE MOST OF YOUR E-MAIL

What is your e-mail? Is it hotgirl2009@xyzmail.com? If so and that's cool for you to give out, then groovy! I would suggest getting an e-mail address that is easy to remember and isn't too self-indulgent. So I'd steer clear from imthebestdancerintheworld@xyzmail.com or yournevergonnagetit@xyzmail.com. Opt for something simple like using your name like sandracolton@xyzmail.com or if you want to add something industry related go for it like hiphoplove@xyzmail.com or reeldesign@xyzmail.com. Whatever you choose, love it and stick with it. Try not to change it too often as you will put people off if they can't reach you.

THE POWER OF YOUTUBE

Some of the best marketing you can do for yourself is free on the Internet. You can post footage of you dancing online and direct people to it. Create a YouTube or Vimeo account by signing up at YouTube.com or Vimeo.com and start uploading footage today. Make sure you have the rights to all of the footage that you post as YouTube will take down any material that you do not have permission to use. This includes the music you use on your footage.

CREATING BUZZ

I've been able to increase buzz and awareness about what I'm doing in the dance industry by creating postcards, business cards as well as sending out my headshots to different casting directors in Hollywood and New York. By creating marketing materials you can handpick the look you want to project with photos of you and add your upcoming performance information. Always make sure to include your contact information or your agent's contact information so people know how to get in touch with you if they want to book you.

MASTER MARKETING: SELLING YOURSELF, IN A GOOD WAY

MARKETING MATERIALS
(NAME, BUSINESS CARDS, E-MAIL LISTS, POST CARDS)

WHAT'S IN A NAME?
The cold hard facts are that sometimes people only read your name and make up their minds about if they like you or not. Just like making a decision off of a picture submission, you could have a great name and be selected for a job. You could also change your name too much to the point that no one knows what to call you. If you have a great name, don't change it. If your name is Hazel and you just happen to have hazel colored eyes, don't change it! If you have a sick b-boy name and have made a signature move that people use your name for, then more power to you. Find what sticks and make it a selling tool.

BUSINESS CARDS
Putting together a business card is a great way to network and keep in contact with people. The more people you network with the better. I've seen a lot of business cards. Some people list themselves as a singer, producer, director, actor…and go on and on and on! It's great to have multiple talents but if you put everything and anything on your business card, people may start to think you are too scattered to focus on any one thing. I recommend putting your mainstay on your business card and your contact info. Simplicity is key.

My business cards are here as an example. They are not the only way to create a business card. I've listed SAG/AFTRA and ASCAP so anyone who reads this will know that I'm an actor, union member and in the music field as well. The back side has full body photo just in case the person needs to know what body type I have and if I fit their project needs.

E-MAIL LIST
Network yourself to a fantastic e-mail contact list. Create a list in your e-mail account. By sending out a mass e-mail you may have a positive or negative reaction by recipients. My advice is to send out a mass e-mail letting everyone know that you will be sending out e-mails periodically about your upcoming projects and if they do not wish to receive these e-mails to let you know and you can delete them from your list of recipients. This way you won't annoy anyone and you can keep everyone updated on your activities. **ConstantContact.com** is an affordable way to put out your own e-news.

CHAPTER ELEVEN

> ### SICK TIP #38:
> ### YOU TOO CAN HAVE A FAX
> In an effort to always stay accessible, get a fax number! You don't need to spend any money to do this and don't even need to have a landline to receive faxes. EFax is a simple way that is free for the introductory service to have a functioning fax line. It's easy to set up and best of all it is free. It will deliver the readable fax to the inbox of your e-mail. Outgoing faxes cost more. Go to www.EFax.com to find pricing information.

YOU'VE GOT MAIL! – POSTCARDS

Some of the best responses I've received were after I'd sent out informational postcards to managers, agents, casting directors, production studios, payroll companies, fellow dancers as well as friends and family! By sending out a postcard you are reaching people where they are and not waiting or expecting them to come to you. Granted, they may toss it in the garbage but you know that they at least, maybe even for one second, had to look at it before they threw it away to see what it was. Here are a few examples of past postcards that I've sent out as announcements.

MASTER MARKETING: SELLING YOURSELF, IN A GOOD WAY

PACKAGING YOURSELF FOR THE PRESS

By living and working in Hollywood, you may work on a film or television project that enhances your profile as a dancer. Remember what your reason was for moving to Hollywood. If that reason included a bit of recognition or dare I say publicity, then listen up!

Another part of your marketing strategy may be to create a portfolio that includes a **press kit**, **electronic press kit** or **EPK** or **press release** to promote your upcoming projects. If you are so inclined and have good writing skills, this is easier than it looks. Because you've already assembled your resume, demo reel, headshot and biography, you're more than half way there. Creating a sleek looking press kit or media kit is no more than the assembly of information. Along your travels, try to create contacts with choreographers. Quotes from professionals in the industry can be included to validate your talent in a press kit. Below is a list of commonly included press kit documents:

PRESS KITS TEND TO INCLUDE THE FOLLOWING:
- Biography   • Photos   • CD/DVD
- Information or fact sheet (one sheet)
- Quotes from industry professionals
- Articles/news items on the individual
- Contact information

Go to www.PRWeb.com to find out more on how to write and distribute a press release or to find a publicist that is right for your project.

BOOK ME! HOW TO BECOME A SUCCESSFUL WORKING DANCER IN HOLLYWOOD

CHAPTER ELEVEN

You will not need to give everyone a press kit at each audition. Most auditions only require a headshot and resume. The people who are looking for more of an in-depth look into what you do may be interested in seeing a press kit. Always bring multiples of what you've got and never give away your last one without having a backup at home or somewhere safe.

SOCIAL NETWORKS FOR DANCERS

Movmnt.net *(a branch of Movmnt Magazine)*, DancePlug.com, DancOn.com and Jon M. Chu's DS2DIO at YouTube.com/DS2DIO are social networks. Some of the most common social networking Web sites that don't just cater to dance enthusiasts are MySpace, Facebook and Twitter. Getting your voice heard on these sites can be somewhat difficult but it is possible if you cultivate your community. Be interactive with the sites and don't limit yourself. Communication is the key!

THE ULTIMATE BRAND IS YOU!

Create your own brand! Find out what works for you and sell it! Don't forego your training and stop learning. Instead be good at something and capitalize on it. Branch out into other areas of entertainment and market to an audience that you may not have thought would appreciate what you have to offer. Simply put, do what you do and figure out how to make it profitable, long lasting, sought after and ultimately enjoyable. Tell people what you would like to do. Shout it from the rooftops! I would like to be cast as the lead in a remake of the iconic movie *Flashdance*. If you never tell anyone your dreams, no one will ever know what you'd like to accomplish! As a dancer who also sings, I've released singles and produced my own album, **JUST DANCE** and music video for *"I Can't Dance"* which are available at www.iTunes.com/SandraColton.

My other passion is writing, of course! My first magazine ***Original Girl®*** was a quarterly lifestyle publication targeting college students and young adults from 18-26. Featuring music, movies and fashion, **O.G.** also covered financial aid, study abroad and career building tips for our readers. An Original Girl is smart, sexy, fashionable, on the go and in the know. She is a *cool cat*, ahead of the times, savvy and ultra creative! The second magazine I created is called DANCE TRACK Magazine and the 3rd was just launched July 2013 called DANCE TEAM Magazine. Please check out the site at DanceTeamMagazine.com.

MASTER MARKETING: SELLING YOURSELF, IN A GOOD WAY

O.G. COVER MODELS: JENNIFER LYNN, RAISTALLA AND VICTORIA PARSONS (L-R)

Above are the Fall 2008, Winter 2009 & Spring 2009 Covers of **O.G. Magazine**. **Dance Track Magazine**, my 2nd publication, debuted online in 2009 & in print in Fall 2010 & my 3rd magazine **Dance Team Magazine** debuted July 2013.

DANCERS USE NAME AS BRANDING TOOL

SPELLMAN SISTERS (Dena and Jenna)

As part of *Iconic* on Season 2 of *Randy Jackson Presents America's Best Dance Crew* on MTV, Dena and Jenna are sisters who are two years apart but get mistaken for twins all the time. Earlier I asked, 'What's in a name?' Well, the **SPELLMAN SISTERS** are capitalizing on their name and have created a brand all their own!

SC: Describe auditioning with the possibility of one sister booking the job and not the other?
SS: We have gone to auditions where one was booked and not the other, but most of the time if one of us isn't right for the job they usually let us both go, because they don't want to book one without the other. But no matter what we still support each other. We have no issues if one of us gets the job and not the other.

SC: Being part of a crew (Iconic) and dancing with one another can be hard to have lives that are separate from your work. Do you get a chance just to be family?

BOOK ME! HOW TO BECOME A SUCCESSFUL WORKING DANCER IN HOLLYWOOD   235

SS: Most of our lives is working, but on the little down time we do have we go out, play or just chill with friends and play some Wii. Movie nights are our big thing with the crew.

SC: Ever felt burned out and felt obligated to continue in order to support the other if called to an audition that was for both of you?
SS: I don't think we've ever had that problem. We both love our craft and want to work as much as possible, so we go to any auditions we can.

LIL' C - "KING OF KRUMP"

Lil' C hadn't really begun to maximize his full potential in the dance industry until a little known movie called *Rize* took over theatres. He instantly was recognized as the leader of a popular movement and the creation of a new dance style. His vision for this style of dance called **krump** has catapulted him into a staple of the genre and has inspired other dance styles to infuse some of its rawness as well. He is known as the *"King of Krump"* and with this title and talent to back it up he has created his own brand.

SC: How did you get the name King of Krump?
Lil' C: I didn't have a ceremony; I kind of had to take the crown. And then everyone looked up and was upset and said, *'How dare you wear that crown?'* Sometimes in order to grow or to fund your mission, if part of your mission is to be the mediator or the intercessor between the progression of civilization and cultivation of your village, then you sometimes have to lead your village. Go out and acquire what you must acquire to come back and share your riches with your village so your village can reap the benefits of your journey.

What I had to do was to basically not be so against swimming in the industry and playing the game of politics. A lot of people from urban subculture didn't understand that and would say, *'Oh, Lil' C's Hollywood! Lil' C's this. Lil' C's that,'* because krump is very underground. A lot of people don't agree that I should be taking krump to the forefront or commercializing it or putting it in videos or whatever the case may be. Those people are blithering idiots because things have to grow. In order for things to survive they have to grow and you have to feed them. That's what evolution is. With that being said, people started calling me the King of Krump because I am the only person and the first person who has ever been able to articulate the art in the room.

People can watch dancers all day but everyone is not blessed with the ability to talk to a 70-year-old woman and help her gain comprehensive understanding of what krump is and what those moves are. So that's when people started to call me the King of Krump. I may not be the best dancer, I'm very skilled, trust me. I'm the King of Krump because I have taken this movement and put it on my back and stood in front of the wiles of scrutiny and criticism and been turned away and laughed at. People don't understand that I am the front-runner of the campaign and I receive all the lashings and everything that comes against it just for the sake of the movement. For the sake of getting people to realize and acknowledge it as a relevant and solid genre. Krump is a relevant branch on the tree of dance. No one else is doing that. People don't know how hard it is to get people to respect something that came from the ghetto. B-boying is just finally getting its justice, but only after a thousand documentaries on b-boying. 89,000 guys spinning on their heads and being all about the battle, and being about the art and the elements of hip-hop. Even through all of that it's almost as if they're arguing a new point because there is no front-running, articulate leader or representative for that genre of dance stepping up to the mic. And I am that! **I am the Obama for Krump!** I'm the guy that can get in there and sit on a panel with everyone who is making five times as much money as me and double me in age. I'm the person that can be on the panel with them, but I'm also the cat that can be in the session with the **beastiest** dancers and get my sh*t off! And I'm also a choreographer.

I also learned how to create krump-ography and take a freestyle and figure out a way to teach other dancers how to embody the sole compass of the style and put the moves in a sort of sequential order so that people can learn it and execute it and feel like they are 'Getting Krump.' I can't teach you the emotion but I can damn sure teach you the moves. All of those reasons are why I'm the King of Krump, not because I've got the illest moves or I've done the most videos. That's all fleeting! I'd rather do something that's going to leave more of a relevant mark or more of a permanent indention.

SICK TIP #39:
OH MY BLOG!

Start your own blog. It's free and you are able to control the content, post photos and information about upcoming projects. Draw traffic to your Web site, MySpace or YouTube page by showcasing your talent in your own creative way. Set up your free blog at www.WordPress.com or www.BlogSpot.com.

CHAPTER ELEVEN

THE TWINZ
(NANDY AND MAYA)

Born in Sydney, Australia, you've seen Nandy and Maya in the film *Moulin Rouge* and as part of the Australian cast of *The Lion King*. They have worked for and been mentored by Prince as singers, dancers and choreographers for two and a half years, including performances in the 2007 Super Bowl Half Time Show and a 6-month run at *3121* in Las Vegas, Nev. The Twinz have also appeared on *Good Morning America, the BET Awards, American Idol* and alongside artists such as Rihanna (MTV *Video Music Awards*), Chris Brown (*BET Awards*), actor Terrence Howard ("*Sanctuary*" video) and Matthew McConaughey in the film *Surfer Dude*.

SC: How often do you gals get called to auditions together?
THE TWINZ: About 90% of the time. Sometimes it's for the same role and others it's for twin roles. It's really interesting when we get called in for twin jobs. The room is usually full of other sets of twin girls. It's really crazy. Everyone has a clone, lol.

SC: What is it like auditioning together? Is it often that one of you is kept or books the job and the other does not? How often are you booked together?
THE TWINZ: Auditioning as twins can be a plus because it helps you stand out in a crowd. Casting agents can and have rewritten roles so they can use both of us and we both book the job. On the other hand, occasionally when we are auditioning for the same role, we feel that sometimes they cast someone that isn't a twin because they can't choose between us. So that can work against us, but if we both aren't seen we'll never know. Gotta be in it to win it.

SC: Any tips you have for dancers, siblings or twins on how to market oneself as a brand?
THE TWINZ: We have headshots together and separate so we can give the casting director either or. As we are singers it is important to brand and market ourselves correctly. First you need to know what product you are selling and what fan base you are marketing to (age group etc.) and start from there. It's important also to have great representation and professionals around you that believe in the product and can advise and guide you in the right direction.

SC: Any tips you have for dancers, siblings or twins on how to market oneself as a brand?
THE TWINZ: We have headshots together and separate so we can give the casting director either or. It is important to brand and market ourselves correctly. First you need to know what product you are selling and what fan base you are marketing to (age group etc.) and start from there. It's important also to have great representation and professionals around you that believe in the product and can advise and guide you in the right direction.

SC: It's hard to have lives that are separate from your work, do you get a chance just to be family?
THE TWINZ: Since we work together, and are sisters, we are together a lot of the time, work and play. We are really close, so we don't really look at our life in parts. We just live and function really smoothly from one to the other.

SC: Has either one of you ever felt burned out by the industry and felt obligated to continue in order to support the other if called to an audition that was for both of you?
THE TWINZ: Well, we are very fortunate that we are both just as driven as the other. Of course, there are times when one isn't feeling well or sick and is unable to function for a time, but we have each other's back and work it out accordingly.

ONLINE CASTING SERVICES

Some of the best marketing you can do for yourself is to make sure that your pictures are online and represent what you look like today. It doesn't matter how fond you were of how you looked last year it matters that you represent on casting Web sites what you look like today. The next few resources could help you land your next job. Make sure to put your best foot forward and keep your information and pictures updated.

L.A. CASTING
www.LACasting.com

L.A. Casting is an online database for both you and your agent to submit you for different projects. Keep your headshot updated online but be careful about the costs associated with the site. Update your resume online and add your demo reel also. Only update your reel when you have specific <u>new</u> demo reel footage to avoid any additional costs. Multiple links to marketing tools such as address labels for casting directors, agents and managers are available. Check out **sides** posted online as well. Even if you are not up for a part in a commercial, television series or film, familiarize yourself with how sides are generally formatted. Print some out and try your hand at cold reading.

CHAPTER ELEVEN

Hollywood
Crossroads of the World
6671 Sunset Boulevard, Suite 1511
Los Angeles, CA 90028
(323) 462-8200 Phone
(323) 462-8131 Fax

In the Valley
Beverly Long Studios
11425 Moorpark Street
Studio City, CA 91602

West Los Angeles
310 Casting Studios
2329 Purdue Avenue
Los Angeles, CA 90064

Los Angeles
200 South La Brea Boulevard
Los Angeles, CA 90036

Other cities have this service such as:
San Francisco Casting   **New York Casting**
www.SFCasting.com   www.NYCasting.com

> *Although it might be great to have your information and pictures listed on multiple sites, be realistic about where you are focusing your career efforts. Don't waste your time posting in cities you will never be able to travel to for work!*

ACTORS ACCESS
www.ActorsAccess.com

Actors Access is an online site that lets you have a free account where you and your agent are able to submit your profile for posted jobs. Not all projects are posted online and you will not always see every project that is available to your agent or to managers. You will either need to pay per project you submit yourself to or you can become a member of Breakdown Services and pay a yearly fee to be able to submit yourself on an unlimited number of projects.

BREAKDOWN SERVICES
www.BreakdownExpress.com

Breakdown Services provides sides for upcoming projects including commercials, television shows and films. If you are submitted by your agent or manager for a project and are asked to read for a part or know a jingle as part of a commercial audition, your agent or manager is able to print out the sides for you to learn from this Web site. If you are a member of Breakdown Services, you will be able to look at sides already listed online and be able to print them out yourself. Not all sides are listed on Breakdown Services. Casting directors choose what sort of access they want project sides to have and this determines if you are given access or not. You can sign up for $90/year for unlimited projects submissions or submit on a per submission basis and pay a fee each time. Fees may change.

Main Office	Exclusive Casting Studios	On Your Mark
2140 Cotner Avenue	7700 Sunset Boulevard	13425 Ventura Boulevard
Los Angeles, CA 90025	1st Floor	2nd Floor
(310) 276-9166 Phone	Los Angeles, CA 90046	Sherman Oaks, CA 91423

IMDB: Internet Movie Database
www.IMDB.com

IMDB is a great source of information. You can post your resume online and update your information regarding television shows and films in which you appear in online. IMDB lists project budgets, films and television shows in production as well as lists of agents, managers, casting directors and so much more. This Web site is a never-ending tool that can help you be in the know and locate some of the heavy hitters in Hollywood.

Casting Frontier
www.CastingFrontier.com

The Casting Frontier is an online site that links your uploaded profile with contact and agency information to your live audition. You will be asked to bring a bar code with you. Most casting facilities that use this service also have computer work stations for you to access your account and print out a bar code if you've forgotten to bring yours. Keep your bar code printed on the back of a grocery store rewards card on your key chain to make things easier on the session director. The basic profile is free and you can upgrade to other packages if you'd like to customize your profile even more. Keep your profile as current as possible.

Showfax
www.ShowFax.com

Create an account to access sides for films and television shows. Stay up to date with all of the current projects listed for a low yearly membership fee of $68 *(This price may change after the printing of this book).*

BOOK ME! WORKBOOK EXERCISES - PART 3

Some **BOOK ME! Workbook** exercise topics from Part Three of this book are listed below. Purchase the **BOOK ME! Workbook** online at:
www.ColtonCollection.com

- Diagnose your skin type and create your daily skin regimen.
- Outline a plan to market your perfect brand identity and sell it!
- Create a list of key contacts that can influence your career path.
- Free yourself from cookie cutter stereotypes - Invent the new you!

CHAPTER ELEVEN

Sandra says...

- Your name is the most important tool in the marketing game. Make it memorable, even if you need an alias.

- Your e-mail and personal Web site are the gateway to the world. Don't change your e-mail all the time. Keep the same account or people won't be able to find you.

- Make a contact list to send out announcements, postcards, headshots and invitations to your gigs.

- Create your own brand.

- Get your name out to casting directors, agents and choreographers. The best thing you can be is busy and the more your name comes across their desk, the better.

- Don't be annoying! If someone asks to be taken off your list, promptly remove them.

> ### POINT TAKEN:
> Last night a postcard saved my life. It was a test run for my latest and greatest mailing blast out to all of my contacts. The test run is my version of simply mailing it to myself to see how long it takes to arrive. I like to make sure that it goes out in a timely manner. Make your contact list and start informing the world of what you've got going on.

PART FOUR

CONTRACTS: YOUR RIGHTS, RATES, RESIDUALS & ROYALTIES

CHAPTER TWELVE

IF YOU DON'T VALUE YOURSELF, YOU BECOME VALUELESS!

The entertainment industry is always in flux. We have an ebb and flow cycle. In the Writers' Strike of 2007-2008, union members from AFTRA and SAG (prior to merger) participated by not taking jobs and joined the picket lines with writers. It is important to know how unions help you and how the benefits of being part of the union outweigh not being involved. Many jobs that dancers are employed to do are non-union (i.e. industrials, music videos and tours.) Below is information on performer unions that represent dancers on jobs covered by their jurisdiction.

UNIONS

It is important to know the value and importance of performer unions in Hollywood. Unions work for and with members to negotiate and enhance contracts for performers. For contact information for the unions listed below, see the Appendix C.

PERFORMING ARTS UNIONS
AEA (Actors' Equity)
SAG/AFTRA: stands for (Screen Actors Guild)
& (American Federation of Television and Radio Artists)
AGMA (American Guild of Musical Artists)
AGVA (American Guild of Variety Artists)

SAG/AFTRA is the union who will represent you on television and film projects once you become a member. For more information on AGVA, AGMA and Actors' Equity contracts, please contact each directly. **SAG/AFTRA merged 3/30/2012.**

CHAPTER TWELVE

1 Union is the effort that helped to merge SAG and AFTRA.

WHAT IS SAG/AFTRA?

"SAG-AFTRA brings together two great American labor unions: Screen Actors Guild and the American Federation of Television and Radio Artists. Both were formed in the turmoil of the 1930s, with rich histories of fighting for and securing the strongest protections for media artists. Our members united to form the successor union in order to preserve those hard-won rights and to continue the struggle to extend and expand those protections into the 21st century and beyond.

We are actors, announcers, broadcast journalists, dancers, dj's, news writers, news directors, program hosts, puppeteers, recording artists, singers, stunt performers, voiceover artists and other media professionals. Our work is seen and heard in theaters, on television and radio, sound recordings, the internet, games, mobile devices, home video: you see us and hear us on all media distribution platforms. We are the faces and the voices that entertain and inform America and the world. SAG-AFTRA is committed to organizing all work done under our jurisdictions; negotiating the best wages, working conditions, and health and pension benefits; preserving and expanding members' work opportunities; vigorously enforcing our contracts; and protecting members against unauthorized use of their work.

A proud member of the AFL-CIO, SAG-AFTRA partners with our fellow unions in the U.S. and internationally to seek the strongest protections for media artists throughout the world. We work with governments at the international, federal, state, and local levels to expand protections for American media professionals both at home and abroad.

It is a core value of SAG-AFTRA that our strength is in our diversity. We are committed to the broadest employment and involvement of our members, regardless of gender, race, age, religious beliefs, disability, nationality, and sexual orientation or identification. SAG-AFTRA strives to educate and engage members so that they may be full participants in the workings of their union. We are proud to be a model of inclusion, democratic organization and governance." (www.sagaftra.org)

IF YOU DON'T VALUE YOURSELF, YOU BECOME VALUELESS!

> *Interviews Prior to SAG/AFTRA merger with Glen Hiraoka, National Director, Dancers Department for SAG and Chris De Haan, Communication Director for AFTRA, the following statements regarding SAG and AFTRA give great insight into the respective unions.*

JOINING THE UNIONS

MEMBERSHIP ELIGIBILITY FOR JOINING SAG/AFTRA

"A performer becomes eligible for SAG-AFTRA membership under one of the following two conditions: (1) proof of SAG or AFTRA employment or (2) employment under an affiliated performers' union." (www.sagaftra.org)

EMPLOYMENT UNDER AN AFFILIATED PERFORMERS' UNION

"Performers may join SAG if the applicant is a paid-up member of an affiliated performers' union (ACTRA, AEA, AGMA or AGVA) for a period of one year and has worked and been paid for at least once as a principal performer in that union's jurisdiction." (www.SAGAFTRA.org/content/steps-join)

UNION INITIATION FEES AND DUES

SAG/AFTRA

    Initiation Fee $3,000.00
    Annual Basic Dues $ 198.00
    Work Dues are calculated at 1.575% of covered earnings up to $500,000.

The current initiation fees for SAG/AFTRA are listed above and are subject to change if an increase is passed after the publication of this book.

SICK TIP #40:
PAY ON TIME OR INCUR THE COST

SAG does not deduct their initiation fee from your first paycheck. If you work a job that requires you to pay the initiation fee, they will not allow you on set until this is paid. AFTRA will allow you to work a job but will deduct your initiation fee from your paycheck from that job if you initial consent/permission to do so when applying.

CHAPTER TWELVE

SUSPENDING YOUR MEMBERSHIP

Union dues for Screen Actors Guild and the American Federation of Television and Radio Artists may be placed on hold if you foresee an extended time period where you will not be performing a union job. For example, your membership may be placed on hold if you go on tour with a recording artist for one year's time. Be diligent in placing this request so that you do not suffer the consequences of paying dues late and incurring fees that ultimately may revoke your membership and force you to start all over again.

SAG/AFTRA
Membership Services Department
5757 Wilshire Boulevard
Los Angeles, CA 90036
(323) 549-6757 Phone

CONTRACTS

As a dancer many times people in entertainment expect you to be shall we say, a bit dense. Yes, people also at the same time expect you to be extraordinary at your craft. There is a delicate balance between asking someone to go to their mark and acknowledging that they have the wherewithal to know what and where that is. As mentioned earlier in the section on key terms for dancers on set, it is a good idea to know what your contract says and make sure your rate is included prior to signing anything. Typically the less people hired for a project means there is generally more money for you to earn. On your contract you may be categorized as a principal, solo, duo or group. Groups may be Group 3-5, Group 6-8 or Group 9+ (which means 9 people or more).

IMPORTANT DISTINCTIONS FOR CATEGORIZING YOUR STATUS

SAG/AFTRA - DEFINITION OF A DANCER

"A professional dancer is a person who is employed primarily to dance either as a solo, or in a group, including both swimmers and skaters when the performance is choreographed. Non-professional dancing, such as by extras, is excluded from this definition. A professional dancer is herein referred to as a Dancer." (sagaftra.org)

FAQ: WHAT IS THE DIFFERENCE BETWEEN A PRINCIPAL AND BACKGROUND PERFORMER?

A **background performer** or an **extra** is a performer who is usually seen on television, film, stage show, etc. in a non-speaking, non-dancing and non-singing role that is normally in the background.

IF YOU DON'T VALUE YOURSELF, YOU BECOME VALUELESS!

A **principal performer** is quite the opposite appearing on screen in a speaking, singing, dancing or special skill capacity.

BACKGROUND VS. PRINCIPAL CONTRACT ISSUES

It is very important that you know the difference from working as a **background dancer** and as a **principal dancer**. When cast as a background dancer you are not to be doing any sort of choreography. If you feel as though you are being featured or asked to do choreography then you will need to talk with a union representative in order to solve the discrepancy. Some situations involve the appearance of being featured but the resulting footage of the project does not reveal you in a featured role. Contact a union representative if you feel as though you should be bumped to a principal role and they will address your concerns from there. Background dancers are essentially paid to perform dance moves that are considered "normal" or "pedestrian" movement. These are the average dance moves you would see at any nightclub or social dance experience such as a wedding or high school prom.

> *The next section is specific to union information. First is information about SAG followed by information about AFTRA and concludes with information about a non-union organization called Dancers' Alliance.) This interview was conducted prior to the SAG/AFTRA merger.*

SAG – GLENN HIRAOKA
NATIONAL DIRECTOR, DANCERS DEPARTMENT

INFORMATION FOR DANCERS WORKING UNDER A SCREEN ACTORS GUILD CONTRACT

"The information contained below is a brief summary. Always contact your local SAG branch office for the full information and the full language of the respective SAG collective bargaining contract for films, television, commercials, industrials, music videos, video games, interactive, etc. The telephone number for the **National Dancers Department** is (323) 549-6864, or for emergencies/after business hours, you may contact the National SAG Offices at (323) 554-1600.

"As of this printing date, the language (of the contract) may change, and new rates may be established. Please contact the SAG Dancers Department for the latest contract information, or check the SAG Web site (www.SAG.org)."

CHAPTER TWELVE

GLENN HIRAOKA DESCRIBES KEY SAG TOPICS

ONLINE ACCESS TO MEMBER EDUCATION, EVENTS AND CONTRACT NEGOTIATION UPDATES

"The Guild's Web site (www.SAG.org,) contains invaluable information for members. If you are interested in the latest information on contract negotiations, SAG events, official press releases, contract information for members, lost residual information, messages from the SAG President, the SAG National Executive Director, contract rates and other dancing conditions in the *SAG Dancers Handbook*, or the *Safety Bulletins* for working in productions, then be sure to check the SAG Web site.

THE ROLE OF THE GUILD AND THE DANCERS DEPARTMENT

"The role of the Guild is to negotiate terms and conditions with producers affecting dancers and other performer groups under the various Guild's collective bargaining contracts (i.e. film, television, commercials, industrials, etc.) The SAG Dancers Department enforces these conditions should a producer fail to properly pay the dancers, work the dancers under less than the required conditions or violate other provisions of the collective bargaining agreements.

ACTIVE UNION PARTICIPATION

"The Guild has a **SAG National Dancers Committee** that reviews issues and concerns that impact dancers on a local and national basis. In the course of identifying these issues, proposals may be developed for the collective bargaining negotiation process, and/or the Guild's staff assists the committee to find solutions to these problems.

"The **SAG/AFTRA National Dancers Committee** is composed of appointed members in good standing with the Guild. There are three divisions of the committee: Hollywood, New York and the Regional Branch Division. The latter division covers branch areas outside of Hollywood and New York. Members interested in volunteering for the divisional committees should contact the respective Chair person. You may contact the National Dancers Department (323) 549-6864 for further information. Additionally, in Hollywood, members and non-members should contact the Dancers Department for the dates of dancer caucus meetings held throughout the year. These meetings will help you connect with other professional dancers in the community, and useful educational information is always provided.

IF YOU DON'T VALUE YOURSELF, YOU BECOME VALUELESS!

ON SET UNION REPRESENTATION

"The Guild's structure is divided administratively into different areas of specialty. For example, a listing of some of the departments at the Guild would be: Membership, Residuals, Legal, Agency, Affirmative Action/Diversity, SAG Independent Films, Research and Contracts. The Contracts division includes multiple smaller departments that oversee various areas of the collective bargaining agreements. For example, Theatrical, TV, Commercials and Industrials, Background and a department for performers groups called **Stunts, Singers, Dancers and Safety**. The latter department also handles music videos. As noted above, the business representatives receive calls regarding contract enforcement, filing claims for violations, and assisting dancers and agents with any questions.

"Should a problem occur on the set with dancers or other performers, the Guild may need to send a field representative to the set for assistance. This can be done on an anonymous basis without placing the caller in an awkward situation on set. A performer may contact the Dancers Department in Hollywood at (323) 549-6864, or for after-business hour emergencies, please contact (323) 954-1600. For assistance in other areas outside of Hollywood, please contact your local SAG branch office.

RULE ONE AND GLOBAL RULE ONE

"The Guild's **Rule One** for members requires members to work for a production that is a current signatory. Failure to abide by Rule One may subject a member to a discipline proceeding, and can result in a fine or other penalties up to and including to a loss of membership. With respect to **Global Rule One**, a policy has been developed by the Guild for members working in a foreign country for a foreign production company. This policy requires that a member must work only for a company that is a current signatory to Screen Actors Guild. A member should contact the Guild for further information before working in a production, and in determining how Global Rule One applies. You may check the signatory status by contacting the Guild at (800) SAG-0767.

"As each situation may be different, we urge you to contact the Guild to ensure that you know the specific rules governing your work and whether an exception may apply. The Dancers Department can direct you to the specific contracts department that may help you clarify whether Global Rule One applies, and whether the production is currently signed to a SAG contract."

CHAPTER TWELVE

NO STRIKE CLAUSE IN THE SAG COLLECTIVE BARGAINING AGREEMENTS

"A no-strike clause in the SAG collective bargaining agreements requires a performer to continue their work obligations for a producer in a situation where another union has conducted a strike due to a contract dispute or with its contract negotiations. As this is a very complex area, the performer should immediately contact the Guild to find out the specific rules that would apply in this situation. If Screen Actors Guild conducts a strike due to contract negotiations, then a member's obligation is to honor the strike order and not work for that company. For example, if the Guild conducted a strike under the SAG Commercials Contract, then a member is responsible to not work for a SAG signatory producer to the Commercials Contract. However, a member can work in a SAG theatrical or television production as the SAG strike order is limited to work only in commercial productions. As this area is extremely complex, members should always contact the Guild to ensure that they have the proper clearance when working in these situations.

INFORMATION REGARDING TYPES OF COMMERCIAL WORK

"The Commercials Contract requires the producer to provide auditioning performers with information on the intended use of the commercial. This is important as it allows the agent and the performer to have an understanding of a possible commercial use (i.e. broadcast television, dealer, wild spot, cable, new media, etc.) and allows the agent and performer to estimate the possible residual monies that can be generated for the commercial. In addition, although the producer has the (obligation) to inform the auditioning performer of the pay rate, other terms and conditions, the performer does not have to accept these terms and has the right to audition and negotiate for better terms and conditions.

COMMERCIAL AUDITIONS AND OVERTIME

"For first and second commercial auditions, the audition language under a SAG contract allows the producer and the casting director to hold the performer for one hour from the call time without going into overtime payments. No payment is due for the first two hours at the third and fourth audition provided that no more than 3 performers are being auditioned per role. If more than three performers are being auditioned then the producer is required to make a minimum payment of \$148.10 for the first two hours and \$37.00 for each additional $\frac{1}{2}$ hour beyond the first two hours. For fourth auditions, the minimum payment is \$296.10 for four hours, with additional payments of \$37.00 for each additional $\frac{1}{2}$ hour beyond the first four hours. *(Due to recent commercials negotiations, this area is subject to change)*."

IF YOU DON'T VALUE YOURSELF, YOU BECOME VALUELESS!

AVAILABILITY VS. HOLD

"Commercial casting directors usually have performers on **"avails"** or availabilities during the audition process. This is considered a professional courtesy for performers and is not considered an engagement. A performer that has a conflicting work schedule that would interfere with the commercial audition call, should notify the casting director. This advance notice will help the casting director make any needed adjustments in the audition process. On the other hand, if a performer is placed on a **"hold"** or given information signifying a firm engagement or booking under the SAG Commercials Contract, then the performer is booked for the engagement. There are certain exceptions to this rule and a performer should contact the SAG Dancers Department for further information.

SIGNING A COMMERCIAL CONTRACT EMPLOYMENT FORM

"A commercial producer is required to give to the performer a written contract within a reasonable time prior to the production. When a performer receives the employment contract, he/she has the right to contact his/her agent or the Guild before signing the document. If the performer is unsure on the contract language, the performer may discuss it with his/her agent or the Guild. In addition, the producer cannot give the performer a blank contract, and the terms and conditions on the standard employment contract form must be completed.

PAYMENTS & OVERTIME CALCULATIONS FOR WORK PERFORMED

"Generally, the commercial session fee covers the work performed during the commercial session. The scale minimum payment rate is for 8-hours of work. Excluding meal periods, the performer receives time and one-half payment for working beyond 8-hours, (i.e. the 9th and 10th hour of work.) For work hours that exceed the 10th hour, a performer would receive double-time payments until dismissal. For work under the TV and Theatrical Contracts, the performer should check the formulas used for day and weekly contract performers."

TIME OF PAYMENT
- **Session Fees** – 12 working days after services rendered.
- **Holding Fees** – The first day of the fixed cycle.
- **Wild Spots** – Residual payments due 15 working days after commencement of a use cycle. Upgrade adjustments under wild spot formula are due 15 working days after the end of use cycle.
- **Local Program** – 15 working days after commencement of a use cycle.
- **Class A Program** – Payment for all Class A program uses that occur within a single week from Monday through Sunday will be made not later than 15 working days after the end of such week.
- **Cable Fees** – Residual payment must be made within 15 working days from commencement of a cable cycle.
- **Internet Fees** – Residual payment must be made within 15 working days from commencement of each period of Internet use." (www.SAG.org)

"Compensation: Subject to performer's consent, an amount not less than an additional session fee is paid for the 8-week cycle use. For use beyond the initial 8-week cycle, the performer shall be paid an additional 300% of the applicable session fee for one additional year's use." (www.SAG.org)

WHAT ARE RESIDUALS?

"Residuals are compensation paid to performers for use of a motion picture or television program after its initial use. For TV work, residuals begin once a show starts re-airing or is released to video/DVD, pay television, broadcast TV or basic cable. For film work, residuals begin once the movie appears on video/DVD, basic cable and free or pay television. Residuals are based on formulas that take into account such things as the contract in place during the specific year, time spent on the production, the production type and the market where the product appears (TV, video/DVD, pay television, basic cable). All performers hired under or upgraded to a principal performer agreement whose performance remains in the final product. This includes performers, professional singers, stunt performers, stunt coordinators, pilots, dancers employed under Schedule J and puppeteers. Background actors do not receive them – unless they are upgraded to principal performers. Initial compensation covers a project's preliminary release for the market in which it was produced. Residuals are due only for re-use of a production (except for the rare re-release into the theatres)." (www.sagaftra.org)

PAYMENT SCHEDULES FOR RESIDUALS

"**Made-For-Television** then released to:
- Network Prime Time - 30 days after air date.
- Non-Prime Time - 30 days after air date.
- Syndication - 4 months after air date.
- Foreign Free TV - No later than 30 days after producer obtains knowledge of the first foreign telecast and never later than six months after that first telecast.
- Basic Cable - Quarterly.

Made-for-Theatrical then released to:
- Network Prime Time - 30 days after initial broadcast, then quarterly.
- Free TV, Non-Network - 4 months after initial broadcast, then quarterly.
- Supplemental Markets - 4 months after initial exhibition, then quarterly."
(www.sagaftra.org)

IF YOU DON'T VALUE YOURSELF, YOU BECOME VALUELESS!

FAQ: WHAT ARE "DEALER A" AND "DEALER B" COMMERCIALS?

GH: The producer or casting director must inform the performer at the time of the audition (or at the booking if there is not an audition) whether a commercial will air as a **dealer commercial**. This will assist the agent and the performer to have full information with respect to the payment structure under the SAG Commercials Contract, and the period for payment and use (i.e. 6-month intervals instead of 3-month or 13 week cycles). With this information, the performer can determine whether they wish to interview or book the commercial.

COMMONALITIES IN "DEALER A" AND "DEALER B" COMMERCIALS

"Generally, both types of 'Dealer A' and 'Dealer B' commercials are made and paid for by a large manufacturer, and distributed to a local company (dealer or dealer association in Type A, or local retail stores or service outlet in Type B) for purchasing commercial time. The commercials are usually delivered to either dealers or local retail store chains for telecasting. The 6-month payment and use is made as the manufacturer has less control over the use, and has delegated the decisions to the dealer or local retail store chains.

DIFFERENCES IN "DEALER A" AND "DEALER B" COMMERCIALS

"In Dealer A, the commercial is delivered by the manufacturer or distributor of a product to a local dealer or dealer association for telecasting. The manufacturer or distributor does not have a 'substantial ownership interest or control' in the dealer. The rates for an on-camera solo dancer is currently $2,128.15 for use in New York (the rates for group dancers are proportionately less.) Under Dealer B, the commercial is delivered to a chain of local retail stores or retail outlets that are owned and operated by the national manufacturer or distributor, either directly, or through a subsidiary company. The dealer rates for an on-camera solo dancer is currently $3,272.15 for use in New York (the rates for group dancers are proportionately less).

DEALER A

"As noted above, the Dealer A commercial is made and played by the manufacturer or distributor and delivered to a local dealer or dealer association for telecasting. An example of a local dealer is illustrated with a Ford commercial. **Example:** A Ford car commercial is produced by the Ford Motor Company and the company is a national manufacturer. The commercial will be made and paid for by Ford. After the commercial is produced and edited as a Dealer A, it will be given to a local dealer association, (i.e. the Southern California Ford Dealer Association) for telecasting."

CHAPTER TWELVE

"The SAG Commercials Contract signatory-advertising agency will pay the performer a flat minimum fee (as defined in the SAG Commercials Contract) every six months for the use of the commercial. In effect, the SAG signatory is using the commercial as a wild spot or a Class B or C program use, but with a specific rate amount for six months of telecasting. The dealer or dealer association is permitted to use the Ford commercial in this restricted manner. Other types of residual payments may be required under the SAG Contract when using the commercial beyond the scope of a dealer commercial.

"The key phrase for a Dealer A commercial is defined as 'an independent company which offers a producer or service for sale to the public at retail which the company manufactures though a distributor has no substantial ownership interest or control.' In the Ford example, the car manufacturer produces the commercial for the Southern California Association of Ford Dealers. Ford does not have substantial ownership control of the dealer and/or the dealer association and the commercial would be classified as a Dealer Type A commercial.

DEALER B

"As described earlier, a Dealer Type B commercial is made and paid for by a national manufacturer or distributor and delivered to a chain of local retail stores or retail outlets owned and operated by the manufacturer or distributor. **Example:** Macy's is a part of a local retail store chain that is owned and operated by a parent company. The commercial is made and paid for by the parent company who then delivers the commercial to the local retail store chain for telecasting. Dealer Type B commercial residual payments would be paid to a principal dancer (solo, duo or group dancers) for the six-month telecasting."

CANCELLED ENGAGEMENTS

"The performer (Day, 3-Day TV, Weekly) has a firm engagement, which binds the studio in the following cases: "Written notice of acceptance:
  • Contract signed by the producer.
  • Script is given to the performer, with intent to hire.
  • When performer is fitted, other than wardrobe tests.
  • When performer is actually called and agrees to report.
"Day performers only: Either party can cancel prior to 12 p.m. on the day before the *'day performer'* is to work if the call for work has only been verbal and none of the above conditions have occurred. 'On or about' start dates are not permitted for day performers." (www.SAG.org)

IF YOU DON'T VALUE YOURSELF, YOU BECOME VALUELESS!

GLENN HIRAOKA ON DANCERS WORKING CONDITIONS IN FILM, TV AND COMMERCIALS

"As noted earlier, the Guild is extremely concerned for the well-being of all performers, and should any safety or emergency issues arise during work hours, members are urged to contact the Guild at (323) 549-6864. Members can also contact the Guild after hours and weekends at (323) 954-1600. For work in other parts of the country outside of Hollywood, please contact the local SAG branch office. The SAG TV/Theatrical and the Commercials Contracts contain requirements for certain working conditions for dancers with respect to dance floor conditions, warm-up spaces, breaks, stage and rehearsal room temperatures, meal periods, emergency treatment and compensation bumps for working under hazardous conditions as defined in the collective bargaining agreement. These workings conditions are located on the following pages. Please ensure that you contact the SAG Dancers Department for any questions.

"Under the SAG Commercials Contract, (and with the addition to the TV/Theatrical Contract), dancing on asphalt and other hard surfaces is included as a hazard condition, and a dancer would receive an additional adjusted payment. For work in smoke, the producer is required to inform the performer in advance, post or provide the list of elements contained in the artificially-produced smoke. The elements of the smoke are contained in the **Material Safety Data Sheet** (**MSDS**). If the dancer is not notified of the artificially-created smoke, then the dancer has the right to refuse to perform under these conditions, and receive his/her session fee, or part of the session fee payment, depending on whether the dancer is working under the Commercials Contract, or the TV/Theatrical Contract. In addition, the set must be periodically ventilated, and the dancer may stay away in a smoke-free environment at appropriate intervals while working in a TV or Theatrical production.

INDUSTRY-WIDE LABOR MANAGEMENT SAFETY COMMITTEE
"*Safety Bulletins* have been developed by the **Industry-Wide Labor Management Safety Committee**. This committee is composed of safety personnel from the above and below line entertainment unions, and safety representatives from studio and production companies associated with the Alliance of Motion Picture and Television Producers (the AMPTP). The committee meets once a month to review and update safety guidelines for the Industry, to create new safety guidelines, and to review any safety issue or problem that may have occurred in the produc-

CHAPTER TWELVE

tion of films, television and/or commercials production. These guidelines are recommendations to be used within the Industry, and can be located on the SAG Web site www.SAG.org or at www.CSATF.org."

This next sections are portions of the 2009-2012 Commercials Contract and 2011-2014 TV/Theatrical Contracts Provisions for Dancers contracted for SAG projects. Please pay special attention to these and know what your rights are when going to do a project under SAG jurisdiction. Rates may change, but your rights are there to protect you. Contact your union representative with questions.

DANCER'S PROVISIONS UNDER THE 2013-2016 SAG COMMERCIALS CONTRACT STATES THE FOLLOWING:

FF. Dancers

1. Definition — Dancers
The term "dancers" shall be deemed to include both swimmers and skaters when the performance of the latter two is choreographed.

2. Working Conditions
*(a) **Standard Floors** – Floors for choreographed dancers must be resilient, flexible and level in accordance with industry standards. Industry standards generally provide for 2" of air space beneath wood flooring or 3" or 4" of padding under battleship linoleum laid over a concrete or wood-on-concrete floor. Floor surface must be clean and free of splinters, wax, nails, etc. Floors should be swept and mopped at least daily with a germ-killing solution. If Producer requires dancing on surfaces which do not meet the foregoing general standards, such work shall be deemed to be "hazardous work" and shall be subject to all the provisions of this Contract concerning hazardous work and performers' safety. In all instances, dancing on concrete, raked stages; elevated platforms or staircases or performing knee work shall be deemed to be "hazardous work" and shall be subject to all the provisions of this Contract concerning hazardous work and performers' safety. As used herein, "knee work" means dancing, sliding or doing a routine on the knees and includes rolling, spinning, falling, balancing, hinging, walking, turning and/or performing a choreographed routine in which the knee comes in contact with the surface, e.g., floor, sidewalk, etc. Dancers will not be required to do knee work without knee pads.*

(b) In the event that dancers will be required to perform on a non-standard surface, notification of such shall be given at the time of audition and engagement.

*(c) **Unusual Work Conditions** – If Producer requires dancing on slippery surfaces, dancing in inclement weather or out-of-season clothing or in costuming by virtue of its fit or nature may subject the dancer to physical injury or health hazard, it shall be deemed to be "hazardous work" and shall be subject to all the provisions of this Contract concerning hazardous work and performers' safety.*

*(d) **General Work Conditions***
*(i) **Warm-up Spaces** – Adequate space must be provided to permit all dancers to warm up (perform limbering exercises) 30 minutes prior to dancing.*

(ii) Breaks – Dancers/Swimmers/Skaters will have at least fifteen (15) minutes rest during each hour of actual rehearsal or shooting unless rehearsal or shooting is of a continuous nature. If so, at the choreographer's discretion, dancers/swimmers/skaters may continue until a total of ninety (90) minutes have elapsed after which time a thirty (30) minute break must be called. If in the opinion of performers or their representatives (e.g., on-site deputy, captain or assistant choreographer, or union representative), continued full-out performance of choreographed dancing/swimming/skating creates a risk of injury, such performers shall not be required to continue performing at full performance level during rehearsal. Examples of such choreography include repetitive lifts, throws, catches and falls.

(iii) Temperature – Stage or rehearsal area temperature for choreographed dancers must not fall below 75 degrees. Air ventilation (circulation) shall be provided at all times but air conditioning is not acceptable unless strictly regulated to prevent drafts.

(iv) Meal Periods – Dancers cannot be required to dance or skate within 30 minutes following a meal. If a producer does not provide meal service and dancers must leave the premises or location to eat, an additional 15 minutes must be allowed both before and after the meal break to permit the dancer to change clothes.

(v) Emergency Treatment – Producer will use its best efforts to have a doctor qualified to treat dancers on call in case of an emergency and will notify the deputy elected by dancers of his/her name and phone number.

(vi) Hazard Pay – The compensation payable to a dancer for hazardous activity shall be $105.40 per day, with a minimum of $162.15 if only one day's services are rendered. **

(vii) It shall be deemed hazardous work when a dancer is required to do any of the following:
• perform complex aerial acrobatics; • perform wire flying; • perform knee work;
• support more than one other person in any manner which affects safe performance of the dance routine;
• dance under conditions where safe performance of the dance routine is affected because sight or breathing is impaired (e.g., by use of a mask or presence of fog, smoke or fire).

(viii) Footwear – Footwear provided by the Producer shall be appropriate to the work and shall be lean, properly fitted, braced and rubbered.

(ix) Any dancer who is directed to and reports with his or her own footwear shall be paid an allowance of $11.30 per day for each pair of shoes utilized in the performance. **

(x) Producer shall exercise care, including prior testing of equipment (breakaway props, etc.) during rehearsal, to avoid injury to the performer.

3. Pension and Health
If a dancer has had earnings in five (5) prior years in SAG, and is employed to work on a commercial as a choreographer, but not as a dancer or in any other category covered by the contract, the Producer shall contribute to the SAG P&H Plan on the choreographer's behalf on the basis of the minimum session fee for principal performers set forth in Section 20.A of this Agreement.

**Rates are from the 2009-2012 Commercials Contract and may increase when they expire if not extended on March 31, 2012.

DANCER'S PROVISIONS UNDER THE 2011-2014 SAG TV/THEATRICAL CONTRACT – SCHEDULE J:

1. Scope of Coverage
This Schedule J shall be applicable only to persons employed as "dancers," as that term is hereinafter defined.

2. Definition
A "dancer" is a performer who is professionally-trained, doing choreographed routines requiring rehearsals, such as ballet, chorus dancing, modern dance, tap dancing, jazz dancing, acrobatic dancing or skating. Exhibition level dancing is also included. Persons engaged to execute the choreographer's dance directions during the development of dance routines of the nature described above are dancers within the meaning of this Schedule, whether or not such persons are photographed in the production.

4. Applicable Provisions of Codified Basic Agreement & Other Schedules
All General Provisions of this Agreement and all of the provisions of the Schedule Applicable to the dancer's employment (e.g., Schedule A for dancers employed by the day; Schedule B, C or F for Dancers employed by the week, etc.), except consecutive employment, shall apply to dancers.

5. Consecutive Employment Not Applicable
The provisions in other Schedules relating to consecutive employment shall not apply to dancers.

6. General Conditions Of Employment
The following shall apply to dancers if they are employed under this Schedule:

A. "Dancers" shall include swimmers and skaters when the performance is choreographed.

B. The compensations payable to a dancer for a hazardous activity shall be $100 per day, with a minimum of $125 if only on (1) day's services is rendered. "Wire flying" shall in all instances be considered "hazardous." In addition, the parties agree that, under certain circumstances, the following work could meet the definition of "hazardous activity:"
1. knee work, including rolling, spinning, falling, balancing, hinging, walking, turning and/or performing a choreographed routine on the knees;
2. performing complex aerial acrobatics;
3. dancing on slippery surfaces (other than ordinary dance floors);
4. when the dancer is required to support more than one other person in any manner which affects safe performance of the dance routine; or
5. dancing under conditions where safe performance of the dance routine is affected because sight or breathing is impaired (e.g., by use of a mask or presence of fog, smoke or fire).
6. dancing on stony and hard surfaces, such as, but not limited to, concrete, asphalt, gravel, marble, tile or sand, as well as dancing on raked stages, elevated platforms and staircases.

A Committee of Union and Producer representatives shall be appointed to develop standards for determining when a floor will be considered 'slippery.'

C. Footwear provided by the Producer shall be appropriate to the work and shall be clean, properly fitted, braced and rubbered. Any dancer who is directed to and reports with his or her own footwear shall be paid an allowance of $10.80 per day for each pair of shoes utilized in the performance.

D. Industry standards for dancers include adequate warm-up area, surfaces free and clean of debris and materials, adequate rest period, and other such precautions as may be necessary to ensure the health and safety of the dancers in light of the nature of the work performed.

1. Floors for Rehearsal Halls and Stages Except when conditions are otherwise required for a scene:
(a) Surfaces should be clean and free of splinters, wax, nails, and
(b) Floors should be swept and mopped at least daily with a germ-killing solution.

2. Warm-up Spaces
Adequate space must be provided to permit all dancers to warm up (perform limbering exercises) thirty (30) minutes, at the beginning of the day (non-working time), prior to dancing.

3. Breaks
Dancers will have at least ten (10) minutes rest during each hour of actual rehearsal or shooting unless shooting is of a continuous nature. If so, at the choreographer's discretion, dancers may continue until a total of ninety (90) minutes has elapsed after which a fifteen (15) minute break must be called.

4. Emergency Treatment
A person or facility located in the general geographical area and qualified under the circumstances to provide medical care on an emergency basis shall be identified and such information shall be made available to dancers at all rehearsals and performances.

5. Safety of Equipment
Producers shall exercise care, including prior testing of equipment (breakaway props, etc.) to avoid injury to the performer.

6. Knee Work
Dancers doing knee work, including rolling, spinning, falling, balancing, hinging, walking, turning and/or performing a choreographed routine on the knees will be permitted to wear knee pads when practical in rehearsal and performance.

E. Dance rehearsals which are held in rehearsal halls shall be conducted on surfaces which are resilient.

F. For dancers engaged as assistant choreographers, Producer shall make contributions to the Pension and Health Funds on the accounts of such individuals who have had prior contributions made in five (5) out of the last ten (10) years as dancers.

**Note that these rates are from the 2009-2011 TV/Theatrical Contract and may increase when they expire if not extended on June 30, 2011.

CHAPTER TWELVE

AFTRA – Chris De Haan (interviewed prior to sag/aftra merger) Communications Director

CONTRACT NEGOTIATIONS
"The first and most important things we do is bring members together and bargain contracts on behalf of performers. We do collective bargaining agreements and then we enforce those contracts. We sit down with the employers and we work out contracts covering television, performing in video games, music videos and award shows also. We bargain those contracts on your behalf so you don't have to and we set minimum rates and safe working conditions for you. We also put into place residual payments, late penalty payments, in case the employer doesn't pay you on time. We do all of those things on your behalf to make sure you are paid and have a career as a dancer. *All of our contracts are negotiated by members. AFTRA staff guides them through the process.*

AFTRA'S LEGAL WORK ON BEHALF OF MEMBERS
"We also do a lot of legal work on behalf of our members if a matter goes to dispute. *For Example:* Let's say someone puts together all of the best moments from the last 75 years of the *Oscars®* and they put that onto a DVD and they (sell it) on a TV channel. The union would go in on your behalf and would arbitrate for payment. That falls under contract enforcement."

MEMBERSHIP BENEFITS
"We provide membership benefits. If you work under an AFTRA contract, we set the percentage rates that the employers contribute above and beyond your salary to the *AFTRA Health and Retirement Funds* on your behalf so you can earn health care and pension benefits. You can earn a pension whenever you work. Also, we serve as kind of a clearinghouse for membership benefits. *Example:* These include discounts on union-made services and products. AFTRA members have access to supplemental health insurance that is often far less expensive than what you would be able to find as an individual. AFTRA members enjoy access to life insurance also. There are a lot of services and benefits that you have access to because we can go in and negotiate on behalf of a large group of people."

MEMBER EDUCATION
"We (provide) membership classes, member education and training events including casting workshop opportunities for members. If you're an AFTRA member and you get an agent, your agent is franchised with AFTRA."

IF YOU DON'T VALUE YOURSELF, YOU BECOME VALUELESS!

FAQ: HOW DOES A PERFORMER KNOW IF A PROJECT IS COVERED UNDER A SAG OR AFTRA CONTRACT?

CDH: AFTRA members work across the media industries including television, radio, cable, sound recordings, music videos, commercials, audio books, non-broadcast industrials, interactive games, the Internet and other digital media. **AFTRA DOES NOT COVER FEATURE FILMS.**

Example: ER is shot on film so that is covered by SAG. *Damages*, is a TV show that is shot digitally, so it could be covered under either union but is currently under an AFTRA contract. The honest case is that in a lot of these instances, when a producer is putting together a pilot for a new show or new series, they have an option to call either SAG or AFTRA. It is at the producer's discretion who they would rather work with.

AFTRA also covers live TV and live broadcasts like the *Golden Globe Awards*, the *Oscars®* and the *Grammy Awards*. We also do cover sound recordings, which include anything from Broadway cast albums to studio albums to audio books. So if you are a voice over actor and you're doing an audio book, you can earn money under an AFTRA contract. We also cover live news broadcasts, from local news stations to *Good Morning America* programs. We cover the late night talk shows including *Jimmy Kimmel, Craig Ferguson* and daytime soap operas as well.

AFTRA NETWORK TELEVISION CODE GROUPS AND CHORUSES RATES

Group Dancers
3 or more (Solo/Duos are paid the applicable principal performer rate)
Rates change yearly - Check Union Sites

Rates for 7/01/11-6/30/14	
30 Minute Programs	$872
60 Minute Programs	$1,084
Extra Rehearsal	$25/hr.

Award Programs in Excess of 60 Minutes	
Rehearsal Day (6 hr./day)	$227
Camera Day (8 hr./day)	$670
Program Minimum	$896
Overtime (7th & 8th hours paid at Extra Rehearsal Rate) (9th hr. and over)	$45/hr.

AFTRA EXHIBIT "A" PROGRAMS 2011-2014 DANCERS DAILY AND WEEKLY RATES:

7/01/11-6/30/12	Daily	Weekly
Solo/Duo	$855	$2,746
3-8	$749	$2,515
9+	$654	$2,289
Rehearsal	$503	

7/01/12-6/30/13	Daily	Weekly
Solo/Duo	$872	$2,801
3-8	$764	$2,565
9+	$667	$2,335
Rehearsal	$513	

7/01/13-6/30/14	Daily	Weekly
Solo/Duo	$889	$2,857
3-8	$779	$2,616
9+	$680	$2,382
Rehearsal	$523	

AFTRA TERMS FOR DRAMATIC PROGRAMS

Primetime network programs A.
Exhibit A of the *Network Code* covers Dramatic Programs made for Network (ABC, CBS, Fox, and NBC) Primetime exhibition. The term *"Dramatic Programs"* includes both dramas and sitcoms, as well as book musicals and plays recorded for television broadcast.

The Term "Performers"
1. The term *"Performers"* under Exhibit A includes Actors who speak, as well as other Performers who sing or dance, On-Camera and Off-Camera Announcers, On-Camera or Off-Camera Narrators, Stuntpersons, Stunt Coordinators and Puppeteers. In addition, under certain circumstances Warm-Up Performers and Choreographers are entitled to Health and Retirement coverage under Exhibit A. Exhibit A operates on a day, 3-day and weekly rate structure.

• Producer must furnish meals in the 11:00 p.m. – 2:00 a.m. or 6:00 a.m. – 8:30 a.m. meal period if no restaurant facilities are reasonably available.

Overtime
Day Performers: The Money Break is 2 times the minimum Day Performer rate per day. Overtime is paid in 1/10th hourly units at time-and-one-half for the 9th and 10th hours, and at double time beyond 10 hours. Performers who are paid more than the money break receive time-and-one-half after 10 hours based on the money break.

Location and Travel Time
A nearby location is one to which a Performer is transported from the studio and returned on the same day. An overnight location is one at which the Performer is lodged at the location for one or more nights.

Travel to Nearby Location:
When Producer transports a Performer, such travel time is work time. Overtime caused by travel to and from a nearby location is computed at time-and-one-half. Mileage is payable at $.30 per mile to a Performer required to report to a location within the 30-mile Hollywood or San Francisco Studio Zones (8-mile zone in New York), figured from the studio to the place of reporting and return. For new 1 hour series; 1/2 hour and 1 hour pilots, no mileage is payable for a 10-mile radius from a point designated by Producer once per season within the 30-mile zone. Distance for which payment will be given must be clearly stated on the production time report. Mileage will be paid and separately identified on your payroll check. Producer may pay in cash.

Cancelled Engagements
If your engagement is cancelled (except where cancellation is for gross insubordination or misconduct by the Performer) the Producer must pay you in full for all contracted time.

Contracts
Standard employment contracts should be available for signature no later than the first day of employment. Provisions which cannot be stated on the standard form may be delivered 4 days after agreement has been reached. You may not be required to sign a contract on the set. If you choose to sign a contract under such circumstances, an extra copy of the contract must be given to you. Failure to deliver contracts within the appropriate time period will cause damages to be incurred by the Producer to the same extent as those for late payment (see Section 16).

IF YOU DON'T VALUE YOURSELF, YOU BECOME VALUELESS!

Time of Payment / Late Payment
Performers employed by the day must be paid within 5 working days after services are rendered. Series Performers must be paid at least every two weeks for all episodes worked, whether or not completed. All other Performers must be paid no later than the studio payroll date (usually Thursday) following the week in which services are rendered. Performers may be paid on Friday when on overnight location. Damages for late payment accrue at the rate of $10 for each working day, to a maximum of 20 working days. Should the Producer fail to issue payment, including damages, within 5 working days of written notice by the Union or the Performer, further damages at the rate of $2.50 per working day are due, retroactive to the date of receipt of the notice. Damages shall continue to accrue without limitation until the delinquent payments, together with late payment damages, are fully paid. No late payments shall accrue for disputed amounts while in dispute. Late payment damages shall accrue commencing 10 working days after the settlement of a disputed claim.

Cosmetic Alteration and Nudity
A Performer required to grow a beard or moustache or shave his head shall be paid a fee of $35. No Performer can be required to appear nude, but you may consent to appear nude after you have had an opportunity to read the script.

Residuals
Domestic Television: The initial base compensation to the Performer constitutes payment in full for one run in each city in the U.S. and Canada. A repeat in any city puts the program into a "replay." The rate due for each replay is a percentage of the applicable basic minimum program fee at the time of the original performance:
1st Replay: 75%, 2nd Replay: 75%, 3rd Replay: 50%, 4th Replay: 50%, 5th Replay: 50%, 6th Replay: 10%, 7th and each additional replay: 5% each

* In the case of replays over a national network: in addition to the rate above, you are also entitled to 20% of your additional rehearsal and doubling fees for the program.

Pay Television:
The Performer's initial compensation permits 10 exhibitions or 1 year's use, whichever occurs first, on a single Pay TV service. Thereafter, Producer will pay 6% of Distributor's Gross receipts, plus AFTRA Health and Retirement contributions, on behalf of the performers on the program. Such payments are made on a quarterly basis. If a Pay TV program is also released to Home Video, the Performer's initial compensation includes payment for the first 75,000 units sold, before additional compensation is due. Thereafter, Producer pays 6%, of Distributor's Gross Receipts, plus AFTRA Health and Retirement contributions, on behalf of the Performers on the program.

Home Video:
The Performer's initial compensation includes sales of 100,000 units of video sales for Made-For-Video product. Thereafter, Producer will pay 6% of Distributor's Gross Receipts, plus AFTRA Health and Retirement contributions, on behalf of the Performers on the program.

The excerpts from contracts relating to dancers for SAG/AFTRA listed with the beige undertone are subject to change. Please contact your SAG/AFTRA union representatives for the most up-to-date contract information.

CHAPTER TWELVE

FAQs ABOUT UNIONS

FAQ: DEFINE SAG-ELIGIBLE AND TAFT-HARTLEY?
SAG-Eligible means that you have met the requirements to join SAG and the offer has been extended to you. You do not have to join unless the specific job requires you to. You are considered "Taft-Hartley" if you are a SAG-Eligible performer and can work on union and non-union productions during a 30-day period following your eligibility. At the end of this period you must join and pay the initiation fee or choose not to join. You are limited to non-union work if you do not join. Your status will remain as SAG-Eligible and you are free to join at your discretion.

FAQ: I'M SAG-ELIGIBLE. THERE IS A FEATURE FILM AUDITION, DO I GO TO THE UNION OR NON-UNION CALL?
My personal opinion is to go to the Union Call but sometimes choreographers need you to be already paid-up with your dues and ready to start immediately. So you may not want to do this. Discuss this with your agent and figure out what works best for your financial situation as well as the wishes of the choreographer.

FAQ: WHAT DOES IT MEAN TO BE 'AFTRA-WILLING'?
"AFTRA-willing" simply means that if cast for the job you are willing to join AFTRA because you wouldn't be able to work the job if you are not an AFTRA member. This means paying the initiation dues.

FAQ: WHAT DOES IT MEAN IF I NEED 'STATION 12' CLEARANCE?
All performers must be cleared for work. It is the responsibility of the producer to clear all dancers for each production. If a member is declared to be 'Station 12,' that means that there is a problem with the membership status of the performer. The producer must get in touch with the performer and correct the problem immediately. The performer will not be allowed to work the project without the problem being rectified. Contact the SAG Station 12 Department at (323) 549-6794.

FAQ: I'M SAG AND AFTRA. I HEARD I COULD DECLARE FINANCIAL CORE IN ORDER TO WORK NON-UNION JOBS. IF TRUE, THEN WHY DOESN'T EVERYONE DO THIS?
By declaring financial core you are giving up your voting rights for the union, but don't think that this is all you are doing. I <u>HIGHLY STRESS</u> that you talk to your union representative before considering this. <u>DON'T TAKE THIS DECISION LIGHTLY</u>. My personal advice is to NEVER to declare financial core. No matter

how much money you think you'll make on non-union jobs, it's not a good decision.

FAQ: WHAT DOES IT MEAN TO BE CATEGORY GROUP 9+?

The category "Group 9+" is just that, nine or more dancers that will be used in the commercial and will all have the same rate. Each project has different rate variables. Generally speaking, less people = more money! **Categories 6-8 & 9+ were combined in the 2013 Commercials Contract, 6+ will be paid at higher rate.** *For Example:* On-Camera Commercial Session fees for performers (8 hr. day) are as follows:

All principal performers, except Group Performers	$535.00
(Solos and Duos are included as principal performers)	
Group Singers or Group Dancers 3 to 5	$391.65
Group Singers/Dancers/Speakers 6 to 8	$346.75
Group Singers/Dancers/Speakers 9 or more	$286.75

These rates are from www.sagaftra.org. Go to the SAG/AFTRA Web site for specific rates with the details of your role or ask your agent for assistance.

FAQ: WE SHOT AN EPISODE A LONG TIME AGO THAT WAS A LITTLE RISQUE BUT IN GOOD TASTE. WHY HASN'T IT AIRED YET?

Your episode may not have aired for many reasons. Your show may have been cancelled, you may not have recognized it, the scene was cut or you may just have the wrong air date. The episode may also be held up by **censors** or **standards and practices**. This department controls what you see on network television, *(i.e. CBS, NBC, ABC and FOX)*, and makes determinations as to what is morally acceptable *(i.e. nudity, sexually explicit language)*. The department is also responsible for making sure there is fair play on shows where there is a prize *(i.e. So You Think You Can Dance, Jeopardy)*. For example, if one couple has one 2-hour rehearsal, every couple is allowed one 2-hour rehearsal.

FAQ: WHAT DOES IT MEAN TO BE PAID TO SCALE?

Being paid to scale is being paid the established union rates. If your agent negotiates your contract for a project where you can command more money, go for it!

FAQ: TERMINOLOGY FOR INTERNET-BASED MEDIUM?

The Internet is being categorized as "new media," "digital media" or "rich media." Performer unions are working to ensure that performers are compensated for their work.

CHAPTER TWELVE

FAQ: WHAT ARE SAG PROJECT BUDGETS?

AGREEMENT	BUDGET
• Codified Basic Agreement	More Than $2,500,000.00
• Low Budget Agreement	Less Than $2,500,000.00
• Modified Low Budget Agreement	Less Than $625,000.00
• Ultra Low Budget Agreement	Less Than $200,000.00
• Short Film Agreement (under 35 min.)	Less Than $50,000.00
• Student Film Agreement	N/A

FAQ: WHY ISN'T THERE A SEPARATE DANCE UNION?

Your guess is as good as mine. SAG and AFTRA take care of the television and film aspects of dance contracts for performers. Many rates that do not fall under these union jurisdictions and are left up to agent negotiations and/or self-imposed industry guidelines established by a non-profit organization called Dancers' Alliance. These are suggested rates and do not and have not always been upheld.

FAQ: DEFINE BEING DOWNGRADED OR OUTGRADED?

Downgrading in basic terms is when you are cast as a principal and shoot a commercial and then for whatever reason your status as a principal is re-categorized but your face still remains in the final on air edit. Your payment and/or residuals will be less because of the final version of the commercial. The performer should receive notice of this downgrading and re-categorization of their status in writing within 60 days from the work and not after 15 days from the initial airing of the commercial. **Outgrading** is when a performer has been cast in a principal role or their voice has been used and for whatever reason they have been cut from the final edit of the project, meaning your likeness is not used at all in the final edit.

SICK TIP #41:
AFTRA AND SAG SHOW SHEETS

Take advantage of resources your union provides. Get the AFTRA and SAG show sheets either online or at your local office. Show sheets detail the shows currently running for dramatic serials, dramas, sitcoms, non-dramatic programs and digital animation programs as well as films in production for SAG and pilots in production. Don't be behind, be proactive and know who's doing what and when.

IF YOU DON'T VALUE YOURSELF, YOU BECOME VALUELESS!

HISTORY OF DANCERS' PARTICIPATION IN UNIONS

BOBBIE BATES (Interview prior to SAG/AFTRA merger)
SAG/AFTRA Dancers' Committee

SC: Can you give a brief history of the involvement of dancers in the unions?
BB: When the Screen Actors Guild was founded in 1933, it included all performers. In the 1940's, the Extras in Hollywood didn't feel like they were being served well by SAG, so they broke off and formed the Screen Extras Guild. That was during the era when Busby Berkeley was doing huge musicals where there were hundreds of dancers waving fans and creating spectacular formations; but they weren't necessarily great dancers. They were pretty girls who moved well more than anything. So when the unions split, dancers had their choice of being part of SAG (Screen Actors Guild) or SEG (Screen Extras Guild), and since most of them were extras, that's where they chose to be (part of SEG). In the 1960s, and even earlier, when they started doing movies like *Bye Bye Birdie*, *An American in Paris* and *West Side Story*, they were using really serious dancers. So, they would hire them under a SAG principal contract. SEG still had the legal jurisdiction over dancers, and only SEG members could go to the dance auditions. It was the hardest union in Hollywood to get into.

When my dance generation came along, all of the variety television show dancers, even the greatest dancers couldn't get into that union. In order to go to the auditions for those jobs, you had to be part of the union and these jobs often ended up being converted to SAG jobs once they started. This injustice prompted my diving into union activism with a passion. A small group of us went to the SAG board, explained our plight, and urged them to get our jurisdiction back. SAG leadership asked SEG to let the dancers go. SEG told them to take all of them, not just a few. That is actually what motivated the first attempt to merge SEG with SAG. It wasn't successful. It was a long battle, sort of my mission in life to get the dancers out of the SEG and into SAG. SEG finally died and SAG assumed the jurisdiction by negotiation. One contract at a time, they negotiated dancers out of the extras agreement and into the principal portions of the contracts.

The change finally happened. It took from 1992 until 1998 for dancers to be covered under all SAG contracts as principals. Once that happened, we were able to move along the working conditions that we had in AFTRA contracts, like hazard pay. In every negotiation we try to improve the contract, like identifying that it is

CHAPTER TWELVE

hazardous to dance on concrete floors and adding the use of wearing kneepads to protect the dancer. We are always fighting to update the language in the contracts. When you are doing something hazardous, make a call to your union. Don't get involved with it yourself, just make the call and they will come down and assess the situation. A lot of dancers never speak up about those things because they are afraid that they won't work for the choreographer again or they'll be called a troublemaker. A lot of the contracts get undercut because the producer says, *'Well, no one else has ever said anything about concrete being hazardous.'* It really takes everybody getting together and being proactive about what is going on, on the set. People complain all the time and say, *'The union didn't do anything for us on the set,'* but at the same time no one ever called the union to even tell them that the job was happening. I used to always call the union before a job and let them know where or when a big dance number was going to happen and (ask the union representative) to come down and take a look. Once they got used to people from the union just showing up they weren't going to pull anything because people representing us would already be there saying, *'You're doing what with those dancers? Sorry, you can't do that!'* A lot of people have never really worked with dancers before so they really don't know what the hazards are for us.

SC: Dancers have long been underpaid for their work in music videos. Are there any new developments regarding union representation for dancers for music videos?
BB: Nothing has happened yet, but AFTRA has been meeting with record company executives working to apply industry standards for covering dancers in music videos under the AFTRA Sound Recordings contract. Currently, the industry doesn't really know what to do and haven't really responded in a serious way. The recording industry is floundering along with the economy and producers remain unwilling to allow this work to be unionized. We won't give up.

BOBBIE BATES ON THE FORMATION OF DANCERS' ALLIANCE

SC: Can you give a brief summary on the formation of Dancers' Alliance?
BB: During the peak of the music video years, early to mid 1980's, dancers made requests to SAG and AFTRA to create a meaningful contract to cover and organize this work, which today still continues to be mainly non-union work. There was no organized group of employers, so it was too difficult to figure out where to start. Ultimately, SAG and AFTRA created and negotiated music video contracts with the major record labels, which could be used by any producers who were willing to use a union contract. The labels didn't require work to be done under these agree-

ments and it was almost impossible for the unions to know when this work took place, thus most of the work was done non-union. The rates for dancers were well below what dancers were used to being paid. This motivated a group of dancers and a few agents to come together to create rates under the name of Dancers' Alliance. **DANCER'S ALLIANCE IS NOT A UNION**, but rather a collective community of dancers and agents uniting in purpose to establish minimum rates and working conditions similar to those in our union contracts, for areas of employment where no union contracts exist, such as; music videos, live stage productions, industrials, promotional tours with recording artists, etc. Dancers came together and just agreed that no one would work for less than the rates created by Dancers' Alliance. By this time most of this work was being booked through the dance agents, who were instrumental in promulgating these agreements. It didn't take very long for the industry to realize that, if you wanted to have the best dancers, you would need to follow the rates outlined by Dancers' Alliance. When AFTRA was called by producers inquiring about music video rates, staff would tell them that they had a contract and give them the rates. Then would then tell them, *'but the professional dancers in L.A. won't work for these rates,'* and would recommend that they contact the dance agents regarding Dancer's Alliance rates to book dancers.

At the 2005 AFTRA Convention in Los Angeles, a report was given on a study done by Cornell University, which included music videos. The study assessed that music video production was in decline, and should be a very low priority to organize. Interestingly, the research found that 90% of music videos were done in L.A., and hundreds a year were still being made. That added up to a lot of work for L.A. dancers. Those of us who attended the convention were aware that there was an abundance of work for dancers in music videos in L.A., which is why we've pushed to add music videos to the sound recording contracts for dancers.

EXTRA CREDIT: SIT DOWN WITH DANCERS' CONTRACTS

I know, I know…it sounds sooooooo boring! This is going to help you before you find yourself in a pinch! I went to an audition and was handed a consent and release form. I contacted my agent as it asked me to input the amount of compensation for the job. My agent told me not to sign it and they would negotiate it. Another girl came in and was from my agency. She asked where my form was and I told her that my agent told me not to sign it and she promptly ripped up the one she'd already signed. Ask your friends to sit down with you and their contracts. Help each other before it's too late!

CHAPTER TWELVE

**As of the printing of this book no additions have been made to the Sound Recordings Contract for AFTRA to include music video language for dancer compensation and/or working conditions.

DANCERS' ALLIANCE

"Dancers' Alliance enables dancers to be a part of a national community and acts as a resource to that community by providing information, recognition and industry support. Through proposals, we establish equitable levels of compensation and conditions in work not covered by union jurisdiction, and represent our community in union proposals and committees. We are primarily a resource and voice for professional dancers, and we are committed to the education of dancers in training and the participation and betterment of the entire national dance community," (www.DancersAlliance.org). If you have any questions about rates or would like more information about the organization please send an e-mail to: dancersalliance@yahoo.com or go to MySpace.com/DancersAlliance.

Dancers' Alliance Rates are industry guidelines for industrials, music videos and live performances not covered currently in the SAG/AFTRA contracts for performers. Rates are listed below.

FITTINGS/WARDROBE RATES
If you are scheduled to attend a fitting for costuming on a day that isn't scheduled for a rehearsal you will be paid for your time.
• Compensation $50 per hour

If you provide your own clothing, you will be paid on a 'per outfit' or 'per pair of shoes' basis.
• Compensation $25 per Outfit
• Compensation $15 per Pair of Shoes

**You will not be compensated if you choose to wear your own clothing on a shoot. You will only be compensated if the wardrobe stylist tells you to wear selections from your wardrobe.

MEAL BREAKS
All dancers will have meals provided in the same time allotment as Principal Performers/Crew/Staff. Every Six Hours of Work will accrue a meal break and will be provided for you on the day of the shoot unless otherwise specified.

RETURNING TO SET – TURNAROUND TIMES
Your turnaround time will be at least twelve hours from your wrap on the shoot day. You will be compensated if required to return prior to the twelve hour minimum at a double-time rate per hour until the twelve hour time period has been reached.

DRESSING ROOMS
Proper climate temperature and separated dressing rooms must be provided.

IF YOU DON'T VALUE YOURSELF, YOU BECOME VALUELESS!

REQUIRED ADDITIONAL FEES/BUYOUT FEES
New media has required new fees to be associated with the rights to the use of your image. Negotiated fees will be appropriated for video or portions of video to be used that includes a performer's likeness for the purposes of CD Rom, Television, Film, DVD, Concert Tour Footage or Commercials. Additional Buyout Fees may be necessary for music videos.
**Music Videos are currently being negotiated with AFTRA and Record Label Executives to include a standard buyout fee for usage.

Buyout Fees vary per project and do not always occur timely. Fees are calculated based on the project's total budget whether it be for the usage of music videos, including but not limited to documentaries, "Making of..." or Behind the Scenes, Film Trailers, Concert Tours, DVDs or CD Rom. However, the use of music videos within the non-promotional television program or feature film, exclude a fee from being required. This also includes when a portion of the music video is selected to be lifted for use in print media or as cover art for an artist.

MUSIC VIDEO REHEARSAL RATES /MINIMUMS (Agency % On Top Of Rates)
Full Day   8 Hours $250
Required Meal Break   1 Hour
Overtime Begins After the Conclusion of the first 8 Hour Period.
Overtime Compensation   Time and ½   or $46.88 per Hour
Rehearsals 12 Hours or Longer   Double Time
Second Meal Break Might Be Required Depending on Length of Extended Overtime Period

Half Day   4 Hours $175
Overtime Begins After the Conclusion of the first 4 Hour Period
Overtime Compensation   Time and ½   or $65.63 per Hour
Rehearsals 12 Hours or Longer   Double Time
Second Meal Break Might Be Required Depending on Length of Extended Overtime Period

MUSIC VIDEO SHOOT DAY (MINIMUMS)
Full Day   12 Hours $550 | 10 Hours $475
Required Meal Break   1 Hour
Second Meal Break Will Be Required if Shoot Continues Beyond 12 Hours
Third Meal Break Will Be Required if Shoot Continues Beyond 18 Hours
Overtime Begins After the Conclusion of the first 12-14 Hour Period
Overtime Compensation   Time and ½   or $71.25 per Hour
Double Overtime Begins After the Conclusion of the first 15-20 Hour Period
Overtime Compensation   Double Time   or $95 per Hour
Over 20 Hours & Less Than 24 Hours Includes an Additional Compensation of One Full Day Rate

Additional Day Overtime Compensation   Day Rate or $475 Full Day Rate x 1
*No additional work may continue beyond the full twenty-four hour period. Keep in constant contact with your agency if your work schedule goes into such long hours.

INDUSTRIAL REHEARSAL RATES (MINIMUMS)
Full Day   8 Hours $250.00
Required Meal Break   1 Hour
Overtime Begins After the Conclusion of the first 8 Hour Period.
Overtime Compensation   Time and ½   or $65.63 per Hour

INDUSTRIAL SHOW RATES (MINIMUMS)
Full Day   8 Hours $350.00
Required Meal Break   1 Hour
Must Be Provided within Six Hours of Call Time
Overtime Begins After the Conclusion of the first 8 Hour Period.
Overtime Compensation   Time and ½   or $65.63 per Hour
Overtime Begins After the Conclusion of the first 12 Hour Period
Overtime Compensation   Double time   or $87.50 per Hour

INDUSTRIAL SHOW RATES (MULTIPLE SHOWS/SINGLE DAY MINIMUMS)
Industrials that include multiple shows in one single day that incur a run time of Ten minutes or MORE can have a maximum of FOUR shows scheduled to run per day.
Industrials that include multiple shows in one single day that incur a run time of Ten minutes or LESS can have a maximum of SIX shows scheduled to run per day.

LIVE SHOW REHEARSAL RATES (MINIMUMS)
Full Day   8 Hours $250.00
Required Meal Break   1 Hour
Overtime Begins After the Conclusion of the first 8 Hour Period.
Overtime Compensation   Time and ½   or $46.88 per Hour

Half Day   4 Hours $175
Overtime Begins After the Conclusion of the first 4 Hour Period
Overtime Compensation   Time and ½   or $65.63 per Hour

LIVE SHOW PERFORMANCE RATES (MINIMUMS)
Full Day   8 Hours $500.00
Additional Shows Within Same Day Compensation $150 per Show

Hazard Pay Compensation $75 per Day (Dancer's Alliance)

AGENCY FEES SHOULD BE ADDED ON THE TOP OF ALL OF THE RATES ABOVE. COMPENSATION CALCULATIONS ABOVE DO NOT INCLUDE YOUR AGENCY FEE. **Visit dancersalliance.org for up to date rates.

IF YOU DON'T VALUE YOURSELF, YOU BECOME VALUELESS!

CHRISTINE COLTON'S
TOP 5 THINGS TO DO BEFORE SIGNING A CONTRACT

"SO THIS IS IT – YOU GOT THE JOB! You feel like the hard work has paid off. You start thinking of what you are going to do. When you get the job you are so excited you may sign your life away just to keep the job. The adrenalin is rushing and you have been chosen by the people you want to work with. Then they hand you this document that seems like 100 pages with the smallest print you have ever seen. Unfortunately, you have to sign this document before you leave for the day.

"You now think 'Oh boy, I need this job and if I don't sign this document I won't get the job.' Everything that went through you mind like 'I can pay my rent now,' or 'I can keep my car for another month,' rushes through your mind and these are important. If I don't sign, I won't get any of these tasks done. So you sign it and wonder, 'What did I just sign?' Well, before you get to that point, here are a couple of tips to keep you from getting involved in a legal nightmare.

#1 - READ THE DOCUMENT

"We have all been in this situation and NEED to have that one job. When you receive your contract, READ THE CONTRACT. It may take you some time but you will actually know what you are getting into. They cannot get upset at you for reading it; they actually expect you to. What are they asking for you to do? What rights are you giving up? If you don't read it and sign the document, the one thing you can be sure of is: You are stating you DID read it.

#2 - LEGAL TERMINOLOGY

"Go online and you can find a million courses on legal terminology. This will help you understand what you are reading. You can search 'legal terminology' on the Internet. Once you find the course you want to take, it will help you when this moment comes. You will understand what the document is requesting you to do. When I searched online, I found www.UniversalCourse.com or www.Dictionary.Law.com. When you find the course you like, take all of your experience and learn the words that have been in the contracts you have signed before. Use these older contracts as reference. I am sure you have seen terms such as 'name and likeness.' Remember, knowledge is power."

CHAPTER TWELVE

#3 - ASK QUESTIONS

"If you do not understand something, ask a question. This will <u>NOT</u> make you look stupid. It will actually make you look like you are concerned and care about what you are signing. Based on your position, you may not have the right to change what is written in the contract. However, understanding what is being asked of you may be an important deciding factor if you want to continue with what they are offering you. If there is something in the contract you **don't** agree with, you can request language to be changed. Now, if the company chooses NOT to change the language, you have the right to NOT sign it. Yes, it may not seem fair but you are also learning what is right for you and your future. What if they want to use your 'name and likeness' for the next 10 years? If the contract states they can, they might take that option. If you are not aware of these terms, you will forfeit some cash in your future.

#4 - REQUEST A COPY

"After you have signed it, make sure you get a copy THAT DAY! <u>Request that the person who had you sign it gives you a copy the same day</u>. If that means you run down the street to make this copy and bring it back; then that is what it takes. Some circumstances may change. What if something is scratched off and agreed to in person, you want that contract as proof if something changes in the future. You also want to be sure that if someone says, 'Oh, I'll fill in your sign-out time after you leave, no problem.' No, you want to get a copy that is fully filled out with all of your dates of work, times worked, meal/break time, etc. What if they fill out the time wrong, or they don't know about an added rehearsal? Later when the production company pays you, then you will have to go back to get the missing payment for the times that were missing on your time sheet.

#5 - VERBAL AGREEMENTS

"Just because they stated, 'Oh yes, we can do that for you,' doesn't mean that they actually can. Make sure you get them to sign the change on the contract. If they will do what they say; it will not be hard to have them sign the change. If they will not take the time to sign off on the verbal agreement, they may not own up to the agreement. Verbal agreements are difficult to prove once a contract is signed. This is because there may be a clause in the contract that states, 'This contract supersedes any verbal agreements.' Therefore, you need to make sure that any changes that are made on the contract get signed off in writing on paper and preferably to the original contract. Nothing states that this is right or wrong. You will not be the 'bad' one out of the bunch by clearing up any problems before they happen."

IF YOU DON'T VALUE YOURSELF, YOU BECOME VALUELESS!

> "These are just a few things to look for before you sign a contract for your next new job! Sometimes, you may have to turn down that 'great job' because the contract wasn't right. However, there will always be the next gig to get you going in the right direction. Your future will be more profitable if you know just a little more about the contracts you sign.

WHAT IS IN A CONTRACT?

Even if you decide to enter into work that is negotiated or handled by your agent or lawyer, you should still know the bare bones of the parts/sections in most contracts. Get familiar with the following sections that are in most entertainment-related contracts, the terminology and come back to this chapter more than once if you have problems understanding it. Knowing how to read a contract is part of your job!

Christine lists <u>READING YOUR CONTRACT</u> as the #1 thing you should do before signing it. So look for the following contract section headings and what they cover.

PREAMBLE

This is the very beginning of the contract that generally states the parties that are entering into the agreement, the title of the project and normally will incorporate the date of the event/project and time as well. Sometimes these details are also listed in subsections. Here is an example of a preamble in a contract:

This is an agreement between Original Girl, LLC (Producer) and Sandra Colton (Talent/Artist) for Project: O.G. Magazine's "Fall Fashion Show" featuring the debut of O.G. Style, and to any and all Original Girl, LLC's associates, assistants, clients, staff or co-staff on this project as a Model/Interactive Dancer/Performer. Show Day is to be July 27, 2009 at the Hollywood Theatre, Los Angeles, CA 90028. Rehearsals are scheduled to be July 21st from 10 a.m.- 6 p.m. Call Time for show date of July 27th to be at 7 p.m.

BODY

The substance of the agreement is in this part of the document. This is where the terms of the agreement will be detailed. All key factors will be mentioned here. This section can include many parts such as: services to be rendered, authority (rights for a manager or agent, rights for use of your name and likeness, etc.), exclusivity, commissions and/or residual/royalties and payout clauses, permissions and waivers, accounting, warranties and representations, releases, indemnity, waivers, notices, publicity and assignments of the contract to a third party, conflict of interest, future agreements, assumption of risks, general provisions, relationship of parties, etc.

SIGNATURES, DATE AND TITLE
This is at the end of the document where you are normally asked to print and sign your legal name and date the document.

EXAMPLES OF CONTRACT EXCERPTS
If you are negotiating your own contract seek counsel from a lawyer.

EXAMPLE #1: KILL FEE
If for any reason, this production is postponed or canceled within 72 hours of the scheduled first rehearsal, except for "ACTS of WAR" or "ACTS of GOD," PRODUCTION COMPANY X will pay a "KILL FEE" of 50% of the ABOVE LISTED FEE to Artist.

The **KILL FEE** is due to you, the Artist. Make sure you look for the opposite fees that you may incur if you have to cancel an engagement such as:

EXAMPLE #2: ARTIST REIMBURSEMENT FEE
If ARTIST cancels for any reason after signing contract and returning, short of "ACTS OF WAR" or "ACTS OF GOD," or a LIFE THREATENING illness, ARTIST will pay Producer any and all invested sums including costume purchases, flights booked and other fees that may have been incurred by the Producer or the Producer's clients and/or associates.

EXAMPLE #3: EMPLOYER NOT RESPONSIBLE
Production Company X will not be responsible for any injury or accident incurred by ARTIST/TALENT during any rehearsals or performance. Performer must carry his/her own health and accident insurance policy.

EXAMPLE #4: LIKENESS RIGHTS (VIDEO/PHOTO RELEASE)
Performer agrees to the recording, use and reuse by the Producer and any of its licensees and assigns in any and all media, whether now known or hereafter devised, worldwide, **in perpetuity**, of Performer's actions, likeness (actual or simulated), name, or voice that are in most entertainment-related contracts, appearance, photograph, picture, silhouette and other reproductions of Performer's physical likeness (appearing in any still camera photograph and/or motion picture film or

tape) and biographical information (collectively "likeness") in and in connection with the production, exhibition, distribution, and/or exploitation of the Program and/or any derivative works thereof, and in connection with any marketing, promotion, publicity, advertisement, merchandising for the Program and/or any derivative works thereof and all other commercial and non-commercial purposes relating to the Program and/or any derived works thereof. Performer agrees that Producer may use all or any part of Performer's likeness, and may alter or modify it, regardless of whether or not Performer is recognizable. Performer releases Producer (and its employees, officers and directors) from liability arising out of its use of Performer's likeness, voice, and/or name as set forth herein. Performer agrees not to make any claim against Producer (or its employees, officers and directors) as a result of the recording or use of Performer's name, voice, and/or likeness (including, without limitation, any claim that such use invades any right of privacy and/or publicity). *In the excerpt on the previous page, you have no claim to any footage/photos taken of you if you agree.*

EXAMPLE #5: CONFIDENTIALITY
The project you are about to work on has been classified as "Project Confidential." Failure to protect the confidential nature of this project may be identified as a security breach and can be grounds for immediate termination. All information that you receive as a part of this project is a strategic asset of the company.

EXAMPLE #6: NON-COMPETE PROMOTION/ENDORSE/SOLICITATION
You will not promote, announce or advance in any way any private endeavors or products of your own or of any organization other than those affiliated with or approved by Production X. This includes but is not limited to master classes, workshops, videotapes, private choreography or other conventions & competitions.

EXAMPLE #7: NOT YOUR EMPLOYER
You agree that you are not an employee of Production Company X for any purpose whatsoever, including unemployment tax, income tax withholding or workers' compensation.

In the excerpt above, you need to understand that as a dancer you will do many jobs where you will not be considered an employee of a company. You are considered an **independent contractor** and will get a 1099 at the end of the year from that job, which will be discussed in Chapter 13.

CHAPTER TWELVE

EXAMPLE #8: COMMISSIONS TO AGENCY
Generally, you are giving your agency the right to take their percentage directly off of the gross compensation, not the net. Make sure that you are aware of the percentage that you are allowing your agent, manager or financial advisor to take as this will affect your net earnings. This will be further discussed in Chapter 13.

EXAMPLE #9: UNION STATUS DOES NOT APPLY
Performer understands and acknowledges that Performer's appearance on the Program does not fall under the jurisdiction of any SAG or AFTRA agreements (whether or not Performer may be a member of either such guild). This is essentially stating, you may be a member of SAG or AFTRA but because the program does not fall under either union's jurisdiction, union rules do NOT apply to this project (i.e. wages, turn around times, etc.)

EXAMPLE #10: REALITY PRODUCER'S ULTIMATE DECISION
In circumstances beyond your control, the voting system may fail to work during a competition reality show. Contracts usually have a stipulation in them that if such an occurrence does happen; the Producer will have the final say as to who moves on in the competition.

EXAMPLE #11: NO UNION COMPENSATION
In some reality-based competition shows, the contestant may have to sign a form stating that they are not now, nor have they ever been part of a performer's union. Be wary of signing this statement as you are agreeing that you are an amateur competitor and not a professional. If you agree that you are NOT a professional and are found to be a professional who is part of a performers' union, you may be fined or placed on suspension by the union.

EXAMPLE #12: EXCLUSIVITY
You may be required to not perform the same functions you have on one program on a "like program" if asked to do so. Generally, this is so you are not seen on two similar programs doing the same thing and promoting competing shows or products. This is the same as having a commercial conflict. You would not want to be seen as the spokesperson for Verizon and Sprint at the same time as this is a severe conflict of interest.

EXAMPLE #13: CREDIT
Credit is in Producer X's sole discretion.

IF YOU DON'T VALUE YOURSELF, YOU BECOME VALUELESS!

SICK TIP #42: KNOWLEDGE IS POWER

Ask for an *AFTRA Member Guide* to the AFTRA Television Contract and the *S.A.G. Dancers Handbook*. Both of these publications are handbooks for working performers and include current rates and rights. These are updated and distributed frequently. Stay informed!

CONTRACTS CAN MAKE YOU STIR CRAZY JUST READING THEM! IT'S OKAY, YOU'RE DONE WITH THIS CHAPTER. SHAKE IT OFF! DO A LITTLE DANCE! NEXT UP IS MONEY!

CHAPTER TWELVE

Sandra says...

- If you become eligible to join SAG or AFTRA take advantage of the union benefits which include project rates, residuals, pension and health insurance.

- Know your union history and dancers' roles in them. We can't move forward without knowing where we came from.

IF YOU DON'T VALUE YOURSELF, YOU BECOME VALUELESS!

- Dancers' Alliance is not a union. Rates created by D.A. are guidelines put together by a group of concerned dancers wanting to protect the rights and rates of dancers.

- Many of the issues on the table for music videos are being negotiated to amend the AFTRA Sound Recordings Contract to possibly include music videos.

- Join the SAG/AFTRA Dancers Committee to be part of the process along with becoming part of ADP: Association of Dance Professionals. Let your voice be heard!

> **POINT TAKEN:**
> Unions are beneficial to dancers but do not always cover every project. To any dancer who is reading this book please get involved in the process. Let your voice be heard about issues that affect you and listen to veterans who have been around the block. Participating the process is the only way to improve upon the current situation.

CHAPTER THIRTEEN

MONEY, MONEY, MONEY! HOW TO MAKE IT, SAVE IT, AND HAVE IT WORK FOR YOU!

THE BUSINESS OF DANCE

Knowing how to organize your receipts, expenditures and income is difficult for regular jobs. It is even more difficult for people in an industry where paychecks tend to come 30-45 days after the completion of a job. Make sure to keep your travel receipts, industry related receipts as well as all contracts and pay stubs for work completed. Keep accurate records of time spent traveling to and from your gigs including mileage from your home to job and rehearsal locations. This information will be valuable to you when it comes time to do your year-end taxes.

It's also good to know some of the payroll companies in town, just in case you need to follow up on a payment for a residual, first payment or late payment. A few are listed below:

PAYROLL COMPANIES
ArtPayroll – ArtPayroll.com
Cast & Crew Talent Services – CastAndCrew.com
Entertainment Partners – EntertainmentPartners.com
Talent Partners – TalentPartners.com

To file for unemployment insurance:
www.edd.ca.gov/fleclaim.htm

To file for disability insurance:
http://www.edd.ca.gov/fleclaimdi.htm

Note: Although the payroll companies (on the left) have offices in Southern California, they may not be headquartered in Los Angeles. Look up the national headquarters for each company as this is often where your checks are being generated and mailed from.

Another resource if you are a union member is the AFTRA/SAG Federal Credit Union. Call (818) 562-3400 or go to www.aftrasagfcu.org for more information.

EARN YOUR KEEP AND SPEND IT WISELY

Often you can find deals when you purchase things at stores with reward cards like Ralph's grocery store, Staples, Best Buy and Office Max. Rewards card are not credit cards. They are cards that allot reward points that you earn with every purchase. Periodically you will receive certificates to redeem in the mail. Apply for a MAC Pro card. If you qualify for one as an entertainment industry professional, you will save 35% off of your purchases from the MAC Makeup Pro stores. Go old school and get a local Los Angeles Library card. Go to www.LAPL.org to find the nearest library. You may save money on Internet costs and check out copies of movies or music for free. Read audition listings in *DANCE Magazine* or *BACK-STAGE* while you're there. Take a leisurely stroll through the isles of the library and find yourself a good book once and a while for FREE!

Deals on audition gear can be found at Walmart, Ross and Out of The Closet thrift stores. Find local addresses in Appendix G. Become a Costco member and save on groceries, buy dance cards in bulk from your favorite dance studios. Carry change in your car to avoid parking tickets. Spare yourself the extra expenses. If you accumulate parking tickets of 5 or more the city can put a boot on your car, which is the cost of your tickets to have one removed plus a boot removal fee of $150. Don't wait to pay it! You'll have 72 hours to pay or the city has the right to tow your vehicle, which will make the total cost ridiculous.

SAVE FOR A RAINY DAY – INVEST IN YOUR FUTURE

When you get paid from your jobs, try to save a little from each check. You never know when the industry will slow down and you want to be prepared to support yourself through a strike or lack of work. The best advice I have ever heard was to PAY YOURSELF FIRST! Open a savings account and have money automatically transferred from your checking to your savings every month. Be good about not touching this money. You may think that you need that extra trip to Jamaica, but in the long run, you will be so much better off if you leave that money where it is and make smart decisions with your spending habits.

KEEP ACCURATE RECORDS

Make the most of your records to cut costs by taking a good hard look at receipts and expenditures.

CHAPTER THIRTEEN

> ## SICK TIP #43:
> ## UNION CARD ACCESS
> Century 8 Theatre in North Hollywood honors SAG Cards that are current for members to view movies there for free. Caution: Policy may change!
>
> Century 8 North Hollywood
> 12827 Victory Boulevard
> North Hollywood, CA 91606
> (800) 326-3264 Fandango (Movie times)
> (818) 508-1943 Phone (Box office)

The U.S. Department of Labor's Bureau of Labor Statistics states:
Professional dancers and choreographers held about 40,000 jobs in 2006. Employment of dancers and choreographers is expected to grow more slowly than the average for all occupations. Employment of dancers and choreographers is expected to grow 6% during 2006-2016. Median hourly earnings of dancers were $9.55 in May 2006. The middle 50% earned between $7.31 and $17.50. The lowest 10% earned less than $6.62 and the highest 10% earned more than $25.75.

Look at the median hourly income for dancers of $9.55/hour and now let's compare it to what you might make on an award show or 60-minute televised program covered under AFTRA jurisdiction. For example, I was on the Season 8 Semi-Final show of *Dancing With The Stars* with Raphael Saadiq. The total you would make for the entire job from rehearsals to show date is $1,052 *(will adjust to $1,084 as of 11/16/09)* for 3+ group of dancers for a variety show. The production can have you for up to 30 hours over 4 days for that rate for a 60 minute variety show program. Break that down and say you worked all 30 hours, you made about $35 per hour, which is well above the median average listed for 2006. The downside of this is that you may only work one show like this in the month or none at all.

AVERAGE MONTHLY EXPENSES IN HOLLYWOOD
- Rent and utilities (apartment/gas/electric/cable/sewer) $900 - $2,600
- Resume (ink and printing) $20 DIY - $50
- Pictures (session fees + 4x6s/uploads to casting Web sites) $150 - $650+
- Audition and rehearsal clothing $100 - $350+
- Beauty regimen (hair/makeup/tanning/teeth whitening) $100 - $300+
- Transportation (car + car insurance/gas/reg. maintenance) $200 - $850+
- Classes (dance/commercial/acting/voice/conventions) $12 - $300+
- Entertainment research (industry publications/movies) $20 - $150+
- Overall maintenance (laundry/food/nightlife/gym) $500+
- Audition materials (music/monologues/scripts/sheet music) $100+
- Marketing materials (demo reels/headshots/cds/flyers/DVDs) $150+

MONEY, MONEY, MONEY! HOW TO MAKE IT, SAVE IT AND HAVE IT WORK FOR YOU!

It is hard to gauge just how expensive your cost of living will be in Hollywood. If you only take class once a week and buy a bulk number of classes well then you are saving money. If you walk instead of drive to the grocery store instead, then you'll save money too! In each of the variables listed regarding the cost of living in Hollywood, there are costs listed on the low end of the spectrum that make life here more manageable. If you have roommates, usually that brings your rent payment down each month. If you live in North Hollywood, rent is considerably less than living in Beverly Hills, Santa Monica, Westwood or in the heart of Hollywood. You may actually find parking there too, which is a bonus! Try to look at what you need and want and then decide on what you can afford. Remember that once you join a union you must factor in paying union dues every quarter as well.

MY BUDGET – HOW DO I MAKE ONE?

The easiest way to make a budget is to get out a pen and paper and write down two lists: #1: List of your expenses. #2: List your income. The goal here is to make more money than you spend. Essentially not living above your means. In creating your budget, you are able to really see exactly where your money is going. This is where starting out your savings plan prior to moving to Hollywood will help. If you guesstimate your expenditures based on averages and what you've seen on your short trips here, then you can save accordingly. Now, once you move to Hollywood, prices may have gone up, gas may have soared through the roof and work may be slow. Remember that you've got a plan, so stick to it. This also means that your plan can be adjusted. Decrease the amount of money that you are spending on gas. Change the amount of times you planned on eating out and put that money toward going to one extra class at the Edge or Millennium. This is your life and your financial future, so take hold of it now!

In writing down your expenses, it's good to do a test run and keep your receipts for a few weeks, then go back to them and write down exactly where you ate, how much you spent on average, and what kind of things you went back to over and over again *(i.e. the laundromat, grocery store, etc.)*. Keep a log of those receipts and if you find that your spending habits don't fall within your projected budget, then it will be there in black and white staring you in the face. This is when you can change your habits and adjust them to work more for you than against you. Learn to compromise.

EXPENSES TO WRITE DOWN IN THE "BOOK ME! WORKBOOK"

Audition expenses, business expenses, personal expenses and travel expenses.

CHAPTER THIRTEEN

INCOME INFO. - YOU NEED IT!
- Date of the paycheck
- Employer and payroll company
- Production company/name of the product
- Casting director/casting company
- Gross total
- Net total

> For each of the jobs that you list income for, make sure to list the work dates as well. This will help you fill in your audition tracker in the **BOOK ME! Workbook** as well. Use Quicken® or Quickbooks® to track expenses!

EXPENSES (IN-TOWN AND OUT-OF-TOWN)
- Transportation (car + car insurance + gas) - for all in-town expenses
- Transportation (car rental fees) for all out-of-town expenses
- Travel accommodations (hotel/concierge/tips/restaurant/flight) - out-of-town expenses
- Industry publications (*Backstage, The Call Sheet, Variety, Hollywood Reporter*, etc.)
- Per diem/meals/laundry (for in or out-of-town expenses)
- Advertising expenses (photocopying, headshots, 4x6s, resumes, casting Web site posts, post cards, flyers, demo reels, etc.)
- Office supplies
- Business gifts (agency holiday gifts, etc.)
- Legal fees (lawyer, income tax filing services, accountant fees, etc.)
- Workshops/classes (acting, dance, voice, comedy lessons, etc.)
- Hair and makeup maintenance expenses (haircut, etc.)
- Studio rental (rehearsal space fees)
- Entertainment research and nightlife (movies, plays, music, etc.)
- Miscellaneous fees (union dues and initiation fees, banking fees, answering service, P.O. box, childcare, medical, dental, IRS tax payments, charitable contributions)

SICK TIP #44:
FOLLOW THE MONEY!

A word to the wise: Hollywood runs on the "honor system." Paychecks for non-union jobs don't always come in on time. It is best to check in with your agent about the money that is outstanding two weeks after your job has completed and follow up with them after the 30th day. For union jobs, paychecks are usually due to go out within 14 business days after the airing of the show or the shoot day. For residuals, production payroll has up to 15 days after the initial airing of a commercial to send out monies due and for films, it could be from 4-6 months. Unions also have a turn around period in which they are to get your residuals out to you, which could be up to 60 days.

DON'T IGNORE YOUR CREDIT!

Now that you've looked at what you can afford, take a look at your credit score. Many people overlook this because they either don't have any credit or have bad credit. Don't ignore this three-digit number. It can make or break you when you decide to move on up to the East side! That deluxe apartment may not be yours if you don't talk finances with yourself and get serious right away. The best thing you can do is take advantage and obtain a FREE copy of your credit report online. The three main credit bureaus are **Equifax, TransUnion** and **Experian**. Go to www.AnnualCreditReport.com or call (877) 322-8228 to obtain a FREE copy of your credit report from each of the three bureaus.

The overall information on these three credit bureaus may be different as they each get different information about you from many places. You CAN correct any inaccurate information on your credit reports! It is in your best interest to correct the information right away. Go online to dispute any of the items you believe have been paid or represent cleared accounts. Your credit score, or your **FICO**, is something else. This is a score that ranges from 300-850 and is calculated based on the amount of money you spend and how good you are at paying your bills. It comes up with a score that is a tell-all to credit lenders about the amount of debt you have and your ability to pay it. To purchase a copy of your fico score go to www.MyFico.com. You'll be glad that you looked at your status before moving to Hollywood and getting into more debt.

IDENTITY THEFT

Identity theft is the most common crime in cyberspace. I have had my bank accounts hacked several times and was fortunate enough to get back the money that was stolen. By placing a **fraud alert** on your credit bureaus you can make sure that anyone who is trying to access your accounts is questioned and you are notified when this occurs. File a police report if you have fraudulent activity on your account. In some cases, there have been a string of these cyberspace crimes and the more the police know, the better they are at tracking down the criminals.

INVESTING IN YOUR FUTURE

Start an **emergency fund** that you can rely on just in case you need it. This is different than savings. Set up a **deductible fund** too, just in case you are ever in an accident. Be prepared to pay that deductible instead of wondering where the money is going to come from. Avoid balance transfers and cash advances from your credit cards to minimize fees. Also try to only withdraw cash from your bank's

ATM machines to avoid other bank ATM fees. My friend choreographer **Brian Friedman** said in his earlier statements to buy property sooner than later. This is one thing dancers forget to do. It's like a light bulb hits around age 30 and people say, "Hey, that's right, I don't own anything and I should!" Sometimes running around Hollywood and busting your butt to be on your gig will have you forgetting that your wealth will come from smart saving, property owning and a good solid work ethic. Winning the lottery doesn't hurt either.

IRS – INTERNAL REVENUE SERVICE (WWW.IRS.GOV)

Dancers will be given a number of forms to fill out while on set. Most of these have to do with the withholding amounts on your tax forms. The following forms are part of that process:

• W-4: EMPLOYEE'S ALLOWANCE WITHHOLDING CERTIFICATE

On this form, you claim allowances for your tax withholding. The more allowances you claim, the higher your net pay will be because the IRS will deduct less. ***Example: If you claim 0, then the IRS takes more money.*** To be conservative and not have a tax burden (bill) at the end of the year, you may want to claim 0 on Line A. But if you want to receive more money throughout the year in your paycheck claim yourself or (1) in the claim box. Ask your tax professional for help.

• I-9: EMPLOYMENT ELIGIBILITY VERIFICATION

This form is used to verify that you are eligible to work in the United States. You can provide your U.S. driver's license and Social Security card or present your passport as verification.

The forms that you will receive at the end of the tax year will be your **W-2** and **1099**. You will receive 1099s from jobs where you were employed as an **independent contractor** and tax was not withheld. Employers have until January 31st to mail your 1099s or W-2 to you. Update each employer with your correct mailing address or else they may end up at the wrong address. Ask payroll companies and your agent for a running total that includes all jobs, their work dates, payments and withholdings. The filing deadline for your tax returns is April 15th. Don't be late. If you know you will be late file for an extension. You may also receive a **W-9** form. Fill out this form completely and return.

PROTECT YOUR ASSETS

If you're a dancer with signature moves, know one thing: You can't patent or trademark a dance move! You can own it by making it your signature step. If you've got a series of moves that you think are SICK, you can film, document and copyright them. Go to www.Copyright.gov and download **Form PA** for **performing arts works** or simply register your work online for $45. Copyright rates are subject to change. Read *Copyright of Choreographic Works* by Julie Van Camp at www.csulb.edu/~jvancamp/copyrigh.html for a detailed look into copyrighting choreography.

> ## SICK TIP #45:
> ## FILING A CLAIM
> You may end up doing a job that does not pay you in a timely manner. For SAG or AFTRA jobs, you can file a claim with the union. They will investigate your claim and follow up on your behalf. Your agent can only do so much to follow the money trail and many times when a production company is late paying talent, the filing of a claim sometimes lights a fire in their belly to correct the error and not repeat the mistake. Please do not ever feel like you are in the wrong when a payment deadline has passed. It is your responsibility to follow up. For non-union jobs it is more difficult to seek payment from employers.

UNION BANKING AND DISCOUNTS
Find yourself a nice interest rate at a few of the industry-affiliated banks. The SAG/AFTRA Credit Union and the Actors Federal Credit Union are two industry-related banks. Visit www.UnionPlus.org for union discounts as well.

INCORPORATE AS A BUSINESS
You are a business so why don't you operate like one. Incorporate yourself by going to www.sos.ca.gov/business.

CHAPTER FOURTEEN

BOOKED SOLID:
Building Your Brand With A Business Plan

Figuring out how to budget your career is made easier in Chapter 13, but figuring out your strategy on how to achieve your ultimate goal may take a bit more planning. Becoming a hot commodity may be something you continually work at, just look at the careers of some of the most famous pop stars like Madonna. Forever reinventing themselves, it takes strategy and ultimately creativity to make your brand last a lifetime.

Creating your brand is part of your marketing plan and marketing is only one part of the overall business plan you will need to outline your future goals. You can say, "I want to be in movies one day." That is a great way to reinforce your goals. As a kid, to harness those goals, I always wrote them down. A great way to build your brand is to create your own business plan to really look into your future and develop a road map that will help you get there. Not only will this help you see where you're going but it will also help you understand the magnitude of your goals and dreams.

Putting to paper your ideas may sound like a daunting task but once you write your ideas down, updating and revising your plan will be easy. In life future employers will ask you, "Where do you see yourself in 5 years? And in 10 years?" In the **BOOK ME! Workbook**, these questions are also there to help you really dig deep and find out exactly what your goals are and how to write them down in an attainable fashion.

BOOKED SOLID: BUILDING YOUR BRAND WITH A BUSINESS PLAN

As a professional dancer or choreographer, you may not think of yourself as a business person. In fact you are an independent contractor on many gigs and must treat your talent as a skill that producers want in their productions. You are a self-run business, which means **you need a business plan**.

The road map begins with your goals. Set them high because if you aim low, you will only reap the rewards you set out for yourself. A business plan can be formatted in plenty of ways. You can make a simple outline, or make your plan very detailed to include your overall finances. At the start of this business plan is your **Executive Summary**. Put into words what you feel are your business attributes. What is your purpose?

Next up is your **Objective**. Talk about what you do? What clientele do you serve? What are your best qualities? Following this list your **mission**. Where do you see yourself in the entertainment industry? Where do you fit in? The **keys to a successful career** are in your hands. List the things you believe necessary to help you move your career in a positive direction. Make your bullet points specific and honest. If you are honest with yourself in the beginning, you will make your career path much more attainable.

Do you have multiple goals? You may have to take a long look at your overall brand. Will all of your goals fit into one business model? Or will you need to separate out your goals into different branding strategies? It is best to make a list of what your aspirations are and then move forward with your business plan accordingly. If you want to be a medical doctor, a film producer and a professional dancer, putting them in the same business plan may have a few kinks to work out. Your path may be different for all three. This is where your strategy comes in and your ability to decide which goal to focus on first is a very important part of your overall plan. You may want to determine if all three fit into the same plan and if you can itemize how you feel your brand incorporates all three. If not, you may need to readjust your plan and separate out portions that don't fit as easily into the brand's identity.

The next portion of your plan needs to include who the **owner** will be, the **location** where you will reside and what **products and services** you will offer. Be specific as to your skills in this section. You may even want to talk about future skills that you will add to increase your brand's effectiveness in the market. Your **strategy and implementation** come into play next. From this point you will need to describe how you will put your plan into action. This may be to describe

CHAPTER FOURTEEN

your move to Los Angeles and the challenges that you face when planning the move (how you will overcome these challenges financially, adjusting to a new city and settling into a new scene). This may involve describing phone calls to prospective agents, creating your reel, taking a headshot and creating a resume. Putting your plan into action is the second step in accomplishing your career goals, the first step is to visualize your goals and put the effort into making a plan.

Following this you will need a **marketing and promotion strategy**. This is where your tools in your tool belt will be utilized. Dancers are always seen and never heard. Use your voice to get your message out. Like Jessie J says, *"Stomp Stomp, I've arrived."* Make your first impression on the entertainment industry a noticeable one. This involves making a detailed guide to the marketing materials you will use to promote yourself. You can create your own YouTube channel and upload choreography from your regular classes, make flyers about an upcoming performance, create a business card or send inquiry letters to agencies. Whatever you do, write it down first. Then make a schedule of when you will use your promotion strategy, the dates of your mailings and keep an accurate record of what is getting you attention and what may have missed the mark.

Try to make alliances with your fellow dancers. In essence make friends. Not superficial, but REAL friends. I've heard people say plenty of times, "Oh, we're friends on Facebook." Know who your true friends are. Ask yourself, who you regularly keep in contact with, who replies to your emails when you send out a performance/event flyer and how many people you actually speak to on the phone or make it a point to meet up with in class or for fun outings. In this business, it isn't about fake friends, this business is about real lifelong relationships.

Create a **Sales Forecast** (include profit and loss) for your business plan. Include how much it will cost to create headshots each year, the photo shoot and the reproduction costs. Include how much your mailings will cost, business cards, mass emailing subscription (MailChimp or Constant Contact), travel costs (i.e. gas and car maintenance) in addition to your phone bill. Your cell phone is your lifeline. Having Internet on your phone will be a lifesaver when being able to receive audition notices and respond right away to your agent or even a friend who has a potential gig in mind for you. This expense is a business expense. Write it down as such.

Finally, determine who will be on your **team**. What management will you have? What agency will represent you? What publicity team will you employ? What marketing team will help you with your efforts? All of these people are part of your team. At first you may not be able to afford a fully staffed team. You know what this means? **YOU ARE YOUR TEAM!** Just because you can't afford them at the beginning of your journey, doesn't mean you shouldn't include them in your business plan. You will be doing the bulk of the work, write down the job functions, the duties involved in each position, then list your name beside the position. You are responsible for these essential aspects of your career.

A major part of your business plan is to incorporate your **financial outlook**. Include what you see for your future for Year 1, Year 2, Year 3, Year 4, Year 5 and Year 10 of your career. This may all be in theory and you can adjust this later, but it is important to grasp that you do see your career longevity. You want to make an affirmative statement about how much you believe in your talent but writing all of this down. By creating a business plan with such depth and detail, you also are committing to being serious about embarking on such a lifestyle and career path. **You are choosing to make your dreams a reality.**

BOOK ME! WORKBOOK EXERCISES - PART 4

Some **BOOK ME! Workbook** exercise topics from Part Four of this book are listed below. Purchase the **BOOK ME! Workbook** online at: www.ColtonCollection.com

- **Budgets are bootilicious! Make a plan to save.**
- **Know your worth - Outline your future in a business plan.**
- **Secure your financial future - Take steps through education.**
- **Put you first - Save a penny, earn a penny.**
- **Understand your rights and the complex language of contracts.**

CHAPTER FOURTEEN

Sandra says...

- Dance is a business and YOU are a business. Invest in Quickbooks® or Quicken® to help track your finances.

- Know when your W-2s and 1099s are coming and prepare for your taxes early.

- Keep accurate records of your income and expenses. Save often!

- It isn't enough to want to retire. Buy property as soon as you can afford it and plan for your future.

- Take advantage of union banking *(i.e. SAG/AFTRA Credit Union)* and their rates on home loans.

- Invest in your future and pay yourself first!

- Take a finance course and don't ignore your credit report!

> **POINT TAKEN:**
> We are all so consumed with getting to the audition and booking the job that we forget to save the money we actually make. The check-to-check mentality that we've grown accustomed to is not the way to save for the future. If you can't count on income, you need to figure out a way to make side income. Think about it now so it will be there in the future.

PART FIVE

CAREER PATHS & THE DANCE COMMUNITY

CHAPTER FIFTEEN

BE PART OF THE DANCE COMMUNITY!

Becoming part of the dance community is crucial to your success within it. Keep seeking knowledge in the community and you will continually grow as an artist. Some of the works showcased by dancers have now become exciting events to attend in the community. Attend monthly events like Choreographer's Carnival, Groove Night hosted by the Groovaloos and various workshops and open jams hosted by the Beat Freaks, Quest Crew and the Jabbawockeez. Don't wait for opportunity to knock, seek out opportunities to be part of the Hollywood dance community.

An event that has taken shape over the last few years is Dancescape. A non-profit organization that showcases dancers and choreographers. The money raised is donated to public school art and music programs. Performances are held at Aqua Lounge in Beverly Hills, Calif. You can find more information about upcoming events on their Web site at www.CheshireMoon.org.

Take master classes and attend benefits and fundraisers for the arts help to continually grow the community and create opportunities for dance to thrive and extend to many more audiences and deserving youth. It isn't enough to cultivate and perform your craft, it is also your responsibility to pass on your knowledge. Supporting fellow dancers and their upcoming projects only creates more avenues for dancers to travel. Without supporting one another, the art will not continue to transform and connect with so many like it has to date. Try to develop your own shows and invite fellow dancers to support your hard work.

CHOREOGRAPHER'S CARNIVAL

The Choreographer's Carnival: "Choreographer's Ball" takes place on the last Wednesday of every month at Avalon in Hollywood, Calif. except for the months of December and August. This event gives choreographers a chance to showcase their work and dancers a chance to be seen by top Hollywood dance agents and their peers. The show begins around 11 p.m. and has two acts consisting of 15-25 dance-driven performances. Incorporating some singers, poets and rappers within their format, Choreographer's Carnival is a great event that showcases new talent and can give new dancers and up-and-coming choreographers an opportunity to obtain footage for their dance reels and generate a bit of buzz about them as well. Carey and Paulette Azizian produce Carnival. Go to the Web site at www.ChoreographersCarnival.com. I have performed at Carnival twice and was excited to have the opportunity to share my hard work with a community that is supportive. Key Club allows 18 and over admission for this event. There is also a show presented in New York, Chicago, London, Sydney and Tokyo each year.

CAREY AND PAULETTE AZIZIAN

"Dance is the greatest form of free expression. A story told through the motion of the body. Love, passion, fear, anger and all of life's journeys can be shown through the art of dance. **This is Carnival.**

"Carnival started nine and a half years ago to give working choreographers and dancers a venue where they can have free artistic expression without the constraints of an artist, a director or a script. Carnival is an event where it features not only choreographers from the film and video industries, but from all over the world: Paris, Japan, New York, Las Vegas, Texas, Florida and many more. Where else can you see a show that highlights not only hip-hop but ballet, funk, lyrical, tap, modern, performance art and spoken word. Only at the Carnival, where you get more dance for your dollar. Thank you for your support throughout the years. This would never be possible without you. **DANCE COMMUNITY UNITE!**"

Much Love,
Carnival Staff

BE PART OF THE COMMUNITY!

PASSION FOR DANCE

I first heard of **Passion For Dance** from Ben Allen when he was choreographing for my first performance at Carnival. A talented dancer and choreographer he has traveled the world teaching and developing dancers through an organization he and co-founder Kristen Marshall created. Ben Allen elaborates on the project by stating, "The Passion for Dance Project is a Los Angeles based cultural non-profit organization. Established in 2004, The Passion for Dance Project awards scholarships to young dancers ages 18-25, who are serious about pursuing a career in the dance industry. The organization seeks to assist those who possess the talent, commitment and dedication to succeed, but lack the financial resources to do so. Through a program called 'The Experience' recipients will receive the training and mentoring needed to sustain a career in the business. The Passion for Dance Project is funded through private donations and corporate grants. If you are interested in supporting the arts, especially in supporting the artists in dance please contact (323) 301-5967 or at www.PassionForDance.org for more information."

Ben Allen describes the vision of the Passion for Dance Project. "Ultimately, our organization was created not only to fund young dancers who are trying to make it in the business, to offer scholarships to help them pursue their dream, but also as an organization to be a resource to help any dancer whether they are just getting their start or already working. We want to be a network of people and information that can be there for the dance community. Why isn't there money out there? If you decide to go to school to be a doctor, you could probably apply for a scholarship at most schools and get money to help pursue your career. So, why isn't there money for the arts, for dance, unless you go to a performing arts school? Or a place like FIDM (Fashion Institute of Design and Merchandising), where it is an institution and you can get scholarship money. When you come out to Hollywood, it is the same. You know what you want to do with your life, this is your career, but there is no money. We want to change that."

CHAPTER FIFTEEN

DANCIN' 4 A CAUSE

In the past year there have been a few sudden losses to the dance community. In efforts to continue to help the families and friends of the dancers who have passed away much too soon we have seen an unforgettable love emerge in the form of **Dancin' 4 a Cause**. This charitable organization is a start-up by former dancer and dance educator Maria Diaz-Estorga. I met Maria in the hospital while visiting Tiffanie Washington. Maria is a giving and generous woman who sees the need for dancers to come together and support one another. By creating an opportunity for choreographers to teach and give their time for free she and others create a loving and warm atmosphere where dancers can come and experience different styles with the proceeds going to help dancers in times of crisis. The organization has most recently helped to raise awareness for two friends and dancers lost. Tiffanie Washington and Gabriel Paige will be missed and their memories live on.

MARIA AND NICHOLAS DIAZ-ESTORGA (FOUNDERS)

"Dancin' 4 a Cause uses dance as a platform, to help the dance community and world in times of need. Dancin' 4 a Cause serves as an organization to inspire and bring awareness and resources to help others that are in need in times of crisis, whether it be a medical diagnosis, drugs/alcohol, homeless, unplanned pregnancy, death, etc. Just through the last few years the dance community has grown rapidly, and more than ever dancers are struggling with lifestyle changes, pressures and finances. Through workshops, events, TV programming, private donations, choreographers, dancers, agents, celebrities and dance studios around the world, we can meet these needs and make a difference! The heart of Dancin' 4 A Cause is to love and inspire others to give back!" (www.Dancin4aCause.com)

It is important that the dance community stay connected because we have each other to lean on in hard times and we need to try to maintain and support an organization such as this one because with unexpected losses like Tiffanie and Gabe, dancers need to have a network of support. Please continue to support Dancin' 4 a Cause even while events are not readily taking place because the support they provide is invaluable and the financial support they give is something that needs to be replenished so that it is at the ready when and if a dancer needs it.

Please continue to support this organization at:
www.Dancin4aCause.com or www.MySpace.com/Dancin4aCause

BE PART OF THE COMMUNITY!

L.A. CHOREOGRAPHERS AND DANCERS
www.LAChoreographersAndDancers.org

Louise Reichlin, founder of L.A. Choreographers and Dancers has been educating dancers and choreographing dance for over 30 years. Louise compiled the **Southern California Dance Directory** at www.LAChoreographersAndDancers.org. "When I put it together, I already had a big list. I was on the board of the Dance Resource Center and I called around and compiled lists of resources. I keep updating it every time we do a mailing. We have e-news now also. If they are a dance school they are not on the list. All listings are resources that have to be professional companies that pay their dancers in some capacity and there are also related organizations like agents or dance studios that rent rehearsal space. I feel very strongly that dancers have to get paid."

DIZZY FEET FOUNDATION
www.DizzyFeet.org

Dizzy Feet Foundation is a new charitable organization founded by Nigel Lythgoe, Katie Holmes, Adam Shankman and Carrie Ann Inaba. Dizzy Feet aims to establish scholarship funds to help disadvantaged youth afford arts education in addition to providing teacher accreditation.

BOOGIEZONE
www.BoogieZone.com

MONIE ADAMSON (Choreographer)
SC: Can you say a little bit about BoogieZone, your studio and how it helps dancers navigate and connect in the dance community?
MA: Focus Dance Center and BoogieZone came together in partnership 4 years ago in an attempt to offer the semi-professional and professional dancer a place to come in Orange County and train with top industry teachers. It has definitely created an environment  where dancers can come and connect to the dance community and make connections with industry choreographers. We are thrilled that it has become a place to be seen and also given the dancer a place to possibly network their way into a dance company or open doors to doing industry work. Focus is also the home of the hip-hop company *Breed* (an extension of BoogieZone) and a studio that offers over 200 classes in all styles of dance and to all ages from the beginner to the professional.

CHAPTER FIFTEEN

DANCE TRACK FOUNDATION

Dance Track Foundation is a non-profit organization created to honor and promote the appreciation, recognition and continued growth of the contributions of dancers and choreographers to American culture – from the artistic and street founders of the past to the yet to be conceived master pieces of future dance professionals. Dance Track Foundation accomplishes this mission through programs and activities that interact and energize the dance industry and artistic community as well as the general public. The Foundation works in partnership with *Dance Track Magazine* to bring attention to crucial topics such as importance of dance and arts education and the necessity of cultivating our diverse and ever emerging young artists and genres of dance. For more information on how to donate and apply for scholarships visit **www.DanceTrackFoundation.org.**

AGENCY SHOWCASES AND CHOREOGRAPHY AUDITIONS

Participate in agency showcases. These events are to gain attention for their clients, dancers and choreographers alike. Support your agency, fellow dancers, choreographers and artists who are putting their hearts and souls into each and every performance. Recording artists, touring shows and upcoming Broadway workshops often ask choreographers to put together an audition piece of their own to be showcased live. By participating in the process you could be given the chance to work with choreographers that you may have been dying to "live" for. Give it your best and you could possibly come out with good footage for your own demo reel and a lasting working relationship with a choreographer and fellow dancers.

ADDITIONAL RESOURCE FOR DANCERS

The Dance Resource Center L.A. is a great place to start. Go to www.drc-la.org/ for more information.

SICK TIP #46:
DANCE AND FAITH - BUILD A COMMUNITY!

Share dance within other facets of your life. Many churches have dance ministries where you can help educate young children with the art of dance. Branch out into the community and share your passion in an inner city school or at an after school program. The community is small but you can help it grow. There are certain challenges with funding in school programs for arts education and by volunteering your time to help underprivileged children you can make a difference in a young person's life. Go to www.CoachArt.org or the Boys & Girls Clubs of America at www.BGCA.org.

DANCE MEDIA AND CRITICISM

By supporting the community this also means one can take a more exploratory view of the world of dance also. The *Los Angeles Times* ended its full time dance critic position in 2008 and the few media outlets that are specifically devoted to dance are dwindling every day. I've chosen, with my background in magazines, to create a new publication that will help to promote dance and all things that it encompasses (i.e. fashion, music and entertainment). I hope with this new publication, **Dance Track Magazine**, that dance will be viewed in a more current fashion exploring the world of commercial dance with fresh new eyes. This publication will give an opportunity for dancers to express themselves with reader submissions, giving young choreographers and dancers another opportunity to be profiled and gain exposure for their budding careers. This will be a media outlet that will also shine a spotlight on the problems facing the industry and ways to find workable solutions. Each career path is different, and in the world of entertainment, genres collide. This new magazine inspires you to find your own dance track. To submit your stories, ideas, comments and suggestions, please send an e-mail to: submission@dancetrackmagazine.com. To subscribe go to **www.DANCETRACKMAGAZINE.com** today! Send all dance-related press releases to: press@dancetrackmagazine.com.

SICK TIP #47:
SUPPORT DANCE THROUGH NATIONAL ORGANIZATIONS: NFAA AND NEA

Two organizations that are supporting the arts are the National Foundation For Advancement In The Arts (www.nfaa.org) and The National Endowment For The Arts (nea.gov). Contributing to these organizations is also a way to continue to see arts programs and individuals thrive on a national stage.

"The mission of the National Foundation for Advancement of the Arts is to identify emerging artists and assist them at critical junctures in their educational and professional development." (nfaa.org) *"The NEA is an independent federal agency supporting artists and arts organizations and bringing the arts to all Americans."* (nea.gov)

CHAPTER FIFTEEN

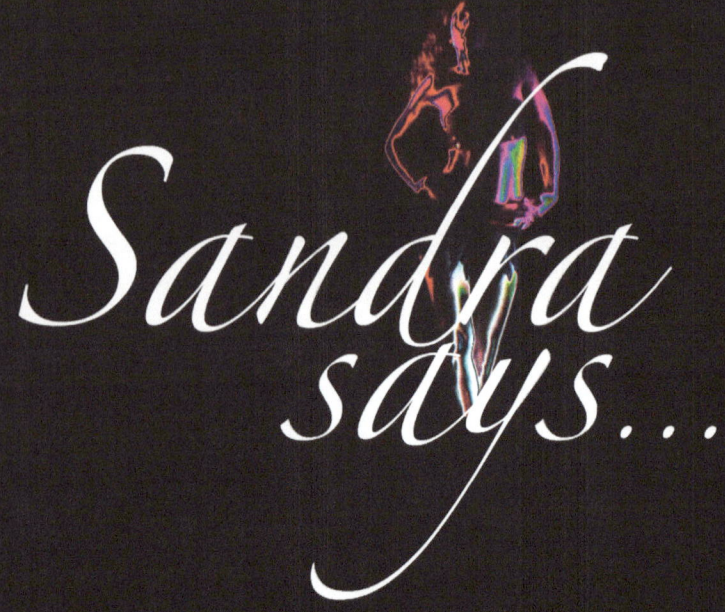

Sandra says...

- Once you make it big, don't forget the people who got you there.

- Give back to the community. Attend events that support dance and the arts.

- Join fellow dancers in support of charitable organizations that benefit dancers and dance-related causes.

BE PART OF THE COMMUNITY!

- *Dancin' 4 a Cause, Art4Life, Passion For Dance, Dizzy Feet Foundation* and the *Sandra Colton Foundation* are a few organizations that do great things to support dancers in need.

- Participate in choreography showcases. Be a part of something special.

- Connect with the online community at BoogieZone.com, DancePlug.com and DanceOn.com.

- Create your own way of contributing to the art form.

> **POINT TAKEN:**
> The secret to dance is that so many people want to share it. The way that the game *telephone* used to work is kind of how the creativity flows with dance. By watching someone perform a piece, you may be inspired to do something great of your own. Dance makes us wake up, think, create and live in a way most other things do not.

CHAPTER SIXTEEN

CAREER LONGEVITY AND TRANSITIONS

TRANSITIONING TO OTHER AREAS OF ENTERTAINMENT

Performers who have many interests make a very big mistake by trying too many things at one time. If you have many interests, it is a great idea to cultivate those interests and try out new and different platforms to showcase your talent. A mistake might be to completely abandon your mainstay for a huge leap to another field. If you are making your living as a dancer and would like to pursue singing for example, don't quit your dance career outright until you start making money as a singer or can support yourself doing that as a profession. It is a huge mistake to hope you will make money at something else just as you did in your profession as a dancer.

The entertainment industry is finicky and doesn't always reward your efforts right away. My advice is to gradually get into other interests and hone your other skills along the way. Protect yourself from going completely broke. Don't give up your main source of income altogether. Be smart about your choices. Make a plan. Have a strategy! Take baby steps toward your goals and live through them by saving money and getting to the next level with a mapped out plan of action. The Actors' Fund is a resource as well as Career Transition For Dancers.

Career Transition For Dancers
www.CareerTransition.org

The Actors' Fund
www.ActorsFund.org

CAREER LONGEVITY AND TRANSITIONS

Career Transition For Dancers is an organization that helps dancers find new and different ways to use their craft and transition themselves into a working environment. Providing educational scholarships, career counseling and more, this organization knows how to nurture dancers and find them a path that will best keep them moving forward.

If you are dead set on continuing in an alternative field of entertainment such as acting, singing, directing or producing – Don't quit your day job! Do what you're best at and cultivate the other area until it is profitable enough for you to stop dancing as a way to make your living. Go back through the early chapters of this book and ask yourself, "What kind of singer am I? What kind of films would I direct?" Set goals, outline a career path for yourself, and go after it. It isn't enough to see yourself as an actor right away without taking a class to determine if you like it. Do your homework and really weigh the pros and cons of any transition.

Take a class (i.e. Groundlings, commercial acting, scene study) to find out if it is something you like before canceling on each audition with your agent because if you do that enough times eventually they won't call you. Maybe you're a natural, maybe you have a gift. It isn't enough in this business to just be talented. I'll repeat that again. It isn't enough in this business to just be talented! You have to want it. You have to dream it. You have to love it. Most of all you have to go after it full steam ahead and have the drive to push through all of the ups and downs you will face. Choreographer Michael Rooney said, on the set of a Subway $5 Footlong commercial that, *"The only way to get to the top is to start at the bottom."* He's right. Appreciate what you have right now, find the humor in the craziness you'll encounter along the way, and don't ever give up. The moment you give up on your dream is the moment you know it will never come true.

I recommend taking Craig Colvin's commercial class, Bob Garrett's musical theatre workshop and Candy Herman's cold reading class. These are not the only classes you can take. Ask your agency who they recommend. Contact the instructor and ask to audit a class to see if you understand their in-class techniques. You may not gel with the teacher and it may end up not being the right class for you. You need to be able to connect and feel safe in the learning environment since you'll be opening yourself up in new and different ways. Find what works for you. Some acting classes feel more like therapy than an acting class. Remember, no teacher should ever tell you they have to break you down before building you back up. Breaking a bad performance habit is not the same as breaking one's spirit.

CHAPTER SIXTEEN

TRANSITIONING TO ASSISTANT CHOREOGRAPHER

JENNIFER GOLDSMITH
DANCER AND ASSISTANT TO MARGUERITE DERRICKS

SC: Most think choreographer's assistants simply teach the steps or provide an example of the movement at an audition or in a rehearsal. Describe your job functions.
JG: Yes, there is a lot more that goes into assisting. While teaching and showing the steps is a very big part of the job, assisting/being an associate entails so much more. First, you have to know the needs and personality of the choreographer whom you are assisting. It's so important to be in tune with them, to know how to read who they are and how you can make their job easier. In my experience assisting Marguerite, I'll give you an example of all the things I do on a typical job with her; I usually go to a meeting(s) with her when projects come up. I take notes to make sure all of her questions and concerns get answered in addition to establishing my role so the producers, directors, actors, etc. become comfortable with me as a part of the choreography team. I then help to gather research materials and other references we need to execute the job.

For instance, if the job is all about disco dancing, we research past video clips, movies and archives for inspiration to create our own movement for the job. We almost always have a prep day to plan out what the movement and choreography will be. If Marguerite holds a casting, I make the phone calls to the agencies to convey what we are looking for so they can make sure their clients get to the audition. I set up the casting sessions and rehearsal sessions with dance studios and keep in contact with production during the duration of the job to make sure they have everything they need on our end and vice versa. Then, when rehearsing with the dancers, I will teach and show the choreography and make sure they remain clean and precise. It's very important for me to retain the choreography and know what's going on at all times, in case Marguerite needs to make quick changes or adjustments. Sometimes these changes need to be made immediately and it's my job to be able to make that happen for her as quickly as possible and very often on the spot. Marguerite values my creative input and opinions as well, which is such a wonderful thing.

SC: Give a little insight into the creative process and how choreographers work, think and create?
JG: I have found that for me, I really need to know the person I'm working for so that I can deliver exactly what they need. And when you work with someone for so long, you know how they like things done, so over time it makes the process of the

jobs a lot more effective and efficient. We have built a solid relationship along the way, and when you spend that much time working on all different types of jobs, you start to learn how the choreographer thinks. Half of the time I know what Marguerite is going to say without her even finishing her thoughts. You must be able to anticipate. Every choreographer has different ways of working and different needs to be met. With Marguerite, I know she likes efficiency, organization, preparation, details and hard workers. For up-and-coming dancers, I would tell them that assisting a choreographer is a fantastic way to learn in this business. It's so hands-on and it's really good training for your own growth as a dancer, teacher and choreographer. It's such a demanding job, but you learn responsibility and work ethic. You also build relationships along the way, which is always crucial. Because of my experience as an assistant, other choreographers, as well as producers and directors know what they can expect of me when they hire me. They know how I work and whom I have worked with and that makes a big difference.

SC: *What qualities do you need to possess as an assistant that go beyond the gift of dance?*
JG: Responsibility, loyalty, patience, listening and communication skills, efficiency and organization.

DANA WILSON
DANCER AND ASSISTANT TO WADE ROBSON

SC: *Most think choreographer's assistants simply teach the steps or provide an example of the movement at an audition or in a rehearsal. Describe your job functions.*
DW: It is the assistant choreographer's role to be the canvas that the choreographer can look to during the creative process. It is their job to remember the details of the choreography so that they can better clean and teach the work to cast members. They may also be called upon to make choreographic decisions in the choreographer's absence, and act as the liaison between dancers, choreographers, directors and other positions of management.

SC: *Who did you start assisting first and is there anything about their creative process that might give a little insight into how choreographers work, think and create?*
DW: The first person I ever officially assisted is Jason Parsons. Since then I have assisted *(in a class setting)* Nick Bass, Brian Friedman, Dee Caspary, Blake McGrath and many others. In a professional setting, Marty Kudelka, Wade Robson and Toni Basil. I have learned that everyone works differently and they do what they do, the way they do it because it works for them. Some create based on a story, some based on a visual, or a picture they have in their head, and some based

CHAPTER SIXTEEN

on feelings. I try my best to fit the mold of whatever their creative process may be as to not actually inhibit them from working at their best.

SC: What qualities do you need to possess as an assistant that go beyond the gift of dance?
DW: Assistants must be organized, punctual, attentive, have good creative problem solving skills, communication skills, and be ready to be the first to get to work and the last to leave!

GINA STARBUCK also had a good piece of advice for dancers looking to become assistant choreographers as she has assisted Brian Friedman, Blake McGrath, Bobby Newberry, Andre Fuentes and many more.

"A good assistant is hard working, remembers choreography, is well-mannered but strong enough to tell the person they're assisting when they've made a mistake. Someone who is patient and good at interacting with their fellow dancer."

FAQ: HOW DOES A CHOREOGRAPHER SELECT A DANCER TO BE THEIR ASSISTANT CHOREOGRAPHER?

FATIMA ROBINSON (CHOREOGRAPHER/DIRECTOR)
"I try and hire people that are strong in what I am not. I like people that are along the same temperature as I am. It really is about the personality and how you gel with someone."

PAUL BECKER (CHOREOGRAPHER)

"Being an assistant, you have to have a special quality because you have to contribute in a diplomatic way. When I look to hire an assistant, I look for someone I can trust. Sometimes assistants are out to get the job(s) of the choreographer. It's not good to overhear things where people claim that they've made up choreography as their own, when you've made up the routines. I had a great assistant for *So You Think You Can Dance Canada* because he makes up for the qualities that I don't have. For example, I'm not good at counting. He's great at that and great at cleaning. A lot of times a choreographer is looking for an assistant that makes up for the qualities and traits that they may be lacking. I usually do because you are only as strong as your team."

TRANSITIONING INTO ACTING

While your transition may be a rocky or smooth one, here are a few words from dancers who have made a successful career move into acting and want to give some advice to others who might choose to do so as well.

BRIANA EVIGAN - STEP UP 2

"Before I got *Step Up 2*, I was ready to put my dancing and acting aside because I was fed up with the rejection of auditions. One of those last auditions I went to happened to be for *Step Up 2* and I ended up booking the role. I was very pleased with this nice surprise that really lead to the start of my (acting) career. It was difficult trying to remember all the choreography and also have the weight of the movie as an actress on my shoulders, but as I always say, 'Ya do what ya gotta do.' Transitioning into acting for me was the most exciting part. Acting is so fun because you get to embody roles and characters that are different from yourself. I'd say it takes a lot of dedication and determination to keep yourself going in the business, especially once you're in. What I would say to anyone that moves to Los Angeles with hopes of succeeding as an actress, dancer, singer, etc. is to be prepared for rejection, but remember if it's what you love to do, you will be seen by the right person. Keep going, stay strong and work your hardest to get your foot in the door. Most of all, don't let the people around you put you down or intimidate you. The best tool you can have is confidence so that when you walk into the room to get that job, it's yours."

GUS CARR - BRING IT ON, ALL OR NOTHING

"It's a lot more specific on TV and film. Directors have different visions. Stage is louder, film is toned down. Start ASAP!! Get in class and start learning. Not every movie is a dance movie. If you want to really transition into acting be ready for all roles. It's a lot of work but a lot of fun as well. Use what you have in front of you, such as your dancing abilities, to give you an up on certain roles. But be ready to do non-dancing roles and have the confidence to kill it just as hard. I wish I would have listened and started my acting career sooner. I was so wrapped up in dance that I lost focus of what I really wanted to do and that's sing and act. Spend your time and money wisely! If acting and singing are your passion, start acting and vocals as soon as possible. Auditions are your best classes. You can learn so much if you pay attention. Dance gives me that one up on other actors going out for the same role but this is Hollywood and everyone does everything. Just always do your best and that's all you can do. Never stop trying to get better and always know there is room for improvement."

CHAPTER SIXTEEN

ROBERT HOFFMAN - STEP UP 2, YOU GOT SERVED

"Doors opened for me with the movie *You Got Served*. I've been playing around making videos on my own since I was a kid, and I developed a comfort level that way.

"I have nontraditional, minimal advice on acting because it is a subjective, personal art and an uncontrollable business. You can't just walk into a room and prove you're the best actor. In dancing you can turn more, flip higher, dance harder...you can prove that you have what it takes to get the job. I initially had no desire to get into the acting business 'cause all I saw was a lot of people who were 'struggling actors.' Dancing was different to me, you may or may not make money, but I could never consider myself a 'struggling dancer,' just a dancer. I realized you have to first admit to yourself what you really want, otherwise you may perpetually feel down if you gauge yourself based on your career path in a business as undefinable as acting. If you love acting, then act - plays, Internet videos, stand up comedy, improv comedy, short films, on the street, in your home, at a party...anywhere. Then you will be happy and with good business tactics a deserved success will follow. If you love the thought of being rich and famous, then you are getting into a situation where you are setting yourself up for disappointment.

"There's no guarantee or way to 'work the hardest' in acting. There's working hard - there's staying true to yourself, and there's expressing yourself completely - and those things will bring you success in the entertainment industry on some level. But 'rich and famous' is not an honorable or realistic goal in my eyes. I believe most of the people in this business have just not admitted to themselves what their goal really is. Usually, their goal is not actually to be the greatest dancer they can be or inspire as many people as possible with their acting - most people's goal is to be rich and famous. And when you are chasing that goal, you aren't truly giving yourself to your art to become the best you can be. These are the many people that have bad things to say about this business. If you really wanted to act then you wouldn't wait to audition for a 60 million dollar movie to come along to do it. You would want to do it regardless.

"Being really good at anything will expose you to other things. Acting is what you make of it. Hollywood is whatever you make of it. Every business has people to avoid. Hollywood is the same, except those types of people are just more exposed because the stakes are higher in Hollywood. Here you don't just get a raise, you could get fame and fortune. Because of this, many people who come to Hollywood are more willing to jeopardize their integrity with the hopes of becoming rich and famous. Manipulative types know that and take full advantage. If you associate with people that your gut tells you are not good people and something bad happens, Hollywood didn't do that to you, you did that to you."

TRANSITIONING INTO TEACHING DANCE

If you want to transition from dancing into teaching dance, remember what your experience was like growing up taking dance class. Take the good and dispel the bad! As a teacher, you are guiding young lives toward their future. Remember this every time you see or watch a class where the teacher is looking more at themselves in the mirror than focusing on helping to train the students in front of them. To some teachers, the class can end up being about them instead of the real reason that teachers should be teaching, to educate and pass on knowledge. Everyone has that one favorite teacher who inspired them to be better and work their hardest. Be that person for every young person and reap the rewards!

TRANSITIONING INTO SINGING

To transition from dancing to singing, you've got plenty of on-the-job training right in front of you. It isn't easy to make the leap because most will always see you as a dancer. Great examples of dancers who've made the leap and succeeded in the singing world are Britney Spears, Jennifer Lopez and Paula Abdul. When performing with a recording artist, it is important to watch from the wings during performances and on tours. Do your job, first and foremost, but when you're waiting around to go back on stage, watch how the artist interacts with the crowd, see what you would like to emulate and take with you as an artist. Develop your on-stage senses for what works and what doesn't in a small venue versus a large arena.

TRANSITIONING INTO STUNT WORK AND HOSTING

BROOKE LONG - Deal or No Deal, Laker Girl

"One thing with dance is that you go to an audition and you've been dancing your whole life, you learn a routine and you go. With hosting and modeling, people just think you stand in front of a camera. When you first started dancing you fell on your butt. You couldn't do anything, you didn't know what a pirouette was, and it's kind of the same thing. The hardest thing for people to realize is that it isn't easy. Take class and put the work in. It doesn't get handed to you. It doesn't happen over night. You also might invest in some martial arts classes as dancers make very good transitions into stunt work or body double work especially if they're a gymnast."

CHAPTER SIXTEEN

TRANSITIONING INTO COMEDY

ANJELAH JOHNSON
ON MOVING FROM DANCE TO COMEDY/ACTING

"I moved out (to L.A.) in 2003 right after the Super Bowl and was working with Clear Talent for about a year and then I stopped going to dance auditions and started auditioning more for commercials. My dance agent sent me on commercial auditions and then after a while you end up doing commercials where you're not dancing, you are an actor in the commercial. That was my first transition out of being called a dancer into just going on regular acting auditions. I took a joke writing/stand up class and the final assignment of the class was that you had to perform at a real comedy club. It went well and since then it just kind of took off for me. I had a video on the Internet (Vietnamese nail salon parody) and from that video people started requesting me at comedy clubs, colleges, churches and all over the place. That's kind of how my stand up career took off and so I had to write new material and be on the road. That lead to getting a stand up agent and a manager. I never thought that when I was an extra on *Friends* that I would be touring with stand up comedy. I never thought being an *Oakland Raiderette Cheerleader* at home that I would later be on *MadTV* with Bobby Lee. Everything happens for a reason. My advice to performers would be to keep yourself grounded in a firm foundation and for me that was Jesus and just knowing that it's not about me. Even though you're booking a role here and there, just remember that it's not about you. Although it is my heart's desire to be in film and television, my main focus is what God's desire is for my life. As long as you put God first then everything else will fall into place. I'm definitely transitioning into more television and film right now and transitioning out of being a touring comedian on the road.

ANJELAH ON PUTTING ON YOUR GAME FACE

"As soon as you hit the stage you have this performance face on and doing stand up I'm being myself on stage but you're still putting on an act. You're still presenting yourself in front of 450 people at a time and then after your show, you do meet and greets and you need to still be able to communicate with people. Just like when you're on stage dancing, even if you're not feeling well, you can't let that show."

ANJELAH ON DEVELOPING A CHARACTER

"I'm very observational. I get my characters from being in life; from my family members or people that I come across that stand out to me. I find that the funniest ones are the ones that are the most relatable. You realize that like with my character **Bon Qui Qui** for instance, everybody has dealt with some fast food employee of that sort. So it's about being observational and taking real life and just magnifying it and exaggerating it a little bit. I'm reading this book right now called, *Talent Is Never Enough*. It's basically talking about how some people try to just get by on their talent and they feel like they're entitled to things because they are talented. There are people who are just talented and then there are people who are talented who also have drive. They are productive,; they're reading and bettering themselves. They're also just getting out there and being proactive and separating themselves from the ones that are just talented."

AFFION CROCKETT

"I grew up in Germany, I was a military brat. We used to get mix tapes, rap music from my cousins in New York. As far as dancing, I got into it when *Beat Street* and *Breakin'* came out. As a little kid, I would watch these cats on screen get down and said, 'Man, I want to do that.' So my older brother and I started dancing. Then I dabbled in rapping back when hip-hop was really hip-hop in the Slick Rick days where you went to a party and really had fun and got on the mic and freestyled. My brother and I had a group and opened up for concerts back in the day for Naughty by Nature in North Carolina.

"When *Def Comedy Jam* came around in the early '90s I was still in school. I thought that I could relate to it because it was like hip-hop comedy. All types were on that show. I saw impressionists and dancers and it made me connect the dots. That's when I started doing stand up comedy. I did stand up for about five years, toured with all the Def Jam guys from Joe Torry to Michael Collier and Dave Chappelle to Tommy Davidson. Then I decided to move to Los Angeles, Calif. I made a good living doing stand up back East but when you move out to Hollywood, they feel like they're doing you a favor by giving you a stage so they don't really pay you very well. They give you like $20 or something. I said to myself, 'Whatever I have to do to survive out here is what I'm going to do.' So instead of going and getting a job waiting tables, I decided to get back into dancing. I would meet a couple of dancers here and there on video sets and they would tell me that they were making pretty good money. $400 for a video as opposed to $20 for a stand up set, it just made sense. So I got fully back in the dance world but I never stopped doing my stand up or acting. A lot of people thought that I came from the dance world and just jumped into acting but it wasn't like that at all. I was simultaneously doing everything; dance, commercials and acting auditions.

CHAPTER SIXTEEN

AFFION ON HOSTING CHOREOGRAPHER'S CARNIVAL
"I used to go to Carnival with a few of my dance friends. I thought it was dope how all the dancers in the industry got together on that one night and just shared the art of dance. I'm also a member of The Goovaloos so when I first got with them, we did a show at Carnival. I was on stage clownin' in the dance number, and after seeing that Carey and Paulette (who put on Carnival) asked if I would host one. So then, Lisa Thompson (former *Fly Girl*) and I hosted it every month for five years doing all types of characters. We just had fun!

AFFION ON BEING A TRIPLE THREAT & BALANCING HOLLYWOOD
"I have always been working as an actor even I was working dance gigs. Honestly, it is what I do and I love it. It's just like a parent who has five kids. How do you balance that? You love each kid for different reasons and you love them all for the same reasons. They're your kids, but you try to nurture each one in a different way based on what their strengths are and what they love. So I look at my gifts as my kids. To me they suit different moods.

AFFION ON "DANCE FLICK"
"It's the Wayans brothers whom I've been fans of since *Hollywood Shuffle* and *In Living Colour*. I just did a TV pilot with them and right after that they told me about this movie called *Dance Flick*, which is a dance comedy. Well, for me, that's right up my alley because I'm a dancing comedian. So, it was a no-brainer!"

TRANSITIONING INTO SPORTS

EVE TORRES - WWE DIVA

"I was on Clippers from 2006-2007. For the past year, I've been one of the backstage interviewers for the WWE after winning the WWE Diva Search. The WWE Diva auditions started as something where I thought, 'Hey, you know I can see myself kind of going this route.' And I knew the girl who won the year before was a *Miami Heat Dancer*. She was super hot and kind of had the same background that I did. So I approached it how I would most auditions by saying, 'OK, well let's give it a shot and see where it takes me.' And they really liked the tape that I sent in. They narrowed it down to 50 girls from all over the country and Canada too. There were rounds of interviews where they put you on the spot, some bikini stuff and I was one of the last eight girls. It was based on fan voting. Going into it, you just kind of had (to have) an open mind

CAREER LONGEVITY AND TRANSITIONS

because it was totally something that 2 years ago I wouldn't have seen myself doing. Now, I absolutely love it, but it wasn't something that I grew up watching. So it really was one of those things where you just never know. I truly believe that I'm meant to be here right now just because of the way everything happened. I was on tour with Mario at the time and had also just booked the Bette Midler show in Vegas. There were things that I had to figure out, like which one I wanted to do. I love dance and it's my passion. We do it because we love it, but there are so many other opportunities that present themselves once you get into it. I really think that dancing helped me because I can perform in front of thousands of people and not be scared. I've done auditions, so going into it, I had much more experience than some of the other girls that came from a wrestling background.

"Being a dancer, I went in and it's one of those businesses where you have to earn your respect. If you go in there thinking you're a DIVA in the WWE and expect to be treated that way, you're in the wrong business. You have to be very humble. You have to work very hard. Traveling can be brutal. Being a dancer in Hollywood is exactly the same. Going into it, I felt prepared. I've been through the really long auditions and I've gone through all the times that you work really hard but you don't necessarily see the pay off. Going into the WWE, I hadn't paid my dues in the same way because I haven't been a wrestler all of my life, but I've been doing something. In dance, I really grinded it out on the audition scene and everything else. It's the first time in my life that I have ever just had one job and this is it. Obviously it's going to present a lot more opportunities but like this is it. I'm totally focused on it. I travel full time now. I'm just thankful that I've had my previous experience to help me cope with it because someone who may be from a different background may have a very hard time adjusting to the lifestyle. You can't just go into things thinking this is all I want to do, you always have to be looking at the bigger picture. And you're not always going to be able to be a dancer. You're not always going to be able to do the physical and someday, it's sad to say, but you're sex appeal is going to die."

TRANSITIONING LEADS TO STARTING A MOVEMENT

GIGI TORRES – ESSENCE MVMNT

"Essence started in November 2005. I went through a really bad break up and I had the opportunity to have my own piece showcased in Carnival at Key Club. During that time, I didn't know what song I was going to perform to and the only ones that came

to mind were the sappy love songs. I started to look into that and did a piece called 'Her Perspective' that was from my perspective on the relationship. It detailed falling in love, when you first meet, getting comfortable and then finding out about the cheating, then getting over it and being better off. During that time, my best girlfriends were there for me and helped me through it. I asked them to be in this piece and that's how Essence was born."

"At that time it wasn't called Essence, but after Carnival we all kind of looked around and thought, 'Hey we like dancing together, we should continue this.' Initially there were 12 girls. People have come and gone in the four years that we've been performing but there is that core group of us that continues to perform and spread the movement. I didn't really know where it was going to go. It was a crew that just wanted to dance together and share the stage. (We were) presented opportunities to dance at community shows, then industry shows and then I started teaching on my own. After a while of teaching, people would ask if the rest of the girls taught as well. So I said, 'OK, let's just start this!' So I kind of forced all of them to start teaching and start choreographing. I just said, 'Next rehearsal, you're teaching.' Everyone was like, 'What?' So, after that we got an opportunity to teach workshops in Vegas and around the area people started asking us (to teach) regularly. Over the last year, people have asked us to teach workshops overseas, in Canada (and) on the East Coast also. It's cool and right now it's nice to know that the girls are booking tours, teaching out of the country and doing their own thing also.

"It's nice to know that it stemmed from Essence. It was kind of hard to come up with the name Essence. We just started naming things. Essence came up because each and every girl has their own essence that they bring to the team, their own strong point, their own quality. To even dig deeper, when you put it all together, it comes together to make the essence of a woman, that person that we strive to be. That's what we're aiming towards.

GIGI ON WORKSHOPS BENEFITTING WOMEN & THE MOVEMENT
"We definitely want to give back. Our theme for a while was, 'Women are the new men.' It's hard, especially in the dance world. Men seem to take over. Honestly, you see that the majority of the roster at dance studios are guys. Well, we can do the same things, and some even better. So we just wanted to step up. It's been something we've been trying to work on for the last four years. We've been teaching and the way that I teach the girls how to teach, we don't just give the choreography. It isn't spitting out 1, 2, 3, 4, 5, 6, 7, 8 and then where's our money? We

actually want to go into places and start up dance communities and start community love and support for each other with dance. A lot of times in this industry, people are just out for themselves. We went to a place outside of Montreal, (Canada) with a very small community. We tried to let them know that they can start a larger community there by just uniting and creating an atmosphere for each other to create."

TRANSITIONING TO THE GLAM SQUAD

Dancers often transition to behind the scenes areas of entertainment like becoming a makeup artist or wardrobe stylist. In Hollywood you can obtain hands-on work experience. Take as much time with this as you did with dance. A friend of mine went back to school at MKC Beauty Academy and really studied the craft. She spent three months and $15,000 at a five day per week 9 a.m. - 5 p.m. training course to become a Certified Makeup Artist. When you make the commitment to change your career path so drastically,; you need to be serious about it.

SICK TIP #48:
WEB SITES FOR CAREERS OUTSIDE OF DANCE

www.Monster.com   www.CareerBuilder.com

A bonus about having a job outside of entertainment is that you get paid bi-weekly as a standard. In the industry, there really isn't a promise that you'll get paid from every job. Yes, it is expected that you'll see your paycheck, but nothing is ever guaranteed to be timely.

CAREER LONGEVITY - THE TRUTH

LANEY FILUK (BLOC AGENT)

"It's not an age factor, it's more the willingness to still keep going to the same types of auditions that take usually a lot of time out of people's day. It's not necessarily by the time I'm in my late 20s - early 30s, I look too old because a lot of dancers look amazing, have great relationships with choreographers and can keep dancing for a long time. It's more they don't want to go to the cattle calls anymore. They get more and more selective and that closes their opportunities in comparison to a younger dancer that will go to everything, that does want to try and audition and get in front of as many people as possible, that still wants to take class three or four times a week and that are still very involved in the dance community. I think it's more that the longevity of a dance career is as long as you're willing to keep out there, training and auditioning."

CHAPTER SIXTEEN

Sandra says…

- Your body probably won't last forever doing crazy spins on your head. It's good to find an alternative career path early on, so you don't have to later!

- Choreographing, acting, singing, teaching and comedy are great avenues for dancers looking to transition.

- Express yourself through spoken word. Become an educator. Teach young dancers as a transition career.

- You can go back to school as another option. Receive help for this from Career Transition For Dancers.

- Don't quit your day job just yet. Work at dance and your alternate career until you can support yourself.

- Stay focused on your new goal and you will be rewarded!

> **POINT TAKEN:**
> I don't want to be a pirate! Sometimes you have to do what you don't want to do. And other times, you get to do something fun like transition from one form of entertainment into another. Entertainment jobs are at your fingertips in Hollywood. Transition with a plan and you'll be so much better off.

CHAPTER SEVENTEEN

Hollywood: The Intersection Of Art And Commerce

Hollywood never ceases to surprise, amaze or excite me! Yesterday, I walked out of my house and went for a jog. Within a block of leaving, I saw a Darth Vador impersonator waving at a Tigger wannabe and then heard a horn honk down the road from a mad Spunge Bob Square Pants to a then dejected Mickey Mouse look-a-like carrying his ears in his hands. This town is full of the famous, infamous and the desperately wanting to be famous! It is also the home to the darkest secrets, hottest stars and all of the hopes and dreams of the lucky few. When I say lucky few, I mean those who make it over night. When I say over night, I mean those who have worked all of their lives and then suddenly are plucked from the chorus and thrown center stage into the limelight. I joke about this, but I know this to be true. I personally have been working professionally since I was 12. It is a very long and hard road for the people who have the persistence to walk it, run it or sprint through it over and over again.

The lure of Hollywood creates an intersection of art and commerce. A sort of tango where the struggle between the two ignites over and over again. It's like the kill at the end of the paso doble, where dreams are crushed and hearts are broken, but the beacon of hope does shine for a few. The conflict between art and commerce lies with the knowledge that in any other field one can make a living at what they have studied and not feel guilty about it. Within the dance community there is a sort of give and take. Make nice with employers in addition to having talent and you may end up with a job. Do a free gig, a bit of pro bono work and you may reap the rewards. The love of dance is the backbone for what you do on the stage, screen, print or Internet. You love what you do, right? You love the feeling you get from performing, the rush of the applause from the audience and the joy you feel when you see the pride on the faces of your loved ones and friends. It is as if you would work for free if you could be on stage every day doing what you love. Here is where our conflict ensues.

The love of dance with regard to Hollywood is being misconstrued with an ability to support oneself with that love. It's like two people in a long distance relationship barely being able to support themselves in the city they each live in, let alone support traveling to and from each other's cities to make things work. It is hard to imagine a world where an average office worker would go into his/her new place of employment and have his/her boss say that they are going to try them out for the week and see how their presentation goes and then at the end of the week they will decide if they will get paid for that work or be asked back. Generally, the people who sign up for these types of positions are interns or students wanting on-the-job training, experience or credit for a class.

The reality of the dance industry in Hollywood is that one might just do three, four or five of these "assignments" before a job where pay is involved actually materializes. Imagine everyone in the United States waiting three, four or five times to see if they will be asked back, hired on or even revisited for another shot at the gig down the road. This is the case with some choreographers and the types of jobs that are available in Hollywood. You should also be aware that the reality exists that even if you are doing your best and should be getting booked you may not be because of outside factors like favoritism, nepotism and simple things like agency preference for picture submissions. You may be asked back on two, three, four or five callback auditions for the same artist because you fit the type, dance the style of the choreographer and perform well. And when not selected it can feel a bit like a waste of time and energy. A feeling that is undeniable and a process that is simply unnecessary. And if necessary, callbacks like these deserve to be paid calls just like union callbacks are for actors.

Some argue that it is alarming to think that a dancer might want to be paid for their skill and should be happy simply working with a choreographer. Unfortunately, in Hollywood that doesn't pay your rent. It may down the road, but you have to pick and choose wisely when and how to give your services away for free. Taking a job just because you want to work or want to dance is great but it also brings down the power of our collective front as dancers. It is unfortunate that at the same time that a dancer may turn down a job for it not paying enough money, another dancer who is new to the industry and hungry, decides to pick up that gig

CHAPTER SEVENTEEN

for free. The intersection of right and wrong, of being able to work on the craft that you love and have it also work for and pay you, makes art = commerce look like a bad math equation. This scenario forces us to look at what we do and our love of dance as a half full and half empty situation. The two sides being: A love of dance that fulfills us for the art of dance and a love of dance that fulfills us with art and also pays us back for our hard work. It isn't bad to think of them both at the same time and accept the two as being important parts of professional dance. Maintaining the idea that 'it is all about the battle' won't continue to grow dance positively either. Competition is grand but it is not what dance is ultimately about.

**SICK TIP #49:
HALF EMPTY VS. HALF FULL**

Try to be a half full type of person. Try not to let the downside affect you.

In an effort to make the dance industry a better place to live, work and communicate, we must all remember that we need to create in order to push dance forward. We must continue to strive to imagine new and different ways to express ourselves. In this effort to create, communicate and push dance forward, we must also recognize that without an appetite for newness, old work will become irrelevant. Irrelevance will make our industry fade and disappear. By holding true to the talent that will move our art form forward, and also recognizing the financial quandary that will forever hold dancers back professionally from ever moving their salaries in a positive direction and commanding headliner box office receipts, we must look at what we do internally with each other when asking dancers to work for free with the promise or hope of booking a job down the road. By saying the dance industry, I'm speaking of those who have built their skills in a way that those skills are a marketable commodity. Just like a doctor goes to school to be able to provide a medical diagnosis, a dancer should be able to capitalize on the skills they learn from an early age or even a not so early age if they are of value.

We must question the practices of some agents who may low ball fees for their clients just to get an account with a certain recording artist or project. We must take a look at why agencies are not held accountable by their clients to stick to the non-union rates put forth by Dancers' Alliance and why there is room to negotiate or accept lower rates. We must ask why we (as dancers) don't increase Dancers' Alliance rates like our unions *(SAG/AFTRA/Actors' Equity)* do. We must inform dancers of the negative effects of those who work for less and the impact it has on us all. We need to evaluate how our economy has put our industry in jeopardy enlisting recording artists to hire less dancers.

HOLLYWOOD: THE INTERSECTION OF ART AND COMMERCE

With so many questions to answer we must also look at the advances we've made in our love of the art form. Contract negotiations that our performer unions have been able to negotiate have increased hazard pay as well as award and variety program rates for dancers. Advances that protect dancers will benefit us all in the long run. The intersection between art and commerce remains in Hollywood and at the forefront of the dance community. If we do not look within, we will never be able to show a united front that can articulate the needs of dancers and the required compensation that is lacking. My conflict is at the intersection of Sunset and Vine, where's yours?

The yellow brick road is a bright and shiny path that has twists and turns which lead to an ending where one has already known their destiny from the beginning. Although there are no ruby red slippers to click because *"There's no place like home,"* there are black diamond-studded stilettos and sweet Fanny Pak kicks to rock at your next audition. And you don't want to go home, you want to make it here. In a line from the song *"New York, New York,"* Frank Sinatra sang, *"If you can make it there, you can make it anywhere."* To borrow the same sentiment, I'd like to propose a new reality check about Hollywood:

CONQUER HOLLYWOOD AND YOU'LL CONQUER THE WORLD!

Take the good and dispel the negative to create your own version of Hollywood. With all of this new knowledge of the entertainment industry, I urge you to remember why you moved or are planning your move to Hollywood in the first place, you're love for dance! The constant hustle and daily grind that makes you go and go until you can't go anymore. When these times come, try to remember your love for dance. Remember how many other people moved here and didn't make it. Think about how many people would love to be doing what you do for a living, how excited your parents and family get when you tell them you're working with a recording artist or will be on an award show. When you think that you don't want to do this anymore, take your favorite class and reignite that sense of urgency inside you. It isn't only beneficial for you but also for those around you. It stinks to have a "Debby Downer" in the room that always complains about everything. You may pull others down with you if you have a sour attitude toward the industry. Always uplift yourself and others to want to do the best job at all times. Find your "thing" that gets you through your tough times. That "thing" may be escaping to a friend's house, going out on the town, phoning home, watching your favorite movie, talking to your agent or for me just a quick trip to the Santa Monica pier. There's nothing like a brilliant sunset to help me put things into perspective.

CHAPTER SEVENTEEN

Once you're successful don't get lazy. Topping oneself with reinvention is difficult but with success you now have new and different challenges financially and personal responsibility to supporters. Once you get to the top, don't forget who helped you get there. It's easy to bask in success and forget about people who were there for you in the beginning and believed in your talent. It's also easy to get trapped by people who are your "new friends" who met you after you gained success and may be there for all of the wrong reasons. Evaluate your friendships because the same people who are there on your way up will be there on the way down. The ones you acquired along the way will fall off like dead leaches.

THE FUTURE OF DANCE

In sharing my thoughts about the dance industry today, I wanted to also share the thoughts of some of the people I've interviewed on the future of dance.

TONY SELZNICK (M.S.A. AGENT)

"I think that you're right in that dance is cyclical. Dance comes in and out. Unfortunately, what happens is that there'll be three good dance films and then one bad one will come out and it kind of shelves everything for a while. What's interesting with the reality shows is that it put dance on the map in such an intense way that I think it's not going to go away in the same way that it's gone before. When *So You Think You Can Dance* came out, it seems like every year they're getting better and smarter in what they're doing. Then every network wanted a dance reality show and then there were a few bad ones. Now I think there's a bit of an over saturation of dance. There hasn't yet been a show that's awarded the winner something that they can actually walk away with. *So You Think You Can Dance*, the first year they offered an apartment in New York and Nick Lazarini didn't take it and the next year they offered Benji Schwimmer a role in the Celine Dion show but he's not a Celine dancer so he didn't take it. They haven't been able yet to match the prize to the dancer the way *American Idol* does because a singing contract makes a lot of sense. One of the things that I thought was great (was) when *America's Best Dance Crew* went into Season 2 they used Jabbawockeez to promote Season 2. I thought that was brilliant because then it gave Jabbawockeez some branding opportunities."

LIL' C (CHOREOGRAPHER)

Scenario #1 for the future of dance: "When mankind finds a new resource, they find every way under the sun to utilize it to where it benefits them but what happens is there is no moderation when it comes to it so we experience depletion. So what is most likely going to happen since dance is a resource right now, it's like, *'Ooh, ooh...a new type of fossil fuel! Let's just use this until it's all gone.'* They're going to extrapolate all the juices and all of the essence because they don't understand it. They want to make money off of it instead of make money for it. They want to exploit it. So what most likely will happen is that there will be dance show after dance show and dance film after dance film to where it will be taken as a joke. Because right now it's not taken seriously. It's just a new way to entertain the uninventive minds of those who watch television all day. People only pay for things that they find interesting. So it's just like music. When it's not hittin' anymore they move on to the next artist. When dance isn't making money anymore; they're going to move on to the next resource. Then what's going to happen is that dance will have been set back 20 years just because we received a little bit of notoriety. (Because) everybody got sidetracked by the money or by the fact that we are a lucrative commodity. It's supposed to be all about the art. But it's going to turn us into hypocrites because we're going to doom ourselves because then we're going to be put into a position where we have no more leverage.

"We have leverage now because no one else can do what we can do as dancers, as people who consider themselves artists - whose art is dance. We have leverage and when you can't get the real thing, people go get the next best thing. But everybody is starting to understand that you can't get an amazing actor who's an amazing dancer because he's not going to be able to pull off the dancing. With dance doubles, it used to work like that, (you'd get) an amazing actor and then cut in shots of amazing dancing. But now people have seen the real stuff just based on *America's Best Dance Crew* and *So You Think You Can Dance*. (That is) what people now think dance really is. People have been mesmerized. You are not going to catch Morris Chestnut spinning on his head or Denzel Washington doing a chest pop.

"Dancers and dance itself have leverage but we are still playing such a huge back role because now it's more about the script. Same script, different dancers. Same storyline, different dancers. Let's do *Stomp The Yard*, but let's do it with tap dancing now. OK, let's do *Stomp the Yard*, but let's do it like *Stomp the Yard* meets *27 Dresses* now. It's going to be turned into this formula that will be sold to the highest bidder. Dance is a tree and each genre has its own respective branch. They are ripping the branches off of the tree and they're not even utilizing all of the sap within them. They're not even taking the chance to understand what they have their hands on.

CHAPTER SEVENTEEN

It could be so much more lucrative if done the right way and really understood.

Scenario #2 for the future of dance:
"Dance could continue to be big and be huge and have a nice little decade run. You never know, especially catering to a human beings' desire these days."

ROSERO MCCOY (CHOREOGRAPHER)

"I've been working on three seasons of *Randy Jackson Presents America's Best Dance Crew* on MTV and I've watched the Jabbawockeez and Super Cr3w win and (how) their careers after that where they have become artists. I believe that dancers are becoming stars again. I want dancers to remember who paved the way. Reality TV has afforded dancers an opportunity but with that opportunity comes a price. The price that comes is that the realness of dance or the coolness of dance might go to that other side if everyone is not careful. If we're not careful it then becomes corny and people don't want to see it for a while."

ADVICE ON THE ENTERTAINMENT INDUSTRY

SERGIO TRUJILLO (CHOREOGRAPHER)

"I started really late and I also was really ferocious about things. I took it seriously. I learned lessons as I went along. Nothing is impossible. You just have to have your priorities straight. Get to know people and let them know what your talents are. You can't expect to come and all of a sudden end up with a job. Don't get defeated by the process, just learn from it. Have a clear goal and don't deviate from that path."

ROBERT HOFFMAN (ACTOR/DANCER)

"Practice your ass off before you get here! It is easier to put in the time and dedicate your life when you don't have the financial pressures. Have your technical training as good as you can and be in a place where you're financially stable before making the move. Save up enough change to live out here for at least three months, at least! That way you'll have time to settle, time to get known at auditions and time to network. Be fun to be around. You can go to auditions and book them, but if you're fun to be around, people will want to work with you over and over again. This is the same with any business. Make sure you are in a good place as a person before you jump in. No amount of training matters if you're just whack to be around. Own your craft and when you're really ready it will happen. Start making videos and put them up on YouTube. You can gauge yourself and you have an audience of infinite size! If you dedicate your life to it, you will be rewarded."

DANA WILSON (DANCER/ASST. CHOREOGRAPHER)

"My best advice is to not take anything too personally. It can be a while before you book, but don't let the 'Thank You' (code for 'NO thank you') get you down on yourself. Keep perfecting your craft, diversify your skills and treat yourself as your own business and you will make it!"

MONIE ADAMSON (CHOREOGRAPHER)

"Always stay true to yourself and be confident with who you are and what you have to offer. Sometimes you just might not have the right look for the job, and maybe that is a good thing, because it could free you up for another opportunity! It is up to you to make your life and career what you want it to be. Become as versatile as possible, train in all styles of dance, learn to act and sing. Try to work in all levels of the industry, from dance companies, stage, to TV, film and always take responsibility for your career. Keep up your training and know that 'No' is an opinion not a fact."

HEATHER MORRIS (DANCER/ACTOR)

"Don't get STUCK in crowds or end up getting too lazy because you're not booking. I know plenty of dancers who get lost in the world of L.A. and don't even end up doing what they came out here to do. Be yourself too! Don't falter by changing your personality because a certain 'so and so' thinks it's cool to act that way and they'll get you further in your career. Be who you are and if you're successful in that all the right jobs will line up for you."

AFFION CROCKETT (ACTOR/COMEDIAN)

"An old manager told me, 'It's going to take you about five to ten years to really make it in Hollywood. More like ten. Five is ambitious but it's going to take you about ten years to really make it. There's no such thing as an overnight success.' When he said that, I was like, 'Nah, don't even try it. I'm about to go out there, people are going to see me. I'm about to blow up tomorrow!' And this is what a lot of, not just dancers, but actors have this thing too! They think it's going to happen right away and when it doesn't happen they give up and they move back home. So what I would say to all the dancers, actors or aspiring entertainers that would like to move to Hollywood is

CHAPTER SEVENTEEN

to come out here with the right mindset. It may not happen in the right time frame for you, but just give it room to happen. Give yourself time to develop and grow. That's imperative!"

"You would rather have a cake that comes out of the oven in an hour as opposed to a cake that came out of the microwave in three minutes. It's simple but a lot of people go home thinking that they failed. It's not that they weren't talented. They had all the right ingredients. Both of the cakes have the same ingredients and the ingredients are all correct. The difference is in the process of preparation. One was prepared in the microwave in three minutes and the other took time to sit in the oven and really develop. That's the one that I want to eat and it's going to be delicious. If it's what you love to do, and you know you're supposed to be here, you can never give it up. It's like breathing. I will be around forever in this industry because it's what I do."

AFFION CROCKETT ON THE LOVE OF DANCE VS. DANCE DIVAS

"Ultimately, I just love dance. We should all love it. Instead, I see dancers who get on TV once and then start wearing shades at Millennium and trying to be cool; thinking that they're better than everyone else. We all share in the dance art form and we all come from the same love. I used to get on stage at Carnival and try to make sense to these cats. I'd be like, *'What? You did one video and think you're the sh*t?'* Or, *'You just toured with Timberlake and now you're at Carnival with a scarf on your neck and shades and you're sitting up in the balcony now? You used to be on the floor getting grimy with all of us!'* I still love dance and so should everyone else even if they have a little success."

SICK TIP #50:
DON'T QUIT 5 MINUTES BEFORE THE MIRACLE!

My mom would always say, *"Don't quit five minutes before the miracle."* If this is your passion, pursue it. Don't give up on your dreams because if you do, then they are guaranteed to not come true. It took moving away from Los Angeles for me to really know that I wanted to pursue my dreams. From the outside looking in, I knew I had to get back to the stage. And I hope to share the stage with you, one day soon!

HOLLYWOOD: THE INTERSECTION OF ART AND COMMERCE
GIVING BACK AND TAKING CENTER STAGE

Make sure to give back. One way that I'm trying to give back to the dance community is through this book. Sharing knowledge and helping up-and-coming dancers do their best is something I hope this book does for novice and professional dancers. Some people told me that I was crazy to write a book and give people tips to help them get a leg up on the competition. They said, *"Aren't you competing with the same people who will read this book?"* I say, *"Bring it on!"* I love the competition and I've loved every minute of writing this book. It really helped me find my love for dance again and made me think and explore every side of this industry in a way that I hadn't thought about before. Because it is part of my job, I just do what I do and don't even think, *"Hey, others should do it to."* I just do things because I've learned them along the way. I also have learned that if you don't help others obtain their dreams, obtaining your own isn't quite the same. Getting to the top and not having anyone to share it with is very lonely. I've never given up on something I've set my mind to and I have my mom to thank for that. I also share each and every small miracle with her regarding my career.

The life of a dancer is very short. Keep this in mind once you've written out that "Hollywood or Bust" sign for the road. The path that you will take is yours and yours alone. Don't veer from it or let yourself wander. Find who you truly are along the way, accomplish the goals you set for yourself in Chapter One of this book and outline more specific ones in the **BOOK ME! Workbook**. It isn't enough to be a great dancer in Hollywood. You must eat, breath and live for the chance to audition, the opportunity to push forward and the great times you get to have along the way. There's no business like show business and I believe that there's no place like Hollywood. There's nothing like being in such a creative environment where you could be sitting in your living room and shout out, "Hey that's Sheila!," as you recognize your friends in commercials and videos. Your friends will say that about you too. The excitement of performing on stage, screen and around the world is right at your finger tips.

Reassuring yourself when times are tough is a challenge and will be something that all dancers will need to do when they get hit hard with rejection. Rejoice when you book your first job! And book the second, third, fourth and so on! Each gig is like a mini-miracle! Be confident in your skills and don't be afraid to share them with the world. In this work, I've given you the tools, resources, advice and most of all in-

CHAPTER SEVENTEEN

sider knowledge about the way you can get in where you fit in and stand out when it's your time to shine! My mom use to say, *"You can't be the plucked from the chorus to play the lead if you're not willing to be in the chorus in the first place."* Basically stating that if you want to be the star but don't want to take part in group numbers because you want the solo; don't complain if all of the opportunities aren't presented to you in the time frame you would like them to be. Life is crazy in this town and I hope that everyone who reads this book remains excited to join our bustling community of artists.

SICK TIP #51:
IF YOU FAIL TO PLAN, YOU PLAN TO FAIL!

My mom also used to say this to me all the time, *"If you fail to plan, you plan to fail!"* It's so true. If you can plan short trips to Hollywood, you'll know your way around when you get here. If you can come out here having put together a good financial plan, you will have saved enough to live off of to get you through the initial period of auditioning and finding jobs. If you set goals for your career, you can make sure that you and your agent are working toward the same thing. You will achieve so much more by planning for the future. Since you are reading this book, you're already on your way. Good luck with your career in dance and let it take you everywhere you want to go!

BOOK ME! WORKBOOK EXERCISES - PART 5

Some **BOOK ME! Workbook** exercise topics from Part Five of this book are listed below. Purchase the **BOOK ME! Workbook** online at:
www.ColtonCollection.com

- **Create and be rewarded** - Accomplish your goals and find new ones.
- **Support outlets** - Link to worthy causes to help you be part of the community.
- **Hollywood is intense environment** - Exercise common sense.
- **Transitions and new career paths** - Explore ideas for your future.

HOLLYWOOD: THE INTERSECTION OF ART AND COMMERCE

YOUR DANCE CAREER IN HOLLYWOOD STARTS NOW! GET BOOKED TODAY!

"I'm not a game player. I've evaluated the system and entered it on my own terms. Take control of your career and paint your picture of dance one stroke at a time."

-Sandra Colton

CHAPTER SEVENTEEN

Sandra says...

- Hollywood is kind and cruel at the same time. Learn from your mistakes and be hip to the game.

- Smarter than the average bear? Be ahead of the curve. Understand the intersection between doing what you love and being compensated for your hard work.

- Seek out a mentor and don't give up on your dream.

- Don't become a dance DIVA or DIVO!

- Whatever you seek, do it your way! There's no prize for second place but you have to remember this isn't a race. Success will come when it is supposed to. Nothing happens overnight!

- Practice, practice, practice! Doug Johnson says, "Practice doesn't make perfect. Perfect practice makes perfect!"

> **POINT TAKEN:**
> Hollywood can steal your heart, eat it for breakfast, regurgitate it and feed it right back to you with a little sticker on it that says, "Thank you for coming, goodbye." The trick is to make sure you didn't have your soul stolen as well! Keep your morals about you. Battered, beaten and bruised is your body but your hunger, your passion still remain.

PART SIX

THE FINE PRINT

Thank You Very Much From Sandra!

Monie Adamson
Ben Allen
Joshua Allen
James Alsop
Frankie Anne
Joey Antonio
Chloe Arnold
Carey Azizian
Paulette Azizian
Brianna Barcus
Bobbie Bates
Paul Becker
Norm Betts
Robert Biro
Adrian Broadhurst
Luther A. Brown
Lisette Bustamante
Matt Cady
Michael Catapano
Gus Carr
Herman Chan
Stephen Chatfield
Rodney Chester
Candice Coke
Kelly Connolly
Lisa Coppola
Affion Crockett
Jon *"Do Knock"* Cruz
Nikki Dalonzo
Crespatrick de los Reyes
Ryan Domigpe
Tabitha D'umo
Napoleon D'umo
Chris Dupre
Pete Engle
Sandra Enriquez
Christopher Erskin
TJ Espinoza
Danny Essin
Maria Diaz-Estorga
Briana Evigan
Laney Filuk
Christopher Freer
Tony G.
Ellenie Galestian
Eddie Garcia
Melissa *"Myrtle"* Garcia
Jennifer Goldsmith
Danele Grant
Cody Green
J.C. Gutierrez
Roy Haidar
Hi Hat

Danielle Hawkins
Keesha Hernandez
Chieko Hidaka
Robert Hoffman
Dorian Holley
Tre Holloway
Galen Hooks
Geo Hubela
Carrie Ann Inaba
Anjelah Johnson
Douglas Johnson
Aakomon Jones
David Kang
Jim Keith
Dominique Kelley
Mary Ann Kellogg
Jamie King
JaQuel Knight
Kelly Konno
Terry Lindholm
Eitan Loewenstein
Brooke Long
Jennifer Lynn
Jessica Lynn
Maya McClean
Nandy McClean
Rosero McCoy
Amber Madison
Kevin Maher
Michelle *"Jersey"* Maniscalco
Kennis Marquis
Kristen Marshall
Mia Michaels
Mister (The Dog)
Jerry Mitchell
Sarah Mitchell
Dalphe Morantes
Heather Morris
Valeska Mosich-Miller
Dalila Muro
Mary Murphy
Jason Myhre
Jeff *"Phi"* Nguyen
Timo Nunez
Adam Parson
Victoria Parsons
Phlex
Raistalla
Liz Ramos
Bradley Rapier
Louise Reichlin
Fatima Robinson
Isla Rose

Apollo Sa'deek
Jason Samuels Smith
Giselle Samson
Anthony Scarano
Jillian Schmitz
Benji Schwimmer
Dave Scott
Leslie Scott
Tony Selznick
Dante Sevin
Harry Shum
Chonique Sneed
Shane Sparks
Dena Spellman
Jenna Spellman
Gina Starbuck
Kevin Stea
Becca Sweitzer
Fred Tallaksen
Sonya Tayeh
Tony Testa
Yanick Thomassaint
Tammy To
Eve Torres
Gigi Torres
Sergio Trujillo
Paula vanOppen
Gustavo Vargas
Roman Vasquez
Tyrell Washington
Dana Wilson
Marcel Wilson
Jason Williams
Jayson Wright
Keith Young

Special Thanks To:
Bloc, C.T.G., D.D.O, Go 2 Talent, M.S.A., Trio, AFTRA (Chris de Haan), Atomic Studios, Break The Cycle Fitness, Christopher Erskin, Danny Essin, David Kang, Joanna Colbert, Tiffen, Ryan Powell, SAG (Glenn Hiraoka, Hope Barkan) and Kevin Levine.

Extra Special Thank You To:
Mom, Brian Friedman, Jeremy Mowe, Chrissy Colton, Abigail Mortimore, Heather Burton & Megan Lokis.

Works Cited

WEB SITES

- AFTRA. Retrieved from www.AFTRA.com on June 1, 2009.
- Chance, Bonnie. *Mission Statement.* Retrieved from www.BonnieChance.com on June 1, 2009.
- Dancer's Alliance. *Working Rates For Dancers.* Retrieved from www.dancersalliance.com on June 1, 2009.
- IADMS. Nutrition Fact Sheet. "The Challenge of the Adolescent Dancer. *Avoiding The Female Athletic Triad.*" Retrieved from www.iadms.org on June 1, 2009.
- IMDB Web site. *Recording Artist Height Listings On Individual Performer Pages.* Retrieved from http://www.imdb.com on June 1, 2009.
- Internal Revenue Service. *W-2, W-4 and I-9 Documents.* Retrieved from www.IRS.gov on June 1, 2009.
- Loewenstein, Eitan. *Polaroid Taking Tips.* Retrieved from www.EitanTheActor.com on November 23, 2008.
- Los Angeles Gay Center. *Your Center & Your Health Information Sections.* Retrieved from www.lagaycenter.com on June 1, 2009.
- National Endowment for the Arts. *Mission Statement.* Retrieved from www.NEA.gov on June 1, 2009.
- National Foundation For The Advancement In The Arts. *Mission Statement.* Retrieved from www.NFAA.org on June 1, 2009.
- *Original Girl Magazine.* Mission Statement. Cover photos (Fall 2008, Winter 2009, Spring 2009). Retrieved from www.OriginalGirlMagazine.com on June 1, 2009.
- SAG/AFTRA. Retrieved from www.SAG.org on June 1, 2013.
- U.S. Food and Drug Administration. *"Food Labeling: Trans Fatty Acids in Nutrition Labeling, Nutrient Content Claims, and Health Claims - Small Entity Compliance Guide"* (August 20, 2003). Retrieved from www.cfsan.fda.gov/~dms/transgui.html on June 1, 2009.
- U.S. Department of Labor's Bureau of Labor Statistics. *Occupational Outlook Handbook* (2008-2009 Edition). Retrieved from www.bls.gov/oco/ocos094.htm on June 1, 2009.

PHOTOGRAPHERS INCLUDED IN THIS WORK:

Jesse Ashton
Atomic Studios
Kimo Bentot
JKay Bradford
Ron R. Carino
Marc Cartwright
Lee Cherry
Lionel Coleman
Christine Colton
Sandra Colton
Kelly Connolly
Craig and Lindsay
Chris Cuffaro
Dahl Photography
Rob Daly
DJ Risk One
Jody Domingue
Shabba Doo
Bill Drake
Jerome Duchange
Kimo Easterwood
Deidhra Fahey
Gerry Frank
John Ganun
Robyn Ganter
Jonathon George
Simon Gluckman

PJ Graham
Ian Hagen
Reto Halme
Michael Higgins
Angie Hill
Chae Hill
Mark Hill
Bonnie Holland
Honey
Galen Hooks
Eric Hyler
Tye Jacobs
Cory Jones
David Kang
Kenzi Kay Photography
Mary Ann Kellogg
Phil Kessler
Leo Lam
Frankie Leal
Jessica Lynn
Carl McClarty
Rosero McCoy
Patrick McKenzie
Felix Mack
T. Matsushita
Jerry Metellus
Sarah Mitchell

ND Capture Photography
Dana Patrick
Cari Lightfoot Pike
Pierre Polak
Ryan Powell
Karl Preston
Mike Quain
Toshi Sakari
Rich Schaub
Michael Sigler
Paul Smith
Rose Spellman
Pamela Springsteen
Edward St. George
Jennifer Star
Mike Sijlek
Storm
Tim Tadder
Tiffen
Vince Trupsin
Miranda Pen Turin
Voyeur Photography
Levi Walker
Tyrell Washington Rebekah Westover
David Wile
Michael Woolley

RECOMMENDED READING

A Practical Guide For The Actor
by Melissa Bruder, Lee Michael Cohn, Madeleine Olnek, Nathaniel Pollack, Robert Previto and Scott Zigler

Dancers with Disabilities
Making An Entrance: Theory and Practice for Disabled and Non-Disabled Dancers
by Adam Benjamin

Dance Medicine and Science Bibliography
Compiled by Ruth Solomon and John Solomon
Find online at www.IADMS.org

Dance Magazine College Guide
Find online at www.DanceMagazine.com/TheCollegeGuide/Intro

Appendix A
Special Skills To Add To Your Repertoire

- Stupid human tricks/unique skills
- Armpit farting
- Balloon animals
- Baton twirling
- Crab walk
- Celebrity impersonations
- Sign language
- Hand puppetry
- Turning eyelids inside-out
- Tie a cherry stem into a knot
- Telling jokes
- Tongue tricks (i.e. Tongue to nose)
- Wiggling your ears
- Flaring your nostrils
- Whistling
- Yo-yo tricks
- Pat head while rubbing stomach/belly
- Make smoke rings
- Burping the alphabet
- Double-jointed body tricks
- One-armed push-ups
- Musical specialty
- Singing
- Beat-boxing
- Rapping
- Yodeling
- Playing instruments
- Specialty dance
- Belly dancing
- Ballet pointe
- Break dancing
- Gymnastics/tumbling
- Rhythmic gymnastics (ribbon, ball)

- Circus skills
- Kick worm
- Cheerleading stunts
- Unicycle
- Stilt walking
- Ventriloquism
- Fencing
- Track and field
- Karate/judo
- Fire breathing
- Juggling
- Magic tricks
- Miming
- Ventriloquism
- Funny laugh *(i.e. Fran Drescher)*
- Cool history of name story
- Crushing cans on your head
- Raise eyebrows (alternating)
- Make farm animal noises
- Bird calls
- Apply makeup in the dark w/o mirror

APPENDIX B
TOP 5 HOLLYWOOD DANCE AGENCIES
(LISTED ALPHABETICALLY)

BLOC
WWW.BLOCAGENCY.COM

(Los Angeles Office)
5651 Wilshire Boulevard Ste. C
Los Angeles, CA 90036
(323) 954-7730 Phone

(New York Office)
137 Varick Street
6th Floor
New York, NY 10013
(212) 924-6200 Phone

(Atlanta Office)
749 Moreland Avenue SE Suite
C-201
Atlanta, GA 30316
(404) 622-4116 Phone

CLEAR TALENT GROUP (C.T.G.)
WWW.CLEARTALENTGROUP.COM

(Los Angeles, CA Office)
10950 Ventura Boulevard
Studio City, CA 91604
(818) 509-0121 Phone

(New York, NY Office)
325 W. 38th Street, Suite 1203
New York, NY 10018
(212) 840-4100 Phone

D.D.O. ARTISTS AGENCY (DOROTHY DAY OTIS)
WWW.DDOAGENCY.COM

(Los Angeles Office)
6725 Sunset Boulevard
Suite 230
Los Angeles, CA 90028
(323) 462-8000 Phone

(Las Vegas Office)
10624 South Eastern Avenue
Suite 577
Las Vegas, NV 89052
(702) 371-7274 Phone
joy@ddoagency.com

(New York Office)
81 Franklin Street
5th Floor
New York, NY 10013
(212) 379-6314 Phone
nyc@ddoagency.com

GO 2 TALENT AGENCY
WWW.GO2TALENTAGENCY.COM

(Hollywood Office)
2817 W. Magnolia Blvd., Suite A
North Hollywood, CA 91505
(818) 848-9800 Phone

M.S.A. (MCDONALD/SELZNICK ASSOCIATES, INC.)
WWW.MSAAGENCY.COM

(Hollywood Office)
953 North Cole Avenue
Hollywood, CA 90038
(323) 957-6680 Phone

(New York Office)
140 Broadway, 46th Floor
New York, NY 10005
(212) 858-7549 Phone

TRIO TALENT AGENCY
WWW.TRIOTALENTAGENCY.COM

1502 Gardner Street
Los Angeles, CA 90046
(323) 851-6886 Phone

Appendix C
Performer Unions

Actors' Equity
WWW.ACTORSEQUITY.ORG

(West Coast Office)
6755 Hollywood Boulevard, 5th Floor
Hollywood, CA 90028
(323) 978-8080 Phone

(New York - National Headquarters)
165 West 46th Street
New York, NY 10036
(212) 869-8530 Phone

American Federation of Musicians of the U.S. & Canada
WWW.AFM.ORG

(West Coast Office)
3550 Wilshire Boulevard, Suite 1900
Los Angeles, CA 90010
(213) 251-4510 Phone

(New York - National Headquarters)
1501 Broadway, Suite 600
New York, NY 10036
(212) 869-1330 Phone

American Guild of Musical Artists (AGMA)
WWW.MUSICALARTISTS.ORG

(West Coast Office)
459 Fulton Street, Suite 305
San Francisco, CA 94102
(415) 552-2800 Phone

(New York - National Headquarters)
1430 Broadway, 14th Floor
New York, NY 10018
(212) 265-3687 Phone

American Guild of Variety Artists (AGVA)

AGVA does not currently have a Web site

(West Coast Office)
4741 Laurel Canyon Boulevard, Suite 208
North Hollywood, CA 91607
(818) 508-9984 Phone

(New York - National Headquarters)
184 Fifth Avenue, 6th floor
New York, NY 10010
(212) 675-1003 Phone

ASCAP
The American Society of Composers, Authors and Publishers
WWW.ASCAP.ORG

(Los Angeles Office)
7920 West Sunset Boulevard, 3rd Floor
Los Angeles, CA 90046
(323) 883-1000 Phone

(New York - National Headquarters)
One Lincoln Plaza
New York, NY 10023
(212) 621-6000 Phone

APPENDIX C
PERFORMER UNIONS CONTINUED

BMI
WWW.BMI.COM

(Los Angeles Office)
8730 Sunset Boulevard, 3rd Floor
West Hollywood, CA 90069
(310) 659-9109 Phone

(Nashville - National Headquarters)
10 Music Square East
Nashville, TN 37203
(615) 401-2000 Phone

SAG/AFTRA
WWW.SAGAFTRA.ORG

(Hollywood - National Headquarters)
5757 Wilshire Boulevard, 7th Floor
Los Angeles, CA 90036
(323) 954-1600 Main Switchboard
(323) 549-6648 For Deaf Performers
TTY/TTD
(800) SAG-0767

(New York Branch)
360 Madison Avenue, 12th Floor
New York, New York 10017
(212) 944-1030 Main Switchboard
(212) 944-6715 For Deaf Performers
Only: TTY/TTD

SAG/AFTRA CONTRACTS DEPT. PHONE NUMBERS:
Dancers: (323) 549-6864
Music Videos: (323) 549-6864
Commercials/Infomercials: (323) 549-6858
Singers: (323) 549-6864
Stunt and Safety Representative: (323) 549-6855
Television: (323) 549-6835
Theatrical Motion Pictures: (323) 549-6828
Background Actors: (323) 549-6811
Industrial/Educational/Interactive: (323) 549-6858
Residual Payment Info Center: (323) 549-6505

SESAC
WWW.SESAC.COM

(Los Angeles Office)
501 Santa Monica Boulevard, Suite 450
Santa Monica, CA 90401
(310) 393-9671 Phone

(Nashville - National Headquarters)
55 Music Square East
Nashville, TN 37203
(615) 320-0055 Phone

APPENDIX D
HOLLYWOOD/L.A. DANCE STUDIOS

Alley Kat Studios
1455 N. Gordon Street
Los Angeles, CA 90028
(323) 462-1755 Phone

The Basement Dance Center
5259 Lankershim Boulevard
Suite C
North Hollywood, CA 91601
(818) 487-0100 Phone
TheBasementDanceCenter.com

Burbank Studios
3800 Burbank Boulevard
Burbank, CA 91505
(818) 843-2262 Phone
ScreenlandStudios.com

Center Staging
3407 Winona Avenue
Burbank, CA 91504
(818) 559-4333 Phone
www.CenterStaging.com

Dance Arts Academy
731 S. La Brea Avenue
Los Angeles, CA 90036
(323) 932-6230 Phone
DanceArtsAcademy.com

Debbie Allen Dance Academy
3631 Hayden Avenue
Culver City, CA 90232
(310) 280-9145 Phone
DebbieAllenDanceAcademy.com

Debbie Reynold's Studio
6514 Lankershim Boulevard
North Hollywood, CA 91606
(818) 985-3193 Phone
DRDanceStudio.com

Edge Pac
1020 North Cole Avenue
4th Floor
Los Angeles, CA 90038
(323) 962-7733 Phone
EdgePac.com

Evolution Dance Studios
(Formerly Synthesis)
4200 Lankershim Boulevard
Universal City, CA 91602
(818) 754-1760 Phone
EvolutionDanceStudios.com

Hama's Dance Center
12117 Moorpark Street
Studio City, CA 91604
(818) 985-8701
Hamadance.com

Hollywood Aerial Arts
3838 West 102nd Street
Inglewood, CA 90303
www.HollywoodAerialArts.com

Hollywood Dance Center
817 North Highland Avenue
Los Angeles, CA 90038
(323) 467-0825 Phone
HollywoodDanceCenter.com

(IDA) Itnl. Dance Academy:
6755 Hollywood Boulevard
2nd Floor
Hollywood, CA 90028
(323) 463-8865 Phone
IDAHollywood.com

Liv'art Dance Studio
5200 Lankershim Blvd.
Suite 100
North Hollywood, CA 91601
livartdance.com

Madilyn Clark Studios
10825 Burbank Boulevard
North Hollywood, CA 91601
(818) 506-7763 Phone
MadilynClark.com

MKM Cultural Arts Center
11401 Chandler Boulevard
North Hollywood, CA 91601
(818) 752-2616 Phone

Millennium Dance Complex
5113 Lankershim Boulevard
North Hollywood, CA 91601
(818) 753-5081 Phone
MillenniumDanceComplex.com

Movement Lifestyle
11135 Weddington Street
North Hollywood, CA 91601
themovementlifestyle.com

PAC – The Annex
7932 Haskell Avenue
Van Nuys, CA 91406
(818) 779-0428 Phone

PAC-Rehearsal Facility
7735 Sepulveda Boulevard
Van Nuys, CA 91405
(818) 908-9001 Phone
WebMarketConsulting.com/PAC

Playback Studios
14547 Erwin Street
Van Nuys, CA 91411
(818) 994-1088 Phone
PlaybackStudioLA.com

Screenland
10501 Burbank Boulevard
North Hollywood, CA 91601
(818) 508-2288 Phone
ScreenlandStudios.com

SIR Studios
6465 Sunset Boulevard
Los Angeles, CA 90048
(323) 957-5460 Phone
SIRLA.com

Appendix E
Commercial Casting Facilities

5th Street Studios
1216 5th Street
Santa Monica, CA 90401

Alyson Horn Casting
1015 North Orange Drive
Los Angeles, CA 90038

Big House Studios
4420 Lankershim Boulevard
North Hollywood, CA 91602

Blanca Valdez
1001 North Poinsettia Place
West Hollywood, CA 91602

Castaway Studios
8899 Beverly Boulevard
Los Angeles, CA 90048

The Casting Studios
200 South La Brea Boulevard, 2nd Floor
Los Angeles, CA 90036

The Casting Suite
12500 Riverside Drive, Suite 202
Valley Village, CA 91607

Chelsea Studios
11530 Ventura Boulevard
Studio City, CA 91604

Cole Ave Studios
1006 North Cole Avenue
Los Angeles, CA 90038

Deborah Kurtz Casting
11751 Mississippi Avenue, Suite 140
Los Angeles, CA 90025

HKM/Casting Underground
1641 North Ivar Street
Hollywood, CA 90028

Lien/Cowan Casting
7461 Beverly Boulevard, Suite 203
Los Angeles, CA 90035

On Your Mark Studios
451 North La Cienega Boulevard
Los Angeles, CA 90036

Session West Studios
2601 Ocean Park Boulevard
Santa Monica, CA 90405

Sheila Manning
508 South San Vicente Boulevard
Los Angeles, CA 90048

Silverlayne Studios
1611 North Las Palmas Avenue
Los Angeles, CA 90038

Sunset Studios
7707 Sunset Boulevard
Los Angeles, CA 90046

Tepper/Gallegos
639 North Larchmont, Suite 201
Los Angeles, CA 90004

Village Studios
519 Broadway Boulevard
Santa Monica, CA 90401

Westside Casting
2050 South Bundy Drive
Los Angeles, CA 90025

Appendix F
Photographers And Reproduction Companies

Barbara Benvil
www.BenvilPhotography.com

Lee Cherry
www.LeeCherry.com

Greg Crowder
www.GregCrowderPhotography.com

Kenneth Dolin
www.KennethDolin.com

Jeff E. Photo
www.JeffEPhoto.com

Eyekool
www.Eyekool.com

Robin Ganter
www.RobinGanterPhotography.com

Nancy Jo Gilchrist
www.NancyJoPhoto.com

Simon Gluckman
www.SimonGluckman.com

Michael Higgins
www.MichaelHigginsPhoto.com

Angie Hill
www.AngieHillPhotography.com

Erik Hyler
www.EHGPhotography.com

JBC Images
www.jbcimages.com

ND Capture Photography
www.NDCapturePhotography.com

Johnny Pena
www.JohnnyPenaPhotography.com

Photofly-Dance by Melissa
http://tribes.tribe.net/photofly-dance

Mike Quain
www.QuainPhoto.com

Tim Sabatino
www.TimSabatino.com

Shutter Dee
www.ShutterDee.com

Paul Smith
www.PaulSmithPhotography.com

Guy Viau
www.GuyViauHeadshots.com

Caroline White
www.CarolineWhitePhotography.com

Scott Young
www.CommercialSuccess.tv

Reproduction Companies

Argentum
6550 Sunset Boulevard
Hollywood, CA 90028
(323) 461-2775

Gray Tone
726 Cahuenga Boulevard
Hollywood, CA 90038
(323) 467-4117

Genesis
5872 West Pico Boulevard
Los Angeles, CA 90019
(323) 965-7935

ISGO
2411 West Magnolia Boulevard
Burbank, CA 91506
(818) 848-9001

Nardulli
1710 North La Brea Boulevard
Los Angeles, CA 90046
(323) 882-8331

Paper Chase
7176 Sunset Boulevard
Los Angeles, CA 90046
(323) 874-2300

Reproductions
3499 Cahuenga Boulevard
Los Angeles, CA 90068
(323) 845-9595

Appendix G
Dance Apparel, Thrift Shops And Book Stores

Applause Discount Dancewear
2180 Westwood Boulevard, Unit 2A
Los Angeles, CA 90025
(310) 470-9836 Phone
www.ApplauseDiscountDancewear.com

Ballerina Dancewear
228 North Glenoaks Boulevard
Burbank, CA 91502
(818) 846-1170 Phone

Beverly Hills Hosiery
801 South Los Angeles Street
Los Angeles, CA 90014
(213) 627-7705 Phone

Broadway Cheerleading Sales
2152 Sacramento Street
Los Angeles, CA 90021
(213) 680-9694 Phone
www.Broadwayalbion.com

Capezio
1777 North Vine Street
Hollywood, CA 90028
(323) 465-3744 Phone
www.CapezioDance.com

Danskin
www.Danskin.com

Danny's Warehouse
5701 West Adams Boulevard
Los Angeles, CA 90016
(800) 552-5385 Phone
www.DannysWarehouse.com

Discount Dancewear
3940 Laurel Canyon Boulevard
Studio City, CA 91604

Freed
www.FreedUSA.com

Karabel Dancewear
3901 West Magnolia Boulevard
Burbank, CA 91505
(818) 955-8480 Phone

Katnap Dance
12932 Venice Boulevard
Los Angeles, CA 90066
(310) 306-7069 Phone

Katrina Active Wear
www.KatrinaWear.com

Red Shoes
1018 Mission Street
South Pasadena, CA 91030
www.TheRedShoes.com

Shelly's Discount Dancewear
2089 Westwood Boulevard
Los Angeles, CA 90025
(310) 475-1400 Phone

The Ballet Shop
1709 Stewart Street
Santa Monica, CA 90404
(310) 315-0486 Phone

The Dance Factory Wear
11606 San Vicente Boulevard
Los Angeles, CA 90049
(310) 826-4554 Phone

The Dance Store
1446 South Robertson Boulevard
Los Angeles, CA 90035
(310) 271-3664 Phone
www.TheDanceStore.com

Worldtone Dance Shoes
2138 Westwood Boulevard
Los Angeles, CA 90025
(310) 234-9100 Phone
www.WorldToneDance.com

Inexpensive Shops/ Book Stores

Hollywood Toys and Costumes
6600 Hollywood Boulevard
Hollywood, CA 90028
(866) 232-1829 Phone
www.HollywoodToysAndCostumes.com

Marshall's
www.MarshallsOnline.com

Samuel French, Inc.
7623 Sunset Boulevard
Hollywood, CA 90046
(323) 876-0570 Phone
www.SamuelFrench.com

Appendix H-1
Popular Female Recording Artist Heights

Female Recording Artists
(Alphabetical By First Name)

Alicia Keys	5'6"
Amerie	5'5"
Ashanti	5'3"
Ashlee Simpson	5'6"
Avril Lavigne	5'3"
Bette Midler	5'1"
Beyoncé Knowles	5'6"
Brandy Norwood	5'7"
Britney Spears	5'4"
Carrie Underwood	5'3 ½"
Celine Dion	5'7 ½"
Cher	5'8 ½"
Christina Aguilera	5'1 ½"
Christina Milian	5'2"
Demi Lovato	5'3"
Faith Hill	5'8"
Fergie	5'1 ¾"
Gwen Stefani	5'7"
Janet Jackson	5'4"
Jennifer Lopez	5'6"
Jessica Simpson	5'3 ½"
Jessie J	5'9"
Katharine McPhee	5'8"
Katy Perry	5'8"
Ke$ha	5'10"
Kylie Minogue	5'0"
Lady Gaga	5'1"
Madonna	5'4 ½"
Mariah Carey	5'9 ¼"
Mary J. Blige	5'9"
Miley Cyrus	5'5"
Missy Elliott	5'2"
Natasha Bedingfield	5'6 ¼"
Nelly Furtado	5'1"
Nicole Scherzinger	5'5"
Nicki Minaj	5'3 ¾"
Pink	5'4"
Rihanna	5'9"
Shakira	4'11"
Shania Twain	5'4"
Taylor Swift	5'11"
Tina Turner	5'4"
Vanessa Hudgens	5'2"

Female Recording Artists
(In Order By Height)

Shakira	4'11"
Kylie Minogue	5'0"
Bette Midler	5'1"
Nelly Furtado	5'1"
Lady Gaga	5'1"
Christina Aguilera	5'1 ½"
Fergie	5'1 ¾"
Vanessa Hudgens	5'2"
Christina Milian	5'2"
Missy Elliott	5'2"
Avril Lavigne	5'3"
Ashanti	5'3"
Demi Lovato	5'3"
Carrie Underwood	5'3 ½"
Jessica Simpson	5'3 ½"
Nicki Minaj	5'3 ¾"
Britney Spears	5'4"
Janet Jackson	5'4"
Pink	5'4"
Shania Twain	5'4"
Tina Turner	5'4"
Madonna	5'4 ½"
Amerie	5'5"
Miley Cyrus	5'5"
Nicole Scherzinger	5'5"
Beyoncé Knowles	5'6"
Jennifer Lopez	5'6"
Ashlee Simpson	5'6"
Alicia Keys	5'6"
Natasha Bedingfield	5'6 ¼"
Gwen Stefani	5'7"
Brandy Norwood	5'7"
Celine Dion	5'7 ½"
Katharine McPhee	5'8"
Katy Perry	5'8"
Faith Hill	5'8"
Cher	5'8 ½"
Jessie J	5'9"
Rihanna	5'9"
Mary J. Blige	5'9"
Mariah Carey	5'9 ¼"
Ke$ha	5'10"
Taylor Swift	5'11"

Appendix H-2
Popular Male Recording Artist Heights

Male Recording Artists (Alphabetical By First Name)		Male Recording Artists (In Order By Height)	
50 Cent	6'0"	Justin Bieber	5'5"
Akon	5'11"	Bow Wow	5'7"
Bow Wow	5'7"	Omarion	5'7"
Busta Rhymes	6'1"	Timbaland	5'7"
Chris Brown	6'2"	Ne-Yo	5'8 ½"
Daddy Yankee	5'11"	Usher	5'8 ½"
Dr. Dre	6'1"	Eminem	5'8"
Eminem	5'8"	Kanye West	5'8"
Flo Rida	6'3"	Nick Lachey	5'9"
Garth Brooks	5'11 ½"	Paul Wall	5'9"
Jason Derulo	6'3"	Pharell Williams	5'9"
Jay-Z	6'1 ½"	T.I.	5'9"
Jesse McCartney	5'10"	Jesse McCartney	5'10"
Justin Bieber	5'5"	Keith Urban	5'10"
Justin Timberlake	5'11 ¾"	Soulja Boy Tell 'Em	5'10"
Kanye West	5'8"	P. Diddy	5'11"
Keith Urban	5'10"	Lionel Richie	5'11"
L.L. Cool J	6'1 ½"	Daddy Yankee	5'11"
Lionel Richie	5'11"	Akon	5'11"
Nelly	6'0 ¾"	Garth Brooks	5'11 ½"
Ne-Yo	5'8 ½"	Justin Timberlake	5'11 ¾"
Nick Carter	6'0 ¾"	50 Cent	6'0"
Nick Lachey	5'9"	Tim McGraw	6'0"
Omarion	5'7"	Nick Carter	6'0 ¾"
Paul Wall	5'9"	Nelly	6'0 ¾"
Pharell Williams	5'9"	Busta Rhymes	6'1"
Ricky Martin	6'1"	Dr. Dre	6'1"
P. Diddy	5'11"	Ricky Martin	6'1"
Soulja Boy Tell 'Em	5'10"	Jay-Z	6'1 ½"
Snoop Dogg	6'4 ¾"	L.L. Cool J	6'1 ½"
The Game	6'4"	Flo Rida	6'3"
T.I.	5'9"	Jason Derulo	6'3"
Tim McGraw	6'0"	Toby Keith	6'3"
Timbaland	5'7"	Chris Brown	6'2"
Toby Keith	6'3"	The Game	6'4"
Usher	5'8 ½"	Snoop Dogg	6'4 ¾"

Appendix I
Must-See Dance Films

Year	Title	Year	Title	Year	Title
2009	Abuelo	2009	Fired Up	1990	Silence Like Glass
1945	Anchors Aweigh	1997	Flamenco	1952	Singin' in the Rain
1933	42nd Street	1983	Flashdance	1983	Staying Alive
1985	A Chorus Line	1984	Footloose	2006	Step Up
1983	A Night In Heaven	2011	Footloose	2008	Step Up 2 The Streets
2007	Across The Universe	1985	Girls Just Want To Have Fun	2010	Step Up 3-D
1979	All That Jazz	2011	Go For It!	2012	Step Up 4: Revolution
1982	Annie	1978	Grease	1991	Stepping Out
2009	B-girl	1982	Grease 2	2007	Stompin'
2013	Battle of the Year	1962	Gypsy	2007	Stomp The Yard
2012	Battlefield America	1988	Hairspray	2010	Stomp The Yard 2: Homecoming
1963	Beach Party/Bikini Beach	2007	Hairspray		
1984	Beat Street	1985	Heavenly Bodies	1943	Stormy Weather
2000	Billy Elliott	2008	High School Musical	2010	Street Dance 3D
2011	Black Swan	1969	Hello Dolly!	2012	Street Dance 2 - 3D
1984	Body Rock	2003	Honey	1993	Strictly Ballroom
2011	Boogie Town	2011	Honey 2	2004	Swing
2000	Bootmen	2008	How She Move	1993	Swing Kids
2000	Bossa Nova	2007	Kickin It Old Skool	2006	Take The Lead
2010	Bouncing Cats	1987	La Bamba	1999	Tango
1984	Breakin'	1990	Lambada	1989	TAP
1984	Breakin' 2: Electric Boogaloo	2011	Leave It On The Floor	1996	That Thing You Do!
1954	Brigadoon			1985	That's Dancing!
2000	Bring It On	2006	Little Miss Sunshine	1996	The Birdcage
2003	Bring It On Again	2000	Mad About Mambo	1978	The Buddy Holly Story
2006	Bring It On: All or Nothing	2005	Mad Hot Ballroom	1991	The Five Heartbeats
2007	Bring It On: In It To Win It	2012	Magic Mike	1990	The Forbidden Dance
2009	Bring It On: Fight To The Finish	2013	Make Your Move 3D	2002	The Freshest Kids
2010	Burlesque	2011	Mao's Last Dancer	1997	The Full Monty
1972	Cabaret	1944	Meet Me In Saint Louis	1988	The In Crowd
2000	Center Stage	2001	Moulin Rouge	2005	The Producers
2002	Chicago	1977	New York, New York	1997	The Tango Lesson
2000	Coyote Ugly	2009	Nine	1977	The Turning Point
1990	Cry Baby	1949	On The Town	1978	The Wiz
1958	Damn Yankees	2007	Planet B-Boy	1950	Three Little Words
2009	Dance Flick	2005	Rent	1991	Truth or Dare
1998	Dance With Me	2005	Rize	1961	West Side Story
1999	Dancemaker	1956	Rock Around The Clock	1985	White Nights
1987	Dancers	2005	Roll Bounce	1983	Wild Style
1992	Danzon	2011	Saigon Electric	1980	Xanadu
1987	Dirty Dancing	1988	Salsa: The Motion Picture	2004	You Got Served
2012	Dirty Dancing	1977	Saturday Night Fever	2011	You Got Served: Beat The World
2004	Dirty Dancing: Havana Nights	2001	Save The Last Dance		
1982	Disco Dancer	2006	Save The Last Dance 2	1946	Ziegfeld Follies
1999	Do You Wanna Dance?	1997	Selena		
1948	Easter Parade	1989	Shag: The Movie		
1980	Fame	1997	Shall We Dance?		
2009	Fame	2004	Shall We Dance?		
1985	Fast Forward	1995	Showgirls		
2007	Feel The Noise	2007	Show Stoppers		

Appendix J
Hollywood Studio Guide

ABC (Prospect)
4151 Prospect Avenue
Hollywood, CA 90027
(323) 671-4554

ABC (Sunset Gower Studios)
1438 North Gower Street
Hollywood, CA 90028
(323) 467-1001

Adventist Media Center
101 West Cochran Street
Simi Valley, CA 93065
(805) 955-7777

Buena Vista Home Video Inc.
350 South Buena Vista Street
Burbank, CA 91521
(818) 295-5200

CBS/Radford
4024 Radford Avenue
Studio City, CA 91604
(818) 655-5000

CBS-TV City
7800 Beverly Boulevard
Los Angeles, CA 90036
(323) 575-2345

Chandler Studios
11401 Chandler Boulevard
North Hollywood, CA 91601
(818) 763-3650

The Complex Studios
2323 Cornith Avenue
West Los Angeles, CA 90064
(310) 477-1938

Culver Studios
9336 West Washington Boulevard
Culver City, CA 90230
(310) 202-1234

Delfino Studios
12501 Gladestone Avenue
Sylmar, CA 91342
(818) 361-2421

Downey Studios
12214 Lakewood Boulevard
Downey, CA 90242
(562) 401-0120

Empire Studios
1845 Empire Avenue
Burbank, CA 91504
(818) 840-1400

Fox Sports Center
5746 Sunset Boulevard
Hollywood, CA 90028
(310) 369-9160

Fox Sports West
10000 Santa Monica Boulevard
Los Angeles, CA 90067
(310) 286-3800

GMT Studios
5751 Buckingham Parkway
Culver City, CA 90230
(310) 649-3733

Hayvenhurst Studios
7021 Hayvenhurst Avenue
Van Nuys, CA 91406
(818) 909-6999

Hollywood Center Studios
1040 North Las Palmas Avenue
Los Angeles, CA 90038
(323) 469-5000

KABC
500 Circle Seven Drive
Glendale, CA 91201
(818) 863-7777

KCAL
5515 Melrose Avenue
Los Angeles, CA 90038
(323) 460-3000

KCBS
6121 Sunset Boulevard
Hollywood, CA 90028
(323) 460-3000

KCET
4401 Sunset Boulevard
Los Angeles, CA 90027
(323) 666-6500

KCOP
915 North La Brea Boulevard
Los Angeles, CA 90038
(323) 851-1000

Appendix J
Hollywood Studio Guide Continued

KTLA
5800 Sunset Boulevard
Los Angeles, CA 90028
(323) 460-5500

KTTV
1999 South Bundy Drive
Los Angeles, CA 90025
(310) 584-2000

L.A. Center Studios
1201 West 5th Street
Los Angeles, CA 90017
(213) 534-3000

Lacy Street Production Center
2630 Lacy Street
Los Angeles, CA 90031
(323) 222-8872

Lindsey Studios
25241 Avenue Stanford
Valencia, CA 91355
(661) 257-9292

NBC
Sunset-Gower Studios
1420 North Beachwood Avenue
Hollywood, CA 90028
(213) 617-0153

Oakridge TV Studios
1239 Glendale Avenue
Glendale, CA 91205
(818) 550-6000

Occidental Studios/Mansfield
201 North Occidental Boulevard
Los Angeles, CA 90026
(213) 384-3331

Paramount Pictures Television
5555 Melrose Avenue
Los Angeles, CA 90038
(323) 956-5000

PKE Studio
8621 Hayden Place
Culver City, CA 90232
(310) 838-7000

Post Group Studios
6335 Homewood Avenue
Hollywood, CA 90028
(323) 462-2300

Production Group
1330 North Vine Street
Hollywood, CA 90028
(323) 469-8111

Quixote Studios
4585 Electronics Place
Los Angeles, CA 90039
(323) 957-9933

Raleigh Studios
640 North Bronson Avenue
Los Angeles, CA 90004
(323) 466-3111

Ren-mar Studios
846 North Cahuenga Boulevard
Hollywood, CA 90038
(323) 463-0808

Santa Clarita Studios
25135 Anza Drive
Santa Clarita, CA 91355
(661) 294-2000

Sony Pictures Entertainment
10202 West Washington Boulevard
Culver City, CA 90232
(310) 244-4000

South Bay Studios
20434 South Santa Fe Avenue
Long Beach, CA 90810
(310) 762-1360

Studio West
2220 Colorado Avenue
Santa Monica, CA 90404
(310) 315-4350

Sunset Stage
6063 Sunset Boulevard
Hollywood, CA 90028
(323) 461-1001

Appendix K
Sandra's Sample Audition Tracker

Date	Client/Product	Agent/Manager	Casting Director/Choreographer	What Project? TV/Film/Print/Commercial	Wardrobe	Callback	2nd/3rd Callback	On Avail.	BOOKED	Dates Worked

APPENDIX L
SAMPLE AGENT INQUIRY LETTER

Sandra Colton
c/o Original Girl, LLC
P.O. Box 824
Hollywood, CA 90078

June 7, 2013

Agency X
Address X
Hollywood, CA 90028

To Whom It May Concern:

My name is Sandra Colton and I am a dancer from Las Vegas, Nev. Currently seeking dance and choreography representation, my background includes tap, jazz, hip-hop, gymnastics and stunt training. My professional experience is extensive and some of the highlights include performing on *Star Search* and winning the Teen Dance Championship as well as opening for Bill Cosby and Lou Rawls on the Las Vegas Strip.

A fun, easy going young woman, I am a hard worker, dedicated to improving my skills and furthering my craft. I plan to move to Hollywood, Calif. on July 1st and would like to set up an interview with you to discuss if you would be the right agency for my needs. Pursuing dance has been my dream and I can't wait to go full steam ahead. If you'd like to catch a glimpse of my show-stopping skills, check me out at www.SandraColton.com or go to my YouTube page at www.YouTube.com/dancegirl2007.

Thank you for your time and if you get a chance to come out to Carnival this month, I'll be performing in the piece choreographed by one of your clients, Choreographer X. Hope to see you there and schedule a meeting with you as soon as possible! Contact me at (310) xxx-xxxx.

Take care and thanks again!

Sincerely,
Sandra Colton

Appendix M
Sample Deal Memo

DEAL MEMO

DATE: 1/1/10

Attn: Original Girl, LLC
P.O. Box 824
Hollywood, CA 90078
editor@originalgirlmagazine.com

From: Talent Agency X
Addresss
Hollywood, CA 90028

Subject: Dancer for Sandra Colton Showcase
Promo Tour & Tour Dates TBD

Work Dates: June 2013 - July 2013

Daily Rate: $500 (Per Show Fee) + 20% Agency
(Multiple day rehearsals TBD - Dancers' Alliance rates will apply and buy out rate will be negotiated if music video is scheduled)

Note: Additional days to be determined and will have a pre-negotiated weekly rate.

Misc.: Expenses shall be paid by company RE: rehearsal rental, audio materials and/or production materials such as props, microphone and/or mic stand, etc.

Cancellation: Fee is 100% of the total job - NO exception.

Sign and Return this agreement to our fax number to acknowledge and agree to this deal memo. We will move forward as if this agreement is accepted by both Original Girl, LLC and Talent Agency X. Any and all cancellations will need to be paid in full. Please contact us with questions, comments or concerns regarding this deal memo.

Agent	Date	Company Representative	Date
Talent Agency X		Original Girl, LLC	

Appendix N
Sample Commercial Ad Copy

In this commercial copy, you are selling a new lotion. As a dancer, you may have to speak and show off a few moves at the same time. Try holding a bottle of lotion and work on this commercial in your spare time.

My life is running a mile a minute, literally. Constantly zipping from one place to the next, my body takes a serious beating. I don't have a lot of time to moisturize my legs after showering. I need a lotion that can keep up with me. With the new Gotcha Brand X Lotion, it lasts all day long. Giving my legs the love they need and the shine too! It works for me and that's all I ask.

THE BACKSTORY

It's 6:35 p.m., what are you doing? "I'm dressed in a naughty school girl outfit ready to go-go at a high profile Mindy Weiss party! Wait, what?" My life and times as a dancer in Hollywood have produced a few of these moments. All you have to do is put the word "naughty" in front of any theme outfit and the word "go-go" in the same sentence and you've got yourself a gig! Try it, "naughty school girl," "naughty vampire," "naughty maid." It's an indestructible combination for a grand ol' time!

I got a call at 4 p.m. from my agent who said, "Hey girl, what are you doing? Where are you right now?" I said, "Oh, I'm at home just fiddling around on the computer." He says, "Can you get over to Center Staging by 5:30 p.m.? Look hot and ready to learn something to sing for a recording artist to be on the *Tonight Show with Jay Leno.*" I said, "Sure!" I jumped in the shower and put on a hot little background vocal dress and headed over to the rehearsal studio. I walked in and was given lyrics to Paulina Rubio's song, *"Ni una sola palabra,"* a song that was of course, all in Spanish. They said, "Can you learn it and perform it?" I along with one other dancer/singer Samantha Lee were to learn it and perform it the next night. I went home and memorized the words. It was interesting because many times you don't think about how in English you may not pronounce a certain word in slang or flow from one word to the next. I got done learning all of the words to the song in Spanish and then realized as I started to listen to the song that half of the words weren't even pronounced fully. I love the song, but had spent so much time learning the words in a way that I wasn't even going to sing them. I should've listened first. It was a learning experience but we looked and sounded great! This was the first time in the show's history I was told that a Spanish-speaking artist has performed a song entirely in Spanish on the show. My agent later told me, "Whoever answered their phone first was the person who was going to get the job." It's all about being available at the right time!

Leotards do not lie! I performed in Europe with Rihanna in a leotard and heels. The sassy backless halter leotard we wore didn't cover anything! We were rockin' those things like they were going out of style. After going to an initial call for Beyoncé, then a callback, another callback, a rehearsal run-through and then another callback in my leotard, that thing wanted and needed a rest. It was in between one of those callbacks that we were asked to provide pictures in sports bras, leotard bottoms and heels to have on file for choreographer Frank Gatson. Call me crazy, but dancers are asked to do a lot of things. Here are a few pics from my own DIY impromptu photo shoot. Just silly!

The Backstory

I went to a casting session for a commercial and as I arrived I noticed another casting for a department store print ad. I went to my own audition before asking the casting director for the print ad if I could audition since I was already there. She said that my hair was a bit too curly for what they had in mind and asked if I could go home and straighten it. I said, "Sure, I'll be back in an hour!" I left, straightened my hair and returned ready to audition. The casting director paired us up in couples and while sitting there for a second time in the waiting room, I saw that there was another casting for a car commercial in the next room. I jokingly said out loud to my audition partner, "Wouldn't that be cool if I auditioned for three things in the same office in one day and booked all three?!" He with a very dry sense of humor said, "Yeah! Cool. You could retire for like a week!" Aww...yes, he brought me right back to reality!

If you are a customer in Target, don't ever wear red. Just an idea.

If you're told you are shooting on a green screen
and you are asked to bring your own wardrobe, don't bring or wear green!

---

25 years old seems young...
until you are next to a hot 17 year old living through the naked audition silence!

My friend Raul said the best thing while watching some ladies sing their hearts out.
He said, *"I'm not a singer, I let my body hit the high notes."*
The words of a true dancer.

I went to an audition for a cellular phone commercial. I had my cute black skirt on, my cute black heels, a tank top and a fresh necklace. My hair was huge and was ready to whip around. I went in and was told to freestyle. I started when the music came on and my necklace got tangled in my hair so badly that more than half of my audition was spent trying to get it untangled. I thought I was so horrible. I left crying. I felt I did that poorly. Then, I got a callback! Crazier things have happened. It just goes to show you that even on your very worst day, you might end up doing better than you think. Stick with it, I'm sure glad I did.

HOW YOU CAN HELP WITH MY NEXT EDITION

I'd love to hear any comments for my next edition. Any additional tips you may have for dancers or stories you think may benefit a dancer moving to Hollywood! Send your questions, suggestions to: sandra@sandracolton.com. You can also send them via U.S.P.S. to:

Sandra Colton
c/o Pinstriped Publishing
RE: BOOK ME!
P.O. Box 824
Hollywood, CA 90078
THANK YOU!

BOOK ME!
SANDRA COLTON
SANDRA@SANDRACOLTON.COM

the end

P.S. THANKS MOM!

PINSTRIPED PUBLISHING
ORDER FORM

Yes, I want to be a successful working dancer in Hollywood...Send me:

Qty:

____ BOOK ME! How To Become A Successful Working Dancer In Hollywood $34.95

____ BOOK ME! Workbook $19.99

ITEM TOTAL:

SHIPPING: _____

TOTAL DUE: _____

Enclose $4.95 per item for USPS flat rate mail ($10 per item if you are outside the U.S.) and mail your name, address, telephone, e-mail address and credit card number including expiration date to:

Pinstriped Publishing
P.O. 824
Hollywood, CA 90078

For the fastest service, please order directly from our Web site at:
www.ColtonCollection.com

Share your experiences about living and dancing in Hollywood by writing to me at: tips@dancetrackmagazine.com. Your success stories just may appear my blog **DANCE 365**. For all dance-related questions e-mail me at: sandra@sandracolton.com. No orders to this e-mail please.

I'll see you on the dance floor!

Love,
Sandra

www.ingramcontent.com/pod-product-compliance
Lightning Source LLC
Chambersburg PA
CBHW042128010526
44111CB00030B/1